Purifying Empire

Purifying Empire explores the material, cultural and moral fragmentation of the boundaries of imperial and colonial rule in the British empire in the late nineteenth and early twentieth centuries. It charts how a particular biopolitical project, namely the drive to regulate the obscene in late nineteenth-century Britain, was transformed from a national into a global and imperial venture and then re-localized in two different colonial contexts, India and Australia, to serve decidedly different ends. While a considerable body of work has demonstrated both the role of empire in shaping moral regulatory projects in Britain and their adaptation, transformation and, at times, rejection in colonial contexts, this book illustrates that it is in fact only through a comparative and transnational framework that it is possible to elucidate both the temporalist nature of colonialism and the political, racial and moral contradictions that sustained imperial and colonial regimes.

DEANA HEATH is a lecturer in South Asian History at Trinity College Dublin. Her work, which endeavours to place South Asia in broader comparative, transnational and global contexts, focuses on a range of issues including imperialism and colonialism, modernity and governmentality, sexuality and the body, and communalism and violence. She is the co-editor of *Communalism and Globalisation in South Asia and its Diaspora* (2010).

Purifying Empire: Obscenity and the Politics of Moral Regulation in Britain, India and Australia

Deana Heath

CAMBRIDGE
UNIVERSITY PRESS

CAMBRIDGE
UNIVERSITY PRESS

University Printing House, Cambridge CB2 8BS, United Kingdom

One Liberty Plaza, 20th Floor, New York, NY 10006, USA

477 Williamstown Road, Port Melbourne, VIC 3207, Australia

314-321, 3rd Floor, Plot 3, Splendor Forum, Jasola District Centre, New Delhi - 110025, India

103 Penang Road, #05-06/07, Visioncrest Commercial, Singapore 238467

Cambridge University Press is part of the University of Cambridge.

It furthers the University's mission by disseminating knowledge in the pursuit of education, learning and research at the highest international levels of excellence.

www.cambridge.org
Information on this title: www.cambridge.org/9780521194358

First published 2010
First paperback edition 2013

A catalogue record for this publication is available from the British Library

ISBN 978-0-521-19435-8 Hardback
ISBN 978-1-107-67659-6 Paperback

Contents

Abbreviations

AAC	Australian Archives, Canberra
AAM	Australian Archives, Melbourne
AAS	Australian Archives, Sydney
ML	Mitchell Library, Sydney
MSA	Maharashtra State Archives
NAI	National Archives, India
NAUK	National Archives, United Kingdom
NLA	National Library, Australia
PROV	Public Record Office of Victoria
SLV	State Library of Victoria
SRC	Sydney Records Centre
WBSA	West Bengal State Archives
WL	Women's Library, London

Introduction: Books, boundaries and Britishness

Boundaries – spatial, cultural, moral – are the fault lines of empires. Such boundaries – which divided 'inner' and 'outer', 'self' and 'other', and 'home' and empire' – became sources of growing concern in the late nineteenth century. At a time when nations were first imagined somatically, as gendered and racialized bodies, and individual bodies were conceptualized in political terms, as waging battles against external enemies, the phenomenal expansion of the material and communicative circuits of the European empires that had commenced in mid-century, while serving to consolidate imperial space and usher in a new 'globalizing' age, also served to undermine and reconfigure the boundaries of rule through which imperial and colonial regimes operated. Such a process was facilitated by particular commodities, although ones rarely analysed as such, namely printed matter such as books and periodicals, which were purveyed through the trade networks of empires in growing numbers. For in addition to being forms of material capital, such printed matter also functioned as cultural capital that served to mark the 'distinction' – and hence worth – of European cultures and norms. It was this latter aspect that made print culture so appealing to colonizing regimes as a means of 'civilizing' subjects. Yet employing books and periodicals as cultural–moral capital posed a problem for these regimes, for the acquisition of such capital by colonized subjects served not only to fracture the boundaries demarcating colonizer and colonized, and nation and empire, but ultimately to diminish the value of such commodities – and with it their power to serve not only as colonizing tools, but as a means of ensuring the 'strength' and 'purity' of European bodies, nations and empires.

Purifying Empire explores the material, cultural and moral fragmentation of the boundaries of imperial and colonial rule in the British empire in the late nineteenth and early twentieth centuries by exploring how a particular biopolitical project, namely the drive to regulate the obscene in late nineteenth-century Britain, was transformed from a national into a global and imperial project and then re-localized in two different colonial contexts, India and Australia, to produce two related but distinct moral regulatory projects.[1] While a considerable body of work, most notably by scholars of gender and sexuality, has demonstrated both the role of empire in shaping moral regulatory projects in Britain and their adaptation, transformation and, at times, rejection in colonial contexts, this book illustrates that it is in fact only *through* such comparative and transnational studies that it is possible to elucidate both the temporalist nature of colonialism (namely the historically differentiated structures and projects of rule in different colonial contexts) and the contradictions (political, racial and moral) that sustained imperial and colonial regimes.[2] Placing two distinct types of colonies, namely a settler and an exploitation colony, within the same analytical framework as their imperial metropole, and exploring how and in what ways a particular metropolitan disciplinary project was transformed in both contexts, serves to reveal not only the continuities and discontinuities in the imperial project, but also the sites of disorder, or the locations in which imperial and colonial states failed to impose order or failed to even attempt to do so. It thus sheds new light on the hierarchies of production, power and knowledge that constituted both imperial and colonial regimes and that linked the local to the global.

Secondly, *Purifying Empire* situates debates about obscenity in the late nineteenth and early twentieth centuries not simply in the realms of law or discourse, where they are generally located, but in the biopolitical

[1] Biopower is a modern form of power that, according to Michel Foucault, works on transforming the lives of individuals rather than operating in relation to a series of acts. It has two poles, discipline and governmentality. While 'Discipline operates on particular individuals in a particular space' (which it does under the aegis of institutions such as schools, families and hospitals, which collect information about an individual and act on it), 'Governmentality . . . operates on particular groups of individuals' (which it does by gathering information by such means as statistical analyses, censuses, and reports on health and hygiene, which it uses, by such means as legislation, to manage population). Moral regulation ('a special kind of social control that has a specific object – the conduct of life of the regulated, and a specific aim – the change of their identity') operates through both formal systems of governance (such as legislation and policing) and informal ones (such as schools, families and hospitals) and is therefore an aspect of the operation of biopower. Tadros, 'Between Governance and Discipline', 78; Ruonavaara, 'Moral Regulation', 289; and Hunt, *Governing Morals*, p. 1. See also Foucault, 'Governmentality', pp. 87–104.

[2] As Richard Phillips contends, 'the complex and multi-layered historical geography of imperial state formation meant that British imperial and colonial states did different things – with respect to the regulation of sexualities for example – in different times and places'. Phillips, 'Imperialism and the Regulation', 341. Such a claim has been richly borne out in the literature pertaining to prostitution and contagious diseases, as demonstrated notably by the work of Philippa Levine, among others. See, for example, Levine, *Prostitution, Race*; Phillips, *Sex, Politics, and Empire*; Howell, 'Race, Space', 229–48; Ogborn, 'Law and Discipline', 25–57; and van Heyningen, 'The Social Evil', 170–97. See also Stoler, *Race and the Education*; McClintock, *Imperial Leather*; and Hall, *Civilising Subjects*.

realm of what Alison Bashford terms 'imperial hygiene'.[3] Like the emissions of the body, sources of impurity and pollution that are 'marginal stuff of the most obvious kind', obscenity, which is the representation of matter that is deemed beyond representation or that is beyond the accepted norms of public display, is the 'marginal stuff' of art.[4] While 'art' symbolizes the transformation and containment of base matter into the higher realms of culture and sentiment, 'obscenity' symbolizes its efflorescence, or its traversal of the boundary of the body – a traversal that not only endangers the production of a rational, coherent subject, but threatens the 'strength' and 'purity' of the national/imperial body.[5] In viewing the drive to regulate the obscene as both *coterminous with* and a *product of* drives to discipline bodies through regulating sanitation, contagious diseases and the white slave trade, this book thus looks at the effects not only of language upon bodies, but of bodies upon language.

Thirdly, *Purifying Empire* examines the nature of imperial and colonial dis-order, namely of the limitations of governmental power and the role such limitations played in shaping conceptions of modernity, particularly the genealogy of the idea of Australia and India as being *more* modern than their imperial metropole. For the British government's failure to institute an effective system to regulate 'obscene' publications in the empire led, in the case of Australia, to the erection of a system of quarantine as a means of making Australia 'purer', 'cleaner' and 'whiter' than Britain. In India, on the other hand, although 'the modernizing impulses of metropolitan Europe were modified by the imperative of producing colonial subject-bodies that were fundamentally different from European citizen-bodies', as James Mills and Satadru Sen have argued, in electing to regulate 'obscenity' – in contrast to Australia – largely through the inculcation of self-governance, the colonial state erased the distinction between European citizen bodies and colonial subject-bodies and enabled Indian elites, like their Australian counterparts, to hijack this particular project of European modernity.[6] Examining the struggles and contestations that took place between not only colonizers and colonized, metropole and colony, or state and society but between different groups *within* each of these categories serves to demonstrate that governmentality was not 'a singular colonial strategy' but was instead part of 'the struggles going on among groups of colonizers and the colonized and between them, not only over the control of

[3] Bashford, *Imperial Hygiene*.
[4] Douglas, *Purity and Danger*, p. 121; Michelson, *Speaking the Unspeakable*, p. xi; and Nead, *The Female Nude*, p. 90.
[5] Nead, *The Female Nude*, p. 2.
[6] Mills and Sen, 'Introduction', p. 11.

governmental technologies but also over their appropriateness, application, and desirability'.[7] Attempts to regulate the obscene could thus be both empowering and disempowering, strategies of rule and – since 'desires emerged, whetted by and in reaction against . . . regulation' – of resistance.[8] Moreover, while linked by a common set of fears, discourses and modes of regulation – and even, as we shall see in the case of translations of Émile Zola's works, by the same 'obscene' texts or other matter – such regulatory projects played out differently in Britain, India and Australia. They all, however, serve to reveal the nature of imperial and colonial power at its most intimate and vulnerable, and most subject to contestation.

Chapter 1, 'Colonialism and governmentality', offers a re-assessment of the nature of colonial governmentality.[9] Beginning with an overview of the concept of 'governmentality', it argues that while the notion of an all-transforming colonial governmentality has for the most part been discarded by scholars of colonialism, governmentality continues to be regarded as a set of technologies that can be effectively applied to virtually any subject(s), context or time period, regardless of the incongruities in its operation. But since colonialism was not a unitary project, then neither was colonial governmentality. Understanding its nature, this chapter demonstrates, requires examining the historically differentiated political rationalities or differentiated structures and projects of rule in different *types* of colonies – particularly in exploitation and settler colonies, which because they are regarded as so dissimilar are rarely placed within the same analytical framework – and then comparing them to each other. It illustrates, furthermore, that since culture is difficult to subject to governmental power, *perceptions* of the nature or functioning of colonial governmentality may in fact have played a more significant role in fashioning colonial modernities than the actual operation of governmentality itself.

Chapter 2, 'From sovereignty to governmentality: the emergence of obscenity regulation as a biopolitical project in Britain', explores how the regulation of obscenity first emerged as a biopolitical project in Britain in the early nineteenth century. It argues that obscenity, in contrast to other forms of libel such as blasphemy and sedition, came to be regarded as a social problem in this period – one that required regulation through both disciplinary and governmental means. Generated by the construction of a new set of relations of ruling (wrought by the emergence of a complex civil society which included not only new print cultures but new civil

7 Pels, 'The Anthropology', 176.
8 Sigel, *Governing Pleasures*, p. 12.
9 The first major assessment of colonial governmentality was offered by David Scott over a decade ago. See Scott, 'Colonial Governmentality', 191–220.

associations that sought to act upon others through undertaking projects to improve their morals), the aim of this particular regulatory project was to manage the bodies of the working classes through the inculcation of self-governance. This chapter demonstrates, moreover, that empire played a key role not only in fashioning an obscene print culture in Britain, but in spurring the transformation of its regulation into a biopolitical project.

But while the empire played an important role in projects to regulate the obscene throughout the whole of the nineteenth century, as demonstrated in Chapter 3, 'Globalizing the local: imperial hygiene and the regulation of the obscene', the last quarter of the century marks a distinct transformation in the regulation of obscenity not only in Britain but in its empire. This was thanks to, firstly, the coming together of moral reform organizations, the newly emergent medical profession and the state in a medico-moral alliance that attempted to shift the focus away from viewing 'purity' as a moral question to regarding it as a medical and racial one and as, therefore, a 'hygienic' problem. Such a transformation was also, however, a product of a growing awareness that the increased intermingling of peoples, things and texts wrought by the expansion of the material networks of the empire, while serving to strengthen imperial ties, also rendered the boundaries between metropolitan and colonial spaces more unstable. For in addition to transporting the diseases, pollutions and impurities of colonial spaces to the metropole, such networks also conveyed 'obscene' publications. 'Obscene' publications from Britain and Europe were, in turn, being purveyed through the trade networks of the empire and were serving to undermine the 'strength' and 'purity' of Britain's empire. But while Britain could no longer be conceived of as ontologically distinct from its colonial possessions, the fashioning of the empire as contiguous space – as, in essence, an imperial body – meant that Britain could erect a cordon sanitaire around it to protect the race, nation and empire. This chapter thus reveals how the regulation of the obscene was transformed into a project of imperial hygiene through the construction of an international system to police the trade in 'obscenities' throughout the empire.

Envisioning the empire as an imperial body that needed to be purified through policing its margins posed problems, however, for the project of imperial hygiene and, in turn, for imperial power. The first difficulty was that the colonies were engaged in undertaking their own social hygiene projects, and while these often intersected with imperial projects – or, in the case of the regulation of the obscene, were in many ways derived from them – their genealogies were often decidedly distinct. As Chapter 4, 'Localizing the global in settler societies: regulating the obscene in

Australia', illustrates, in the case of Australia the regulation of the obscene emerged as part of the 'White Australia' policy, which was initially designed to keep non-whites out of the geographical boundaries of the nation-state in order to protect Australia's racial and cultural 'purity'. However, with its evolution in the early twentieth century into an endeavour to bar eugenically 'unfit' Britons, the regulation of the obscene was in turn transformed into a project to construct Australia as more hygienic – as, essentially, 'whiter' – than the imperial metropole through the construction of a system of quarantine to keep out 'impure' publications from Britain. Since such a project was largely undertaken by the state, sovereign and disciplinary rather than governmental power thus predominated in Australia as a means of regulating the obscene, which as this chapter demonstrates reveals a lack of faith in the self-governing capacities of Australia's citizens.

The second problem for the project of imperial hygiene was that some margins, as in the case of India, could be policed more rigorously than others. As illustrated in Chapter 5, 'Localizing the global in exploitation colonies: regulating the obscene in India', this was not due to the Indian government's reluctance to intervene in indigenous custom or because of the difficulties (cultural, economic, and so on) in doing so, although these of course played a part. The rationale was instead more contradictory and complex. On the one hand, the colonial government was opposed to taking an active role in regulating the obscene because it had, by the late nineteenth century – thanks in part to its employment of the governmental technology that Henry Schwarz has termed 'aesthetic imperialism' – become convinced of the self-governing capacities of its subjects, or at least of those exposed to Western education.[10] But on the other hand, it opposed undertaking such a regulatory project because the disorder that threatened the imperial body served to justify the civilizing mission of colonialism. Purifying and containing all of the margins of empire would, in short, undermine the social order of the entire imperial/colonial project. But in failing to erect an effective cordon sanitaire around India to keep out 'obscene' publications emanating from Britain or conveyed to India from other parts of the empire, or to effectively police them within India, both British culture and the empire that purveyed it became perceived as a threat to the strength and purity of the Indian 'race' and 'nation'. As in Australia, a tension thus emerged between colonial modernity and national desire, in which the latter sought to dissociate itself from empire and justify its authority through declaring the nation the true, legitimate and authentic bearer of modernity.

[10] Schwarz, 'Aesthetic Imperialism', 563–86.

For since the emergence of bourgeois society was one of the major cultural factors linking metropoles and their colonies in the nineteenth century, colonialism was therefore engaged in the (unintended) project of fashioning modern bourgeois subjects who, in turn, were engaged in fashioning the bourgeois self – which entailed policing boundaries, ensuring racial purity and, in turn, regulating the obscene. Thus, rather than appearing as an agent of modernity, in failing not only to eradicate India's own 'obscene' print culture but in opening up India to the obscene effluvium of the whole empire, Britain became conceived of not only as anti-modern, but as hindering the production of a distinct 'Indian' modernity. As in the case of Australia, 'margin' and 'centre' were thus effectively reversed as Britain's Indian subjects strove to define themselves as more modern than their ostensible colonizers.

The expansion of the material and discursive networks of the British empire began roughly a century before what is generally perceived to be the beginning of the era of 'globalization'. In offering a radical re-assessment of processes of cultural transmission and exchange beginning in the globalizing era of the nineteenth century, *Purifying Empire* disrupts such ahistorical narratives of globalization. Through focusing on three discrete contexts, one metropolitan and two diverse types of colonies, it also challenges theories of both globalization and imperialism that embrace a centre–periphery model in elucidating processes of cultural transmission and exchange. For although the particular regulatory project explored here was initially exported from metropole to colonies, it assumed new life in the process, becoming appropriated, distorted and resisted in ways that not only served colonial interests but that were antithetical to, and undermined, the interests of the metropolis. It thus de-centres the metropolis from the histories of imperialism and globalization. Lastly, in illustrating not only the tensions and insecurities of imperial power, but the emergence of new forms of resistance to it, *Purifying Empire* reveals the importance of culture as a factor in destabilizing empires – often decades before their political and military collapse – while at the same time demonstrating why aspects of imperial cultures such as languages, literatures and knowledge systems, as well as moral and bodily norms, were embraced by colonized peoples around the world even in the face of, and often in conjunction with, their rejection of the political, military and economic aspects of imperialism. In an era witnessing not only an escalation of processes of globalization but the emergence of a new 'new' imperialism, including new forms of resistance, this book thus serves both as a cautionary tale and as an emblem of hope – for the fracturing of the cultural–moral boundaries through which empires are constructed and maintained serves, ultimately, to undermine them.

1 Colonialism and governmentality

Since the work of Michel Foucault, the concept of governmentality has become central to understanding power not simply as repression, but as an epistemological (practical and discursive) phenomenon that normatively produces subjects. The chief concern of governmentality is to apply economy, which Foucault regards as 'a form of surveillance and control as attentive as that of the head of a family over his household and goods', to the maintenance of a healthy and productive population.[1] Enacted under the aegis of a series of institutions (the judiciary, the school and the family), discourses (medicine, criminal justice and demography) and procedures and analyses (surveys, statistics and regulations), what is distinctive about this form of power 'is not its relation to capitalism, but its point of application', which is the '*conditions* in which [the] body is to live and define its life' (emphasis in original).[2] In subjecting them to 'rational' principles governmentality seeks to foster an identification of interests, a 'contract between the technologies of domination of others and those of the self', that ensures that subjects are obliged to transform themselves in an 'improving direction' to do as they ought.[3] It thus serves to construct the normative regularities of civil society.

Although not a universal form of power – it emerged, as Foucault made clear, in European society at a specific time and then became

[1] Foucault, 'Governmentality', p. 102. Foucault defines governmentality as 'The ensemble formed by the institutions, procedures, analyses and reflections, the calculations and tactics that allow the exercise of this very specific albeit complex form of power, which has as its target the population, as its principal form of knowledge political economy, and as its essential technical means apparatuses of security'. Foucault, 'Governmentality', p. 92.

[2] Scott, 'Colonial Governmentality', 201.

[3] M. Foucault, 'Technologies of the Self', p. 19. As Alan Hunt cogently elaborates, 'others' are governed through 'rationalized programmes, strategies, tactics and techniques directed towards acting upon [their] actions'. These include surveillance, constraint and coercion, all of which are aimed at stimulating the governance of the self through 'those voluntary practices by which people not only set for themselves rules of conduct, but seek to modify the social presentation of their selves' by acquiring certain socially visible behavioural characteristics. Hunt, *Governing Morals*, pp. 185, 155.

gradually more important – scholars of colonialism have traced the emergence of governmental power in colonial contexts through the projects of modernization initiated by colonial regimes.[4] Analyses of the operation of governmental power through localized theories and historically specific accounts, or projects, that focus on the particular technologies or sites through which colonial states sought to manage their populations, have demonstrated the ways in which physical exploitation was accompanied and followed by an epistemological one as colonial regimes, bringing with them new conceptions of space and time and new understandings of economy, society, history and progress, set about enumerating, demarcating, and classifying colonized peoples.[5] In doing so they sought to tame the unruliness of difference, delineate the unstable boundaries of rule between colonizers and colonized and facilitate the management of populations. Nationalist movements in turn appropriated governmentality in an effort to 'purify', 'strengthen' and reform their own societies to challenge the project of colonial modernity and make colonized subjects capable of self-rule.

Through exploring how a particular governmentalizing project, namely the regulation of the obscene, was transformed from a national project in Britain to a global and imperial one, and was then translated, reformulated and localized in India and Australia, this book aims to shed new light on the operation of governmentalities not only in colonial contexts, but in the West as well – and of how these shaped each other. Colonialism was not, as David Scott argues in his seminal article on colonial governmentality, a unitary project, which means that 'something called "*the* colonial state" cannot offer itself up as the iteration and reiteration of a single rationality' (emphasis in original). What is

[4] Foucault argues that the transformation from an understanding of power as repression to an understanding of it as a science of government, forged by the population (the object of analysis and manipulation), the government (the political means through which this manipulation is performed) and the economy (the field of action through which population and economy are connected), occurred in European states during the seventeenth and eighteenth centuries. It was not until the nineteenth century that the two poles of biopower, discipline and governmentality, became connected in concrete ways and which, along with sovereignty, formed a triangulated balance of power. Foucault, *The History of Sexuality*; and Tadros, 'Between Governance and Discipline', 91–2, 99.

[5] As Alan Hunt defines it, 'A "project" is a process of governance, practices directed towards the control of some other social agents, institutions, or other social entities'. All governmentalizing projects, according to Hunt, have five main components: agents (ranging from the state to voluntary bodies such moral reform organizations); a target (individuals – or sometimes entire populations or particular segments of those populations – whose behaviour is deemed in need of regulation); tactics or techniques (such as legal measures or the publication of guides to marriage or child-rearing); discourses (which are used in government documents, treatises, texts and so on); and a political context. Hunt, *Governing Morals*, p. 28.

therefore needed, according to Scott, is to explore 'the different political rationalities, different configurations of power, [which] took the stage in commanding positions' within 'the structures and projects that gave shape to the colonial enterprise as a whole'.[6] Such a proposal serves to highlight the temporaneous and localist nature of colonialism. However, in ignoring the connections and similarities *between* political rationalities in different colonial contexts it limits the possibility of generating new understandings of the particular *universalities* of colonial power.[7] Elucidating the connections between both the particular and the universal demands examining the historically differentiated political rationalities or differentiated structures and projects of rule in different *types* of colonies – particularly in exploitation and settler colonies, which because they are regarded as so dissimilar are rarely placed within the same analytical framework – and then comparing them to each other.[8]

Such a comparison also illustrates that while colonial regimes prided themselves on the successful adaptation, operation and transmission of governmental power even in the face of the malleability, subversion and transformation of concepts such as civility and morality, *perceptions* of the nature or functioning of colonial governmentality may in fact have played a more significant role in fashioning colonial modernities than the actual operation – however imperfect – of governmentality itself. For although regarded as universal, the concepts of civility and moral purity that sustained such regimes were in fact highly malleable and subject to constant critique, appropriation and subversion. As Frederick Cooper and Ann Stoler rightly note, for colonized societies 'The intrusion of European models into "private" domains did not necessarily reproduce bourgeois civility but gave rise to diverse efforts ... to find new and original ways for expressing ideals of a domestic domain, for demonstrating status, and indeed for showing that a man or a woman could be "modern" in a variety of ways'.[9] Such efforts led in turn to a constant redrawing of the boundaries between self and other, colonizer

[6] Scott, 'Colonial Governmentality', 197. Scott defines political rationalities as 'those historically constituted complexes of knowledge/power that give shape to colonial projects of political sovereignty' and that characterize 'those ways in which colonial power is organized as an activity designed to produce effects of rule'. Scott, 'Colonial Governmentality', 193.

[7] While I agree with Scott's aim of fracturing the universality of the concept of colonialism, such a concept is, however, meaningless unless it embodies *some* universals.

[8] Since there are seven different types of colonies, and multiple forms of colonialism often coexisted in the same colony, many other comparative possibilities also exist. See Osterhammel, *Colonialism*.

[9] Cooper and Stoler, 'Between Metropole and Colony', p. 32.

and colonized.[10] The boundaries defining European selves were also subject to continual reworking in colonial contexts. By the early twentieth century Australians could thus view themselves as morally – and hence racially – 'purer' than their Anglo-Indian counterparts, who were deemed to be so 'pigheaded and spoilt by the servility of the natives of India, that they are actually not fit to mix with white men'.[11]

Comparing different colonial contexts to each other illuminates, lastly, not only the continuities and discontinuities within colonialism, but the linkages between the local and the global. It therefore has broader implications for the study of imperial and colonial history, especially on the role of imperialism and colonialism in shaping global processes. Like its precursor world systems theory which, while placing colonies in a broader global context (namely the development of the capitalist world system), reduced them to a peripheral status and denied agency to the colonized, globalization theory threatens both to grant too great a transformative power to imperialism, and to veil the emergence of imperialism in new guises.[12] Moreover, as Peter Van der Veer argues, 'there is not a world-systemic teleology that connects imperialism of the past with globalisation in the postcolonial world today' – indeed, increasing global integration, rather than undermining the ethnic and religious divides wrought by imperialism, has instead served to magnify them.[13] In illustrating why some metropolitan discourses resonated in some colonies and others did not, or how notions of the modern were being played out, comparing governmentalizing projects in different colonial contexts thus offers insights into the nature of the relationship between imperialism, colonialism and globalization.

Rethinking colonial governmentality

While the notion of an all-embracing colonial governmentality that, in Homi Bhabha's famous phrase, 'appropriates, directs, and dominates its various spheres of activity' has for the most part been discarded by scholars of colonialism, governmentality continues to appear in such scholarship as a set of technologies that are effectively applied to a variety

[10] As Simon Gikandi observes, despite the considerable body of theory on the dialectic that exists between colonizer and colonized 'it has never been clear where the identity between colonizer and colonized ends and the difference between them begins'. Gikandi, *Maps of Englishness*, p. 2.

[11] *Parliamentary Debates: Commonwealth of Australia*, 6 December 1909, p. 7076.

[12] Ania Loomba *et al.*, 'Beyond What?', pp. 1–38.

[13] Van der Veer, *Imperial Encounters*, p. 11. For further insights into the relationship between globalization and ethno-religious divides in South Asia see Heath, 'Communalism, Globalization'.

of subjects in different contexts and time periods.[14] Yet modern power was not mapped as easily – nor as homogeneously – onto colonial contexts as the above framework implies.[15] There were, in fact, several key incongruities in the way governmental power operated in colonial contexts. To begin with, while colonial governmentality, like its Western form, developed as a means of managing population, of cultivating its resources and maintaining its health, colonial states tended to evince little actual interest in regulating the bodies of their subjects – at least of their indigenous subjects – in order to maintain a healthy and productive population. Simple financial expediency often undermined their desires to do so, as is clear in the reluctance of the state in British Malaya to introduce public health measures among prostitutes and the labouring population until it became clear that the cost of replacing labourers was greater than that of providing for their health care.[16] The fear of rousing indigenous opposition likewise played a role, although when colonial states had the will to undertake such regulatory projects these anxieties become noticeably less pressing.[17] The need to appear progressive while maintaining both indigenous and colonial structures of power arguably generated greater constraints, as is evident in the dilemmas faced by colonial states in managing sexual relations between European soldiers and indigenous women.[18] Since the class status of European soldiers purportedly rendered them incapable of self-control, colonial

[14] Bhabha, 'Difference, Discrimination', p. 154.

[15] This is not to argue that governmental power was mapped easily onto European contexts but rather to question its purported universalism. Moreover, as Nicholas Thomas argues, in overlooking Foucault's argument that governmentality is 'a historically specific, non-functionalist analysis of political knowledge', scholars of imperialism and colonialism often 'lapse into a reifying functionalism more reminiscent of some Marxist theory than Foucault'. Thomas, *Colonialism's Culture*, pp. 42–3.

[16] Manderson, 'Colonial Desires', 380. The health of British troops, on the other hand, remained of paramount importance to the colonial state. Racial factors also, of course, clearly played a role in generating such economic decision-making, as is evident in the British preference for building residential quarters outside and upwind of Indian towns rather than cleaning up what they perceived to be the filthiness of Indian urban spaces. Collingham, *Imperial Bodies*, p. 82.

[17] As David Arnold reveals in his study of British efforts to eradicate plague in late nineteenth-century India, when the call for intervention was pressing, in this case literally a matter of life or death (most notably for the British themselves), they were willing to override their fears of opposition to intervene in even the most intimate aspects of Indian bodies and lives. Arnold, *Colonizing the Body*, pp. 391–426.

[18] Thus, as Veena Das has argued in the case of the East India Company's efforts to regulate sati in the 1820s (both because it challenged the state's attempts to establish a monopoly over violence and because evidence of Indian 'barbarity' served to legitimize colonial power), such efforts, by lending support to *shastric* custom, instead led to the promotion of sati (predominantly in Bengal) and hence undermined attempts to fashion a colonial governmentality – which led the Company to resort to banning the practice in 1829. Das, 'Gender Studies', 64, 66. See also Mani, 'The Debate on *Sati*', pp. 88–126.

states regarded it as their responsibility, on the one hand, to provide them with 'clean' women to consort with, and on the other to prevent interracial liaisons in order to protect the purity and moral authority of the governing 'race'. State cooperation in indigenous regulatory projects, or the merging of indigenous and colonial projects, was one way out of some of these difficulties, as in the case of state involvement in the physical culture movement in Bengal in the late nineteenth century.[19]

Such problems demonstrate not only that the will to undertake governmentalizing projects was thus expedient and contingent, but that the maintenance of colonial structures of power, rather than of a healthy and productive population, was ultimately the chief concern of colonial authorities.[20] The Indian state's passage of numerous legislative enactments in the nineteenth century centring on women, for example, presents evidence of a state that encouraged female emancipation.[21] But while couched in the language of civilization and progress, such measures were instead a means of justifying colonial rule through contributing to the reinvention of Indian 'traditions', the denigration of Indian masculinities and the strengthening and refashioning of both colonial and indigenous patriarchies.[22] Women were thus merely the grounds on which the ideological struggle between colonial and indigenous elites was waged – and, for the colonial state, a means of intervening in matters pertaining to the personal realm while alleging that its intentions were otherwise.[23]

[19] Rosselli, 'The Self-Image', 137–41. The result of such selective disciplinary intervention, however, was that a set of institutions emerged to protect segments of the indigenous elite – more intimate details about whom, moreover, were often collected than would have been permissible in Europe – 'while the rest of the population was left to the more distanced normalisation of colonial government'. Legg, *Spaces of Colonialism*, p. 28.

[20] Ballhatchet, *Race, Sex*, p. 9. Thus in colonial Queensland, while legislation regulating contagious diseases was never applied to the indigenous population, the colony maintained legislation to regulate contagious diseases long after the rest of the British empire had abandoned such efforts out of fears that diseased Aboriginals would infect the white population – an example that illustrates, according to Philippa Levine, that 'Medical care in the colonies was aimed primarily at the British military and at resident colonists'. The brothel was in fact one of the few places in European colonies where the colonized (at least colonized women) were given access to medical care. Levine, 'Public Health', p. 165.

[21] Such enactments include the banning of widow immolation in 1829, the legalization of widow remarriage in 1856, the prohibition of female infanticide in 1870 and the raising of the age of consent from eight to twelve years in 1891.

[22] As Mrinalini Sinha contends, 'the official policy toward women was often contradictory in nature because it could seldom be divorced from the dictates of the colonial situation'. The dictates of the colonial situation, Sinha concludes, led the government to claim to be advocates of female emancipation while reinforcing the oppression of Indian women. Sinha, 'Gender and Imperialism', p. 219.

[23] Ashwini Tambe argues that, for the colonial state in India, 'appearing to hold back from matters relating to the personal realm and posing as a regime which honored local customs was merely politically expedient'. Tambe, 'Colluding Patriarchies', 589.

Such struggles between contending patriarchies demonstrate another incongruity in the operation of colonial governmentality, namely the difficulty of generating a confluence of interests between the governance of others and of the self. It is for this reason that colonial projects designed to regulate the bodies of the colonized were often more effective in regulating those of the colonizers. Rather than transforming Indian bodies to produce Macaulayesque versions of brown Englishmen, the project of Anglicization in early nineteenth-century India, for example, arguably had more of an impact on British bodily norms.[24] Similar effects are evident in settler colonies, as is clear in the case of the efforts of Australian feminists to transform Koori women into responsible and productive members of colonial society, which had a greater transformative impact on the nature of Australian feminism and on its understandings of the colonizing nature of Australian masculinities than on the behaviour of Koori women.[25] Such governmentalizing projects could likewise rebound back to imperial metropoles and transform European subjectivities.[26] Thus British attempts to put a stop to the practice of clitoridectomy in Kikuyu society in the 1920s not only served as a spur to Kikuyu nationalism (and with it a proliferation in the practice of clitoridectomy), but had a profound impact on the discussion of sexual matters in the public realm in Britain.[27]

In addition to fostering the self-governance of the colonizers, colonial governmentalizing projects and processes therefore often had an equal – and at times possibly greater – impact on the fashioning of that of the bourgeoisie in Europe. In the case of agitation by members of the European community in India over the 1883 Ilbert Bill, for example, which sought to amend the Code of Criminal Procedure to give Indian officials in the administrative service a degree of criminal jurisdiction

[24] Collingham, *Imperial Bodies*, p. 51. The project, according to Collingham, served to mark a 'shift from an open to a closed and regimented body'. Collingham, *Imperial Bodies*, p. 4.

[25] Lake, 'Colonised and Colonising', 377–86.

[26] Rather than being targeted at colonized populations, much of what is generally labelled 'colonial discourse' was actually directed at public opinion in imperial states. As John Mackenzie illustrates in his study of British imperial propaganda, such propaganda had a greater impact in 'creating for the British a world view which was central to their perceptions of themselves' than it did in transforming the world view of Britain's colonial subjects. Mackenzie, *Propaganda and Empire*, p. 2.

[27] Pederson, 'National Bodies', 647–80. Concerns with metropolitan sexuality often underlay such colonial regulatory efforts. As Antoinette Burton has argued in the case of one of the most widespread imperial campaigns of moral regulation in the nineteenth century, against the Contagious Diseases Acts, the real goal of abolitionists seeking to overturn colonial acts was the fear that they might be reimposed in Britain. Burton, 'The White Women's Burden', pp. 137–57.

over Europeans living in *mofussils*, or country areas, such agitation served to reinforce racial and gender hierarchies in Britain as well as India.[28] So too did efforts to manage bourgeois sexualities in colonial contexts. In addition to generating a profusion of discourses around pedagogy, parenting and child sexuality that sought to discipline the bourgeois body and distinguish it from both non-whites and poor whites, such efforts served to *produce* middle-class sensibilities.[29] Rather than simply being imported from Europe, such sensibilities were thus formed in European colonies and exported back to imperial metropoles – making the relationship between the production of colonial and European subjectivities one of 'mutual imbrication and contamination'.[30]

That colonial governmentality served to foster at least some identification of interests between colonizers and colonized is clear, however, in the fact that the colonized undertook their own governmentalizing projects. But they also drew upon indigenous traditions of self-subjection in fashioning such technologies.[31] In the case of Indian nationalist attempts to create an 'Indian therapeutics' based on indigenous cultural norms, for example, Western-educated elites combined indigenous forms of self-governance, such as the embodiment of 'femininity' (envisioned as asexual, self-sacrificing and nurturing) and the practice of *brahmacharya* (designed both to preserve sperm and to master control over the senses), with Western forms – evidence that indigenous populations sought not to *mimic* but rather to *transform* the terms of colonial governance.[32] Furthermore, while they often ostensibly sustained governmentalizing projects enacted by colonial states, indigenous elites

[28] Sinha, *Colonial Masculinity*, p. 42. The bill provoked a 'white mutiny' from members of the European community, who challenged it through an intersection of gender and racial ideologies that contrasted the supposed effeminacy of the Bengali *babu* with the 'manliness' of the Englishman. The role of white women, who made a rare foray into the public sphere in India to protest against the bill, posed a further challenge to those hierarchies, and led them to be reconfigured in new ways. Sinha, *Colonial Masculinity*, pp. 33–4.

[29] Stoler, *Race and the Education*, p. 99.

[30] Gikandi, *Maps of Englishness*, p. xviii. Colonies were thus ' "laboratories of modernity", in which recognizably modern conceptions of social discipline and culture were initially produced before being exported to European environments'. Mort, *Dangerous Sexualities*, p. xxii.

[31] As Nicholas Thomas argues in response to theories of the 'pervasive efficacy' of colonialism, such a contention 'excludes the possibility that "natives" often had relatively autonomous representations and agendas, that might have been deaf to the enunciations of colonialism, or not so captive to them that mimicry seemed a necessary capitulation'. Thomas, *Colonialism's Culture*, p. 57.

[32] Prakash, *Another Reason*, p. 145. In the process of this embracing of Indian difference, such a project also opened up Western medicine to revision and reformulation, and altered the relationship between the state and the society it sought to govern.

frequently deployed the language of colonial governmentality to critique colonial rule. Thus tribal leaders in Uganda managed to skilfully rework the colonial campaign to combat syphilis to both assert greater social and political control and condemn the British for exposing them to syphilis and undermining the strength and morality of their culture.[33] Although initially sharing the same ground, governmentalizing projects in the colonies could therefore often fragment and generate competing projects.[34]

Such incongruities demonstrate not only that colonial governmentality emerged in part in spite of, rather than from, the desires of colonial regimes, but that it was not simply, as Gyan Prakash argues, 'the tropicalization of its Western form, but rather ... its fundamental dislocation'.[35] There are three main reasons this is the case. The first is that, as Stephen Legg contends, 'colonial governments operated in a more intimate relationship with the violence of *sovereign* power' (emphasis in original), a relationship in which 'violence became the language of right and exception became the structure of sovereignty'.[36] While it is clear that exploitation colonies were virtually permanent states of exception, so too, although to different degrees, were settler colonies, which were not only shaped by foundational violence but perpetuated violence through legitimating forms (although these were largely targeted at particular populations) and through an imaginary embodied in the state. As in the case of exploitation colonies, settler colonies also, moreover, marked space through violence, rituals and 'the spatial insignia of sovereign power, such as boundaries, hierarchies, zones and cultural imaginaries'.[37]

33 Tuck, 'Venereal Disease', pp. 191–204.

34 Thus in the case of the battle over education in colonial India in the latter half of the nineteenth century, while the colonial government was initially happy to let Indians assume responsibility for opening schools and colleges in the belief that a Western-style education and new institutional structures would, as Partha Chatterjee asserts, 'correct the deficiencies in knowledge and character inherited by the students from their native culture', with the rise of Indian nationalism it sought instead to make the schoolroom an extension of the state. It failed, however, to do so, since 'education institutions, especially in Bengal, had by then largely passed into a disciplinary domain where the discursive forms of a specifically nationalist modernity were already in command'. However, since nationalists regarded such institutions as alien, as disseminating a foreign culture and morality, they sought to construct them as part of the 'inner' domain of the family. Education thus became a contestatory site for competing colonial and nationalist governmentalizing projects. Chatterjee, 'The Disciplines', pp. 11–12.

35 Prakash, *Another Reason*, p. 125. Prakash likewise argues that the governing of colonized peoples 'as modern subjects required colonial knowledge and colonial regulation to function as self-knowledge and self-regulation', which was impossible under colonialism. Prakash, *Another Reason*, p. 127.

36 Legg, *Spaces of Colonialism*, pp. 21, 22.

37 Legg, *Spaces of Colonialism*, p. 22.

The second reason governmentality was dislocated in colonial contexts was the despotic nature of colonial rule, which made colonial states 'incapable of fulfilling the criterion of representativeness – the fundamental condition that makes modern power a matter of interiorized self-discipline, rather than external coercion'.[38] Since their primary concern was to increase the economic strength of the state and enhance the wealth of the colonial rulers, they did not consider population to be wealth. Rather than producing the 'citizen-individual' necessary for the tripartite sovereignty–discipline–government nexus to emerge, colonial regimes thus sought instead to create what Uma Kalpagam refers to as 'an individual who by being forced into a new sphere of commercial exchange would become the *Homo economicus* of the market economy'.[39]

Governmentality was also dislocated in colonial contexts, lastly, by the operation of what Partha Chatterjee has termed 'the rule of colonial difference', which in reproducing difference between the colonizers and colonized served to further undermine the generation of a confluence of interests between the governance of others and the governance of the self.[40] The rule of colonial difference meant that the attitude of colonial regimes towards the generation of such a confluence, or indeed towards the production of modern subjects, was in fact highly ambiguous since they needed to maximize economic exploitation without undermining colonial rule.[41] Colonial regimes negotiated this difficult problem by altering the relationship between the state and its subjects. As Mark Brown argues, while in the West the relationship between state and subject is marked by a progressive elaboration of the latter's civil, political and social rights, in colonial contexts virtue, rather than right, structured relations between state and subject.[42] The colonial subject

[38] Chatterjee, 'The Disciplines', p. 8.

[39] Kalpagam, 'Colonial Governmentality and the "Economy"', 420.

[40] Chatterjee, *The Nation and its Fragments*, p. 10. The rule of colonial difference meant, furthermore, that colonial discipline was forced 'to define the limits of its ambition through an orientalist discourse that blamed the [colonized] for the very measures required to police them'. Howell, 'Race, Space', 238–9.

[41] The distinction drawn by Mitchell Dean between what he terms 'governmental self-formation' (in which authorities attempt to shape the behaviour, desires, requirements, and capabilities of individuals) and 'ethical self-formation' (by which individuals endeavour to know and act on themselves) would appear to alleviate this tension. I agree, however, with Alan Hunt's contention that such a distinction serves to conflate morals and ethics and to assume that 'the external imposition of a moral code is mirrored in internal processes of self-formation' (a tendency Hunt rightly notes is also clear in Norbert Elias's account of the civilizing process and Émile Durkheim's of the 'moral order') – processes that in colonial contexts were often highly disparate. Hunt, *Governing Morals*, p. 16. See also Dean, '"A Social Structure"', 145–68 and *Governmentality*; Elias, *The Civilizing Process*; and Durkheim, *Moral Education.*

[42] Brown, '"That Heavy Machine"', 44–5.

was required, according to Brown, to be 'an agent of obligation before being a recipient of rights': to conform, in other words, to notions of morality, rationality, integrity, prudence and self-control without receiving counterpart rights.[43] For Brown the rule of colonial difference thus operated not through markers such as race, but through an ethical capacity ordered and defined through virtues.[44]

Yet although colonial regimes may have altered the relationship between the state and its subjects, they nonetheless opened up a space for the colonized to enter, critique and transform governmentalizing discourses and practices. For since the subjects brought into being by statistics, Western medicine and alien institutions were also located in indigenous knowledges and conditions, 'The colonization of the body had to operate as the care of the native body'.[45] Colonial regimes were thus forced to occupy two positions at the same time, namely both a Western and an indigenous one.[46] While generating tremendous tensions in the operation of colonial governmentality, since the colonized were viewed as incapable of self-governance, on the one hand, but on the other as being capable of being made 'self-governing in spite of their will' through the application of modern technologies, such duality also created a space for linking the state and the people.[47] This linkage was largely obscured, however, by the aesthetic of colonial governmentality – what Zahid Chaudhary, in his study of colonial photography, has termed the 'phantasmagoric aesthetic'. Such an aesthetic served to manage population through rendering the violence of colonial governmentality invisible by veiling existing social relations, in particular relations of production.[48] But it also served to make visible the self-estrangement and alienation wrought by colonial governmentality upon *both* the

[43] Brown, '"That Heavy Machine"', 46. As Veena Das contends, one of the benefits of administrative knowledge is that it did not 'have to address itself to the problems of the rights of people'. Das, 'Gender Studies', 59.

[44] Brown, '"That Heavy Machine"', 46. Such a concept helps to explain, furthermore, the seeming contradiction practised by the colonizers of 'high ethical standards accompanied by brutality'. Brown, '"That Heavy Machine"', 47.

[45] Prakash, *Another Reason*, p. 127.

[46] For the British the Indian body, according to Prakash, was 'a spectral body composed of unhygienic habits and superstitious beliefs upon which modern knowledge and tactics were to be applied in order to reform it and restore its health and well-being'. *Another Reason*, p. 128.

[47] Prakash, *Another Reason*, p. 143. Such a space was created, for Prakash, by the concept of population, which 'permitted the application of modern technologies on inhabitants who were otherwise seen as unfit for and incapable of reason and progress'. *Another Reason*, p. 144.

[48] Chaudhary, 'Phantasmagoric Aesthetics', 72. The violence of colonial governmentality penetrated colonized societies through the development of statistics and population management.

colonized (through objectifying and imposing 'foreignness' upon them) and the colonizers (through emphasizing their own foreignness and by generating a sense of superiority in the face of colonial difference) – and to undermine, in turn, the efforts of colonial governmentality to construct and maintain such categories.[49]

Yet while governmentality was clearly dislocated in a colony such as India, was this also the case in settler colonies, particularly those that were self-governing? The logic of colonial governmentality was clearly at work in regard to the relationship between settler states and their indigenous subjects, but what about the relationship between such states and their (white) citizen-subjects? Or between imperial states and their settler subjects? Although 'settlers left some of the most lasting legacies of colonialism', as Peter Pels acknowledges, the Australian historian Angela Wollacott justly contends that scholars 'have barely begun to supply the insights of post-colonial theory and critical colonial studies to Australia and other white settler colonies of the British and other European empires'.[50] It is in part the notorious difficulty of interpreting the nature of settler colonialism that has led to its virtual exclusion from postcolonial studies, including the work on colonial governmentality. But the emphasis on difference in postcolonial studies at the expense of explorations of similarity or congruity has also played a role, since it has served to preserve rather than undermine the binaries of colonialism (such as self/other, colonizer/colonized and modernity/tradition).[51] Because settlers were both subjects and citizens, colonizers and colonized, and were hence complicit in colonialism even in the face of the most strident resistance to it, such resistance could not be directed purely at an external object. It entailed, therefore, a division of the self.[52] Colonial binaries thus shed little light on the nature of settler societies' coloniality. It is precisely the *ambivalence* of settler colonialism that

[49] Chaudhary, 'Phantasmagoric Aesthetics', 99.

[50] Pels, 'The Anthropology of Colonialism', 173; and Wollacott, 'White Colonialism', p. 50. There have been numerous attempts since the publication of Bill Ashcroft, Gareth Griffiths and Helen Tiffin's *The Empire Writes Back* to incorporate settler colonies more fully into the domain of postcolonial studies. Such attempts have made little impact, however, on the field as a whole, although the racial dynamics within settler societies (particularly relations between white settlers and indigenous populations) has drawn a considerable amount of attention from postcolonial scholars.

[51] Slemon, 'Unsettling the Empire', 33. This is not to argue for the abandonment of analyses of difference, particularly in regard to settler colonies. Indeed, as Lorenzo Veracini maintains, in light of the settler colonial trope of articulating their difference as new worlds divorced from corrupt old worlds such analyses are particularly pressing. See Veracini, 'Historylessness', 271–85.

[52] Slemon, 'Unsettling the Empire', 38, 39.

illustrates what Stephen Slemon terms 'the radical ambivalence of colonialism's middle ground'.[53]

The existence of such a 'middle ground' demonstrates that we cannot talk about colonial governmentality in the singular. Not only did different governmentalities exist in both exploitation and settler colonies, but *within* such colonies. The operation of the rule of colonial difference offers a case in point. While such a rule was clearly at work in settler attitudes towards indigenous subjects, it could also be argued that what we might term a 'rule of settler difference' operated in imperial attitudes towards settler subjects. As Lawrence Buell argues in his study of what he regards as 'the postcolonial anxiety' of nineteenth-century canonical American writers, which is evident in their efforts to 'define themselves over against the prior cultural hegemony of the former ruling power', such apprehension stemmed from British attitudes towards the thirteen colonies and later the United States (namely that American civilization lacked refinement, that it was unphilosophical, that it had no language and that Americans tended to irrationality).[54] The operation of such a 'rule of settler difference' leads Buell to make the daring claim that settler societies such as the thirteen colonies found cultural colonization harder to resist than colonies such as India, since although the former did not experience the degree of political and military domination exerted by the British in the latter, 'the extent of cultural colonization, from epistemology to aesthetics to dietetics, was much more comprehensive'.[55]

But whatever form governmentality took in different colonial contexts, it opened up spaces through which both imperial and colonial regimes could be critiqued and subverted. Moreover, attempts to prevent or alleviate the possibilities of subversion, such as the employment of virtue rather than right as a means of structuring relations between states and their subjects, were not only largely unsuccessful, they served to further undermine such regimes. The utilization of virtue as a means of cultivating what I would term, in contrast to Brown, *moral* rather than ethical subjectivities was arguably, in fact, the ultimate flaw of colonial

[53] Slemon, 'Unsettling the Empire', 34.

[54] Buell, 'Postcolonial Anxiety', p. 199.

[55] Buell, 'Postcolonial Anxiety', p. 199. Such cultural colonization, Buell insists, persisted in the literary–cultural sphere well beyond independence, which he believes helps to explain both the nature of American anxieties and America's transformation into an imperial power. He thus concludes that 'this continuum between colonial and imperial mentalities . . . seems inextricably bound up with its antecedent history, as the creation of a colonial project'. Buell, 'Postcolonial Anxiety', p. 213. For a more comprehensive overview of the nature of the postcoloniality of the United States see Stoler, 'Tense and Tender Ties', 829–65.

governmentalities.[56] Since what marks the relationship between virtue and rights in colonial contexts is not simply that virtue was used as a yardstick to measure rights – such a yardstick existed, for example, in Britain as well as its colonies – but that the *equation* between virtue and rights differed in both exploitation and, to a smaller extent, settler colonies, colonized peoples had to attain a higher standard of virtue in order to acquire lesser rights.[57] While this model does not appear to hold for settler colonies such as South Australia or New Zealand, which in the late nineteenth century extended rights to white settlers that were unavailable to British citizens (such as female suffrage), the right or ability to govern the self was, as we shall see, often deemed considerably more lacking in such contexts than in a conquest colony such as India. Furthermore, when Indians, Nigerians, or Australians *did* attain such virtue – when they were deemed, in other words, capable of governing the self – the falsity of the relationship between virtue and rights became evident, particularly in exploitation colonies, in which indigenous elites continued to be denied the right to self-government. The denial of such rights further undermined, therefore, the moral legitimacy of imperial and colonial regimes.

Yet what was most problematic in fashioning a relationship between virtue and subjectivity was that it necessitated that the colonizers possess the moral legitimacy to hold themselves up as the yardstick by which the colonized could be judged. Although considerable attention has been devoted to attempts to regulate sexuality in European colonies, the broader socio-political implications of the operation of what Lenore Manderson terms the 'moral logic of colonialism', namely the sanctioning of acts, policies or behaviours that Europeans regarded as immoral, has received relatively little consideration. Such a logic functioned as a double bind, for while 'immoralities' such as prostitution or obscenity were sanctioned by the colonizers to uphold the moral–political order of colonialism, in doing so they ultimately undermined their claims to a superior morality – and with it the right, and ability, to govern. As Manderson demonstrates in her discussion of the colonial state's efforts to manage contagious diseases in Malaya, one of the most common arguments put forward to defend the sanctioning of prostitution was that 'morality was relative', since it is 'dependent on influences of climate,

[56] The two are, however, intimately related, since, as Valverde argues, the aim of moral reform, a particular discourse and practice of governmentality, 'is not so much to change behaviour as to generate certain ethical subjectivities that appear as inherently "moral"'. Valverde, 'Moral Capital', 186.

[57] Brown, '"That Heavy Machine"'. For an analysis of the relationship between virtue and rights in late-Victorian Britain, see Petrow, *Policing Morals*, pp. 7–27.

religious belief, education and the feeling of society'.[58] Prostitution was thus seen as inevitable, a 'necessary palliative' for a society that did not deem it immoral. Metropolitan intervention into the regulation of colonial sexualities, such as the forced repeal of the Contagious Diseases ordinances in Britain's colonies, was therefore viewed as evidence of 'an inappropriate English morality that failed to account for the realities of the social and sexual life of the people of the region'.[59] They regarded it, in short, as undermining the 'critical moral-imperial universe' necessary for colonialism to function, for in spite of ensuring that their troops were provided with ('clean') prostitutes, it was essential, as Philippa Levine argues, for the British to 'monopolize the moral ground' – which they did through declaring their colonial subjects uncivilized, amoral and effeminate.[60] But maintaining – or even obtaining – this ground was precarious, and they began to lose it increasingly from the last quarter of the nineteenth century onwards as Indians, Malays and Ugandans began to turn the tables against them and accuse them of failing to uphold the morality and civility with which they claimed the right to rule.[61] So too did Britain's settler colonies, which assessed their moral geography vis-à-vis that of the metropole and often found the latter wanting.[62] As testified by the emergence of colonial nationalisms, the moral legitimacy of colonialism was thus beginning to wane precisely at the moment when governmentality was coming into its own as a tool

58 Contagious Diseases Regulation (Perak and Malay States), Copy of Correspondence relative to proposed introduction of Contagious Diseases Regulations in Perak or other Protected Malay States, cited in Manderson, 'Colonial Desires', 382. While, as Dane Kennedy rightly argues, the development of the concept of moral relativity in Britain in the late nineteenth century was a result of a growing consciousness of the non-Western world, such a concept was embraced much earlier by colonial officials faced with irrefutable evidence of its existence. Kennedy, *The Highly Civilized Man*, p. 207.

59 Manderson, 'Colonial Desires', 381–2. Although attempts to regulate prostitution in Britain during the mid-nineteenth century had served to normalize prostitution and a double standard operated there vis-à-vis acceptable moral behaviour for men and women, evidence of colonial states' sanctioning of relative morality in British colonies was always vehemently opposed – even to the point, as Philippa Levine argues, of threatening the collapse of the British government in the 1890s, and of severely undermining that of its Indian counterpart. Levine, 'Rereading the 1890s', 585–612.

60 Cited in Levine, 'Rereading the 1890s', 591, 603.

61 Indian newspapers, Levine comments, 'were not shy about pointing to the flagrant prostitution on London's streets, to the bastardy rates in Britain, and . . . to the loutish behavior of English soldiers on Indian soil'. 'Rereading the 1890s', 605.

62 As the Methodist preacher and South Australian parliamentarian John Carr argued in opposition to the introduction of contagious diseases legislation in South Australia, he had 'seen more immorality in certain streets of Liverpool in half an hour than he had seen or heard of during the whole of his sojourn in Adelaide', and he regarded the latter as 'one of the best-conducted cities in the world as far as police supervision, good order, and general morality were concerned'. Cited in Phillips, 'Imperialism and the Regulation', 349.

of governance – a result, in part, of the alienation wrought by colonial governmentality.

While the tendency of colonial discourse is to 'recast culture as a whole in terms of government', as Simon Gikandi argues, 'one of the most fascinating aspects of colonial rule was its uncanny generation of narratives that refused to fit into the hierarchies of colonial government and rule, narratives that dislocated the colonial project itself or called its central assumptions into question'.[63] The existence of such narratives implies that culture was, in fact, difficult to subject to governmental power in colonial contexts, an argument borne out by James C. Scott in his discussion of the ideologies, methods and tools of modern state-building. States, Scott argues, seek to transform population, space and nature through 'techne', or 'settled knowledge', which is organized into a set of 'systematic and impersonal rules . . . [that] facilitate the production of knowledge that can be readily assembled, comprehensively documented, and formally taught'.[64] The fashioning of formal order is dependent, however, on 'metis', or informal processes and local knowledges, which unlike techne is 'contextual and particular'.[65] The problem for states is that while they can partially create metis, they cannot maintain or control it. Since culture is part of the realm of metis, it is thus difficult to render it subject to techne, particularly in multilinguistic, multicultural contexts such as India in which the socio-cultural divisions between techne and metis were so acute. While 'culture' and 'colonial dominance' are thus mutually implicated, it is not possible, therefore, to reduce one to the other.[66]

Some aspects of culture, such as obscenity, are, however, even more impervious to techne than others. Because 'the best analogy for a society's stock of metis is its language', and obscenity is partly a linguistic problem, it was difficult to subject to governmental power in colonial contexts.[67] Moreover, since dirty words instilled ideas of pollution into aspects of sexuality far more than other forms of language, they thus broke down the boundaries mediating both language and sexuality, public and private, self and other, and home and empire. Attempts to regulate the obscene thus exposed the moral logic of colonialism even

[63] Gikandi, *Maps of Englishness*, p. xiii.
[64] Scott, *Seeing Like a State*, pp. 82, 320.
[65] Scott, *Seeing Like a State*, p. 320.
[66] 'The governmentalization of culture', as Nicholas Thomas argues, is not productive since 'colonial discourse cannot be construed as a unitary or stable archive in the fashion of a set of official statistics or reports'. Thomas, *Colonialism's Culture*, p. 46. For works that regard culture and government as virtually synonymous see, for example, Bhabha, *The Location of Culture*; and Cohn, *Colonialism and its Forms*.
[67] Scott, *Seeing Like a State*, p. 332.

more effectively than efforts to regulate sexuality. While to fail to regulate European-language or imported publications threatened to 'corrupt' and 'pollute' both colonizers and colonized alike, to undertake their regulation served to highlight the 'impurity' and 'degeneracy' of the culture of the colonizers (or, in the case of settler colonies, of the imperial metropole). Such regulatory endeavours demonstrated that, furthermore, rather than 'uplifting' and 'purifying' indigenous societies – or, in the case of settler societies, 'strengthening' and 'protecting' the white 'race' – the colonizers were instead corrupting and polluting societies to which such forms of 'corruption' were either obscure or entirely unknown. Similar problems beset attempts to regulate indigenous publications. In exploitation colonies the moral logic of colonialism dictated that indigenous 'obscenities' should not, in fact, be regulated, and attempts to do so could thus be greeted with charges of both hypocrisy and moral prudery (particularly if non-indigenous-language matter was left untouched). Yet neglecting to regulate the cultures of the colonized also laid colonial states open to charges of failing to protect the racial strength and purity of their subjects and of thus, again, undermining the civilizing mission that they purported to uphold. Similar charges were made against imperial metropoles for failing to assist settler colonies to regulate obscenity within their borders. When it came to regulating the obscene, whatever the course taken, it thus served to undermine the moral legitimacy of the colonizers and/or imperial metropole – and with it, that of imperial/colonial rule.[68]

Comparing colonialisms: the political rationalities of governmental rule

In spite of the fact that comparable political rationalities operated in both settler and exploitation colonies in which race and sex served as markers of inclusion and exclusion, the personal was linked to the political, and the cultivation of the self was allied to that of the body politic, exploitation colonies such as India and settler colonies such as Australia are rarely placed within the same analytical framework thanks to their differing political and economic histories and development. While exploitation colonies are regarded as a more common form of colonialism, one in which land, natural resources and labour were appropriated by colonial powers and subjected to indirect control through a 'thin white line' of administrators, soldiers, merchants and

[68] For insights into how obscenity continues to undermine postcolonial regimes, at least in Africa, see Mbembe, *On the Postcolony.*

missionaries, settler colonies are viewed as distinct because they were characterized by larger-scale European settlement, the development of more complex political and economic infrastructures and the attainment of political independence from their metropoles.[69] Yet as Penny Edwards argues, the 'bifurcation between "settler" colonialism and its hypothetical antithesis – the presumed conundrum of a colonialism without settlers', is more artificial than real, 'a legacy of colonial mapping which still structures much contemporary thinking, both within and without academe'.[70] Part of the reason for the ongoing predominance of this binary, according to Edwards, is the varying terms that were used to describe Europeans in different colonial contexts. In a context such as Australia, Europeans were referred to as 'settlers' as a means of claiming the land, fixing their location and securing identities that were destabilized through migration and colonization – by, in essence, their mobility (a factor that the language of 'settlement' sought to deny through defining Europeans, in contrast to the indigenous inhabitants, as civilizing, settled and sedentary). In spite of patterns of long-term settlement, Europeans in India, on the other hand, were referred to by terms such as 'Anglo-Indians', 'Domiciled Europeans', or 'half-castes', terms 'which allowed distinctions between class, race and, perhaps most importantly, mobility' but which, like the term 'settler', were highly contested and variable concepts.[71] For Edwards there is, in fact, little to distinguish settler from non-settler colonialism apart from 'differences in demographic scale and in timing', since what united all colonial populations was 'a common, elemental preoccupation with making a home on foreign land'.[72]

While Edwards elides some of the very real differences in hierarchy and power in settler versus exploitation colonies she is right to question the continued prevalence of colonial mapping in shaping contemporary understandings of colonialism, particularly in relation to settler colonies. As Daiva Stasiulis and Nira Yuval-Davis contend, it is necessary to resist

[69] Stasiulis and Yuval-Davis, 'Introduction', p. 3.

[70] Edwards, 'On Home Ground'. It does so, according to Edwards, through 'an assumed moral hierarchy of colonization, where "settler colonies" occupy the abyss and "non-settler colonies" have somehow secured an unspoken moral high-ground' (para. 53).

[71] Edwards, 'On Home Ground', paras. 11, 5.

[72] Edwards, 'On Home Ground', para. 53. Such different types of colonies as Australia and India were also, of course, tied together via empire. Since the East India Company had a monopoly on trade in the Pacific up to 1833, as Beverley Kingston argues, 'the fortunes of Australia were linked with those of India' from its very founding. Moreover, 'A vast network of imperial connections in government, administration, the army, the church, the law, education, and enterprise, extended from India to the Australian colonies' until well into the twentieth century. Kingston, 'The Taste of India', p. 36.

'drawing an unambiguous line of demarcation between settler and other (colonial, post-colonial or metropolitan) societies' because 'circuits of power are vastly more complicated both globally and in specific locations than any binary division allows'.[73] Australia offers a case in point, for while in contrast to a colony such as India (which until its independence from British rule was subject to a system of autocratic government by alien rulers) the Australian colonies had achieved self-governance by the mid-nineteenth century and by 1901 had federated to form a new nation-state, Australia nonetheless remained a colonial society. An Australian cultural ethos had come into being by the late nineteenth century but Australian culture, as Stephen Alomes has argued, actually became 'more colonial at the very moment of national self discovery and self confidence'. Moreover, although imperial sentiment actually peaked in the interwar period, Australian culture remained predominantly Anglo-Celtic until at least the 1950s.[74] The Australian government was in fact so reluctant to sever imperial ties that it did not ratify the 1931 Statute of Westminster, which accorded independence to Britain's dominions, until the Second World War.[75] This is not to say that the relationship between Australia and its imperial metropole was not often a contentious one. Indeed, although they were linked together in what Frank Mort refers to as a 'puritan sexual diaspora', demarcating the boundaries of 'whiteness' between Australians and Britons was often as fraught as that between settlers and the indigenous population.[76] Unlike the case of the former, delineating the borders between the latter remains, however, an ongoing process. The continued colonial dispossession of its Aboriginal population means that Australia has yet, in fact, to fully sever itself from its colonial past, rendering it 'Caught in that liminal, always undecided state between a colonial past and a postcolonial future'.[77]

[73] Stasiulis and Yuval-Davis, 'Introduction', p. 3.

[74] Alomes puts forward a number of arguments to explain why this was the case, but the most important was undoubtedly the growing interconnectedness of the empire. Alomes, 'Australian Nationalism', 324.

[75] Although the Commonwealth finally acceded to the statute in 1942, the individual Australian states were not formally severed from Britain until 1986. Considerable doubt also remains as to the pervasiveness of an Australian cultural ethos from the late nineteenth century, since, as Martyn Lyons and Lucy Taksa have revealed, most Australians favoured reading the works of British authors over those of their Australian counterparts up to the Second World War. Hudson and Sharp, *Australian Independence*; and Lyons and Taksa, *Australian Readers Remember*, ch. 4. See also Davison, 'Sydney and the Bush', 191–209; Stewart, 'Journalism and the World of the Writer', pp. 174–93; Nesbit, 'Literary Nationalism'; and White, *Inventing Australia*.

[76] Mort, *Dangerous Sexualities*, p. xviii.

[77] Curthoys, 'Identity Crisis', 166.

What, then, were the political rationalities that shaped the emergence and operation of governmental power in Australia? The first was the timing of Australia's nationalist movement. While by the early twentieth century the 'good' citizen had been conceptualized as the healthy citizen in all Western contexts, in Australia this was also the period of concerted nation- and citizen-formation – at least of 'white' Australian bodies.[78] Thus while the Federation Conferences of the 1880s and 1890s sought to delineate the political boundaries of the new nation-state, a corresponding string of Australasian sanitary conferences sought to demarcate the hygienic boundaries, notably through the elaboration of a federal quarantine system to keep pollutants (both physical and moral) outside its borders. The power of quarantine, which was used to keep not only undesirable bodies out of the Commonwealth but also, as we shall see, 'obscene' publications, was in fact the only public health power granted to the federal government.[79] Questions of health and hygiene therefore became deeply imbricated in the formation of Australian national identity.

The second factor shaping the political rationality of governmental power as it developed in Australia was Australia's geography, and the role it played in fashioning 'whiteness'. Not only was Australia a 'European' nation moored in the 'East', but with an 8,000 mile coastline it had the most porous and unpoliceable border in the world. But that geography also gave Australia an immense advantage in attempting to create a new, model society through protecting it from contamination, and not just from those forms of contagion that were perceived to emanate from Asia. Indeed, the 'tyranny of distance', as Geoffrey Blainey has memorably phrased it, while creating a 'gap between geographical and cultural-historical codes of belonging' in Australia, also enabled Australia to 'protect' itself from the diseases, impurities and corruptions of the 'Old World' as well, including those of the 'mother' country.[80] For the problem for Australia was that it was not a 'geographical expression' – all those within the boundary of the nation-state were not citizens, and all those outside were not foreigners.[81] The national quarantine line, which was also the border of the new nation-state, thus served to produce Australia as a geo-body.[82] While British ethnic identification actually increased in Australia in the late nineteenth century, quarantine became a knowledge-practice through which Australia was

[78] Bashford, *Imperial Hygiene*, p. 117.
[79] All other health powers were left to the states.
[80] Blainey, *The Tyranny of Distance*; and Curthoys, 'Feminism, Citizenship', 20.
[81] Rosecrance, 'The Radical Culture of Australia', p. 293.
[82] Bashford, *Imperial Hygiene*, p. 116.

imagined and a means of protecting the 'uncontaminated' island nation from threats to its purity, including, by the First World War, threats to its whiteness by the 'morally unhygienic and contaminating Briton'.[83]

That Australia was able to erect such a powerful quarantine barrier to protect its 'purity' was thanks to the final key factor distinguishing the political rationality that fashioned governmental power in Australia. This was the fact that the state obtained legal hegemony there earlier than it did in many other colonial contexts, at least in New South Wales, the oldest of Australia's six colonies.[84] As Lauren Benton has argued, multicentric legal systems within imperial and colonial polities, in which the state is one among many legal authorities, were replaced during the course of the nineteenth century with state-centred legal authorities in which states sought (although did not always attain) dominance over other legal authorities. Although the timing of such a shift varied in different colonial contexts, in each case the 'jockeying over alternative visions of the plural legal order contributed to the formation of the colonial state as an arbiter of internal boundaries'.[85] Benton argues that in New South Wales conflicts over the legal rights of emancipists coincided in the 1830s with a redefinition of Aborigines as colonial legal subjects rather than as members of a separate community, which marked a shift from a policy of legal pluralism to one of state hegemony.[86] The fact that, as George Nadel has argued, Australian nationalism is 'ethical' rather than political, a result of the elaboration of an Australian nationhood before the existence of an Australian state, also contributed to an instrumental view of the state, in which the purpose of the state was envisioned as that of imposing an ulterior unity on the nation.[87] This also led to a conception of the state as 'collective power at the service of individualistic "rights"', which diminished opposition to the

[83] Bashford, *Imperial Hygiene*, p. 139; and Day, *Contraband and Controversy*, pp. 73–4.

[84] Studying law is important for understanding the nature of governmental power since, as Victor Tadros claims, 'Law operates as a field through which techniques of governance can intervene in the disciplinary network', although 'by connecting itself to both of the poles of bio-power law, in justifying itself . . . [law] masks the need of each of these forms of power to legitimate themselves'. Tadros, 'Between Governance and Discipline', 79.

[85] Benton, *Law and Colonial Cultures*, p. 23.

[86] Benton, *Law and Colonial Cultures*, p. 184. Such a shift was brought about, Benton illustrates, through the struggles of emancipists to secure the legal and political rights of other whites, which entailed an emphasis on the cultural gulf between whites and Aborigines. But the state also secured legal hegemony in New South Wales earlier than was the case in India thanks to the perceived nature of the relationship between settlers and the land in settler colonies, in which the land was viewed as a purported historyless *terra nullius* unframed by social relations. This led the founders of political orders in settler colonies to 'see themselves carrying an inherent and unprecedented sovereignty'. Veracini, 'Historylessness', 274.

[87] Nadel, *Australia's Colonial Culture*, p. 273.

reliance of the 'individual' upon state power.[88] State hegemony coupled with an instrumentalist view of the state meant that the state assumed an early responsibility for policing Australia's 'whiteness'. Thus although the governmentalization of the colonial state in the late nineteenth century led to the 'quantification, distribution and administration of an indigenous white "settler" population' and the production of 'new kinds of subjects for rule', the elaboration of a system of quarantine at a time when such methods of containment were being abandoned as medically and morally ineffective elsewhere reveals that the biopolitical state did not have faith in the self-governing capacities of its citizens.[89] This meant that while governmental technologies were increasingly adopted to fashion pure, clean and moral Australian bodies from the late nineteenth century onwards, sovereign and disciplinary rather than governmental power continued to predominate.

The political rationality surrounding the development of governmental power in India in the late nineteenth century was more complex. As an exploitation rather than a settler colony, India was not, of course, self-governing – indeed, although the emergence of India's nationalist movement was roughly coterminous with Australia's, India did not become a nation-state until half a century after Australia. Indians were, however, gradually incorporated into the governing process from the 1860s onwards, and while India was undoubtedly culturally colonized, the cultural differences dividing rulers and ruled, in addition to the colonial state's abnegation of interference in the socio-cultural realm, meant that, pace Buell, Indian culture was arguably *less* colonized than its Australian counterpart.[90] Moreover, the institution of a hegemonic state took much longer to evolve in colonial India and remained subject to greater contestation than in Australia.

For the early East India Company state the role of governance was inconsequential. The techniques of government were gradually instituted with the acquisition of the administration of police, justice and revenue, and by the early nineteenth century regular and centralized forms of administration began to evolve and the state began to stake

88 Hancock, *Australia*, p. 62.

89 Bashford, *Imperial Hygiene*, pp. 34, 118. By 'governmentalization' I am referring both to 'those discourses and practices whereby something comes to be regarded as a suitable object to be governed, and . . . the means of governing through a complex of more or less rationalized programmes, strategies, tactics and techniques directed towards acting upon the actions of others'. Hunt, *Governing Morals*, p. 185.

90 Although an Australian cultural ethos had come into being by the late nineteenth century, Australian culture was still, nonetheless, a derivative culture. India, on the other hand, could lay claim to an ancient culture, a multitude of indigenous languages and a rich literary heritage.

claims to its legal hegemony.[91] But it was not until the second half of the nineteenth century, following the transferral of the governance of India from the Company to the crown, that legal and political control became more firmly established (through such measures as increasing control over criminal law, an intensification of supervision of policing and tighter control of 'frontier' areas), administrative procedures became more systematized, the project of knowing India 'scientifically' was launched (through such means as censuses, surveys, anthropological studies and so on), and population became the chief concern of the state.[92] Unlike in Australia, the attainment of state legal hegemony thus coincided with the governmentalization of the colonial state as it sought, through statistical methods, to enumerate, classify and demarcate population. In the process new categories were delineated, and while categories such as caste and tribe continued to remain obdurate in their differences, they 'rendered it possible to conceive of narratives and counter-narratives of modernity and progress, and in so doing brought "India" within the discursive fold of universal science and universal history'.[93]

But although the unruliness of difference was to some extent tamed, the political rationalities of colonial rule meant that the implementation of colonial governmentality in India nonetheless played out very differently from the way it did in Australia. To begin with, the state was subject to greater contestation than it was in Australia. In the case of law, for example, the attainment of state legal hegemony in the second half of the nineteenth century led to state hegemony in the realm of political economy but not in that of moral economy.[94] Moreover, in the process of translating British legal norms into the Indian colonial context, of absorbing Indian law into modern British law and marking a shift from status to contract, those norms were subject to opposition, re-negotiation and transformation.[95] Such processes produced an Indian

91 Kalpagam, 'The Colonial State and Statistical Knowledge', 150.

92 Benton, *Law and Colonial Cultures*, p. 150. Kalpagam argues that while the desire to know India scientifically first emerged in the eighteenth century, population was not the main focus of concern until the late nineteenth. Such a shift can be explained in part through the changes brought about by the 1857 Revolt. Arguably more important, however, was the changing nature of India's political economy from a focus on revenue collection to the production of raw materials and a market for British goods during the course of the nineteenth century. Kalpagam, 'The Colonial State', 49.

93 Kalpagam, 'The Colonial State', 49.

94 As Nicholas Dirks illustrates in his study of the impact of the Permanent Settlement on southern India, while the political import of the gift of property declined as a result of the legal redefinition of property relations, the moral economy did not. Dirks, 'From Little Kingdom', pp. 175–208.

95 For transformations in Indian law see Galanter, *Law and Society*; and Cohn, *Colonialism and its Forms*.

legal order that, according to Benton, was 'idiosyncratic', in which the state actually promoted 'a kind of Indian exceptionalism that exaggerated distinctions between India's written legal traditions and other non-western legal systems'.[96] Unlike in Australia, therefore, the legal order in India continued to remain plural, and while religious difference was its organizing principle, such boundaries were fragile and impermeable in the face of other categories (particularly gender and ethnicity) and groups (such as state officials, Westernized elites and so on).[97]

Secondly, the state's interest in and ability to regulate population in colonial India was more limited than that of the state in Australia. Colonialism may have justified itself as a civilizing tool, but in reality the state had no interest in fashioning moral colonial subjects – namely those who were 'civilized' and thus capable of self-governance – beyond the needs of political and administrative economy. This is because, unlike in Australia, the governmental state in India was not engaged in the task of nation-building and of hence assuring the strength and purity of the Indian 'race', although it evinced such concerns when it came to policing whiteness and in delineating those Indian groups amenable to British rule. The state's promise post-1857 to refrain from imposing its own notions of universal reason in the socio-cultural realm and its subsequent abrogation of the realm of personal law, while ostensibly a measure of appeasement, served in fact to further the interests of the colonial state and enabled it to focus on sites of intervention that served to advance colonial rule (leaving Indians, crucially, to engage in their own projects of social and moral reform). Such intervention not only fostered unforeseen transformations in the Indian socio-cultural realm, but put the impetus on Indians to *make* the state intervene in the socio-political realm. The accordance of relative autonomy to Indians to establish their own socio-cultural boundaries while denying them political power meant that, as Tanika Sarkar has presciently argued, 'the community – if it had any hegemonic aspirations – was forced to constantly explain itself'.[98] It did so through the public sphere, which Indian groups used to pressure the colonial state to intervene in the socio-cultural realm of Indian society and enact regulatory projects on their behalf.

Despite the desire of the colonial state in India to choose specific sites of intervention, colonial governmentality therefore produced or served to facilitate outcomes that had not been intended, such as the production

[96] Such a separation was reinforced, according to Benton, by the systems of colonial governance in which the India Office was isolated from that of the Colonial Office. Benton, *Law and Colonial Cultures*, p. 152.

[97] Benton, *Law and Colonial Cultures*, p. 162.

[98] Sarkar, *Hindu Wife*, p. 231.

of an Indian public sphere and, more significantly, Indian nationalism.[99] This leads us to the third key distinction between the political rationalities of governmental power in India and Australia, namely the linkage between state hegemony and nationalism. While in the Australian case nationalism emerged after the attainment of state hegemony but before the formal construction of a nation-state, in India nationalism was produced by the governmentalizing practices deployed in an effort to attain that hegemony – by, in other words, all of the statistical, enumerative, administrative and technological means through which India was made known and thus imagined.[100] Since Indian nationalists (as well as social reformers of many stripes) sought to enact their own governmentalizing projects to delineate the boundaries of the Indian 'race' and nation and to improve their 'strength' and 'purity', the project of colonial governmentality became more fragmented than its Australian counterpart as the state attempted to implement particular governmentalizing projects and Indian groups endeavoured to undertake their own, which they sought to implement in part through the state. The state thus became a battleground for competing projects.

The state resisted undertaking such projects in part because it lacked sufficient legibility in regard to Indian society, as well as the economic means to acquire it. But more imperative was that governmentality requires a confluence of interests between rulers and ruled, and in the Indian context this was more frequently lacking than in Australia. More troubling from the perspective of the colonial state was that Indian governmentalizing projects were often contrary to its interests, for in the process of fostering the strength and purity of Indians they often undermined those of the British. For the British, who established embodied legitimacy through the cultivation of a self-disciplined, bureaucratic body, the governance of the self became reified as a means of establishing distance between the bodies of the colonizers and those of the colonized,

99 The Indian public sphere, as Uma Kalpagam has argued, was produced in part by the statistical practices of colonial governmentality, since Indian newspapers routinely documented and debated the transactions of the imperial and provincial governments. According to Kalpagam 'Governance thus entered the public discourse in a new way inviting the various publics to a "public use of reason" '. Gyan Prakash makes a similar argument about the relationship between governmentality and Indian nationalism, namely that 'the struggle for the nation was at once both a product of colonial modernity and an attempt to steer it in a different direction'. For Benedict Anderson the genealogies of *all* colonial nationalist movements should in fact 'be traced to the imaginings of the colonial state'. Kalpagam, 'The Colonial State', 52; Prakash, *Another Reason*, p. 179; and Anderson, *Imagined Communities*, p. 163.

100 Although understandings of the origins of Indian nationalism have largely shifted from an emphasis on the role of Western education and British constitutional initiatives to a focus on drives to transform the inner or 'spiritual' realm of Indian society to protect it from the depredations of colonialism, the role of the state remains paramount. See, for example, Seal, *The Emergence of Indian Nationalism*; and Chatterjee, *The Nation*.

and of ultimately *undermining* the self-governing capacities of Indians.[101] The role of the body as a basis for social categorization and distinction could be destabilized, furthermore, through the cultivation of physical strength or other techniques of self-rule through which ethnic and even racial lines could be subsumed and the body thus rendered a site of resistance.[102] Considerable efforts were therefore directed at preventing Indians from developing such a body through imposing 'Indian' codes of behaviour on them and punishing transgressions against these. The prestige of the British body was further shored up through the adoption of aristocratic rather than middle-class sensibilities that permitted the gaze of outsiders to intrude into the realm of the private.[103] Since the legitimacy of the body of the colonizer needed to be maintained at the expense of enhancing the self-regulatory abilities of the colonized, colonial governmentality in India thus generated a tension between the legitimacy of the body of the colonizer and that of the colonial state.[104]

But it was also possible for the colonial state in India to abdicate responsibility for fashioning self-governing subjects because, unlike its Australian counterpart, it actually had more faith in the ability of its subjects to regulate themselves. Since by the late nineteenth century colonialism had already intervened in India in the spheres of government, the economy and the judiciary – the spheres that, according to David Scott, 'the political rationality of governmental power sought at once to *construct* and *work through* in order to induce its improving effects on colonial conduct' (emphasis in original) – then a direct intervention on the part of the state was no longer necessary for governmentality to achieve its improving effects on the conduct of Indian bodies.[105] This

[101] The body was always subject to greater contestation in India than in other colonial contexts because Anglo-Indian bodies lacked embodied legitimacy, particularly for Hindus, for whom they were ritually impure. But Anglo-Indian bodies also lacked legitimacy in the eyes of the 'home' country, and hence there was a tension evident from the beginning of British rule as to whether Indian or Anglo-Indian society was in greater need of 'civilizing'. Collingham, *Imperial Bodies*, p. 78.

[102] Budd, *The Sculpture Machine*, pp. 85–93.

[103] Collingham argues that, unlike in Britain, among Anglo-Indians the bathroom and bedroom did not develop into private spaces, which, through the use of body servants, was a means of maintaining prestige. *Imperial Bodies*, p. 143.

[104] The complexity of this dilemma is evident in the treatment of European prostitutes in colonial contexts such as India, where their 'whiteness' ensured that, unlike indigenous prostitutes or their counterparts in Europe, they were to some extent 'rehabilitated'. See Levine, 'The White Slave Trade', 140.

[105] Scott, 'Colonial Governmentality', 208. Although governmental power had also intervened in such spheres in Australia, the complications of colonial Indian body politics – including both the role played by virtue and the fact that the state was not engaged in upholding Indian bodily purity – led, ironically, to the belief that state intervention in Indian bodily regulation was no longer necessary.

was evident in the implementation of a host of moral and social reform projects from the late nineteenth century onwards. While these often worked against the interests of the state, they illustrated that the political rationality of governmental power had made the production of moral colonial subjects, individuals such as Mohandas Gandhi, possible.[106] It was not until the Indian project of nation-building began to be implemented *through* the state, from the 1920s onwards, that Indians started to conceive of *themselves* in governmental terms as incapable of self-governance, and the state thus began to assume greater responsibility for regulating their behaviour.

An examination of the operation of colonial governmentality in two distinct contexts thus illustrates that self-government is not synonymous with governance of the self, and that government as a form of power can be *perceived* to operate more effectively in states that are not self-governing than in those that are. A focus on governmental power thus illustrates the importance, as Saurabh Dube warns, of both 'guard[ing] against fetishizing the state as a mere panoply of institutions and policies, [as] a locus of abstract power', *and* against 'lyrically portray[ing] communities and traditions as outside the realms of disciplinary imaginings and state power'.[107] Only by looking at the structure of power within and around the colonial state in all of its manifestations, by focusing on governmentality in different colonial contexts and by comparing these different governmentalizing processes to each other, can we gain a clear understanding of how colonialism functioned.[108]

106 For Gandhi the reformation of sexuality was necessary for India to obtain national liberation.

107 Dube, *Untouchable Pasts*, p. xiii.

108 In challenging such concepts, we must be wary, however, of inadvertently re-affirming them. Modern techniques of governing are generally assumed to have been introduced in colonial contexts by the colonizers and later adopted by the colonized – part of the epistemological conquest carried out by colonial states through new institutions, a shift in knowledge content and new methods of knowing. While it is important to ask, with Uma Kalpagam, how it is that 'modern' knowledge acquired 'its legitimacy and its universal character', it is equally important to illustrate what techniques may have emerged prior to or independent of colonialism. Kalpagam, 'The Colonial State', 39, 43.

2 From sovereignty to governmentality: the emergence of obscenity regulation as a biopolitical project in Britain

Between the late eighteenth and early nineteenth centuries a new biopolitical genealogy for regulating the obscene emerged in Britain.[1] Its origins were three-fold. The first was interacting social, economic and political apprehensions among the propertied classes wrought by the effects of both the Industrial and French Revolutions, in particular fears about the socio-moral conditions of the working classes, which 'created "the social" as a focus for debate'.[2] The second, tied to the discovery of the social, was the emergence of a new governmental rationality that relied on regulatory strategies to transform the behaviour of working-class bodies.[3] The third was the manifestation, between the 1820s and 1840s, of a new set of 'relations of ruling' wrought by the emergence of a complex civil society, including new print cultures, which while undermining the prevailing tripartite state–church–property nexus served to enhance the power of the state through providing an infrastructure which enabled the expansion of administrative systems.[4] It also, however, forced the state to take account of the web of new civil associations that linked the propertied classes with the growing middle and artisan classes. Prominent among these were moral reform organizations that sought to act upon others through undertaking regulatory projects – including the regulation of the obscene – designed to improve the morals

[1] 'Regulation' refers to the mechanisms for examining 'cases, risks, danger and crises in society in order to calculate the probable norm at which society should function', and to 'normalize' those that were unfavourable. Legg, *Spaces of Colonialism*, p. 9; see also Foucault, 'Governmentality', pp. 87–104.

[2] Hunt, *Governing Morals*, p. 58.

[3] The making of the social as an object of conscious inquiry is exemplified in such projects as Arthur Young's statistical undertaking the *Annals of Agriculture* (1784–1815) and inquiries into the conditions of the rural and urban poor that began in the 1790s and that culminated in reform of the Poor Law in the 1830s.

[4] Hunt, *Governing Morals*, p. 58. While the generation of a new complex of relations of ruling first emerged, according to Hunt, in the 1760s, it was consolidated between the early 1830s, with the reform of parliament and the new Poor Law, and the 1840s, with the repeal of the Corn Laws. Hunt, *Governing Morals*, p. 59.

of the populace, most notably those of the working classes, through the inculcation of self-governance.

The term 'morality' served as a referent for a series of codes and practices about the art of government, in particular for the conduct of the individual.[5] 'Immorality' thus signified practices that fostered ungovernable behaviour, such as a lack of self-reliance, ignorance, dishonesty, disloyalty or sexual impropriety, all of which were deemed attributes of working-class life. Since the Enlightenment understanding of the body as having porous boundaries that opened it to both physical and moral contagion had yet to be replaced in the early nineteenth century by the conception of the 'biomedical body' (which came to predominate by the 1870s), in which the skin served as a relatively sealed boundary, immorality was also regarded as being contagious.[6] Immorality, it was believed, could be absorbed into the skin through corpuscles (which bore the mark of a person's moral and physical condition) in the atmosphere around bodies.[7] The problem posed by moral contagion was thus one of boundaries – between the mind and the body, the inside and the outside, and the self and the other – all of which obscenity transgressed. It is the very embodiedness of obscenity, and the crisis of boundary order that it thus generates, that made it a particularly potent form of moral contagion. Unlike 'art', which seeks to contain the body, 'obscenity' is a celebration of bodily excess, one that revels in 'the base matter of nature' rather than transforming it 'into the elevated forms of culture and spirit'.[8] It thus serves to undermine the ability of individuals to govern their own bodies and, in turn, to destabilize the boundaries of culture and society.

Beginning in the late eighteenth century, however, a range of new possibilities for controlling and enjoying bodies – and by extension obscenity – began to emerge: possibilities that expanded in the early

[5] Mort, *Dangerous Sexualities*, p. 29. The relationship between morality and governance means that morality is often conceived in terms of citizenship. Bashford and Hooker, 'Introduction', p. 8.

[6] Contagion, as Alison Bashford and Claire Hooker explain, 'implies absorption, invasion, vulnerability, the breaking of a boundary imagined as secure, in which the other becomes a part of the self'. According to the 'atmospheric' or 'miasmatic' approach to contagion, which remained the orthodoxy of the public health movement into the mid-nineteenth century, the atmosphere became changed with an epidemic influence under particular circumstances, and could become malignant when it united with the effluvia produced by the decomposition of the earth's organic matter. The miasma that ensued in turn infected the body. Bashford and Hooker, 'Introduction', p. 4; and Mort, *Dangerous Sexualities*, p. 23.

[7] Forth, 'Moral Contagion', p. 63.

[8] Douglas, *Purity and Danger*, p. 121; and Nead, *The Female Nude*, p. 2. It is for this reason that the body, particularly the nude female body, has long served as a boundary marker between art and the obscene.

decades of the nineteenth century with socio-political shifts such as industrialism and utilitarianism that served to depose older conceptions of the moral–spiritual body.[9] The 1820s and 1830s were particularly pivotal decades, according to Anthony Budd, that marked the beginning of what he terms the 'age of the sculpture machine'. The era witnessed not only the rise of democracy, the emergence of national popular cultures, the growth of the European empires and the consolidation of capitalism, but the creation of new systems of mechanization, organization and discipline that both increased the value of the labouring body and led to the emergence of new forms of bodily oppression.[10] In addition to facilitating the governance of others, such shifts also fostered the governance of the self, at least for the emergent middle classes, who sought to define themselves as opposite to the purportedly immoral and degenerate labouring classes by cultivating, through the interlinked themes of health, hygiene and procreation, 'the respectable middle-class representative body'.[11] The rituals and restraints the bourgeoisie placed upon their own bodies were designed, in turn, to secure their hegemony over the social body.

Securing such hegemony necessitated a wide programme of intervention into the culture and society of the labouring classes, which was achieved through the coming together of the state, medicine, evangelical religion and philanthropy with new professional knowledges and apparatuses, as well as procedures of social inquiry such as blue-book investigations into health and sanitation and reports from Poor Law commissions and factory inspectors. Rather than acting autonomously in selecting the targets, technologies and procedures for regulating the morals of the populace, the state therefore operated in conjunction with organizations and movements designed to act upon the morals of the poor through developing an intimate link between the governance of others and of the self.[12] Such organizations and movements brought

[9] Budd, *The Sculpture Machine*, p. xi.

[10] Budd, *The Sculpture Machine*, p. xii. The period also witnessed contending views of the rights of individual bodies and fears of the impossibility of controlling them. Thus working-class attempts to control their own bodies by, for example, the Luddites, were met with bourgeois efforts to exert control over those bodies, as incidents such the banning of trade unions and Peterloo demonstrate. Budd, *The Sculpture Machine*, pp. 7–9.

[11] Budd, *The Sculpture Machine*, p. 3.

[12] Hunt, *Governing Morals*, p. 15. Such an alliance demonstrates that moral regulation is not synonymous with political regulation, since it is undertaken by a wide range of different agents both within and outside political and state institutions, and since it can manifest itself in guises ranging from medical projects to religious imperatives. Moral regulation therefore *coexists* rather than purely derives from political and economic forms of regulation. Hunt, *Governing Morals*, p. 17.

together diverse agents, from both the state and civil society, to undertake such a task.[13] Although such a project was in part undertaken through the emergence of more dispersed techniques of discursive power, the law continued to dominate the socio-moral field, but it did so in productive ways (such as seeking out and redefining forms of 'immoral' behaviour). There was thus no clear distinction, as Foucault contends, between discursive and juridical forms of power.[14]

Moreover, rather than being anti-modern, the discourses (such as the language of decline and degeneration, or of the fall from a mystical golden age or era of national greatness) and practices (namely the strategies, tactics and procedures aimed at acting upon the behaviour of others, such as surveillance, constraint and coercion) that tied together the moral reform movements that emerged in the early nineteenth century were a product of the anxieties generated by modernity in the face of the emergence of new cultures coupled with the decline of traditional authorities such as the church or ruling classes.[15] The cultivation of a moral order, promoted through the generation of governmental self-formation, was seen as vital to the maintenance of a social order undergoing such tremendous transformations – although unfortunately for moral reformers, the imposition of a moral code was not always reflected in the cultivation of self-governance. As the case of obscenity serves to reveal, since 'the medico-moral concern for … boundaries, literary, social, and personal, was imbricated within a middle-class ideology that feared contamination of the treasured cultural body', obscenity, in contrast to blasphemy and sedition, came to be viewed as a social problem – one that needed regulating through both disciplinary means, such as moral reform organizations, and governmental methods,

[13] To take an example from the late nineteenth century, the National Vigilance Association (NVA), one of the most powerful moral reform organizations in the 1880s and 1890s, had an executive committee consisting of such luminaries of socio-moral reform as Samuel Smith, MP (parliamentary spokesman for a number of socio-moral reform causes and organizations and advocate of women's rights), W. T. Stead (a prominent British journalist, editor, Nonconformist, social reformer, purity campaigner and pacifist with links to organizations ranging from the Salvation Army to the Law and Liberty League), the noted feminist Millicent Fawcett (who later became a prominent suffragist and head of the National Union of Women's Suffrage Societies) and Dr Elizabeth Blackwell (not only the first woman doctor, but the organizer of the National Health Society in Britain and the School of Medicine for Women, an author of books on health, morality and sexuality, and by the time of her association with the NVA a Christian socialist). Such organizations thus brought together the various strands (forms of knowledge, narratives, practices, rationalities, mechanisms and so on) of socio-moral reform and forged new relationships between them.

[14] Mort, *Dangerous Sexualities*, p. 116.

[15] Hunt, *Governing Morals*, pp. 10–11.

most notably the law.[16] But while such a regulatory project served to suppress some practices, it also served to encourage others, including new techniques of evasion and resistance – techniques that would, it was feared, not only contaminate the social body in Britain, but undermine Britain's ability to govern its empire.

Defining the obscene

Since it encompasses a variety of purported threats to an existing social order, 'obscenity' is defined 'wholly in relation to what it threatens'.[17] It is thus a genre united only by its phenomonenology, by its desire to stimulate the senses. Furthermore, 'such words as "indecent", "lewd", and "obscene" can be defined only in terms of one another, producing a closed system that thwarts even the most assiduous inquiry into what any part of it might mean'.[18] While it is therefore impossible to generate a coherent or universal definition of the term, there is a set of criteria under which texts, images and objects have historically been rendered obscene in Western culture.[19] One of the most basic criteria is that the obscene, as used in the 'Greek sense' by Peter Michelson, is the 'bringing onstage what is customarily kept offstage', or, in the words of Lynda Nead, the representation of 'matter that is beyond representation', or 'which is beyond the accepted codes of public visibility'.[20] While such a conception clearly encompasses representations of or references to sex or sexuality, it also serves to include other representations that have commonly been viewed as unrepresentable, such as images of or references to the excremental functions or to certain degrees or forms of violence. All pornography is thus clearly obscene (since 'Pornography is the representation of sexuality so as to make its obscenity conspicuous, to the point of evoking its transgression of conventional taboos') but all obscenity is not pornographic.[21] This is evident based upon our second criterion under which works have commonly been deemed obscene in the West, namely the espousal of 'unconventional moral attitudes'

[16] Pease, *Modernism*, p. 50.
[17] Gilmore, 'Obscenity', 607.
[18] Kendrick, *The Secret Museum*, p. 160.
[19] By 'historically' I am referring to the period from the seventeenth century when, as Joan DeJean demonstrates, obscenity both re-emerged (after a 'centuries-long disappearance of words used to designate the concept of sexually transgressive material') and was re-invented, first in France and then later elsewhere in Europe (notably Britain) – a product of the emergence of new types of literature, new readerships and new (notably secular) forms of literary regulation. DeJean, *The Reinvention of Obscenity*, p. 7.
[20] Michelson, *Speaking the Unspeakable*, p. xi; and Nead, *The Female Nude*, p. 90.
[21] Michelson, *Speaking the Unspeakable*, p. xii.

such as free love or homosexuality.[22] In the case of this conceptualization of the obscene it is subject matter rather than language or imagery that is the source of contention. The third and final criterion is mode of representation. Under this criterion, language could become the basis for rendering a work obscene, as in the case of advertisements or texts relating to medical matters (generally of a sexual nature) that employed 'colloquial' rather than 'scientific' language.[23] But by the late nineteenth century form was often the most important consideration in classifying a work obscene in Western aesthetics, particularly in the case of art and literary works. Thus Aubrey Beardsley's sketches or James Joyce's *Ulysses* were able to evade being labelled 'obscenity' (although only after considerable ordeals) by virtue of the highly stylized nature of their works.[24]

The ability to judge whether the form, language or content of a particular work rendered it obscene was dependent on what in Western aesthetics was deemed to be the antithesis of the obscene, namely art. As Lynda Nead reveals, form and framing are central to Western conceptions both of art, 'defined in terms of the containing of form within limits', and of the obscene, 'defined in terms of excess, as form beyond limit, beyond the frame and representation'.[25] The importance of form can be traced back to Plato, for whom objects were merely the reflection of absolute forms which lie beyond the realm of the senses. The dichotomies that Plato established – between form and matter, mind and body, ideal and real – became the basis of the Enlightenment reformation of aesthetics, rendering it a discourse of the body – one which sought to foreground the surface of the body and to delineate the threshold between inner and outer.[26] In the defining text of Enlightenment aesthetics, Immanuel Kant's *Critique of Aesthetic Judgment* (1790), Kant sought to distinguish between contemplative pleasure (which was predicated upon reflection of an object) and sensory pleasures (which were not and hence were less refined). Crucial to the experience of contemplative pleasure is that the observer should remain a disinterested subject during the act of contemplating an object, while the object itself, in order to be labelled art, should exist for no other purpose than to be subject to contemplation. But art was also, according to Kant, defined by form.

22 St John-Stevas, *Obscenity and the Law*, p. 2.

23 See, for example, Sarch, 'Those Dirty Ads!', 31–48.

24 As Leigh Gilmore argues in her analysis of two novels about lesbianism, Radclyffe Hall's *Bildungsroman The Well of Loneliness* and Djuna Barnes's experimental novel *Nightwood*, it was the form of Hall's work that dictated the legal responses towards it and that enabled Barnes's to evade legal action. Gilmore, 'Obscenity', 605–6.

25 Nead, *The Female Nude*, p. 20.

26 Chaudhary, 'Phantasmagoric Aesthetics', 90.

As Nead argues, for Kant 'what is bad, what is outside of or goes beyond aesthetic taste and judgment, is matter – that which is motivated, which seduces, embarrasses, or leads the viewer astray, away from the proper consideration of intrinsic form'.[27] By the nineteenth century such arguments had come to be used to distinguish between art and obscenity, with the latter being denied the status of art because it not only invited *interested* rather than disinterested contemplation but, in promoting action or arousal, engendered embodied viewers or readers.

Obscenity is therefore not inherently intrinsic to an object – an object becomes obscene, in part, by virtue of the response of the viewing subject. How an individual responds to a given object, as Pierre Bourdieu has argued, is dependent on the cultural capital of the viewer, which is largely contingent upon class.[28] Emerging out of the rise of industrial capitalism in the late eighteenth century, aesthetic judgment, or taste, became a means through which gentlemen could conceptualize themselves as apart from or outside of the realm of material experience and hence capable of disinterested, socially generous behaviour. 'High' culture, predicated on a rational disinterested pleasure, was seen as distinct from 'low' culture, predicated on the pleasures of the appetite; elevating high over low culture thereby served to assert an individual's cultural distinction. As Alison Pease reveals, the problem with the obscene (particularly in its most iniquitous form, the pornographic) was not only that it was associated with the working classes and hence 'threatened the class hierarchies upon which aesthetic theories of the eighteenth century rested by exposing common experience in bodily sensation', but that 'the selfish individualism that pornography celebrated was viewed as pestilential to civility'.[29] Since in an increasingly egalitarian society the acquisition of civil liberty was equated with self-control, the loss of self-control threatened, quite literally, the body politic.[30] For conservative social theorists such as Edmund Burke, fashioning the social order through a typology of aesthetic responses was thus proof against revolutionary upheavals. While by the late nineteenth century social theorists such as Matthew Arnold, John Ruskin, William Morris and Oscar Wilde were attempting to inculcate a rapidly expanding reading public with a 'high' cultural aesthetic, as Linda Dowling has demonstrated, they also feared that this would debase elite

27 Nead, *The Female Nude*, pp. 24–5.
28 Bourdieu, *Distinction*.
29 Pease, *Modernism*, p. xii.
30 Bataille, 'Sexual Plethora and Death'.

culture in the process.[31] The danger was that objects, images and words would all take on new meanings through their contamination by the masses – and, as we shall see in the following chapter, by colonial subjects – who had yet to cultivate disinterest.

Pornography and print culture

Theories vary regarding the emergence of an obscene print culture in Britain, but most scholars agree that while sexually explicit publications had appeared in Britain well before the nineteenth century, it was not until the period between the late eighteenth and early nineteenth centuries that the infrastructure for the production, distribution and consumption of a British obscene print culture emerged.[32] Although such a culture has become conceptualized as part of the Victorian 'underworld', during the nineteenth century the gap between the 'respectable' and 'unrespectable' publishing worlds was far from distinct, as 'Writers and audiences, ideas and attitudes, genres and conventions overlapped between the sub rosa and aboveboard, creating a mixture more heady and potent than either alone'.[33] While a growing body of work has examined the intersections between these worlds, it focuses primarily on pornography rather than obscenity.[34] The genealogy that has emerged on Britain's obscene print culture is therefore far from complete, particularly since 'the extent to which empire was crucial to the trade's pleasures, powers, and profits' has only begun to be elaborated.[35]

[31] Dowling, *The Vulgarization of Art*.

[32] Colligan, *The Traffic in Obscenity*, pp. 4–5. Theories on what led to the emergence of an obscene British print culture include the impact of eighteenth-century literary forms on the emergence of the 'obscene' novel; the influence of the French trade in 'obscene' publications (which emerged earlier than its British counterpart); the construction of 'secret museums'; and the role of political radicalism following the Napoleonic Wars. See Colligan, *The Traffic in Obscenity*; DeJean, *The Reinvention of Obscenity*; Gamer, 'Genres for the Prosecution', 1043–54; Darnton, *The Forbidden Best-Sellers*; Hunt, *The Invention of Pornography*; Hunter, Saunders and Williamson, *On Pornography*; Kendrick, *The Secret Museum*; Marcus, *A Study of Sexuality*; Mudge, *The Whore's Story*; Bristow, *Vice and Vigilance*; and McCalman, *Radical Underworld.*

[33] Sigel, *Governing Pleasures*, p. 10.

[34] Lisa Sigel, for example, employs the term 'pornography' instead of 'obscenity' to discuss the works that she examines, arguing that she 'consider[s] as pornography works that people wrote, published, printed, legislated, and collected as pornography'. Since during the nineteenth century most of the material that she analyses was termed 'obscene' rather than 'pornographic' – such a term did not become part of popular parlance, particularly of moral reformers, until the 1880s (with Richard Burton taking pride of place in making the first English attempt, through the 'Terminal Essay' of his monumental translation of the *Arabian Nights*, to theorize pornography) – this is a problematic term, particularly when it is extended to materials such as scatological postcards. Sigel, *Governing Pleasures*, p. 4.

[35] Colligan, 'Obscenity and Empire', p. 37.

According to such a genealogy, the first phase in the development of an 'obscene' print culture in Britain – what Iain McCalman has termed 'revolutionary pornography' – emerged in the 1810s as part of the English radical movement following the Napoleonic Wars.[36] Spurred by pressmen, publishers and agitators such as William Dugdale and George Cannon, this early English pornography shared, along with the larger radical movement, aims such as reforming parliament and separating church and state, but it 'used these goals to create a political platform that attacked old sexual and social standards and promoted new possibilities for society through sexuality'.[37] By the 1830s the radical pornographers had become established and opened shops in London, a shift which, according to Lisa Sigel, '[made] pornography a London problem'.[38] As the century progressed, however, the 'obscene' novels, journals and prints issued by such publishers, while continuing to convey libertine ideas (particularly on the use of sexual pleasure as a means to the attainment of socio-political revolution), began to deploy such ideas merely as tangents to sexual titillation.

By the mid-nineteenth century a new obscene print culture had thus emerged in Britain – one characterized by what Ian Hunter, David Saunders and Dugald Williamson refer to as 'biblio-erotics', or book sex.[39] This new print culture also marked a shift in the representation of women from subjects to objects, as well as a growing categorization of people and behaviours as a means of 'delineat[ing] objective truth in the natural world'.[40] Such transformations presaged the emergence, in turn, of what has been variously labelled 'empirical and imperial pornography' or 'esoteric pornography'.[41] A product of the expansion and consolidation of British imperialism, this was one of the most visible and controversial forms of obscenity produced in the nineteenth century because it was generated and consumed by the intellectual, economic and political elite. The works of writers, scholars and imperial administrators and adventurers such as Richard Burton, Algernon Charles

36 McCalman, *Radical Underworld.*

37 Sigel, *Governing Pleasures*, pp. 15, 16. Thus Dugdale, while beginning his career as a radical agitator in the 1820s, participating in the Cato Street Conspiracy and publishing a variety of political tracts, was also one of the most prolific pornographers, publishing such classics as *The Lustful Turk* and several editions of *The Memoirs of a Woman of Pleasure.*

38 By the mid-1830s there were an estimated fifty-seven bookshops dealing with 'obscenity' in London. Sigel, *Governing Pleasures*, p. 21.

39 Biblio-erotics, according to Hunter, Saunders and Williamson, was a specific sexual practice wrought by a redeployment of 'the ethical and literary techniques of conscience-formation'. *On Pornography*, p. 40.

40 Sigel, *Governing Pleasures*, p. 49.

41 Sigel, *Governing Pleasures*, pp. 50–80; and Colligan, 'Obscenity and Empire', pp. 116–35.

Swinburne and Richard Monkton Milnes, all of whom belonged to intellectual societies such as the Anthropological Society, the Royal Geographic Society, the Royal Asiatic Society and the Athenaeum Club, focused on the relationship between race and sex, particularly on the sex lives of the colonized. Through deploying a scholarly apparatus (such as footnotes and citations) and a new narrative voice (that of the objective, impersonal observer), and 'invok[ing] an objective "nature" and "truth" to bracket and support [their] decisions', texts such as Richard Payne Knight's *A Discourse on the Worship of Priapus* (1865) and Burton's translation of *The Kama Sutra* (1883) functioned as both science and pornography.[42] In generating a framework in which purported sexual difference – between men and women, British and foreign, colonizer and colonized – translated into racial difference, such works also served to fashion race and sex as biological categories.[43] Unlike the radical, libertine obscene print culture of the first half of the nineteenth century, which sought to level social divisions, such an elite literature endeavoured to construct new social hierarchies – ones that, furthermore, served to legitimize imperial conquest and control.

Such literature was, however, both legitimized and displaced by the emergent disciplines of psychology, anthropology and sexology, as well as by a new, popular genre of obscene print culture in the form of pornographic postcards, stereoscope slides and mutoscope images.[44] Emerging between the 1880s and 1914, this genre was a product of shifts in the publishing industry, including the formation of a tight network of entrepreneurial publishers (such as Charles Carrington, Edward Avery, Leonard Smithers, Harry Sidney Nichols and William Lazenby); the professionalization and internationalization of the trade (as traders, driven by a crackdown in Britain, fled to the continent to conduct their trade); new methods of distribution (such as postal services); transformations in consumption (in particular the emergence of a new mass consumer market); the use of new technologies (such as the reproduction of multiple images from a single negative); and commodity fetishism (which celebrated desire for its own sake).[45] Changes in the

[42] Sigel, *Governing Pleasures*, p. 62. Such claims to respectability were marred, however, by the fact that the works published by empirical pornographers were often issued anonymously or pseudonymously and under false imprints.

[43] Sigel, *Governing Pleasures*, p. 79.

[44] Sigel, *Governing Pleasures*, p. 80.

[45] With the gaining of full authorization from the Congress of the Universal Postal Union in 1886, postcards soon came to dominate this trade in 'obscene' ephemera. Approximately 140 million postcards were sent globally between 1894 and 1919, with the sale of postcards in England alone totalling 800 million by 1909. Sigel, 'Filth', 861.

trade were in turn accompanied by a change in the style of pornographic works, as the literary features in such texts (such as plot, characterization, tension and resolution) were stripped away and replaced by a formulaic focus on sex acts.[46]

The social impact of popular ephemera such as pornographic postcards and photographs was, Sigel argues, profound. On the one hand, matter such as scatalogically themed postcards, many of which depicted gentlemen, ladies or the clergy engaged in acts of defecation or urination, created a more equitable system of objectification through subjecting social hierarchies to scrutiny and undermining the symbolic order of the purified and hygienic body.[47] But in offering up images of women as passive, sexual objects, and of colonial subjects as both racialized and sexualized, such material served, on the other hand, to reinforce the importance of the body as a site of meaning, as well as the need to police the boundaries of gender, class and race.[48] Moreover, the focus on sex acts and the elaboration of the pathological not only engendered fears of the social impact of a consumer culture in which all kinds of desire could be met (as demonstrated by the major sex scandals of the 1880s and 1890s), but served to overemphasize the 'normal'.[49] Such ephemera thus made possible 'the transgression of social hierarchies without the reordering of society'.[50]

The emphasis on sex as a means of self-constitution was mirrored in the emergence, in the same time period (although growing more prominent in the 1920s), of what Peter Michelson has termed 'aesthetic pornography'. Authors such as D. H. Lawrence (*Lady Chatterley's Lover*, 1928) and James Joyce (*Ulysses*, 1922), Michelson argues, incorporated pornographic tropes into their works in an attempt to alter the central tenets of Western aesthetics by inscribing the body rather than the mind as the source of aesthetic disinterest. As in the emergent discipline of sexology, the focus on sexuality in such works was seen as a means not only of inquiring into the self but of creating a healthy social body.[51]

46 Sigel, *Governing Pleasures*, p. 82.
47 Sigel, 'Filth', 871.
48 In contrast to images of white women, the bodies of the colonized were also, Sigel notes, shown not as individuals but as objectified 'types'. Sigel, 'Filth', 864.
49 Such sex scandals included the furore over the 'Maiden Tribute of Modern Babylon', W. T. Stead's exposé on juvenile prostitution (1889–90); the Cleveland Street male brothel affair (1889–90); and the Oscar Wilde trial (1895).
50 Sigel, *Governing Pleasures*, p. 98.
51 As Hunter, Saunders and Williamson note, 'erotic writing and reading became the instruments for a novel kind of work on the self' – but only for the 'little band equipped with the cultural capacity to make them into serious ethical endeavours'. *On Pornography*, p. 96.

What eventually exempted such works from being labelled obscene (after an initially hostile reception) was their form, which provided the aesthetic distancing necessary to the contemplation of art. But while aesthetic pornography ultimately sought to control sexuality and make it 'safe' for high culture by submitting it to formal constraints, in reconstituting 'traditional signifiers of the obscene ... to assume the function of traditional signifiers of the beautiful' it required more complex reading practices – practices that, it was believed, only the cultural elites for whom it was intended were capable of.[52] This collapse in distinction between pornography and 'serious literature' thus generated uncertainty as to how such works should be regulated – uncertainty that, beginning with the 1888 trial of Henry Vizetelly for publishing translations of the works of Émile Zola, manifested itself in the great literary 'show' trials of the period.[53]

Obscenity and empire

As Ronald Hyam and others have demonstrated, British sexuality, including its 'obscene' print culture, had become both understood and represented in a broader imperial and explicitly raced context by the nineteenth century. Not only were most of the 'classics' of British obscene literature written by men who were widely travelled in the empire, but empire, as Colette Colligan argues, 'critically underscored the emergence, development, and expansion of England's obscene print culture in the nineteenth century', not to mention the production of ephemera such as 'obscene' snuff boxes or ballads.[54] But since obscenity is a cultural form that borrows liberally from other genres, its contribution to discourses about both sexuality and empire varied throughout the nineteenth century depending upon when it appeared, the form it took, or the market for which it was intended.[55] Harem obscenity, one of the

[52] Michelson, *Speaking the Unspeakable*, p. ix.

[53] The Vizetelly trial will be examined in Chapter 3.

[54] Hyam, *Empire and Sexuality*, p. 90; and Colligan, 'Obscenity and Empire', p. 2. Such 'classics' included *Fanny Hill, or the Memoirs of a Woman of Pleasure* (1748–9) by John Cleland, who had been a consul at Smyrna and worked in the legal department of the East India Company at Bombay for thirteen years, and the *Romance of Lust* (1873–6), penned by an anonymous author who was knowledgeable about both India and Japan (and who died in India in 1879). Even the obscene magnum opus of the nineteenth century, the twelve-volume *My Secret Life*, was written, again anonymously, by an author who had been not only to every country in Europe but to Russia, the United States, Egypt and possibly Lebanon. The great erotic bibliographer Henry Spencer Ashbee had also travelled to India, China, Egypt and Tunis. Hyam, *Empire and Sexuality*, p. 90.

[55] Colligan, 'Obscenity and Empire', p. 39.

earliest genres of British obscenity, offers a case in point. While in the early nineteenth century it offered fantasies about the Ottoman empire (of 'Oriental' exoticism, sexual conquest and power and the thrill of transgressing sexual, racial and national identities), by the century's end it had come to emphasize European mastery over the harem and, with it, the 'Orient'.[56]

Harem obscenity also served to fuel concerns about an emergent mass reading public and about the difficulties in preventing such a public from gaining access to 'obscene' matter. Although obscenity was first criminalized in England in the early eighteenth century, works that were deemed obscene had an uncertain legal status due to the operation of copyright law, under which, thanks to the prevailing belief that 'there can be no property in what is publicly injurious', they were denied copyright.[57] Thus when in 1823, for example, Byron obtained an injunction against the radical publisher William Dugdale for publishing pirated editions of cantos 6 to 8 of *Don Juan* (the cantos set in the harem, which were issued several years after the first five) Dugdale, in a brilliantly audacious response, successfully challenged the injunction in a court of equity on the grounds that the poem was 'immoral in the highest sense of the word, most calculated to taint the mind of the public, licentious, in every way dangerous, and most destructive to the morals of the community at large'.[58] Cantos 6 to 8 were denied copyright, in short, because they were deemed *too obscene* to merit legal protection. The irony of such a verdict was not lost on critics, as publishers scrabbled to produce copies of the 'obscene' cantos and Dugdale himself went on to dominate the English trade in obscenity (a position he held until the 1860s).[59]

Although the 'Orient' had long had a reputation in England for being morally questionable, it was the introduction of the harem, perceived as a site of decadence and transgression, to an expanding working-class readership that ultimately rendered *Don Juan* obscene.[60] Since in the early nineteenth century an octavo sold for between twelve and fourteen shillings and a quarto could cost as much as two guineas, literature

56 Colligan, 'Obscenity and Empire', p. 87.
57 Colligan, 'Obscenity and Empire', p. 54. See also Phillips, 'Copyright in Obscene Works', p. 138; and Saunders, 'Copyright, Obscenity', 431–44.
58 *The Times*, 9 August 1823, cited in Colligan, 'Obscenity and Empire', p. 71. Dugdale did not defend his own role in publishing an obscene work because he was not on trial for obscene libel.
59 Colligan, 'Obscenity and Empire', p. 51. By 1832 no fewer than eighteen popular editions of cantos 6 to 8 has been published.
60 Colligan, 'Obscenity and Empire', p. 74.

was the prerogative of the middle and upper classes.[61] Publishing such a work in formats that made it accessible to working-class readers, such as in weekly instalments or on poor paper in a duodecimo (often with 'obscene' engravings) rendered it, therefore, a site of class tension. While middle-class readers, as a critic for the *Quarterly Review* avowed, 'would have turned with disgust from its indecencies, and remembered only its poetry and wit' (making '*Don Juan* on a quarter and on hot-pressed paper ... almost innocent'), working-class readers 'would treasure up all its evil, without comprehending that it contains of good' (making the work, in a 'whity-brown duodecimo[,] ... one of the worst of the mischievous publications that have made the press a snare').[62] Thus, while the contaminatory effects of empire could be resisted by middle-class readers, who had the cultural capital to prevent 'infection', the effects of such print culture on a new class of readers – one that was unable to distinguish good from evil, pure from impure, art from obscenity and 'English' sexual–moral codes from those of imperial 'others' – were profound. As another critic of *Don Juan* declared:

> But only let the poetry of Lord Byron become the staple commodity of the realm, and its profane and libidinous sentiments sway the national taste – and neither religion nor law, nor constitution; neither dignity in war, nor reputation in woman, shall ever more give lustre to this devoted land, nor shall the British Empire be, as heretofore, a terror to the kingdoms around nor by the power of her arms, but, by the prevalence of her corruption, a scorn, and a proverb, and a contaminating nuisance.[63]

From its inception, therefore, obscenity and its regulation were intimately bound up with debates over Englishness, nationalism and empire, and about how to protect both of the former from contamination by, and in turn contaminating or undermining, the latter.

Regulating the obscene

Before analysing these debates in greater detail, I would like to examine the nature of such 'censorship'. Until recently censorship was understood largely in terms of what Michel Foucault has termed the 'repressive hypothesis', in which authority intervenes, most notably through the operations of law, to curtail the freedom of individuals to access materials

[61] Murray published the first two cantos of *Don Juan* in a lavish quarto edition that sold for the princely sum of one and a half guineas. Colligan, 'Obscenity and Empire', p. 50.
[62] *Quarterly Review* (1822), 127–8, cited in Colligan, 'Obscenity and Empire', p. 55.
[63] Revd George Burgess, *Cato to Lord Byron or the Immoral and Dangerous Tendency of His Writings* (1824), cited in Colligan, 'Obscenity and Empire', pp. 74–5.

deemed to be obscene, seditious or blasphemous.[64] According to proponents of the repressive hypothesis, the censorship of obscenity in Britain emerged in the seventeenth century in conjunction with the growing suppression of sexuality. Although the explanations for the origins of such repression vary (from socio-religious factors such as the decline of medieval ecclesiastical jurisdiction over moral offences and the state inheritance of such jurisdiction, to economic shifts such as the development of capitalism and of sexuality's perceived incompatibility with an intensive work imperative), most advocates of the repressive hypothesis concur that censorship remained relatively 'liberal' until the passage of the portentous Obscene Publications Act of 1857. Following this the dark days of prudery, hysteria and repression purportedly set in, as exemplified by a series of censorship trials such as the landmark *R.* v. *Hicklin* in 1868. What is deemed particularly notable about such trials is their targeting of 'serious' scientific and literary works, as in the case of Henry Bradlaugh and Annie Besant's prosecution in 1877 for republishing Henry Knowleton's *The Fruits of Philosophy*, or of Henry Vizetelly in 1888 for publishing translations of Émile Zola's novels. The late nineteenth century is in fact a crucial period for advocates of the repressive hypothesis, for as Norman St John-Stevas claims, this was the period 'when the Victorian synthesis was breaking down and when Forster's Education Act had created a vast new reading public', a factor that instituted what many commentators on British censorship regard as a 'moral panic'.[65] Once the stable door had opened on the prosecution of types of literature that had never been censored before, the horse had supposedly bolted, particularly following the 'banning' of D. H. Lawrence's *The Rainbow* in 1915, and the censorship of a spate of 'literary' works in the 1920s such as *Ulysses* in 1923, *The Well of Loneliness* in 1928 and *Pansies, Lady Chatterley's Lover* and *The Sleeveless Errand* in 1929. The dark days of prudery continued, the theory concludes, until the 'age of enlightenment' in the 1960s, following which (barring some minor aberrations), freedom of speech reigned.[66]

In this approach censorship is inseparable from law and, as such, its 'severity' or 'pervasiveness' is charted through a series of 'show trials' that are made to stand in for all forms of censorship activity. Such show

[64] Foucault, *The History of Sexuality*, p. 5.
[65] St John-Stevas, *Obscenity and the Law*, p. xix.
[66] For works that posit obscenity and its regulation in Britain as a product of the repressive hypothesis see, for example, Marcus, *The Other Victorians*; Kendrick, *The Secret Museum*; Travis, *A Long Time Burning*; Tribe, *Questions of Censorship*; Siebert, *Freedom of the Press*; Sutherland, *Offensive Literature*; Thomas, *The Victorian Underworld*; de Grazia, *Girls Lean Back*; and Travis, *Bound and Gagged*.

trials were, however, few and far between, the types of works they sought to censor shifted over time, and the trials were grounded in particular historical circumstances that render it problematic to throw them all together to form a coherent history of censorship.[67] The regulation of obscenity in Britain has not, in short, been a unified historical project – not only did the objectives and the specific targets of censorship change over time, but so did the means of censoring and the particular agents involved in carrying these out. Censorship cannot, therefore, be reduced purely to prohibition or equated simply with silencing.

During the past two decades a substantial body of scholarship has emerged, inspired in part by Foucault, that challenges the 'repressive hypothesis'. According to Foucault:

> What sustains our eagerness to speak of sex in terms of repression is doubtless this opportunity to speak out against the powers that be, to utter truths and promise bliss, to link together enlightenment, liberation, and manifold pleasures; to pronounce a discourse that combines the fervor of knowledge, the determination to change the laws, and the longing for the garden of earthly delights.[68]

Rather than repression, Foucault argues that what occurred in Western European culture at the end of the sixteenth century was a discursive explosion about sex. While by the eighteenth century sex had become a 'police matter', part of the emergence of 'population' as an economic and political problem (which entailed an expurgation of the authorized vocabulary, the monitoring of sexual behaviour and the development of new relations of discretion between parents and children, teachers and students and so on), such regulation fuelled rather than undermined an incitement to speak about sex.[69] What emerged were multiple discourses about sexuality, both institutional (through disciplines such as medicine, psychiatry, criminal justice and demography) and social (through a variety of social controls that emerged in the later nineteenth century).

[67] Saunders, 'Victorian Obscenity Law', pp. 154–70.

[68] Foucault, *The History of Sexuality*, p. 7.

[69] Foucault, *The History of Sexuality*, p. 7. This is not to say, however, that repression did not play a part in such regulation; Foucault maintained that when the bourgeois techniques for the deployment of sexuality developed in the late eighteenth century had spread throughout society by the end of the nineteenth, 'Henceforth social differentiation would be affirmed, not by the "sexual" quality of the body, but by the intensity of its repression'. Foucault arguably did not, however, give enough credence to the power of such repression, since some discourses excluded competing ones and were thus hegemonic. Alan Hunt offers as an example the sex manuals that were produced in Britain from the early nineteenth century onwards that were designed to subvert some of the dangers of unregulated sexuality but that 'were so locked into the refusals and repressions of the dominant discourse that they were literally unable to write or speak the necessary words'. Foucault, *History of Sexuality*, p. 129; and Hunt, *Governing Morals*, pp. 88, 89.

For Foucault and his followers censorship is therefore more productive than suppressive.[70] It is also '*distributive* rather than repressive', since instead of being uniform in their application acts of restriction hinge upon access.[71] Terms like *obscenity* and *indecency* are thus socially determined concepts that, as far as those responsible for regulating them are concerned, change according to who is reading or viewing the work in question and when and where they are doing so. We can see such thinking at work in the first English case to criminalize obscenity (and thus remove it from the purview of the church courts), the 1727 trial of Edmund Curll for publishing an obscene libel in the form of *Venus in the Cloister; or, The Nun in Her Smock*.[72] As Colin Manchester reveals, 'the court was not concerned with penalizing obscenity in literature as *obscenity*' but with 'obscenity's relationship with two other factors, religion and breach of the peace'.[73] The obscenity in question threatened to breach the peace because of the widely disseminable format in which it was purveyed, namely in a printed work.[74] Obscenity law thus first emerged 'in a complex technical environment formed by the overlap of a new governmental distinction between public and private spheres and the spread of a specific cultural technology and competence'.[75]

That censorship was concerned with *limiting* access to the obscene rather than *prohibiting* it is evident in what became the 'test' of obscenity in Britain and throughout the empire, namely the judgment passed in 1868 by Lord Chief Justice Sir Alexander Cockburn in *R.* v. *Hicklin*. According to Cockburn, in a ruling that became known as the Hicklin test, the obscenity of a given work was determined by 'whether the tendency of the matter charged with as obscenity is to deprave and corrupt those whose minds are open to such immoral influences' – those who, in other words, were deemed to be incapable of self-control.[76] In practice this included children, women, the working classes and, since the judgment became the standard 'test' of obscenity throughout the

70 As Richard Burt argues, censorship should be understood as a process, as productive as it is prohibitive, of '*dispersal* and *displacement*', since it involves a variety of regulatory agents and methods of regulation (emphasis in original). Burt, 'Un-Censoring in Detail', p. 17.

71 Hunter, Saunders and Williamson, *On Pornography*, p. 52.

72 While Joan DeJean argues that obscenity was first 're-invented' in France in the mid-seventeenth century (through a conjunction of new forms of print culture, new readerships and new secular modes of regulation), Curll's conviction (which made obscene libel a common law misdemeanour) demonstrates that in England such a re-invention occurred considerably later. DeJean, *The Re-Invention of Obscenity*, p. 12.

73 Manchester, 'A History of the Crime', 41.

74 Saunders, 'Victorian Obscenity Law', p. 437.

75 Hunter, Saunders and Williamson, *On Pornography*, p. 51.

76 *R.* v. *Hicklin*, LR 3 QB 360, 1868.

British empire, Britain's colonial subjects. Determining the 'competence' of particular individuals or social groups to partake of the 'cultural technology' of the printed word was not simply a question of gender, class or age, but also of practices of reading, which meant that different groups were conceived of as being endangered by a variety of texts at different times based on notions of how the group in question was perceived to read or utilize such texts – what Hunter, Saunders and Williamson refer to as the notion of 'variable obscenity'.[77]

Censorship targeted, however, not only particular types of individuals but specific kinds of spaces, which meant that obscenity was also a *spatial* problem. London's Holywell Street, for example, a narrow Elizabethan thoroughfare near the Strand, had by the mid-nineteenth century become regarded as a 'spatial aneurism' in the body of the metropolis – not simply because it was part of the congested route linking the east to the west of the city (and hence its commercial and administrative cores) but because it was the centre of the trade in 'obscene' publications.[78] Purifying the metropolitan body thus necessitated not merely cleansing the street of its contaminants (through such means as the Obscene Publications Act of 1857, which in the aftermath of its passage was deployed almost solely against Holywell Street traders), but by the century's end of replacing it with a new, straight road that would 'act as a "ventilating duct", circulating and cleansing the physical and moral environment of the district'.[79]

While Foucaultian approaches to censorship have thus vastly enhanced understandings of what censorship is and how it works, they have also complicated and problematized it in new ways. The chief difficulty lies in the way in which power has been conceptualized, for Foucaultian scholars have largely abandoned the focus on the legal constraints upon speech to focus on power itself as an object of study – of how it is constituted, of the intersections of resistance and domination through which it is exercised, and of how discursive and disciplinary practices are enacted. Censorship has thus become viewed as a technique through which discursive practices are maintained; as Pierre Bourdieu argues, censorship is 'constituted by the very structure of the field in which the discourse is produced and circulates'.[80] In this reading all discourse is a product of censorship and hence censorship is the norm rather than the exception since it is, quite literally, everywhere.

77 Hunter, Saunders and Williamson, *On Pornography*, p. 10.
78 Nead, *Victorian Babylon*, pp. 174, 163.
79 Nead, *Victorian Babylon*, pp. 197, 164.
80 Bourdieu, 'Censorship', p. 137.

Such approaches to understanding censorship have offered important insights into its productive nature, but its omnipresence poses a problem. As Frederick Schauer argues, 'Once we acknowledge that our abilities to express and to communicate are so dependent on the actions of others . . . to continue to speak of some of those actions as censorship appears odd'.[81] For Schauer censorship is, in fact, 'a conclusion masquerading as an analytic device', for why, he asks, do we characterize the words of Salman Rushdie as the target of censorship and the Ayatollah Khomeini calling for a fatwa against Rushdie as censorship even though words were all that the latter employed? Or why do we regard it as censorship when library boards seek to keep certain books out of libraries but not when librarians do?[82] Seeing censorship as everywhere thus makes it impossible, Schauer implies, to distinguish between different types, means and degrees of censorship; between, for example, the suppression of speech caused by state legal action, market forces or dominant discourses, or between what we might refer to as 'soft' forms of censorship (such as literary criticism or the ways in which pornography serves to 'silence' women) and 'hard' forms (such as imprisonment or death). These represent different mechanisms of silencing and different kinds of power, as well as different methods of constructing subjects. As Judith Butler posits, 'implicit' forms of censorship (namely 'operations of power that rule out in unspoken ways what will remain unspeakable') may not only be more effective than 'explicit' forms such as state policy in making certain kinds of speech unspeakable (particularly since the latter tend to proliferate the very terms that they seek to suppress), they also 'make certain kinds of citizens possible and others impossible'.[83]

Obscenity and governmentality

It was the desire to make certain kinds of citizens possible – both those capable of governing the nation and empire and those capable of being governed – that led to efforts to regulate the obscene in Britain. The convergence between the emergence of a working-class reading culture (one that, moreover, was in part shaped by empire) and new regulatory strategies fostered efforts, beginning in the late eighteenth century and expanding in the early decades of the nineteenth, to regulate print culture in an effort to control the bodies of the working classes.

[81] Schauer, 'The Ontology of Censorship', p. 149.
[82] Schauer, 'The Ontology of Censorship', p. 160.
[83] Butler, 'Ruled Out', pp. 250, 257.

While the state played a role in such efforts through legislative and judicial means, as the copyright case involving *Don Juan* demonstrates, it served more as a mediator between contending print cultures and bodily norms rather than playing an active role in shaping them.[84] Thus, although it deemed the purveyors of obscene wares to be 'person[s] of most wicked lewd depraved and abandoned mind and disposition and wholly lost to all sense of decency chastity morality and religion' – who were, moreover, intent on 'corrupt[ing] the morals of the liege subjects to indecent obscene and immoral practices and to debauch poison and infect the minds of the youth of the kingdom' – it left the regulation of obscenity largely to moral reform organizations such as the Proclamation Society.[85] Founded by the evangelical and anti-slavery advocate William Wilberforce out of the conviction that the only way that vice could be combated in a free society was through voluntary association, the Proclamation Society initiated, as Edward Bristow puts it, 'Britain's first sustained campaign against smut'.[86]

With the absorption of the Proclamation Society in 1802 by the Society for the Suppression of Vice (SSV), a formula emerged that established the nature of the relationship between the state and moral reform organizations regarding the regulation of the obscene that was to prevail throughout most of the nineteenth century: such organizations deployed what Bristow terms 'vigilance networks' to maintain surveillance of working-class print culture and pressured the state to initiate legislation, which they then used to prosecute the sellers of 'obscene' matter (since only the sale, not the production or possession of such material, was indictable) at their own expense.[87] While the state could take

[84] Since the repeal of the Licensing Act in 1695, the state in fact had no effective means of regulating obscenity in print.

[85] Such vilification was directed by the crown to the hapless publisher William Dugdale, who in the 1830s was forced to serve two consecutive sentences for selling obscene publications. Yet in spite of such convictions the state remained, as Frank Mort affirms, 'a relatively subordinate and often passive partner in the dialogue' with social purity groups, who were not only 'central to the enactment of criminal law legislation' but in 'petitioning the state to act'. Sigel, *Governing Pleasures*, p. 22; and Mort, 'Purity, Feminism', p. 210.

[86] Bristow, *Vice and Vigilance*, p. 39. The immediate cause of the foundation of the Society was George III's Proclamation for the Encouragement of Piety and Virtue, and for the Preventing and Punishing of Vice, Profaneness and Immorality, issued in 1787 at Wilberforce's urging. Harrison, 'State Intervention', p. 305.

[87] As Colin Manchester argues, in the case of obscene libel, while law officers of the crown could prosecute such offences, 'Instituting a criminal prosecution was normally a matter for the private individual, although cases were brought in the name of the King, and it seems that few individuals felt sufficiently aggrieved by the dissemination of pornography to go to the trouble and expense of instituting proceedings'. The Proclamation Society, and later the SSV, were the first organizations to make any efforts to do so. They entrapped sellers of 'obscene' wares by buying goods from them and arresting them, following which

over a prosecution for obscenity initiated by moral reform organizations it rarely did so before the 1880s; instead the primary responsibility for such actions during the course of the nineteenth century lay with the SSV.[88] Thus when in 1854 the magistrates of the Court of Chester wrote to the Home Office (the department responsible for dealing with obscene publications) to request reimbursement for prosecuting three men for printing and selling 'obscene and indecent publications', whom they had prosecuted for fear of their effects on 'the corruption of the morals of the people more especially of the rising generation in the manufacturing districts', they received an unsympathetic reply. As far as the Home Office was concerned, there were certain areas of law, such as libel, that the government did not pay to prosecute; in the case of obscene libel, 'no such Prosecution has been carried on at the public expense – it has been left to the Society for the Suppression of Vice'.[89]

Scholars of British censorship have attributed the rationale behind the state's reluctance to take a more active role in regulating the obscene to such factors as the initiative taken by the SSV, the inadequacy of the law and the overlapping system of courts responsible for regulating obscenity.[90] I would argue, however, that the state abrogated primary responsibility for the regulation of the obscene to moral reform organizations such as the SSV because it was caught between the demise of a particular type and form of regulation (religio-moral, conducted by the church courts and the Stationers' Company) and the rise of a new (biopolitical, enacted by moral reform organizations, the state and later the emergent medical profession), and between older and emergent forms of print culture, readerships, and body politics.[91] The problem for the state was that the two poles of biopower, discipline and governmentality, had yet

they were obliged to pay for the prosecution unless the defendant was made to pay costs. While the SSV managed to secure a change in the Vagrancy Act in 1824 to make the display of obscene publications subject to summary conviction before a magistrate (a less expensive and time-consuming method of securing conviction than a prosecution on indictment for publishing obscene libel), and the establishment of the Metropolitan Police in 1829 transferred responsibility for arrest to the police, the SSV was still obliged to pay costs if they failed to secure a conviction or if the police declined to assume responsibility for a prosecution. Hence it is not surprising that the SSV only sought convictions in cases where they were sure of success; of the 159 prosecutions they had undertaken by the 1850s, all but five had succeeded. Manchester, 'Lord Campbell's Act', 224–5; Sigel, *Governing Pleasures*, p. 22; and Bristow, *Vice and Vigilance*, p. 43.

88 As Bristow rather superciliously notes, 'until 1880, this voluntary agency [the SSV] remained the Victorians' chief legal deterrent against the demon smut'. Bristow, *Vice and Vigilance*, p. 33.

89 HO 45/5453, NAUK.

90 See Sigel, *Governing Pleasures*, pp. 21–2; and Bristow, *Vice and Vigilance*, p. 45.

91 With the demise of the so-called bawdy courts in the seventeenth century (which dealt with 'moral' crimes such as bastardy, adultery, incest, homosexuality and brothel-keeping), the

to become connected 'in the form of concrete arrangements ... that would go to make up the great technology of power in the nineteenth century'.[92] Sovereignty, rather than biopower, was still the key concern of the state in the early nineteenth century. As Sigel astutely observes, in the early nineteenth century '*The Crown* saw the publication of ... pornographic works as attacks on the religious and social order, which undercut the monarchy's *sovereignty*' (emphasis added).[93] Regulating the obscene had not, in short, become a biopolitical project, for rather than seeking to regulate the obscene as a means of managing population, the state still regarded obscenity largely in terms of a threat to its sovereignty, and hence sought to regulate it through deployment of the law. In an insightful analysis of the relationship between governmentality and the law, Victor Tadros argues that the law, alongside sexuality, was one of the key institutions through which the connection between discipline and governmentality was made during the course of the nineteenth century. Prior to this connection 'the law presented itself as a threshold of transgression and as the right of the Sovereign to use violence where the laws that constituted his sovereignty were violated' – hence the sale of obscenity (but not its publication or consumption, which did not constitute a social threat that undermined the power of the sovereign) was punished with imprisonment, often with hard labour.[94] Once the connection between discipline and governmentality was made, however, the law began to operate 'as a field through which techniques of governance ... intervene[d] in the disciplinary network', which it did through acting 'as an interface through which governmental decisions ... [took] effect by adjusting the operations and arrangements of the disciplinary mechanisms'.[95] Since by the early nineteenth century obscenity law

state inherited the task of punishing religious and moral offences. It was the inadequacy of state institutions to contain such social disorder that led to what Bristow terms 'the first wave of vigilantism' in Britain, namely the emergence of moral reform organizations. One of the reasons for such inadequacy in the case of the obscene was that obscenity was to some extent regulated through the state's efforts to police blasphemy and sedition, particularly in light of the relationship between obscenity and working-class radicalism. Fears of the contaminatory effects of French culture actually led, by the end of the eighteenth century, to the equation of sexual disorderliness with disloyalty. Bristow, *Vice and Vigilance*, pp. 11–12.

92 Foucault, *History of Sexuality*, p. 140.

93 Sigel, *Governing Pleasures*, p. 22.

94 Tadros, 'Between Governance and Discipline', 87.

95 Tadros, 'Between Governance and Discipline', 79. Not only, therefore, was there no clear distinction between juridical and discursive forms of power, but 'The law was itself productive: seeking out and redefining forms of dangerous or deviant sexuality, organising the cultural experience of dominated groups and stimulating their political demands'. Mort, *Dangerous Sexualities*, p. 116.

served as a tool that moral reform organizations used to discipline the culture of the working classes, and the state not only cooperated with such disciplinary mechanisms but gradually altered the law to serve more governmental ends, what was occurring in the early nineteenth century was thus the emergence and gradual evolution of the biopolitical regulation of the obscene.

That *population* had by the early nineteenth century become the chief concern in efforts to regulate the obscene is clear in the types of materials and groups targeted for regulation. From the beginning of the formation of the SSV in 1802 it was the ephemera consumed by the working classes, rather than pornographic novels or 'empirical' and 'aesthetic' pornography, that was the primary source of concern.[96] In the early nineteenth century such ephemera included 'obscene' pamphlets, tracts, illustrated papers, prints, drawings, advertisements, toys, snuff boxes, mirrors, cigar cases and playing cards.[97] As the century progressed and as technology, consumption and bodily norms evolved – along with the biopolitical drive to regulate the obscene – matter such as advertisements (for products such as aphrodisiacs and abortifacients and 'quack' cures for venereal diseases), various 'rubber goods' (which included both sex toys and condoms), sexology texts and 'obscene' illustrations, postcards and photographs were added to the list.

The cost of such ephemera, while not as exorbitant as for literary obscenity, was nonetheless high, and thus still prohibitive for the working classes. Yet as studies of working-class culture such as Henry Mayhew's *London Labour and the London Poor* (1861) demonstrated, the working classes undoubtedly consumed obscenity, which they did in part through pooling their economic and intellectual resources.[98] Mayhew described

[96] Although it is true that, as Lisa Sigel contends, the cost of 'pornographic' literary texts was generally exorbitant before the 1880s, with even a 'shoddy pamphlet' such as 'Kate Handcock' costing as much as three shillings, and a privately printed and extremely rare work such as the anonymous *My Secret Life* selling for as much as £100, making them luxury commodities, access to which was restricted by class, gender, and income (as well as illiteracy and the lack of languages skills, since they were frequently written in foreign languages or contained phrases in Latin, Greek, or French), such works constituted a microscopic amount of what was considered obscene, and precisely because of their upper-class readership were, moreover, rarely targeted for regulation. Sigel, 'Filth', 860.

[97] The SSV launched an investigation into the sale of such ephemera as soon as it was formed, and uncovered what it believed to be a vast network for the manufacture of such items. Bristow, *Vice and Vigilance*, p. 42.

[98] As Henry Mayhew discovered in his study of working-class labour in the mid-nineteenth century, an 'obscene' item such as a snuff box with a coloured picture of a nude woman cost in the realm of 2s 6d, well out of the reach of working-class pockets. However, 'obscene' pamphlets, which were available for as little as sixpence, were readily accessible through the pooling of resources. *London Labour and the London Poor* (1861), cited in Colligan, 'Obscenity and Empire', p. 9; and Bristow, *Vice and Vigilance*, p. 43.

how costermongers, for example, 'would gather in pubs where one of their literate members would read aloud from salacious texts'.[99] It was not only Londoners who engaged in such practices; unlike the trade in literary 'obscenity', which for most of the nineteenth century operated largely out of shops, the trade in 'obscene' ephemera was itinerant in nature, conducted throughout the country by networks of often foreign hawkers such as Lascars and Chinese.[100] This meant that not only was the entire working class purportedly under threat of moral and physical corruption, but since much of the material they consumed was imported they faced being corrupted – particularly through 'colonial intruders', who were regarded as playing a particularly important role in 'creating the conditions in which low culture thrive[d]' – by 'foreign' immorality.[101] The importance of the 'foreign threat' in generating fears of the obscene and of efforts to regulate it has been vastly underestimated in studies of British censorship. Yet from the formation of the SSV onwards, the perception that obscenity was 'a lower-class social problem imported by itinerant foreigners' served to generate drives to regulate the obscene.[102] As George Pritchard, a member of the SSV, reported to the Police Committee of the House of Commons in 1817:

> It was early ascertained, from indubitable testimony, that several foreigners (having their head quarters in London) of apparent respectability and considerable property, were united together in partnership for the principal, and almost exclusive purpose of carrying on an extensive traffic in obscene books, prints, drawings, toys, & c. The agents, by whome [sic] the partners of this house disseminated their merchandise, were about thirty in number, chiefly consisting of Italians, under the assumed character of itinerant hawkers, by whom they established a systematic trade throughout the great part of the United Kingdom.[103]

While by 1805 the SSV had disrupted the trade and secured the imprisonment of hawkers such as Baptista Bertazzi, sentenced to six months in prison for selling obscene prints in a girls' school, it continued to warn police constables 'to keep a watchful eye upon Foreigners and others exposing pictures on walls', especially with the resurgence of obscene matter from the continent following the end of the Napoleonic wars.[104]

[99] Colligan, 'Obscenity and Empire', p. 10. See also Altick, *The English Common Reader*, pp. 91, 319–25.
[100] Colligan, 'Obscenity and Empire', pp. 7–8; and Nead, *Victorian Babylon*, p. 152.
[101] Nead, *Victorian Babylon*, p. 152.
[102] McCalman, *Radical Underworld*, p. 10.
[103] *Society for the Suppression of Vice*, cited in Colligan, 'Obscenity and Empire', pp. 7–8.
[104] *The Constable's Assistant* (1808), cited in Colligan, 'Obscenity and Empire', p. 12.

In addition to keeping a watchful eye on foreigners, police constables were also warned to 'apprehend Ballad singers, particularly such as sing indecent, lewd, and seditious songs, in the public streets'.[105] For the SSV it was clearly the streets, the purview of the working classes, that were regarded as the chief source of contagion to the social and – as the fear of 'foreign' immorality demonstrates – emerging national body, for although shopkeepers selling obscene wares were periodically targeted by the SSV, their primary aim was to drive 'working-class bawdry ... from the streets'.[106] The danger of such contagion was, apparently, extreme, for the 'obscene' specimens obtained by the SSV were kept 'in a tin box secured by three different locks; one of the keys of which is kept by the treasurer, one by a member of the Committee, and one by the secretary; so that the box can at no time be opened, but with the concurrence of these three persons'.[107] While critics of the SSV (one of whom dubbed it 'the society for suppressing the vices of persons whose incomes do not exceed £500 a year') charged it with class bias, the nature of its union with the state meant that the law began to increasingly evolve as a key field through which techniques of governance came to intervene in the disciplinary network constructed by moral reform organizations such as the SSV around working-class culture.[108] From the passage of statutes such as the Vagrancy Act of 1824, which carried a conviction as a 'Rogue and Vagabond' for anyone 'wilfully exposing to view, in any street, road, highway or public place, any obscene print, picture or other indecent exhibition' and the Town Police Clauses Act of 1847, which carried a penalty of 40 shillings or fourteen days' imprisonment for 'Any person who in any street to the obstruction, annoyance, or danger of residents or passengers offers for sale or distribution any profane or indecent book, paper, print, drawing, painting or representation', the primary target of obscenity law was thus to manage population through regulating the culture and bodies of the working classes.[109]

It was concern with population that led to the passage of the Obscene Publications Act of 1857, which became the chief legal tool for the regulation of obscenity in Britain until the 1950s and served as a model

[105] *The Constable's Assistant*, cited in Colligan, 'Obscenity and Empire', p. 12.

[106] Bristow, *Vice and Vigilance*, p. 44.

[107] *Society for the Suppression of Vice*, cited in Colligan, 'Obscenity and Empire', p. 8.

[108] Sydney Smith, *The Edinburgh Review* (1809), cited in Colligan, 'Obscenity and Empire', p. 11; and Bristow, *Vice and Vigilance*, p. 43.

[109] HO 45/20912, NAUK. See, for example, the East Ham Improvement Act (1898, s. 80), the Leyton Urban District Council Act (1898, s. 81), the Indecent Advertisements Act (1889, 52 and 53 Vict. C. 18) and by-laws of the London Council made under the General Powers Act (1890 and 1896).

for colonial legislation pertaining to obscenity. The Act, initiated by Lord Chief Justice Sir Colin Campbell, was designed not to target literary obscenity (the 'high price' of which, according to Campbell, 'was a sort of check' on its consumption by the working classes), but matter such as penny papers and other ephemera, which 'had a far greater tendency to demoralize the public'.[110] While moral reform organizations such as the SSV had assumed primary responsibility for regulating the obscene for the past half-century, their efforts had proved a notable failure, particularly since under existing law only the sale of obscene matter constituted an offence and conviction could only be secured through bringing a criminal prosecution against the sellers of such material.[111] Attempts to 'purify' working-class print culture through organizations such as the Pure Literature Society (founded in 1854) had likewise met with little success.[112] Although it created no new offences, Lord Campbell's Act shifted the regulatory balance between moral reform organizations and the state by granting magistrates the power to issue warrants to the police to search for and seize obscene publications and to secure their destruction before a magistrate (as well as the destruction of plates and type, which put a serious damper on trade). It also served to further embody the offence through increasing punishment to a maximum of two years' imprisonment with hard labour.[113]

Considerable attention has been devoted to the opposition surrounding the Act, particularly to fears that it would encompass 'serious' literature; critiques of the powers it accorded to police; and concerns about the liberty of the individual and the relationship between public and private, state and society. As one critic averred, while the bill was 'likely enough to be beneficial if judiciously administered', it was nonetheless 'bordering upon the dangerous frontier which divides private right

[110] *Hansard*, Vol. CXLVI (9 July 1857), c. 1154; and Roberts, 'Morals, Art and the Law', 613. Walter Kendrick notes that the Act 'also presupposed, without saying so explicitly, that obscenity came in from outside, mostly France'. Kendrick, *The Secret Museum*, p. 119.

[111] Evidence of sale, however, could only be secured through the sale of obscene matter directly to a member of the police or the SSV. The laxness of the law meant that the SSV only brought legal action against the major traders in obscenity, although even successful prosecutions had little impact on their trade. William Dugdale, for example, served no fewer than nine prison terms for obscenity and maintained his business through the help of family members. It was the failure of such efforts to curb the activities of traders such as Dugdale that led Campbell to introduce the Obscene Publications Act. Manchester, 'Lord Campbell's Act', 225–6.

[112] Roberts, 'Morals, Art and the Law', 613.

[113] Saunders, 'Victorian Obscenity Law', p. 157; and Manchester, 'Lord Campbell's Act', 227.

from public requirements'.[114] In addition to ignoring the considerable support the bill received outside parliament (which not only made Campbell persevere with the bill, but made it impossible for parliament to drop it), such attention has in fact overlooked what was really at issue in debates over the bill, namely a two-fold anxiety over the governmentalization of the moral realm and the governmentalization of the state. Modelled on legislation to regulate gaming houses and inspired by the passage of an Act to restrict the sale of poisonous drugs (for Campbell the Act was designed to control a 'poison more deadly than prussic acid, strychnine, or arsenic – the sale of obscene publications and books'), as David Saunders argues, British obscenity law emerged in conjunction with 'the elaboration of social programmes in public health and sanitation, domestic economy, education (in literacy and morality) and penality' as part of the development of the governmental state.[115] Unlike blasphemy and sedition, which 'were never medicalised into a social problem', obscenity law extended the 'normative domain of sexual medicine into the governmental sphere' in order to protect certain vulnerable populations from moral and physical contagion.[116] The debates over the Obscene Publications Act thus reflect disquiet with the shift that was taking place in the operation of the law during the course of the nineteenth century: a shift from a juridical concern with aberrant acts to the deployment of law as a governmental tactic for constructing the modern subject – and, with it, altering the relationship between the individual and the state.[117]

In the immediate aftermath of the passage of the Obscene Publications Act such concerns appeared to be unfounded. Barring an initial flurry of regulatory campaigns that put an initial damper on the trade (the activities of the Dugdales were eventually undermined by both the death of William Dugdale in 1868 and the seizure of 35,000 copies of 'obscene' books, pamphlets and lithographic stones), the ongoing difficulties in regulating the obscene led the state to continue to leave such a task largely in the hands of moral reform organizations.[118] Although from mid-century onwards a variety of social, economic, political and

[114] Roberts, 'Morals, Art and the Law', 623.

[115] *Hansard*, Vol. CXLVI (9 July 1857), c. 1154; and Saunders, 'Victorian Obscenity Law', p. 160.

[116] Saunders, 'Victorian Obscenity Law', pp. 163, 164.

[117] Tadros, 'Between Governance and Discipline', 93.

[118] While initial regulatory activities had a considerable impact on the trade in 'obscenities' – particularly in London's Holywell Street, where much of the matter was produced and sold – it was able to recover to some extent thanks to the deployment of new techniques of distribution and sale, particularly through the medium of the post. Nead, *Victorian Babylon*, pp. 195, 197; and Manchester, 'Lord Campbell's Act', 232–3.

intellectual pressures began to erode both the ideal and the reality of a limited state, the reluctance of the state to serve as moral regulator of obscenity was a product of the British notion of the ideal state, which was conceived of until the Edwardian era largely as a limited one. As the philosopher and economist John Stuart Mill warned in *On Liberty*, published two years after the passage of the Obscene Publications Act, the increasing governmentalization of the state threatened to 'stretch unduly the powers of society over the individual' through 'prescrib[ing] general rules of conduct, and endeavour[ing] to make everyone conform to the approved standard'.[119] For Mill there were two forms of power, both of which operate through using sanctions to discourage individuals from committing certain acts: the power of the state, which operates through the threat of legal punishments, and social power, which operates through social mandates. Since 'Over himself, over his own body and mind, the individual is sovereign', maintaining the sovereignty of the individual required defence against both forms of power.[120] The freedom of the individual could therefore only be secured through restraining the actions of others; while compelling an individual to act in a certain way was not justified (the only justification for interfering in the liberty of the individual, according to Mill, was self-protection and the prevention of harm to others), Mill nonetheless maintained that society should prevent an individual from acting in a way 'calculated to produce evil to someone else'.[121] Mill thus sought to enunciate a juridical understanding of power in which laws are directed at acts rather than individuals and power cannot be exercised in the space of freedom allowed by those laws. The problem for Mill, however, was that 'juridical power cannot go to the heart of individual action' – while power can limit the actions of others it cannot encourage certain types of behaviour or actions.[122] Mill was therefore forced to fall back on faith in 'disinterested benevolence' to 'encourage' people to behave as they ought, without elaborating on how to distinguish between 'encouragement' and 'prohibition'.[123] For Mill, not only was the distinction between liberty and power therefore 'merely a distinction between one arrangement of

[119] J. S. Mill, *On Liberty*, cited in Petrow, *Policing Morals*, p. 7.
[120] Petrow, *Policing Morals*, p. 8.
[121] Tadros, 'Between Governance and Discipline', 83. Mill also maintained that, through such means as education, society had complete power over an individual before he or she reached adulthood. Petrow, *Policing Morals*, pp. 8, 9.
[122] Tadros, 'Between Governance and Discipline', 84.
[123] Mill thus insisted that 'It was essential for "the moral health of society" that individuals were not compelled but chose to form "virtuous habits of conduct"'. Petrow, *Policing Morals*, p. 9.

power relations and another', but the traditional site of juridical power was ultimately usurped by disciplinary power, which meant that there was, in truth, no free space for what he regarded as 'spontaneous' and 'natural action' to occur.[124]

The space opened up by Mill in his (largely unconscious) acknowledgement and support of the development of the governmental state was expanded by his most vociferous critics. While Matthew Arnold feared that England was heading towards anarchy and needed more government interference in the liberty of the individual, the jurist James Fitzjames Stephen argued not only that it was 'only under the protection of a powerful, well-organized, and intelligent government that any liberty can exist at all', but that it was the responsibility of the state to protect and enforce the nation's morals, if need be through 'the most powerful and by far the roughest engine which society can use for any purpose', namely the criminal law.[125] Although the development in the 1870s of what David Vincent refers to as the 'non-bureaucratic bureaucracy', a Civil Service organized on the basis of the cult of the gentleman rather than on a legal code, created what he considers a 'culture of secrecy' in the British establishment and a rarefied notion of the duties and functions of the servants of the state – of which policing morals was not deemed to be a part – as Stephen Petrow argues, 'after 1870 the balance of opinion was tipping in favour of Stephen's view that the state, by which was usually meant the government, the bureaucracy, and the police, should compel individuals to act in the best interests of society'.[126] With social and political shifts such as the rise of the social purity movement in the 1860s and 1870s, the growth of Nonconformism and, by the last decade of the century, the emergence of New Liberalism and Liberal Imperialism, both of which favoured state-sponsored social and moral reform, the governmentalization of the socio-moral realm by the state had come to be regarded as vital for the maintenance of the 'strength' and 'purity' of the British nation – and also its empire.

As has been demonstrated, empire played an important role in the beginning of attempts to regulate working-class print culture in the early

124 Tadros, 'Between Governance and Discipline', 86. Tadros notes, however, that 'because of their unspectacular symbolic manifestation, these disciplinary techniques escaped the juridical necessity of legitimacy'. Tadros, 'Between Governance and Discipline', 90–1.

125 J. S. Mill, *Liberty, Equality, Fraternity*, cited in Petrow, *Policing Morals*, p. 10.

126 Vincent, *The Culture of Secrecy*, p. 49; and Petrow, *Policing Morals*, pp. 12, 14. Another reason that moral regulation was not conceived of as part of the duties of the state was that 'a system directly responsive to community feeling was [believed to be] one likely to be more respected than one activated by public officials'. Roberts, 'Blasphemy, Obscenity', pp. 148–9.

nineteenth century. But as the debates over the Obscene Publications Act demonstrate it was also vital in spurring the transformation of obscenity regulation from a juridical to a governmental form of power. While amendments to the bill and public support undoubtedly played a part in securing its passage, a more vital role was played by a particular crisis of empire, namely the Indian Revolt (or, as British commentators referred to it, Mutiny) of 1857. Campbell's initial presentation of the bill to the House of Lords was so disastrous that it left little hope for securing its passage – until, however, news of the Revolt reached London two days later.

As M. J. D. Roberts argues, the Revolt

> made an impact on both sides of the moral divide in domestic politics. It strengthened the resolve of Evangelical interventionists to purify the home society to make it worthy of its imperial mission. It also immensely hardened the general public mood against 'sentimentality' in matters of social control, including the sexual. In a process significant for the future development of 'liberal' attitudes toward social regulation, it helped to detach a section of the progressive elite from the libertarian ranks of domestic political tradition and to make it more receptive to a paternalist-imperial set of social priorities at home as well as abroad.[127]

It hit home, in effect, the collapse of space between metropole and colony, and of the role of empire in constituting the national and – as it was increasingly becoming perceived – imperial body, a collapse of which Campbell was well aware when he compared, in his first report on the enforcement of the Act, the police 'siege of Holywell-street' with the 'siege of Delhi'.[128] Such a collapse led to the dissolution of fears of the development of the governmental state, and irretrievably bound empire, obscenity and governmentality together.

[127] Roberts, 'Morals, Art and the Law', 626. An imperial connection had, however, existed prior to the Revolt, since one of its chief supporters in the Commons was Sir Erskine Perry, a Liberal MP and former Chief Justice of Bombay (and future member of the Council of India).

[128] *Hansard*, Vol. CXLVIII (7 December 1857), c. 227. The *Daily Telegraph* extended this imperial metaphor by referring to the police efforts to 'clean up' the trade in obscene publications in Holywell Street following the passage of the Act as a 'razzia' – an Arabic term that had come to denote imperial conquest – which, as Nead contends, illustrates 'that the struggle over Holywell Street . . . assume[d] the significance of a highly concentrated and localised fight over imperial authority'. Nead, *Victorian Babylon*, p. 197.

3 Globalizing the local: imperial hygiene and the regulation of the obscene

In 1888 the publisher Henry Vizetelly was given the hefty fine of £100 (plus £200 for keeping the peace) for publishing English translations of three novels by Émile Zola: *Nana* (1880); *Pot Bouille* (published as *Piping Hot*, 1882); and the worst offender of the three, *La Terre* (published as *The Soil*, 1888), regarded by the judge (and author of the Hicklin verdict) Chief Justice Sir Edward Cockburn as a work of 'bestial obscenity'.[1] The case had initially been brought by the National Vigilance Association (NVA), a relatively new contender among Britain's moral reform organizations but one that would play the most significant role in the governmentalization of the obscene in Britain and in making such a project, moreover, an imperial one. Once the NVA secured a summons against Vizetelly for publishing the works in question, however, the Home Office decided to take over the case.[2] The verdict that thus ensued was, in the words of one Home Office official, 'epoch-making' – although not, perhaps, for the reasons he surmised.[3] For while the passage of the Obscene Publications Act had forged a link between obscenity, governmentality and empire in Britain it was not until the 1880s that regulating the obscene became a project of imperial hygiene. In making apparent the linkages between the English language, the national body and imperial space the Vizetelly trial not only served as a marker of the dangers to both nation and empire should they become 'corrupted', but provided

[1] *Pall Mall Gazette*, 31 October 1888, 1. Vizetelly was also ordered to withdraw the offending works from circulation.

[2] The Attorney-General had initially decided that it was 'undesirable' that proceedings should be instituted against Vizetelly out of fear both of failing to secure a conviction and of the unwanted advertising such a prosecution would accord to Zola's works. Once the Home Office took over the case, however, the prosecution was ably conducted by future Prime Minister Henry Asquith. HO 144/192/A46657, NAUK.

[3] Note by W. F. B., 8 November 1888, HO 144/192/A46657, NAUK. Later commentators have concurred as to the significance of the trial but have attributed this to the beginning of prosecutions for 'serious' literature in Britain, in spite of the fact that the next such prosecution did not take place for another thirty-five years (with the trial of Radclyffe Hall's *Well of Loneliness* in 1922). See, for example, Bristow, *Vice and Vigilance*, p. 207.

a means for a new technique of governing the obscene to enter the disciplinary network.

The problem with Vizetelly's translations of Zola's works was twofold. They were, firstly, translations of realistic novels. While the literary merits of all foreign works, the NVA organ the *Vigilance Record* opined, were 'apt to be blurred by translation', such 'blurring' was considerably exacerbated in the case of realistic works, whose explicit attention to detail of 'national life, manners, and habits of thought' – and, although this was rarely mentioned explicitly, sexual mores – were 'not appreciable to the foreigner'.[4] This meant that 'In a realistic French novel the literature is far more, and probably the vice is less, to a Frenchman than to an Englishman'.[5] Secondly, Vizetelly published his translations in inexpensive, one-volume editions, which rendered them accessible not only to readers who had no knowledge of French, but who were of a gender, age, social status or – thanks to the fact that, as the NVA's mouthpiece in the House of Commons, Samuel Smith, declared, such translations were being sold throughout the empire and in India were 'bought in tens of thousands, and were regarded as samples of European civilization' – 'race' that lacked the requisite aesthetic sensibility to respond 'safely' to such texts.[6] The act of translation from French to English

[4] *Vigilance Record*, 15 June 1889, 55. Émile Zola referred to his literary style as *naturalisme*, or naturalism. While English devotees of Zola such as George Moore praised naturalism for 'the truthfulness of the picture' it afforded, critics regarded its explicit references to 'appetites' and 'sensation' as 'the victory of ... matter over mind'. It was, in particular, the fusion of Zola's radical representation of sexual 'immorality' (namely that it was a product of the corruption of human nature by modern society) with fiction that generated a shocking confusion of both form and boundary order – a problem that was rendered more acute by the fracturing of linguistic boundaries. Hence even for Zola's admirers such as George Gissing, 'everyone, without exception, capable of reading him [Zola] *as literature* would take the trouble to read him in French, and only those who sought pornography would fall on the English version' (emphasis in original). Zola, *Piping Hot!*, pp. vi, xiii, xvii; W. S. Lilly, 'The New Naturalism', *Fortnightly Review*, 45 (August 1885), 24; and Cummins, 'The Transmission of Émile Zola', p. 114.

[5] *Vigilance Record*, 15 June 1889, p. 55. Translations of Zola's works thus threatened, it was feared, to drive 'any young man who had not learned the Divine secret of self-control' to commit 'some form of outward sin within twenty-four hours' of perusing them. Such anxieties about the corrupting influences of French culture were by no means, of course, unique to Zola; indeed, for the British *Bildungsroman* 'Withstanding Parisian seduction' had long been regarded as 'one of the decisive passage rites of a young Englishman'. But, as Franco Moretti demonstrates, Vizetelly began publishing his translations at a time when translations of foreign novels had virtually disappeared from the British literary marketplace (not to mention from the shelves of circulating libraries) – a product, for him, not simply of British nationalism and xenophobia but of 'hostility to foreign [literary] forms' such as realism. *Pernicious Literature*, p. 6; and Moretti, *Atlas of the European Novel*, pp. 30, 157.

[6] *Hansard*, Vol. CCCXXV (8 May 1888), c. 1713. While Smith had previously raised concerns about 'obscene' publications in the Commons he was provoked to take direct action against Vizetelly and Co. by an article in the *Pall Mall Gazette* in which Henry

therefore served not only to 'pollute' and transform English – and to demonstrate the permeability and corruptibility of 'Englishness' – but to undermine the very role of English and Englishness in 'civilizing' Britain's colonial subjects. Since 'Nations that abandon themselves to such practices slowly decline, and by an inevitable law of Providence are swept away by manlier and purer races', the corruption of the individual ('to the very core of his being') through reading such 'obscene' texts thus threatened to undermine not only the strength and purity of Britain, but its ability to govern a vast empire.[7]

The response to Vizetelly, a descendant of Italian immigrants publishing translated French realistic works of dubious morality and selling them not only to the lower classes in Britain but to Britain's colonial subjects, thus served to unite xenophobia – a long-standing fear of the role of the foreigner, or outsider, in corrupting the national–imperial body through the production and dissemination of obscene texts – with a new fear, the role of 'Englishness' in fostering the moral corruption of Britain's colonial subjects.[8] Vizetelly's transgression of so many of the boundaries through which the British national–imperial body was defined meant that when, in an effort to recoup his fine and redeem his business through issuing re-expurgated translations of the three novels for which he had been convicted – translations that, according to his son and translator Ernest, 'were sufficient to satisfy everybody except fanatical Puritans' – he was brought to trial a second time in May of the following year (in a prosecution initiated, once again, by the NVA and taken over by the Home Office) and was once again convicted.[9]

Vizetelly declared that he was selling a thousand volumes per week of translations of Zola's works. Cummins, 'The Transmission', p. 89; and *Pall Mall Gazette*, 24 March 1888, 2.

[7] Samuel Smith, letter to the *Standard*, reproduced in the NVA journal the *Vigilance Record*, 15 August 1888, 80. The *Vigilance Record* had previously alerted its readers to the imperial dangers of realistic literature by declaring that it had brought France 'into a condition resembling that of Rome in the time of the Caesars'. 'Corrupt Literature', *Vigilance Record*, May 1888, 42.

[8] The printer, engraver and journalist Henry Vizetelly (1820–94) was a lively figure on the British literary scene. In addition to co-founding the *Pictorial Times* and the *Illustrated Times* he also edited journals such as the *Welcome Guest* and worked in France as a correspondent for the *Illustrated London News*. He set up the publishing firm of Vizetelly and Co. in 1884 with two of his sons, and one of their specialities consisted of translations of foreign works of a 'high' literary character (by authors such as Fyodor Dostoyevsky, Leo Tolstoy, Edmond About and Prosper Mérimée). His inability, however, to secure a readership for such works led him to try his luck with translations of realistic and naturalistic novels by authors such as Gustave Flaubert, the Goncourts, Paul Bourget, Guy de Maupassant and, of course, Émile Zola. Decker, 'Zola's Literary Reputation', 1140–1.

[9] Vizetelly, *Émile Zola*, p. 286. Vizetelly was also indicted for publishing titles by Paul Bourget, Alphonse Daudet, Gustave Flaubert and Guy de Maupassant. Coote, *A Romance*, p. 47; and NVA Executive Minutes, June 1886 to April 1890, 4/NVA/104, WL.

A sick old man in need of constant medical attention and rendered a pauper by the first prosecution against him, Vizetelly could not summon the money to pay the fine for his second conviction and was sentenced to three months' imprisonment in Holloway, Britain's model panoptical prison. But he was mysteriously sent to the notorious Pentonville instead, where on arrival he completely collapsed and had to be rushed to the prison infirmary.[10] In light of his father's illness, Ernest Vizetelly petitioned the government for his release, and while 'two or three of the newspapers were already beginning to think that matters had been carried too far' his petition was denied (although Vizetelly was transferred to Holloway).[11] The draconian regulations introduced at Holloway in the 1880s, however, meant that three months of incarceration there were enough to send Vizetelly – whose trial, like that of the later Holloway inmate Oscar Wilde, was a 'labelling [process] of a most explicit kind drawing a clear border between acceptable and abhorrent behaviour' – to an early grave.[12]

Vizetelly's body had clearly become a site on which competing fears and social forces converged. Ernest Vizetelly firmly believed, long after his father's death, that his father had been chosen by the government and the NVA as their 'victim' – 'the wreckers', he claimed, 'had resolved to ruin him, and had succeeded to their hearts' desire'.[13] Although there is little evidence that either the government or the NVA sought to

10 The reason why Vizetelly was sent to Pentonville was a mystery even to the prison's deputy governor, who informed Ernest that 'Why he was sent [to Pentonville] I do not know; we have no accommodation for first-class misdemeanants. None has ever been sent here before.' Vizetelly, *Émile Zola*, p. 293.

11 Vizetelly, *Émile Zola*, p. 297. The petition was signed by 125 prominent writers, statesmen and other notables. Frierson, 'The English Controversy', 542.

12 Weeks, *Sex Politics*, p. 103; and Marsh, *Word Crimes*, p. 146. In addition to the physical discomfort generated by 'plank beds, flogging, and the forbidding of outside gifts of food, warmth, and money' at Holloway went a mental one spawned by the regime of constant surveillance and the use of the 'silent' system (which denied prisoners the right to speak to each other or their guards). As was later the case with Wilde (whose two years at Holloway sent him to an early grave), Vizetelly's exposure to such a regime completely shattered him, and he lived in pain and poverty until he died in 1894. Marsh, *Word Crimes*, p. 146.

13 Vizetelly, *Émile Zola*, p. 286. The NVA prided itself that 'No victory could have been more complete or far-reaching' than the outcome of the Vizetelly trials since they had a 'marvelous effect' not only upon booksellers in Britain but in Australia and India as well. It was clearly, however, somewhat uncomfortable with the outcome of its actions, for the NVA organ the *Vigilance Record* carried several articles following Vizetelly's trials in which it asserted that the verdicts were neither 'too severe' nor 'a vindictive punishment', since at his age Vizetelly 'ought to have known better' (although it admitted concern that Vizetelly's 'imprisonment may not unduly affect his health'). NVA, *Work Accomplished*, p. 3; 'Conviction for Publishing Obscene Literature', *Vigilance Record*, 15 November 1888, 114; untitled article 15 June 1889, p. 54; and Executive Minutes.

consciously make an example of Vizetelly, such claims seem justifiable, for while other publishers and booksellers were selling Zola's works only one ever appears to have gone to trial, and none was ever punished with what Walter Kendrick regards as such 'ferocity'.[14] Kendrick in fact asserts that 'no other case in the history of Anglo-American trials offers a comparable example of determined hostility and ruthlessness towards an individual'.[15] Moreover, concerned that Vizetelly's Zola translations had been 'sold to a considerable extent throughout the country', and convinced that his conviction would 'strengthen the hands of the police' in dealing with obscene publications, in 1888 the Home Office took the unprecedented step of notifying the mayors of all of the major cities in England of the outcome of Vizetelly's first prosecution and urging them to initiate prosecutions against sellers of Zola's works.[16]

While the passage of the Obscene Publications Act of 1857 marked the advance of the governmental state and bound empire, obscenity and governmentality together, the British government had continued to leave the task of regulating the obscene primarily to moral reform organizations such as the NVA.[17] Its success in securing convictions against Vizetelly, however, bolstered confidence in its ability to deal with the threat posed by 'obscene' publications not only to the British 'race' and nation, but to the whole empire.[18] Although neither the NVA nor the government had intended to use the Vizetelly trials to launch a moral crusade against obscenity throughout the empire this was essentially their result. Not only did they serve to spur the deployment of new modes and forms of regulation, in particular the creation of a cordon sanitaire to keep 'obscene' publications out of national and imperial space, but as we shall see in the following chapters the repercussions of

[14] See Coote, *A Romance of Philanthropy*, pp. 43–5. Prosecutions were brought by the NVA against publishers W. George and the Temple Publishing Co. and booksellers W. Smith and E. Roberts for works by Zola and other French authors.

[15] Kendrick, *The Secret Museum*, p. 166.

[16] HO 144/192/A46657, NAUK.

[17] The Home Office had become particularly wary of undertaking prosecutions against 'obscene' publications following its prosecution of Charles Bradlaugh and Annie Besant in 1877 for re-issuing Charles Knowleton's birth control pamphlet the *Fruits of Philosophy* (originally published in 1832), since the failure to secure a conviction turned a relatively obscure work into an instant bestseller (with a sale of over 200,000 copies by the early 1880s). Although the trial, which took place before the inventor of the Hicklin test, Lord Chief Justice Alexander Cockburn, did succeed in redefining contraception 'as not simply immoral, but obscene', the Home Office thereafter dealt with other publications that it desired to regulate, such as the periodical *Town Talk* (for an article on homosexuality) and the *Pall Mall Gazette* (for its articles on white slavery) through 'informal pressure'. Foster, 'The Collins Prosecution', 76; Bland, *Banishing the Beast*, p. 191; and HO 144/160/A4150 and HO 144/154/A40202E, NAUK.

[18] Bland, *Banishing the Beast*, p. 191.

these two seemingly obscure trials in Britain reverberated throughout the empire. They also served to reveal the degree to which the empire had become culturally interconnected by the late 1880s, a development that, rather than fostering the strength of Britain and its empire, could assume a frightening aspect when elements of the culture that served as the source of that interconnectedness had become 'degenerate'.

Protecting the future fathers of the 'race', nation and empire

> To the literature of Britain; to that literature, the brightest, the purest, the most durable of all the glories of our country; to that literature, so rich in precious truth and precious fiction; to that literature which boasts of the prince of all poets and the prince of all philosophers; to that literature which has exercised an influence wider than that of our commerce and mightier than that of our arms; to that literature which has taught France the principles of liberty and has furnished Germany with models of art; to that literature which forms a tie closer than the tie of consanguinity between us and the commonwealths of the valley of the Mississippi; to that literature before the light of which impious and cruel superstitions are fast taking flight on the banks of the Ganges; to that literature which will, in future ages, instruct and delight the unborn millions who will have turned the Australasian and Caffrarian deserts into cities and gardens. To the literature of Britain, then! And wherever the literature of Britain spreads may it be attended by British virtue and British freedom![19]

The Vizetelly trials may have ignited the spark that alerted the British government to the national and imperial danger posed by 'obscene' publications and boosted its confidence in its ability to manage such a threat, but it was ultimately revelations about the circulation of 'obscene' literature from the continent among public schoolboys – the future fathers of the 'race', nation and empire – that impelled the British government to act to create a new imperial regulatory regime to contain such contaminants.[20] That concerns about schoolboys should drive the British government to alter its long-standing reliance on moral reform

[19] Macaulay, *The Miscellaneous Writings*, p. 327.

[20] The concern about schoolboys coincided with an escalation of anxieties over masturbation. A product of what Steven Marcus terms a 'spermatic economy' ('to spend' was, notably, a common colloquial term for orgasm), in which the body was conceived of 'as a productive system with only a limited amount of material at its disposal', the effects of such a loss of self-control on both the individual and the national body were perceived to be dire. Complaints received by the Home Office from the headmasters of Britain's top public schools in the early 1890s regarding the reception of 'obscene' matter from overseas by their pupils were therefore regarded as matters of state, and precipitated the launching of a protracted process of negotiations with European governments to try to put a stop to the trade in such matter at its source. Porter and Hall, *The Facts of Life*, p. 151; Marcus, *The Other Victorians*, p. 22; and HO 144/192/A46657D, HO 45/24805, FO 371/70/2089, and FO 371/667/10035, NAUK.

organizations to regulate the obscene and usurp this governmentalizing project was the result of a number of interconnected factors concerning both nation and empire. The first was fears about racial and national degeneration. First coined in 1857 'as the medical label for a process by which men and women were destroyed through ... "moral and physical poison"', 'degeneration', in Sander Gilman's apt phrase, was the 'dark side of progress'.[21] It was the far-reaching social transformations of the 1870s and 1880s (in the economy, the nation-state, national culture, gender and class relations, the environment and, most problematically, in the beginning of a dramatic decline in the birth-rate) that gave the term particular resonance in Britain, for while contributing to a sense of living in a uniquely modern age and spurring faith in the power of scientific and socio-moral 'progress' and the greatness of the British 'race', nation and empire, such transformations also engendered anxieties about weakness and decay.[22] Although mid-Victorian science, particularly Darwinism, had facilitated a gradual shift in viewing race in biological rather than cultural terms, the social theory of degeneration drew more from the socio-evolutionary models evolved by Herbert Spencer and Jean-Baptiste Lamarck, for whom socio-moral ills such as disease, malnutrition and alcoholism could be reversed through 'scientifically' sound social policies.[23] The poetics and politics of degeneration thus sought to make 'individual bodies ... the true wealth of the state'.[24]

Such beliefs legitimated intervention into even the most intimate domains of the domestic life of the working classes.[25] But in the late

[21] Mosse, *Nationalism and Sexuality*, pp. 34–5; and Gilman, 'Sexology', pp. 72–96.

[22] The declining birth-rate was a cause of particular concern. Although Britain's population increased by almost 50 per cent between 1871 and 1911 (from 31 million to 45 million), the birth-rate dropped from 34.1 per 1,000 in 1871–2 to 24.5 per 1,000 in 1910–12. Infant mortality, moreover, remained high, all of which generated anxieties both about how to stem the decline and how to improve the quality of the existing racial stock. Harris, *Private Lives*, pp. 46–50.

[23] Harris, *Private Lives*, p. 243. Empire also played a key role both in the biologization of race in the second half of the nineteenth century and in fuelling concerns about the birth-rate. As one Home Office official declared in a debate on contraceptives, 'the great colonizing and industrial work done by the British race has been due to their prolific increase, which causing a pressure of population at home, has sent them to occupy lands abroad; and historically it has always been those nations which have had increasing populations which have played the greatest part in the world's history'. Such concerns became particularly prominent in the 1920s and 1930s in the face of mounting evidence that the rate of growth of non-white peoples in both the British empire and the world at large was greater than the rate of growth of whites. HO 144/192/A46657C and HO 45/15753, NAUK; and Ittmann, 'Demography as Policy Science', 417–48. See also Hall, '"From Greenland's Icy Mountains"', 212–30.

[24] Budd, *The Sculpture Machine*, p. 22.

[25] Since the poor were believed to suffer a greater burden of disease than other classes, a product of both environmental and moral conditions, it was deemed to be 'the duty of

nineteenth century it was arguably the effects of degeneration on bourgeois male bodies, particularly from forms of moral contagion such as 'obscene' publications (which, in exacerbating debilitating bodily practices such as masturbation undermined the cultivation of self-control in young bodies) that generated greater concerns.[26] Since masculinity was conceived of not simply as an array of attributes and capacities but as a project of self-formation that entailed the acquisition of 'character', moral contagion, in acting not only upon the embodied self but upon the unconscious (through 'a double capitulation to the outer world of "contagious" ideas and to the inner world of affects and drives'), threatened the elimination of selfhood – an effeminizing and, in turn, degenerative process.[27] Moreover, since 'character, active citizenship and "public spirit"' became perceived as being 'the indispensable building-blocks of a well-ordered society and a virtuous state', the linking of the character of the state with that of its citizens, particularly from the 1880s onwards when citizens became increasingly viewed as the building blocks of a new imperial race, meant that such a process of effeminization undermined the 'strength' and 'purity' of the 'race' and nation.[28]

The second factor that led the British government to generate a new system for regulating the obscene was the emergence of new discourses and new forms of print culture pertaining to sexuality, such as advertisements for contraceptives and abortifacients. As one Home Office official bemoaned in 1895, 'All newspapers bought by the common people teem with these advertisements', a situation that, as another lamented over a decade later, was 'having a profound effect on the development of the

government to intervene at this crucial (and vulnerable) point in the chain of causation of disease', particularly in light of what was regarded as one of the chief causes of societal degeneration and decay – a new 'urban type' whose culture and behaviour were believed to be markedly different from that of earlier generations of city-dwellers. Pelling, 'The Meaning of Contagion', p. 25; and Harris, *Private Lives*, p. 45. See also Jones, *Outcast London*.

26 While the morals of working-class men were a source of concern for late nineteenth-century moral reform movements, their primary concern was arguably regulating the bodies of those upon whom the fate of the nation and empire was believed to rest, namely middle- and upper-class men. Hunt, *Governing Morals*, pp. 158, 189. See also Hunt, *The Invention of Pornography*, pp. 12–13; Foucault, *The History of Sexuality*, p. 123; and Beisel, 'Morals Versus Art', 145–62.

27 Forth, 'Moral Contagion', p. 63. Emerging in social discourse in the mid-nineteenth century as a form of social and moral capital that involved the embodiment of particular moral characteristics, most notably self-restraint, the concept of 'character' that came to predominate in the 1860s and 1870s had its roots in classical humanism. In contrast to evangelical concepts, the attainment of virtue was believed to be possible through an act of will, namely through mastering certain codes of behaviour, freeing the mind and body from sexual passion and 'sublimat[ing] sensuality into leadership of society and nation'. Mosse, *Nationalism and Sexuality*, p. 13.

28 Harris, *Private Lives*, p. 250.

race'.[29] Popular sexology works generated similar concerns. Generated by pioneers such as Ivan Block, Magnus Hirschfeld, Charles Féré and Havelock Ellis, the newly emergent field of sexology laid the discursive, medical, psychological and anthropological basis for a new ethics of sexuality, including that of 'deviant' sexualities such as homosexuality (a process fostered by works such as Richard Burton's lavish ten-volume translation of the *Arabian Nights* and translations of Arab sex manuals, which offered a way of speaking about a subject such as homosexuality under the guise of Orientalist anthropology while conveniently deflecting its practice onto another culture).[30] While 'obscene' advertisements threatened the integrity primarily of working-class bodies, it was the strength and purity of middle-class bodies that were at stake in the case of sexology works.[31] A product of a shift in middle-class sexuality in the late nineteenth century in which the middle classes strove to differentiate themselves from the working classes 'not by the "sexual" quality of the body, but by the intensity of its repression', the larger aim of such works was to inculcate bodily self-control.[32] Their frank discussion of sexuality threatened, however, to undermine the very project that they sought to sustain, especially, it was feared, among middle-class youth. 'Scientific' works on homosexuality, or works that sought to expose or eradicate it, were a particular source of anxiety.[33] Hence, while Burton may have regarded

[29] HO 144/192/A46657C and HO 45/10932/157111, NAUK. The chief problem with contraception was not that it led to the production of fewer offspring, but that it weakened self-restraint and thus fostered racial degeneracy (a reason why advertisements for 'preventives' tended to be regarded as obscene). Loopholes in the law and uncertainty as to the likelihood of securing convictions meant that action against such advertisements (or against those for abortifacients) was, however, only taken when they were sent to minors or distributed unsolicited through the post. But since prosecutions generally failed and proposals for new legislation were repeatedly rejected, by the turn of the century the general approach of the Home Office to dealing with such matter was simply to have a 'quiet word' with the editor of an offending newspaper or to issue warrants against dealers in such wares. Bland, *Banishing*, p. 200; *Report from the Joint Select Committee on Lotteries and Indecent Advertisements* (1908), p. 36; and HO 155/192/A46657C, HO 155/238/A52539B and HO 45/10932/157111, NAUK.

[30] Gilmore, 'Obscenity', 605; and Kennedy, *The Highly Civilized Man*, p. 24.

[31] Sexology works were, therefore, subject to greater regulatory endeavours (ranging from prosecutions to restricting their access to members of the medical profession) than was the case with 'obscene' advertisements, although aesthetic quality, authorial intent and readership played a role in whether or not the Home Office decided to initiate proceedings against a work.

[32] Foucault, *The History of Sexuality*, p. 129.

[33] HO 144/160/A4150, NAUK; Gilmore, 'Obscenity', 607; and Wee, 'Trials and *Eros*', pp. 147–8. The inclusion of the notorious Labouchère Amendment, which criminalized all homosexual activity (both public and private) in the 1885 Criminal Law Amendment Act undoubtedly contributed to the criminalization – or at the very least, marginalization – of literature pertaining to homosexuality. So too did Oscar Wilde's trial a decade later, although Leigh Gilmore argues that it was in fact the representation of the homosexual

his translations as advancing the project of imperial governmentality (since they served both to undermine what he regarded as unhealthy British sexual norms and to provide knowledge about Muslim cultures), they were perceived to have quite the opposite effect.[34]

The third factor that played a key role in spurring the British government to implement a new regulatory regime for obscenity was concern about the impact of the empire in undermining 'Englishness'. Imperial space had long been conceived of as space that served to secure, even to invent, English identity, and to provide the stage on which the values of Englishness – and by extension Britishness – such as the rule of law, morality, emotional and physical restraint and bourgeois domesticity could be played out, contested and defined.[35] Englishness thus sought to assert its authenticity by denying the role of colonial spaces in its constitution. The 'paradox of Englishness', namely the 'need to define the national character against a colonial other that it must then disown', meant that English culture was fashioned through a narrative of exclusiveness.[36] But since Englishness was a cultural rather than a racial category, such exclusiveness was difficult to maintain in the face of new technologies of transport and communications and the fashioning of imperial spaces and places in the empire such as gothic architecture and cricket fields that served to preserve 'the Englishness of the English *and* to realize the extra benefit of Anglicizing the empire's sometimes unruly subjects'.[37] As 'webs of trade, knowledge, migration, military power and political intervention', empires, while underlain by systems of power and domination that served to construct and maintain racial, gender and class hierarchies, nonetheless 'functioned as systems of exchange, mobility, appropriation and extraction'.[38] Such processes were accelerated in the second half of the nineteenth century in the face of an expansion not only of the material networks of empire but of the discursive ones, as the 'differentiated knowledges' of various sites within

as someone who challenged gender roles and functions that was criminalized as 'obscene' in Britain rather than the discussion of homosexuality itself. Weeks, *Sex, Politics and Society*, p. 102; and Gilmore, 'Obscenity', 611.

34 Kennedy, *The Highly Civilized Man*, p. 229.

35 In the nineteenth and the first half of the twentieth century 'Englishness' and 'Britishness' were generally perceived to be synonymous – a product in part, as numerous scholars have demonstrated, of the 'complex pattern of antagonistic relationships with the external, supra-national, and imperial world' wrought by empire. Gilroy, 'Cultural Studies', p. 190. See also Anderson, 'Long-Distance Nationalism', pp. 58–74; and Colley, *Britons*.

36 Gikandi, *Maps of Englishness*, pp. 55–6.

37 Baucom, *Out of Place*, p. 20. 'Englishness' (and, by extension, 'Britishness') was perceived largely in cultural terms until the First World War, although biological notions of race gain growing credence from the 1860s onwards. Harris, *Private Lives*, p. 234.

38 Ballantyne and Burton, 'Introduction', p. 3.

imperial networks 'were connected by the communicative circuits of empire' forged through nodal points such as newspapers, telegrams, dispatches, letters, travel reports, parliamentary commissions, personnel – and 'obscene' publications.[39] Thus while the fashioning of the British empire as contiguous space served to strengthen imperial ties, the presence of so many non-English individuals in English places and spaces in the colonies also served to both destabilize and reformulate the very Englishness that those sites were designed to sustain – and in turn to render the boundaries that both united and divided the imperial metropole from colonial spaces and places more unstable.

In the nineteenth century, print culture (or what Benedict Anderson has termed 'print capitalism') came to play an important role in the creation of the 'imagined communities' not only of nations (through fostering the generation of both national languages and literatures), but of empires (through being employed by European official nationalisms as a means of concealing the discrepancies between the nation and dynastic realm – for the British a particularly daunting task in light of the geographical reach of the British empire).[40] It also served as an important 'civilizing' tool in European colonies, a 'mask of conquest' that, for the British, was designed to produce indigenous subjects who were 'English in taste, in opinions, in morals, and in intellect'.[41] But what the British had not accounted for was that Englishness would be transformed through exporting English literature to non-English contexts and using it as a colonizing tool, although this was virtually inevitable in light of the precarious and constricted vision of Englishness that such literature embodied. In contrast to literatures such as the classical or American, which aspired to 'the martial aggrandizements of the epic',

[39] Lester, *Imperial Networks*, p. 6. Cheap paper thus played as important a role in British imperial expansion in the nineteenth century as the gunboat, while new technologies such as the telegraph served to strengthen imperial ties. While it took an average of four months for a letter to reach Britain from India in the 1820s, by the turn of the century a telegraph could cover that distance in seventy-four minutes. By the First World War not only did an 'All Red' telegraph route exist that passed only through British territories, but Britain owned or had an interest in 80 per cent of the world's submarine cables. Kaul, *Reporting the Raj*, pp. 31, 34 and 49. See also Innis, *Empire and Communications*; and Ogborn, 'Historical Geographies', pp. 43–69.

[40] Anderson, *Imagined Communities*, pp. 110–11. Print languages, according to Anderson, created integrated fields of exchange and communication, gave a new fixity to language, and created what he terms 'languages-of-power'. Print capitalism, on the other hand, 'made it possible for rapidly growing numbers of people to think about themselves, and to relate to others, in profoundly new ways'. Anderson, *Imagined Communities*, pp. 44–5, 36.

[41] Viswanathan, *Masks of Conquest*; and Macaulay, 'Minute of 2 February 1835 on Indian Education', in *Macaulay, Prose and Poetry*, p. 729. For the British, English education, as Alistair Pennycock asserts, was 'at the heart of colonialism'. Pennycock, *English and the Discourses*, p. 2.

English literature, as Peter Conrad illumines, aspires towards the pastoral – a pastoral which is, moreover, a lost or imperfect Eden. Characterized by 'reticence', 'quietism', and a 'mystic fatigue' in which the self is annihilated in nature, the English pastoral envisions England as a land of mediocrity that, following the loss of a purported golden age, has become inhospitable both to the gods and to heroic, god-like deeds.[42] While holding out the promise of a future paradise, it thus embodies a spirit of renunciation, insulation and defeat; instead of paradise, the English 'must spend the interim on one island, vainly imagining another'. Although English literature may protest against such literal and metaphorical islanding, including the placing of a 'sanitary cordon' around privacy, attempts to challenge it are always frustrated.[43] In English literature Englishness therefore remains, according to Conrad, always 'quietly aggrieved'.[44]

The use of English literature as a colonizing tool further destabilized this vital yet precarious signifier of Englishness, particularly following the growth in readership of English literature among Britain's colonial subjects in the late nineteenth century thanks to developments such as the emergence of colonial libraries.[45] Launched by the publishing firm of John Murray in 1843, colonial libraries consisted of inexpensive single-volume editions of both fiction and non-fiction works, mostly reprints, that were generally of an inferior quality to texts designed for home consumption (in part because the paper used in colonial editions had to be much lighter to save on shipping costs).[46] By the end of the century close to twenty firms were producing colonial libraries, the most successful of which was undoubtedly that of Macmillan and Co.[47] While

[42] Conrad, 'The Englishness', 160.

[43] Conrad, 'The Englishness', 168.

[44] Conrad, 'The Englishness', 173. Conrad overlooks, however, the role of empire in fashioning such tensions regarding the nature and meaning of Englishness in English literature, in particular the relationship between containment, isolation and the annihilation of the self.

[45] As we shall see in Chapter 5, in India the colonial state also played a key role in cultivating a new readership for English literature.

[46] Murray launched his Home and Colonial Library – out of fear that American publishers were infiltrating the empire and damaging the loyalty of imperial subjects to the Queen – following the passage of the 1842 Copyright Act, the aim of which was to put a stop to the flourishing market in cheap American piracies of British copyrighted works. Joshi, *In Another Country*, p. 94. See also Barnes, *Free Trade in Books*.

[47] This estimate is based on a general but by no means exhaustive survey of colonial libraries. In addition to Macmillan, other firms that published colonial libraries included Bentley and Co.; Cassell and Co.; Frederick Warne; George Robertson; Petherick, Sampson, Low and Co.; Kegan Paul and Co.; Longman's; Greening; Milne; Collier and Co.; Alston Rivers; Duckworth and Co.; John Long; Heinemann; Bell; Walter Scott Publishing Co.; and Constable and Co.

Macmillan catered to settler markets such as Australia by including works by popular Australian authors, it was primarily the firm's desire to 'satisfy the tastes of their Indian readers' that led it to launch a colonial library in 1886.[48] Since over 90 per cent of the 680 titles published in Macmillan's Colonial Library between 1886 and 1916 were new fiction titles by popular authors, it thus played an important role in cultivating Indian tastes for British literature.[49]

But instead of the novels of 'serious standards' (by authors such as Scott, Richardson, Austen and Eliot) that were advocated as appropriate 'civilizing' tools for colonial readers, the bulk of the English novels consumed by colonial readers were far more ephemeral – and, in the Indian case, decidedly melodramatic and non-realistic – works by popular authors.[50] As the Sydney bookseller C. T. Clark lamented in 1899, the advent of the colonial edition was a particularly regrettable development, since 'Before it was inaugurated price prevented the immediate purchase [in Australia] of the novel or other work exciting attention in London', whereas now, 'getting the volume hot from the press we have to take it largely on trust, and it is undeniable that along with much that is good we get much that we could well do without'.[51] Yet while the colonial edition may have transformed the reading habits of colonial readers – although not always, as critics such as Clarke professed, to their benefit – their impact was by no means one-sided, for colonial literary consumption also served to transform publishing practices in the metropolis.[52] Colonial readers influenced the particular works published in Britain and, in the case of Indian readers, even the form of such works, as publishers with a large Indian clientele such as Macmillan developed a fiction list heavy in popular, melodramatic and non-realistic fiction to

48 Joshi, *In Another Country*, p. 30. Macmillan and Co. had begun cultivating the Indian literary marketplace in the 1860s through the publication of textbooks and educational materials in both English and an impressive twenty-one Indian languages. By the end of the century India had become the firm's most important overseas market. Joshi, *In Another Country*, p. 98.

49 Joshi, *In Another Country*, p. 104. Macmillan published no less than a third of the most popular authors in India. Joshi, *In Another Country*, p. 109.

50 Indian readers favoured works by authors such as F. Marion Crawford, Mrs Oliphant, Mrs Humphry Ward, Ouida and – the biggest British bestseller in India – G. W. M. Reynolds. Such readers were, however, hardly alone in their taste for melodrama, since it remained the dominant literary form throughout Europe. Joshi, *In Another Country*, pp. 4, 29; and Moretti, *An Atlas of European Literature*, pp. 176–7.

51 'The Book Trade in New South Wales: A Paper Read Before the Library Association Conference', *Sydney Morning Herald*, 9 February 1899, clipping in Miscellaneous Papers 1899–1934, Mss. 3315, ML. Australia needed to be protected, Clark maintained, from the barrage of cheap fiction emanating from Britain.

52 Joshi, *In Another Country*, p. 94; and Lyons and Taksa, *Australian Readers Remember*, p. 44.

cater to their tastes.[53] Colonial readers' uncivil consumption habits, which in addition to popular fiction included more titillating fare such as 'the worst class of French novels' (through which, according to NVA spokesman Samuel Smith, Indian readers were 'first acquainted with [British] literature') and 'filthy photographs', thus served to undermine not only the 'civilising mission' of colonialism but Englishness itself.[54] Macaulay's conviction that English literature 'exercised an influence wider than that of our commerce and mightier than that of our arms' may therefore have had considerable justification, but by the late nineteenth century whether or not English literature was still 'the brightest, the purest, the most durable of all the glories' of Britain – and whether it should be used as a 'civilizing' agent – had thus become less certain. Instead of furthering the project of enriching the empire from her own cultural traditions, the use of English literature as a civilizing tool had instead come to underscore the fundamental contradiction of official nationalism and to demonstrate 'the inner compatibility of empire and nation'.[55]

But if English literature had become such an unstable bearer of Englishness and civility, there was hope that the English language could step up to meet the task. During the course of the nineteenth century, the 'golden age of vernacularizing lexicographers, grammarians, philologists, and litterateurs', the English language came to be seen as embodying 'Englishness' more effectively than English literature, particularly following the publication of the first volume of the *Oxford English Dictionary* in the 1880s.[56] Through 'produc[ing] the rude and hardy Saxons as Englishhood's direct linguistic ancestors, fit progenitors of the master race', what the *OED* offered that English literature could not was 'the promise not only of a return to origins ... but of racial purity'.[57] Combined with a growing loss of faith in the literalness of the Bible following the publication of the new Revised Version of the King James Bible (1881–4), the study of the English language led to a new '"faith" in "Englishry", [and a] trust in the "English-speaking" "race" and the "English-speaking" "soul"'. It thus came to be perceived as an antidote to racial, national and imperial degeneration.[58]

53 Joshi, *In Another Country*, pp. 120–1. The use of the novel as a colonizing tool supports Edward Said's contention that the novel and imperialism 'are unthinkable without each other'. Said, *Culture and Imperialism*, p. 70.
54 *Hansard*, Vol. CCCXXV (8 May 1888), cc. 1708, 1707.
55 Anderson, *Imagined Communities*, p. 97.
56 Anderson, *Imagined Communities*, p. 77; and Marsh, *Word Crimes*, p. 204.
57 Marsh, *Word Crimes*, p. 205. The first volume of the *OED* was published in 1884.
58 Marsh, *Word Crimes*, p. 206. For an analysis of the revolution in the use of language in England that occurred during the course of the nineteenth century and of attitudes towards it see Joyce, 'The People's English', pp. 159–90.

But as revealed in the fourth factor that drove the British government to initiate a new regulatory regime for 'obscene' publications – namely the new international and imperial nature of the threat – the 'purity' of the English language, and in turn its virtue as a bearer of Englishness and civility, was also open to doubt. For by the late nineteenth century, not only was the emergence of new forms of 'obscenity' ranging from sexology texts to sexually explicit postcards, photographs, mutoscope reels and stereoscope slides intimately tied to empire, so too were new patterns of production, distribution and consumption, including the development of imperial networks for both the dissemination and regulation of obscenity.[59] While the driving of British traders in obscenity to the continent in the late nineteenth century had made it 'difficult for any-one [sic] to procure in London obscene literature or prints', they were soon able to obtain them elsewhere thanks to the post.[60] '[S]eizing every means for increasing [their] profits' through 'those facilities of expansion, of publicity and of communication so widely opened up to human activity by modern discoveries', dealers in 'obscenity' solicited clients through the post and operated transnational networks of correspondents, travellers and depots 'in the most important towns in every country' – including throughout the British empire.[61] By the end of the nineteenth century the long-feared spectre of networks of foreigners who had invaded and pervaded the geographical boundaries of the British nation-state hawking their wares had been replaced by that of expatriate Britons who operated international networks for whom borders and boundaries – national, moral and racial – were irrelevant and who operated through surreptitious, imperceptible and virtually undetectable means.[62] Based in countries such as France, Spain, Switzerland, Germany, Belgium, Hungary and Italy, from which they operated networks of local, national and transnational production and distribution, such traders were also extremely mobile, moving about from country to

[59] As Ronald Hyam pithily observes, by the 1880s there was thus a growing awareness that Britain 'did not merely sell cotton clothes to all the world: it also exported nude photographs'. Hyam, *Empire and Sexuality*, p. 3.

[60] Memo on 'Indecent Publications', HO 45/10930/1149778, NAUK. British- and European-owned bookshops in cities such as Paris also began to cater to British tourists seeking English-language material that was no longer available in Britain. See, for example, FO 371/455/15341, NAUK.

[61] 'Correspondence respecting the International Conference on Obscene Publications and the White Slave Traffic', Paris, April and May 1910, GB/106/4/NVA/S.88/K Box 107, WL.

[62] By the 1890s the British Home Office had come to the conclusion that 'there has been of late a greatly increased use of the international post for the purpose of introducing obscene matter into this country'. Under Secretary of State for the Foreign Office to the Secretary of State, Home Office, HO 144/238/52539B, NAUK.

country throughout Europe as they were hounded by the police (often at the behest of the British government).[63]

While sellers of obscene books and other ephemera, such as Edward Avery, 'trad[ed] considerably with the Colonies', others based more safely on the continent, such as Harry Nichols, could assure potential customers in their catalogues that 'Export orders for England and her Colonies, India, America, and other Foreign Lands, [would be] executed with intelligence, care, and promptitude'.[64] Colonial inhabitants unable to avail themselves of such services, such as Zulus with a taste for 'obscene' photographs, Basothos with a penchant for brass finger rings containing photos of nude white women, or southern African peoples desirous of obtaining purportedly obscene gramophone records in their own dialects, could exploit postal networks through local traders.[65] Such matter was purveyed throughout the empire through nodal points such as Port Said, which, as one critic complained to the NVA in 1905, was 'a perfect sink of iniquity, a vile plague spot' for the sale of obscenity and, since it was 'situated well upon the highway of all the intense shipping traffic to the east', for the dissemination of 'obscene' material throughout the empire.[66] The British empire had thus become a vast system for the purveyance of 'obscenity', and although critics such as the editor of the Victoria *Geelong Advertiser* complained that the metropole dominated imperial communication networks (which meant that inhabitants of Victoria knew 'more of what happens in Berlin than we do of what happens in Perth'), by the end of the First World War such networks operated not simply between metropole and colonies but between

63 See, for example, FO 371/1032/7221 and FO 83/2101, NAUK. By 1912 the Home Office had managed to compile a list of forty-one of the most notorious 'Dealers in Indecent Wares on the Continent who are Known to attempt to do business in England through the Post', although, in light of the mobility of such dealers and the many aliases they employed, the accuracy of the information it contained is questionable. HO 144/10130, NAUK.

64 *Report from the Joint Select Committee*, p. 40; and Colligan, 'Obscenity and Empire', p. 248. By the 1920s there was also a trade in pornographic films between Britain and its colonies, and customers included Indian royalty who were purportedly 'willing to pay big sums for dirty films'. *John Bull*, 29 March 1924, n.p., clipping in file MEPO 3/386, NAUK.

65 *Vigilance Record*, September 1911, cited in Colligan, 'Obscenity and Empire', p. 250; and DO 119/865 and DO 35/571/10, NAUK. The case of the gramophone records is particularly interesting, since they were apparently made by the Columbia Gramophone Company and sold in a number of British African colonies. Uganda successfully prosecuted the company and its local representatives for selling such records in 1941, and the Colonial Office requested its African colonies to establish a censorship of gramophone records in conjunction with the gramophone companies.

66 Letter by C. E. Barlow to the NVA, 19 January 1905, 4/NVA/S.88/RI Box 108, WL.

colonies.[67] 'Obscene' pictures, photographs, postcards and books from Singapore were to be found in Burma, 'obscene' pamphlets from India in Mauritius, Zanzibar and Southern Rhodesia and 'obscene' pictures from Madagascar in Tanganyika.[68] That British colonies played a vital role in the material and discursive networks through which 'obscenity' permeated the British empire is clear in cases such as that of the south Indian moneylender in the Unfederated Malay States who was found in possession of two hundred obscene postcards of French origin that he had obtained from a Chinese hawker in Malacca.[69]

Not only, however, was 'obscene' matter circulating between colonies, but such matter from Britain's colonies was making its way back to the metropole. While the Australian amateur sexologist William Chidley sought to market his treatise *The Answer* (which aimed to rectify the incorrect manner in which, according to its author, mankind was having sex) in Britain prior to the First World War, it was not until after the war that Indian sexology texts, known as *kamashastra* literature (which were formerly 'impossible to get except through secret channels') had become 'openly advertised and published' and were obtainable almost anywhere – including the imperial metropole.[70] The contraction of imperial space, while advancing the cultural consolidation of the empire, had also, therefore, brought the pollutions and impurities of colonial spaces 'home'.[71] Since the purity of Britain's domestic space could no longer be conceived of 'as ontologically different from [that of] its colonial possessions', by the late nineteenth century the British empire had come to be conceived of as a source of spatial, cultural and moral contagion

[67] Transcript of a meeting between R. Lewis James of the *Geelong Advertiser* and the Minister for Home Affairs, King O'Malley, 24 February 1911, A2, 1913/1053, AAC.

[68] See the League of Nations' annual reports on 'Traffic in Women and Children and Obscene Publications' for 1931, 1932–3, 1935–6 and 1937–8, in FO371/17387/W1409, FO 371/18533/W923, FO 371/19669/W8989, CO 323/1432/1 and CO 323/1656/5, NAUK.

[69] See, for example, FO 371/17387/W1409 and FO 371/18533/W923, NAUK. While Stephen Fuchs contends that networks 'are not of one piece' but have 'various bounded parts', including a core and peripheries, viewing Britain as the core of the networks through which 'obscenity' permeated the empire is thus problematic in light of the ways in which such matter actually circulated by the early twentieth century. Fuchs, *Against Essentialism*, p. 274.

[70] MP341/1/0, 1913/9411, Box 157, AAM; and George Grierson to Sir Arthur Hirtzel, 27 August 1925, Home Department 669/25, NAI. The Punjab Sanskrit Book Depot, for example, sent advertisements for an English translation of the *Kama Sutra* to Britain in 1922. Kaul to Home Department, 2 October 1922, 106/1922, Judicial, B, Home Department, NAI.

[71] Such pollution was particularly problematic for a city that had, by the late nineteenth century, come to be conceived of (at least by the British) not only as 'the chief city of England, nor even of the British Empire, but as "the capital of the human race"'. Harris, *Private Lives*, p. 22.

and as a threat, therefore, not only to the British nation, but to its ability to maintain and govern its empire.[72]

To draw upon Ann McClintock's terminology, the contraction of imperial space fostered, on the one hand, 'an *excess* of boundary order and fantasies of unlimited power', a sense of empowerment that led – since the body was 'the most intimate colony, as well as the most unruly' – to British bodies being increasingly laid open to empire, to occupying imperial spaces, consuming imperial goods and defining themselves against the imperial other.[73] But, on the other hand, they also fostered 'the simultaneous dread of catastrophic boundary *loss* (implosion), associated with fears of impotence and infantilization', a fear of disempowerment that fostered attempts to shore up the boundaries of the body through 'fetishes, absolution rituals and liminal scenes'.[74] The consolidation of imperial space thus served to both fragment and infect the British national–imperial body. But that the preoccupation with boundaries became so intense in Victorian Britain, particularly those pertaining to the body, was the result, in part, of a new medico-scientific understanding of the body as a corpus, a secularized entity subject not only to dissection but also to reconstruction – a development that marks a 'shift away from thinking of the body in terms of its "being" to a conception of what it "ought to be"'.[75] Such new conceptions of the body in turn fostered the imagining of the British nation and empire somatically, as a gendered and racialized body, and of individual bodies in political terms, as waging battles against external enemies.[76]

In imperial spaces this fear of disempowerment simultaneously closed off British bodies against processes of acclimatization or indigenization as tropical climates and racial mixing became regarded as threats to the British 'race'.[77] British authority became increasingly grounded 'in the bodily difference between ruler and ruled', and bodily practices

72 Gikandi, *Maps of Englishness*, p. 106.

73 McClintock, *Imperial Leather*, p. 27; and Ballantyne and Burton, 'Postscript', pp. 406–7.

74 McClintock, *Imperial Leather*, pp. 27, 33. Such a reinforcement of the boundaries of the body was perhaps inevitable in light of the fact that, as Philip Holden observes, 'the act of regulation of the self was analogous to the regulation of the colony' since 'both actions imposed discipline upon necessary natural forces, producing a free market of the soul in parallel with that of trade'. Holden, *Modern Subjects*, pp. 116, 118–19.

75 Budd, *The Sculpture Machine*, p. 13.

76 While the body, as Mary Douglas contends, 'is a model which can stand for any bounded system', or 'for any boundaries which are threatened or precarious', it was only from the 1860s onwards that 'the human body and its diseases supplied an increasingly potent model and metaphor for the understanding of the wider "body politic"'. Douglas, *Purity and Danger*, p. 113; and Harris, *Private Lives*, p. 60. See also McClintock, 'Family Feuds', and Martin, 'Toward an Anthropology'.

77 Collingham, *Imperial Bodies*, p. 177; see also Harrison, *Climates and Constitutions*.

in the empire were brought into closer alignment with those in the metropole.[78] Women's bodies – 'at once more completely concealed by clothing and more intimately probed by science' – became particularly subject to regimentation in the empire and at 'home', both to mark the distinction of the bourgeoisie and to serve as a sign of British moral superiority (and of the moral superiority, therefore, of British colonial rule).[79] Reproductive bodies also assumed greater significance as the century drew to a close and population became construed as a national resource. Evidence of a declining birth-rate, rising infant mortality rate and a dramatic drop in family size fostered eugenic conceptions of motherhood as a national duty and child welfare as the duty of the state, and led to science usurping the role of the church as the guardian of normality and morality.[80] Revelations of the poor health of the future soldiers of empire, namely the working classes, and astonishingly high rates of venereal disease among British troops in the empire added further impetus to fears that the imperial 'race' was degenerating.[81]

It was such fears that led to the transformation of the regulation of obscenity into a project of imperial hygiene, which according to one colonial health official was 'development by sanitation', or 'colonizing by means of the known laws of cleanliness rather than by military force'.[82] While earlier in the century obscenity had been conceived of primarily as 'a threat to the procreative behaviour, well-being and public decency of the popular classes', by the late nineteenth century it had come to be viewed as 'a pathological agent invading bourgeois homes and schools' – and a problem, therefore, of social hygiene.[83] Not only did obscenity thus become increasingly subject to regulation but, with the coming together of moral reform organizations, the newly emergent

[78] Collingham. *Imperial Bodies*, p. 8.

[79] Budd, *The Sculpture Machine*, p. 12. As Jenny Sharpe has revealed, that the English woman served as a sign of the moral superiority of British colonialism is evident in the British interpretation of the Indian Revolt of 1857 as a sex crime against 'their' women. Sharpe, 'The Civilizing Mission', p. 68.

[80] Davin, 'Imperialism and Motherhood', p. 88. With the secularization of British society during the course of the nineteenth century the prestige of science rose, which led to morality being given a new scientific basis. Bland, *Banishing the Beast*, pp. 84–91.

[81] By 1896 venereal disease rates among British troops in India had reached the astonishing rate of 522.3 per thousand – a terrifying spectre when the British constituted only 170,000 of the 294,000,000 of India's populace. Ballhatchet, *Race, Sex and Class*, pp. 90, 6.

[82] Bashford, *Imperial Hygiene*, p. 13.

[83] Hunter, Saunders and Williamson, *On Pornography*, pp. 52–3. The social hygiene movement, which emerged in the 1890s with the quest of linking medicine to the service of the nation-state to maintain the health, strength, and 'moral hygiene' of the population, led to the formation of 'an hegemonic alliance' with the military and the state health administration to promote racial 'fitness' and 'national efficiency'. Samuel, 'The Discovery of Puritanism', p. 237; and Hunt, *Governing Morals*, p. 103.

medical profession, and the state in a medico-moral alliance that attempted to shift the focus away from viewing 'purity' as a moral question to regarding it as a medical and racial concern, the regulation of the obscene became part of the biopolitical project of imperial hygiene as a means of preserving the 'strength' and 'purity' of the British 'race', nation and empire.[84]

Obscenity as a project of imperial hygiene

The overwhelming majority of the authors of this country desire to write and publish books which are uplifting and which make for the welfare of this nation, and are in accordance with the principles of 'safety first'.

You have tremendous responsibility, you who write, more than we who speak for your writings go into every home and are read by every kind of person ... Remember what the nation means to the well-being of the Empire, and the civilisation of the world. London is the heart of the whole. The tone of the Empire comes from you the authors of our land. If the tone is pure, the blood will go on pulsating through the whole world carrying with it purity and safety. If the stream of the blood is impure, nobody can tell the effect it will have right through our Empire.[85]

Beginning in 1851 a series of international sanitary conferences – which marked what W. F. Bynum has termed the emergence of 'medical internationalism' – met to address a range of health issues generated by the increased mobility of peoples, and various imperial and colonial authorities started to coordinate to help manage forms of contagion such as cholera, plague, leprosy and venereal disease.[86] With the focus, particularly in the early conferences, on quarantine, such public health measures operated as a spatial form of governance that sought to erect 'lines or barriers drawn *across* these global, local, and bodily circulations and connections', a series of cordons sanitaires that sought simultaneously to police public health – to separate the diseased from the clean, and the fit from the unfit – and to manage racial barriers, in particular

[84] While the term 'purity' nominally referred to the campaigns against prostitution, it was in fact applied to a wide range of moral and social crusades.

[85] Speech by Home Secretary William Joynson-Hicks to the Authors' Club, *Daily Telegraph*, 11 December 1938.

[86] Bynum, 'Policing Hearts', 422. Such sanitary conferences offer evidence of what Tony Ballantyne and Antoinette Burton refer to as 'the ways in which the development of global empires have been entwined historically with bodies in contact'. The first international sanitary conference, which met in Paris, was notably held in the same year as both the Great Exhibition in London and the first international conference on statistics in Brussels – all of which contributed to both the emergence and the globalization of governmentality. Ballantyne and Burton, 'Introduction', p. 8. See also Harrison, 'Quarantine, Pilgrimage'.

the construction of whiteness.[87] It was through such efforts to manage contagion and construct whiteness, in particular through the international campaigns against the 'white slave' trade, that obscenity was fashioned as a project of imperial hygiene.[88]

First launched by purity crusaders and feminists in 1879, following disclosures about young British girls trapped in Belgian brothels, the white slavery movement was the manifestation of a range of discourses and fears – of non-marital sexuality, prostitution, the women's movement, racial degeneration and, since contagion had come to be regarded largely as an external threat brought by 'foreigners' or 'aliens' who were polluting the geo-body of the British nation-state, of xenophobia – into the image of the weak and innocent woman in need of protection.[89] While a national movement emerged to tackle the 'white slave' trade, by the century's end there was growing evidence that 'the increased and cheapened facilities of railway and steam-boat communication' had facilitated the creation of a global prostitution market.[90] This led to the development of an international system to regulate the trade in women, which, while initiated by the NVA, was taken over by the imperial government by the early twentieth century and transformed into a project of imperial hygiene.[91]

87 As Michael Hardt and Antonio Negri argue, the construction of hygienic 'protective barriers' was a product of the 'horror of unlimited contact, flow and change – or really the horror of contagion, miscegenation, and unbounded life' – wrought by European conquest and colonialism. Hardt and Negri, *Empire*, pp. 135–6.

88 Although in the 1830s 'white slavery' emerged as a referent for the conditions of employment of factory girls, by the end of the nineteenth century it had come to connote prostitution, particularly the transportation of women (with or without their consent) to foreign brothels. Petrow, *Policing Morals*, p. 158.

89 Hunt, *Governing Morals*, p. 179. The social purity movement, an alliance of feminists, evangelicals and socio-moral reformers of various hues, originated in the 1880s out of the campaigns against the Contagious Diseases Acts (which aimed to ameliorate the problem of venereal disease in the British army through the administration of a system of state-regulated prostitution). The term 'purity' has a complex etymology, but as used by the campaigners of the late nineteenth century it entailed the avocation, through a mixture of evangelical and scientific language, of sexual restraint and self-control (particularly for men) and the stigmatization of prostitution and other forms of non-marital sexuality. The movement, which targeted three main avenues of socio-moral reform (prostitution, the white slave trade and the trade in 'obscene' publications), thus represented a shift in the targets and means of moral regulation from the suppression of vice to the governmentalization of sexuality. Samuel, 'The Discovery of Puritanism', p. 233; and Hunt, *Governing Morals*, pp. 78, 91.

90 T. W. Snagge, 'Memorandum on the Origin and Evolution of the Movement for the Suppression of the White Slave Traffic', MEPO 2/558, NAUK.

91 Coote, *A Romance*, pp. 200–1. Although the abolition of the Contagious Diseases Acts and the enshrining of a more governmental approach to sexuality with the passage of the great triumph of the social purity movement, the Criminal Law Amendment Act of 1885, seemed to signal the withdrawal of the state from the sexual field, in enshrining

Concerns about obscenity, not only, as Edward Bristow asserts, 'developed [in] parallel with anxieties about the white-slave traffic', but the transformation of obscenity into a project of imperial hygiene emerged directly from the efforts to manage white slavery.[92] In addition to being a sideline business for bullies or souteneurs, obscene publications were regarded by the NVA as 'a direct stimulus to prostitution' by luring young men to brothels and by driving young women to flout the conventions of marriage and embrace a life of immorality.[93] The 'connection between the prostitute, the bully and obscenities' through international networks made all three, therefore, 'a moral pest of which all civilized countries wish to be rid'.[94] This view of the traffic in women and 'obscenities' as interlinked forms of contagion led to the construction of an international regime to regulate the obscene that, in addition to being modelled on the system to regulate white slavery, remained linked to it until well into the twentieth century – and which Britain used to police the trade in 'obscene' publications throughout its empire.[95]

Hygiene connected the governance of the self to larger governmental projects and thus became a means of imagining and embodying the strength and purity of the individual, community, nation and empire. That by the late nineteenth century regulating obscenity had become viewed as a hygienic project is clear from the language used to denote the dangers of publications deemed to be obscene or simply 'immoral' (such as that they were a 'moral epidemic' or a 'contagious disorder of soul and body' that served to '[undermine] the sense of continence and self-control in the individual which is essential to a sound and healthy State'); in the types of material targeted for regulation (such as contraceptive and

a new host of sexual 'crimes' and according greater powers to intervene in matters pertaining to sexuality the Act also appeared to mark a move to greater state involvement in the regulation of sexuality. The reality, in fact, was a mixture of both, for while the state began to play an increasing role in the governmentalization of the sexual field from the 1880s onwards, it was not by any means a coherent project.

92 Bristow, *Vice and Vigilance*, p. 200. Philippa Levine highlights a more literal connection, arguing that the prototype for the white slave trade emerged from obscene literature. Levine, 'The White Slave Trade'.

93 GB/106/4/NVA/S.88/B, Box 107, WL. As NVA stalwart the Earl of Meath (later Lord Shaftesbury) opined in a debate on 'indecent literature' in the House of Lords, factory girls and servants were first 'demoralised' by 'harpies' purveying obscene works, following which they 'fell a ready prey' – presumably to 'white slavery'. 'Indecent Literature and the House of Lords', 15 August 1888, *Vigilance Record*, 8.

94 GB/106/4/NVA/S.88/B,Box 107, WL; and FO 371/13389/W5405, NAUK.

95 FO 371/1028/480, NAUK. Most of the signatories to the international agreements to regulate white slavery also signed those to regulate obscene publications, and from the 1930s onwards the reports on the trafficking in both women and 'obscene' publications, which signatories were obliged to submit annually to the League of Nations, were even filed jointly and printed together by the League.

sexology literature and advertisements); in the agencies responsible for carrying out such regulation (such as health agencies and customs departments, which drew upon their powers of detention and quarantine to keep 'unhealthy' literature outside the geographical boundaries of the nation-state); and in the means required to regulate it (such as the need for a censorship system that functioned in the nature of a 'sanitary system' or, as one proponent described it, as 'a quarantine to prevent plagues which would interfere with the moral health of the people').[96]

Because so much of the 'obscene' matter circulating in Britain came from overseas, including the material found at boys' schools, the first step the British government took to create a hygienic system to regulate the obscene was to attempt to put a stop to the trade at its source. The initiation of a furious diplomatic campaign with almost a dozen European countries to urge them to clean up the trade within their own borders proved, however, an unrewarding task, both because European governments often refused to cooperate in such an undertaking and because they lacked either the sufficient legal machinery or other regulatory powers necessary to do so.[97] Since 'The management of contagion has always involved ... the drawing of lines and zones of hygiene' through such means as quarantine, isolation or containment, the failure of such efforts spurred the British government to create a system of 'quarantine' to keep 'obscene' publications out of Britain.[98]

[96] Lord Mount-Temple, 'Demoralizing Publications', *Vigilance Record*, 15 September 1888, 86; St Loe Strachey, review of *Anne Veronica*, 1909, cited in Bristow, *Vice and Vigilance*, p. 217; and 'Report of Proceedings of Deputation to the Hon. T. W. White, Minister of State for Trade and Customs, RE Censorship of Books', Mss. 9148, NLA. The relationship between 'obscenity' and hygiene was made tangible in the case of Hygienic Stores Ltd in Charing Cross Road, which in addition to offering 'hygienic' productions for sale also had a reputation for selling 'obscene' publications. HO 45/24805 NAUK.

[97] See, for example, HO 144/192/A46657D, FO 83/1786, FO 83/2101, FO 371/746/20081, FO 371/1032/5583 and FO 371/1032/7221, NAUK.

[98] Bashford and Hooker, 'Introduction', p. 9. The British government had more legal means at its disposal to regulate the trade in 'obscene' publications than its continental counterparts, ranging from the 1824 and 1838 Vagrancy Acts, the 1839 Metropolitan Police Act, the 1843 Libel Act, the 1843 Theatres Act, the 1847 Town Police Clauses Act, the 1857 Obscene Publications Act, the 1870 Post Office Act and the 1884 Post Office Protection Act, the 1875 Public Health Act, the 1889 Indecent Advertisements Act, the 1876 Customs Laws Consolidation Act, laws under the London Council (General Powers) Act of 1890 and 1896, and – with the re-establishment of an Obscene Publications Branch at New Scotland Yard in the same decade (it had first been formed in 1863 but was later disbanded) – invaluable assistance in putting these laws into effect. There were, however, numerous loopholes in the law. Neither the Post Office Protection Act of 1884 nor the later Post Office Act of 1908 applied to the sending of obscene matter in closed packets, while the 1889 Indecent Advertisement Act only applied to advertisements displayed in public places (and hence not to

While continuing its diplomatic efforts, beginning in the early 1890s the Home Office developed a new method to prevent obscene literature from making its way to, and contaminating, Britain's shores, namely the warrant system.[99] Warrants were issued against both individual publications sent through the post and postal matter sent from (and even, for a short period of time, to) known overseas traders in obscene wares.[100] All 'obscene' matter found through this violation, as postal officials saw it, of 'the secrecy of the post', was destroyed.[101] By 1906 E. A. Henry, the Commissioner of Police at New Scotland Yard, could boast that the system had proved successful, since 'Within the last few years . . . van loads of filthy publications have been seized and destroyed, and at the present time it would be difficult for any-one [sic] to procure in London obscene literature or prints.'[102] Such matter could still, however, be procured with relative ease from abroad, since while 'The facilities between this and Continental Forces had been made full use of' and a number of known dealers in foreign countries prosecuted, 'this remedy [for dealing with the problem] is a cumbrous one, uncertain in its incidence, and tardy in its application'.[103] Moreover, the laborious system of employing British ambassadors to intervene in the internal affairs of foreign governments by alerting them to the activities of international traffickers in 'obscene' wares within their borders or petitioning them to prosecute such traders was a cumbersome procedure not only when it came to protecting the geo-body of the British nation-state, but

advertisements in newspapers). Moreover, the legal procedures required to convict a purveyor of obscene wares were extremely complicated. Yet despite such dissatisfactions with the law, government officials were rarely in favour of changing it to accord them greater powers. HO 45/20912, HO 45/9752/A59329, HO 45/100/10048/A62697 and HO 45/13296, NAUK.

99 'The Stoppage of Letters to or From Dealers in Obscene Matter', HO 45/9752/A59329; and HO 45/10510/129433, NAUK.

100 Although the Customs Department also had the power, under the Customs Laws Consolidation Act of 1876, to seize 'Indecent or obscene prints, paintings, photographs, books, cards, lithographic or other engravings, or any other indecent or obscene articles', from 1900 onwards all such items found were handed over to the Post Office to deal with in order that 'the importation of any indecent or obscene matter by post may be more effectively repressed'. CUST 46/199, NAUK.

101 Postal officials strongly objected to using the Post Office to regulate 'obscene' matter and were often uncooperative in assisting the Metropolitan Police officers (members of the Confidential Inquiry Branch) assigned to help undertake the task. This problem was somewhat resolved in 1909 when the Post Office handed the duty of dealing with 'obscene' postal items back to the Customs Department. HO 45/10510/129433 and CUST 49/1638, NAUK.

102 E. A. Henry, Commissioner of Police, New Scotland Yard, to Home Office, 11 April 1906, HO 45/10930/1149778, NAUK.

103 E. A. Henry to Home Office.

even more so when it came to protecting that of its empire.[104] Preserving the purity of both thus necessitated the erection of a cordon sanitaire around the whole empire.[105]

Although the 1908 Joint Select Committee on Lotteries and Indecent Advertisements became the first government body to advocate the development of an 'international arrangement' as a means of regulating the transnational trade in obscenities, moral reform organizations, particularly those that coalesced around the purity campaign to overturn the Contagious Diseases (CD) Acts in the 1880s, provided both the model and the framework for the development of this particular project of imperial hygiene.[106] Aware that 'The empire was as much a system of prostitution networks as it was ... a web of submarine cables', following the repeal of the CD Acts in Britain purity campaigners such as Josephine Butler – who maintained that 'England has been sending forth to all ... parts of the world two streams, one pure and the other foul' – launched a campaign to abolish the CD Acts throughout the empire, with India as their primary target.[107] They also sought to tackle 'obscene' publications. Not only did campaigners such as Alfred Dyer set sail for India out of fear that 'obscene photos would set off another mutiny in which all the white women would be ravaged', but the NVA, the foremost anti-obscenity crusader in the late nineteenth century, established a branch in India and forged links with purity organizations in Australia such as the Public Morals Association of New South Wales.[108] The NVA also began holding international conferences on the trade in obscene publications in conjunction with continental associations such as the Swiss Association

[104] See, for example, FO 83/1786 and HO 45/20913, NAUK.

[105] As Krista Maglen demonstrates, while by the 1870s the key method of disease control in Britain had shifted from quarantine to sanitary reform (since the former was viewed as both ineffective and a hindrance to commerce), quarantine nonetheless remained an important tool (if at times merely a psychological one) of socio-moral reform, particularly in the case of projects of imperial hygiene (since Britain's colonies were perceived to lack the necessary 'hygienic' conditions to offset the effects of contaminants such as 'obscenities'). Maglen, 'A World Apart', 197.

[106] *Report from the Joint Select Committee*, p. vii. The Joint Committee on Lotteries and Indecent Advertisements was convened to deal primarily with the problem of 'obscene' advertisements (a particular cause of complaint for the Headmasters' Association), although no further legal remedies ensued.

[107] Hyam, *Empire and Sexuality*, p. 212; and Butler, *Revival and Extension of the Abolitionist Cause*, cited in Phillips, *Sex, Politics, and Empire*, p. 26. Butler also went on to found a branch of the Association for Moral and Social Hygiene in India.

[108] Bristow, *Vice and Vigilance*, p. 87; 4/NVA/S.88/Box 107 and 4/NVA/S.88/Box 108, WL. Dyer also abandoned his editorship of the influential purity paper the *Sentinel* to assume the editorship of the *Bombay Guardian*, through which he served as 'a vehicle for the diffusion of purity campaigns from England to, and then within, India'. Phillips, *Sex, Politics and Empire*, p. 43.

Against Immoral Literature.[109] Such organizations thus laid the foundation for the development of an international system to regulate the trade in 'obscenity'.

Although it was not until the early twentieth century that sufficient pressure was exerted on European governments to initiate such a system, the fifteen countries that came together in 1910 to generate an International Agreement for the Suppression of Obscene Publications (which was modelled, significantly, on the agreements to regulate white slavery) were convinced that 'to a trade which has become international it is necessary to oppose international measures – suitable for baffling its artifices'.[110] While the British government was initially unsure of the efficacy of such an endeavour, the failure of its own efforts to establish an international regulatory system for 'obscene' publications and the growing need for a larger imperial one led it to assume a prominent role in the 1910 Congress. Frustrated, however, by the failure of the Agreement, and by the fact that the trade in 'obscene' publications made a stunning recovery after the war (which led to a 'considerable increase in the number of indecent books and other articles imported from abroad'), the British government advocated the convening of an international treaty convention on 'obscene' publications in 1923.[111] The treaty was designed primarily to extend the provisions of the 1910 Agreement but the British government also hoped that it would both generate enthusiasm for a cause that most of the signatories to the Agreement appeared to have completely lost interest in and that it would 'bring as many States as possible within the international movement'.[112]

On the face of it, international enthusiasm for regulating the trade in 'obscene' publications did seem to have improved the second time around, since an impressive thirty-six states were represented at the 1923 treaty convention. The provisions of the treaty were also broader

[109] The first conference, organized by Swiss and French purity groups in 1888, led to the formation of an International Committee charged with developing an 'International League against licentious literature and immoral works of art'. Further conferences followed, with the 1908 conference attended by representatives of no fewer than eighty-six different purity organizations. 'International Conference', *Vigilance Record*, 15 November 1888, 112; Executive Minutes, 28 January 1890, 4/NVA/104 and 4/NVA/S.88/K Box 107, WL; 'Report of the Fifth Committee to the Third Assembly', FO 371/8334/W8196, NAUK; and 'Report by M. Tang Tsai Fou', FO 371/8334/W8544, NAUK.

[110] 'Correspondence respecting the International Conferences on Obscene Publications'.

[111] FO 371/9417 and FO 371/8334/W8544, NAUK. Since the 1910 Agreement was only administrative in nature and did not require signatories to institute legislative changes in order to enable them to comply with its provisions, it was therefore largely ineffective.

[112] FO 371/8334/W7586, NAUK.

(including photographs and films), and provided for the creation of rogatory commissions in member states to enable them to extradite any of their citizens who were engaged in the trafficking of obscene publications in other countries.[113] Despite good intentions, however, although twenty-eight states had signed the treaty by 1929 most of them failed to implement it. As the League of Nations complained to the Australian government in 1935, 'for some years past only a little over half of the Members of the League had sent in annual reports on traffic in women and children and even fewer countries on obscene publications'.[114] The League certainly had cause for complaint, for Australia did not get around to ratifying the treaty until that same year, while France waited until it was in the throes of war in 1940.[115] The British government, on the other hand, was not only one of the first signatories to the treaty, it also ratified the treaty on behalf of thirty-seven colonies, dominions, protectorates and mandated territories (including Northern Ireland, the Union of South Africa, India, and Canada).[116] In addition to dutifully submitting its annual report on obscene publications to the League in painstaking detail, Britain exerted continued pressure on colonial governments to comply with and enforce the treaty in their territories and to notify the British government of all possible infractions against it.[117] The treaty thus afforded the British government the ability to regulate the production, dissemination and consumption of 'obscene' publications throughout the whole empire.

By the Second World War forty British colonies, dominions, protectorates and mandated territories were regularly supplying the British government with reports on the trade in 'obscene' publications within their own borders and on their attempts to regulate it. But to be successful this particular project of imperial hygiene necessitated the generation or transformation of systems to regulate the obscene in Britain's colonies, and the problem for Britain was that although such systems were to a large extent derived from its own, their genealogies – and, more

[113] FO 371/9417, NAUK.

[114] Memorandum from League, 4 June 1932, A425/126, 1943/2649, AAC.

[115] The animosity in France over what was perceived to be excessive interference by Britain in the French book trade, particularly during the tenure of the rather zealous Home Secretary William Joynson-Hicks, may have played a role in the reluctance of the French government to sign the treaty. See, for example, FO 371/12657/W11318 and FO 371/14118/W815, NAUK.

[116] FO 371/9417, NAUK.

[117] The premise of the British government's reports to the League was always consistent: moral contagion always came from without, rarely from within, and thus while Britain could continue stemming the flow it was up to its colonies or fellow signatories to stop the trade at its source. See, for example, 'Reply to Questionnaire on Obscene Publications', 9 March 1931, A981/4, LEAGUE OBS 2, AAC.

significantly, their goals – were often decidedly distinct. For rather than seeking to consolidate imperial power, the objective of the moral regulatory projects that were undertaken in Britain's colonies in the late nineteenth and early twentieth centuries was to construct indigenous cultural, racial and national boundaries. Revelations about the permeation of 'obscene' publications throughout the empire, rather than furthering Britain's project of imperial hygiene, thus served instead to undermine it. While Britain continued to make valiant efforts to police the morality of its empire, by the early twentieth century India and Australia, Britain's two foremost colonies – and, moreover, its largest literary markets – had come to conceive of it as a font of 'dirt' and 'impurity' – not only a source of their own corruption and degeneracy but a hindrance to the production of their own distinct modernities.

4 Localizing the global in settler societies: regulating the obscene in Australia

By the end of the 1880s the Australian colonies had become not only Britain's foremost colonial literary market, but the largest single market for British books and periodicals.[1] During the following decades the trade grew to be worth over a million pounds a year to British publishers and booksellers, a sum greater than that of the print trade between Australia and all other foreign countries combined.[2] Since 'There is a tendency on the part of the English press and the English trade to neglect or, if noticed, to snub anything Australian', as the Melbourne publisher George Robertson bemoaned in 1875, the trade was, moreover, highly unequal.[3] By the Second World War, when only 15 per cent of the books sold in Australia were of indigenous origin, the efforts of British publishers to corner the Australian market had led to the virtual destruction of the indigenous publishing industry.[4]

The dominance of the Australian literary market by British publishers spurred the British government to make more vigorous efforts to

[1] The value of book and periodical exports to the Australian colonies trebled during the 1870s (from £130,000 in 1870 to £330,000 in 1876). British publishers also began opening branches there during this period. Nowell-Smith, *International Copyright Law*, p. 92.

[2] Coghlan, *Annual Statement*; and *Parliamentary Debates: Commonwealth of Australia*, 24 February 1926, p. 1078. In 1893, for example, the value of imports of books and periodicals from Britain to New South Wales was twenty-eight times higher than the value of such imports from the United States, the colony's second-largest supplier. Coghlan, *The New South Wales Statistical Register*, n.p.

[3] Letter from Henry Parkes to George Robertson, 13 September 1875, cited in Hergenhan, 'English Publication', p. 62. Britain's exports of books and periodicals to New South Wales for 1893, for example, were twenty-nine times higher than those of New South Wales to Britain, and by the end of the Second World War Australia was importing forty-eight times as many books and periodicals from Britain as it exported there. Coghlan, *The New South Wales Statistical Register*, n.p.

[4] Lyons and Taksa, *Australian Readers*; and Lyons, 'Introduction', p. xviii. The British takeover of the trade was so successful that by the 1960s Australia was importing a quarter of total British book production, which in the mind of one commentator had produced a situation in which 'the minds of Australians are conditioned 90 per cent by imported books'. P. R. Stephenson, *Sydney Morning Herald*, 18 July 1962, cited in Trainor, 'British Publishers', 99.

regulate the obscene in Australia than in any of its other colonies. Although the Australian colonies had federated in 1901 to form a self-governing dominion, which afforded Britain little legal power to undertake such a project, the strong socio-cultural ties that bound Australia to its imperial metropole made it amenable to receiving 'advice' on such a matter. By the mid-1920s a Scotland Yard detective with the rather apt name of A. Crapper was not only alerting the Australian government to infractions against the Obscene Publications Treaty committed by its populace (thanks to discoveries made through the British government's system of postal regulation), but advising it on how to prevent such infractions in the future and suggesting, furthermore, the specific course of action that should be taken in regard to the individuals who were caught purveying or purchasing such matter.[5] Since the Australian government had long since prohibited the importation into Australia of any publications against which warrants had been issued in Britain, and did its utmost to ensure that 'obscene' publications from Australia did not pervade Britain's shores, it not surprisingly demonstrated little hesitation in carrying out such advice.[6]

The Australian government was, furthermore, one of the first signatories to the 1910 Obscene Publications Agreement, and at the 1923 treaty convention it 'generally support[ed] British views'.[7] It took, however, twelve years to ratify the ensuing treaty, and was in fact the last member of the empire to do so.[8] But rather than demonstrating a lack of interest in regulating the trade in 'obscene' publications, the Australian government's reluctance to sign the treaty stemmed instead from a

[5] When Crapper discovered, for example, that one Mr J. Mendes of Flinders Lane, Melbourne, had ordered a work from Britain with the evocative name *Forbidden Fruit* he advised the Australian government 'to have some inquiry made as to [Mendes'] identity and occupation' in order to determine whether he was a dealer in 'obscene' wares. Letter from Crapper to Secretary, Prime Minister's Department, 7 October 1925, A981/4, AAC.

[6] The Australian government took such a course of action even prior to the passage of the Obscene Publications Treaty. When in 1913, for example, the British government requested the Australian government to take action against William Chidley's *The Answer* (after Chidley sent a copy to the sister of the Lord Chancellor), the Australian Postmaster-General accordingly declared that the book 'was of a character indecent, obscene and grossly offensive within the meaning of the Post Office Act and Regulations and [that] he would be glad if criminal proceedings could be taken against the sender or senders with a view to stopping any further copies from reaching the United Kingdom'. Chidley was thus fined £3 plus costs for publishing an obscene book, and London was duly informed that the required action had been taken. MP341/1/0, 1913/9411, Box 157, AAM. For the prohibition of publications proscribed under British warrants see, for example, Crapper to Secretary, Prime Minister's Department, 28 May 1924, A981/4 LEAGUE OBS 6, AAC.

[7] A981/4, LEAGUE OBS 4, AAC.

[8] A981/4 LEAGUE OBS 1, AAC; and A432/86, 1934/959, AAC.

conviction that 'no further legislation is required in the Commonwealth of Australia regarding this subject' because a system for 'a very strict examination of literature' was already in place there, one that was so thorough in comparison to other regulatory systems elsewhere in the empire that 'books prohibited in Australia are sold openly, not only in foreign countries, but in other parts of the British empire' – including the imperial metropole.[9] Moreover, since so much of the print matter circulating in Australia actually came from Britain, or was conveyed to Australia through British imperial networks – including 'obscene' publications – while the Australian government may have readily accepted Britain's help in keeping such publications from Australian shores, it had long since come to conceive of the imperial metropole as one of the chief threats to its efforts to do so.

A 'lovely colonial jewel in the imperial publishing crown': Australian print culture[10]

British publishers had been able to corner the literary market in Australia thanks to three key factors. The first was that, contrary to the myth of Australian anti-intellectualism, Australia – which by the end of the nineteenth century had a 95 per cent literacy rate – was a reading-oriented society.[11] This is clear not only in the volume of newspapers consumed (a per capita consumption five times as high, the British writer Richard Twopenny claimed in 1882, as in Britain) but also, as demonstrated by the vast network of lending libraries catering to all classes of readers, of books.[12] Although the reading habits, or lack thereof, of those who lived outside the ambit of lending libraries were often mocked (according to Miles Franklin's heroine Sybilla Miles the only reading in the bush consisted of 'the "*Penny Post*" and the Bible or a circular from Tattersall's'), bush dwellers were also catered to through

[9] Memo, Deputy Comptroller-General to Secretary to the Prime Minister, 15 July 1927; Director, Commonwealth Investigation Branch to Department of External Affairs, 6 November 1929, A981/4, LEAGUE OBS 4, AAC; Memo, Director, Attorney-General's Department to Department of External Affairs, 20 January 1930, A981/4, LEAGUE OBS 4, AAC.

[10] Max Harris, Australian Broadcasting Corporation, Radio Special Projects Broadcast, 28 January 1973, cited in Nile, *The Making*, p. 40.

[11] Lyons and Taksa, *Australian Readers*, p. 8. As Ken Stewart argues, Australia was in fact 'a highly literate community which enjoyed more free time, and could afford to buy more books *per capita*, than those of most other countries'. By 1870 there were no fewer than thirty-one booksellers in Sydney and an astonishing eighty-six in Melbourne. Stewart, 'Journalism and the World', p. 176; and Kirsop, 'The Four Phases', p. 13.

[12] Stewart, 'Journalism', p. 180. See also Lyons and Taksa, *Australian Readers*; and Arnold, 'Choose your Author'.

a wide range of borrowing networks and schemes.[13] The most ambitious of these was the Bush Book Club, which was founded in 1909 to provide 'high-class literature to dwellers in the Bush districts of New South Wales, who live beyond the reach of any School of Arts'.[14] While such a desire was ostensibly driven by 'a debt of gratitude' from those who had 'chosen the safer, easier life of the cities ... [to those] who, braving the loneliness of great distances, are holding the outposts of Empire', its less explicit goal was to fortify those 'outposts of Empire' through providing 'An antidote to the poisonous literature now in circulation among the lonely settlers of Australia'.[15]

The second crucial factor that facilitated British publishers' infiltration of the Australian market (as well as the Bush Book Club's fortification of the 'outposts of Empire') was Australia's communications network. The spine of this network was the overland telegraph, for which, as Jennie Gunn describes in her classic memoir of life in the 'Never Never' at the turn of the twentieth century, 'a clear broad avenue, two chains wide, was cut ... through bush and scrub and dense forests, along the backbone of Australia'.[16] When completed in 1872 the telegraph served to connect not only Darwin to Adelaide (a distance of 1,800 miles) but the island continent to the wider world. The telegraph thus made it possible for bush dwellers to 'shake hands with "Outside"'.[17] For Gunn the heart of the communication network binding the bush to the 'Oustide' was, however, the postal service, which she regarded not only as a benevolent presence uniting the bush but one that brought an even greater spiritual succour than the telegraph was able to offer, namely books, periodicals and letters.[18] While townsfolk had their mail matter 'doled out to them, like men on sick diet', eight hundred times a year, those out in the bush had to be content with a mere handful of deliveries. Thus when the post came, Gunn reveals, 'like thirsty

[13] Franklin, *My Brilliant Career*, p. 62.

[14] Bush Book Club of New South Wales, Minute Book 11/12/09–15/3/11, Mss. Q027.6/3, ML. The club was notable both for the scale of its operations (by 1928 it had 2,252 distribution centres) and the lengths it went to get books to what it referred to as 'Isolated Subscribers' – individuals who lived so far from other human habitation that they were not expected to forward the books that they were sent. *Eighteenth Annual Report*, 1928, Mss. 027.6/B, ML.

[15] *Thirteenth Annual Report*, 1923, Mss. 027.6/B, ML; and 'Gratitude of Lonely Settlers', *Sydney Morning Herald*, 25 April 1929, newspaper clipping in Mss. 027.6/B, ML. The club's Book Selection Committee was responsible for 'censor[ing] all the books sent away'. *Seventh Annual Report*, 1917, Mss. 027.6/B, ML.

[16] Gunn, *We of the Never Never*, p. 58.

[17] Gunn, *We of the Never Never*, p. 58. The 'Never Never' was a referent for the remotest regions of the outback.

[18] Gunn, *We of the Never Never*, p. 59.

camels we drank it all in – every drop of it – in long, deep satisfying draughts'.[19] The importance of such succour was undoubtedly clear to the postal department, for whom delivering mail to rural outposts was an almost Herculean task. The postal route for 'the Fizzer', the 'Hard, sinewy, dauntless and enduring' Northern Territory postman who made deliveries to Gunn's station, was no less than a thousand miles long and took six weeks to complete, much of which was through such dry and sweltering land (with temperatures that reached up to 160 degrees) that there was no water for the horses. Such a route was nothing less than a 'dice with death' – one that the previous postman had lost.[20] Yet 'the Fizzer' made such a phenomenal trip eight times a year in order to carry 'his precious freight . . . to the yearning, waiting men and women hidden away in the heart of Australia' and to deliver their letters for the world 'Outside' – and all for tuppence a letter.[21]

The third primary reason for the dominance of British publishers in the Australian market was the effect of such a network in fostering ties of sentiment between metropole and colonies. For the development of a communications network through such means as the telegraph and postal service, rather than simply erasing regional identities in favour of a national one (a process that K. T. Livingston refers to as 'technological nationalism'), served instead to 'add layers of collective identity' that were to prove as beneficial to British imperialism as they were to Australian nationalism.[22] As Stephen Alomes contends, 'The cable, train and steamship which helped spread the *Bulletin* worldview around the continent also brought British syndicated articles and imperial calls to war' – and in a matter of hours rather than weeks or months – calls that Australians responded to with increasing alacrity from the late nineteenth century.[23] They also ventured to the imperial metropole in growing numbers in order to take advantage of the cultural and intellectual opportunities available there, including its vibrant publishing scene.

The British endeavoured, in turn, to capitalize on the business opportunities such cultural ties fostered. British publishers played a particularly important role in fostering such ties of sentiment by producing not

19 Gunn, *We of the Never Never*, pp. 104–5.
20 Gunn, *We of the Never Never*, pp. 103, 107.
21 Gunn, *We of the Never Never*, pp. 106, 109.
22 Livingston, *The Wired Nation*; and Denoon and Mein-Smith, *A History of Australia*, pp. 191, 192. Technological developments such as the telegraph also brought a greater dependency on empire, for while 'the Darwin–Adelaide link naturally dominated Australian awareness of the [Overland] telegraph . . . relay stations in India played an equal part in ensuring that the link was maintained'. Kingston, 'The Taste of India', p. 40.
23 Alomes, 'Australian Nationalism', 321.

only colonial editions of their books but, from the mid-nineteenth century, colonial editions of their journals. They also produced journals that were designed for sale specifically in the colonies which, as in the case of *Saunders, Otley and Co's Oriental Budget*, sought to 'help to paint the map red' through highlighting the 'political, social, domestic [and] literary' achievements of British colonists throughout the empire.[24] As the *Budget* maintained, in addition to being in 'the interests of the mother country' to know, such information also served to assure British residents in the colonies that they were important members of the British cultural community.[25] By the early twentieth century even publications that were not designed specifically for sale in the colonies sought to include 'a little something' for colonial readers – whom the editor of a series of comic papers pictured in gendered terms as 'bronzed, burly, honest, strong and manly, with a laugh one would travel a hundred miles to hear' – since the bond forged between the brawny colonist and his comic paper would help to preserve 'the social and sentimental ties between the colonies and the homeland'.[26] The *Bystander*, which proclaimed with pride in 1908 that no matter how remote the place, 'it is not too out of the way a district not to have a *Bystander* reader', sought to preserve such ties through the inclusion of a photography feature in each issue that depicted purported *Bystander* readers (such as drovers in the Australian outback or British troops on campaign in north-western India) perusing the paper.[27]

In Australia such cultural colonization had two major effects. On the one hand, it served to foster imperial loyalty by socializing Australians into empire, a process advanced through many means from the late nineteenth century ranging from science to sports, monarchism to militarism and religion to ritual, not to mention through schooling. As Elizabeth Kwan has demonstrated, until as late as 1939 children in South Australian primary schools were taught that although Australia

[24] 'Who's Who Amongst English Houses', *The Colonial Bookseller, Newsletter and Stationer*, 1, 2 (1908), 37, and *Saunders, Otley and Co's Oriental Budget*, December 1859, 1. By the turn of the twentieth century even some of the daily newspapers, such as the *Daily Mail*, were producing overseas editions. Kaul, *Reporting the Raj*, p. 59.

[25] 'Who's Who Amongst English Houses'; and *Saunders, Otley and Co's Oriental Budget*, December, 1859, 1. In addition to soliciting contributions from readers, the *Budget* carried book recommendations (hence in December 1859 readers resident in East Africa were encouraged to read Dr Knapp's *Travels in Eastern Africa*, while residents in India were offered J. Ballantyne's *Christianity Contrasted with Hindu Philosophy: An Essay* either in English or, interestingly, in Sanskrit) and a list of newspapers available for export (which totalled roughly fifty by 1861).

[26] *The Colonial Bookseller, Newsletter and Stationer*, 2, 1 (1908), 86. The comic papers referred to include *Puck, Jester, Chips* and *Comic Cuts*.

[27] 'In Tropic Zones', *Bystander*, 5 February 1908, 293.

was their country, they were nonetheless British – citizens of a greater Britain.[28] The fact that 'The British imprint on a book sold in Australia added to its authority, popularity and sales' offers evidence of the success of such efforts of cultural colonization.[29] So too does the popularity of British magazines and journals, particularly women's magazines and boys' comics such as *Gem* and *Magnet*, which offered not only the thrill of adventure but were regarded as 'a guarantee of respectability'.[30]

Such cultural colonization also served, on the other hand, to foster Australian nationalism, in particular the drive to create a national literature. Although the ability of such cultural colonization to foster both imperial loyalty and Australian nationalism may appear dissonant, since Australian nationalism was based more upon loyalty to state and territory (and was hence more akin to patriotism) than a desire for ethnic differentiation, as Douglas Cole has argued, it was not incompatible with an imperial ideology 'based upon the unity of blood, language, ancestry and tradition' – or at least, as we shall see, not entirely so.[31] The impetus to create a national literature had begun to emerge in the 1850s and 60s, generated in part by resentment of British domination of Australian culture. As numerous critics argued from the mid-nineteenth century onwards, such domination was dire not only for Australian writers but for the nation, since it deprived Australians 'of all chance of developing any sort of national spirit'.[32] But it was not until the 1890s, when Australian writers really began to both defer to and become

[28] Kwan, 'Making "Good Australians"', 38.

[29] Johanson, 'Cultural Cringe', 80–1.

[30] Lyons and Taksa, *Australian Readers*, pp. 85, 92. A British imprint gave cultural cachet not only to British publications, but to Australian publications printed there – Marcus Clarke's *For the Term of his Natural Life,* for example, sold poorly in Australia but as a colonial edition sold 41,376 copies. Such a phenomenon offers evidence that increasing cultural interconnections between metropole and colonies could induce a 'cultural cringe' (a term first coined by A. A. Phillips in 1950) that sowed doubts about the value of Australian cultural production. Johanson, 'Cultural Cringe', 80–1.

[31] Cole, 'The Problem of "Nationalism"', 177–8. Cole contends that, rather than coming to an end with federation, the linkages between nationalism and imperialism in Australia actually intensified (with the latter in fact becoming an extension of the former), because it was possible to celebrate Australia's ethnic kinship with Britain once the goal of creating a nation-state for 'white' Australians had been attained. Since Australia remained dependent on Britain for both physical protection and economic survival, such kinship in fact *had* to be re-asserted in order to protect the nascent nation-state. As the *Daily Telegraph* rightly prophesied in 1900, 'the increased political solidity which Federation gives will tend to augment our loyalty to the Crown and to the nation which gave the Australian colonies their birth'. Cole, 'The Problem', 161; and 'Our Duties to the Commonwealth', *Daily Telegraph,* 9 July 1900, 46.

[32] Senator Cameron, 'Revised Estimates', *Parliamentary Debates: Commonwealth of Australia*, 5 December, 1939, p. 2041.

inspired by the country's 'otherness', that they began to generate such a spirit.[33] The means through which they chose to articulate it was realism, which in the hands of radical nationalists such as J. F. Archibald, Francis Adams, William Lane, William Astley (Price Warung) and Henry Lawrence served, in contrast to romanticism (which 'was often employed in Australia not to intensify reality, but to impose fantasies on a perceived vacuum') to fashion a literature of protest or commitment (albeit one that was largely lacking in political self-consciousness).[34]

The allure of realism for Australian writers was the same as that for its proponents elsewhere, namely its purported 'scientific' and hence 'progressive' nature, which meant that through truthfully 'mirroring' Australia – its landscape, people and society – it would play a key role, in the words of one of its greatest proponents, the Sydney *Bulletin,* in the 'working out of the civilization of the future'.[35] The works of European realists such as Émile Zola were therefore better received in Australia than in England, where critics were wary about the challenge such works posed to English literary conventions.[36] They were not, however, fully embraced. What Australian writers and critics instead sought to do was to 'save the concept of "Realism" while disparaging contemporary realists' – to embrace, in other words, its qualities of analysis and description while disapproving of the particular realities (the 'gutters' and 'noisome sewers') so analysed and described.[37] As a nationalist project such a literary mode was thus problematic, since while it offered a means of obtaining cultural independence from Britain in exposing

33 Stilz, 'Nationalism before Nationhood', 238.

34 Morgan, 'Realism and Documentary', p. 238.

35 'Marginal Notes', *Bulletin,* 19 February 1881, cited in Stilz, 'Nationalism before Nationhood', 479. Realism had come to be regarded as the characteristic literary form of democracies since the publication of Alexis de Toqueville's *Democracy in America* (1840). Jarvis, 'Realism', pp. 37–40.

36 The *Bulletin,* for example, declared Zola's *Nana* to be a 'work of genius' and praised the author for being 'radical, rationalistic, [and] communistic', while the *Australasian* lauded Zola for offering 'a photographic transcript of the actual conditions of ... life' and for 'mak[ing] us feel how universally the law of strife and rapine which prevails throughout nature prevails also throughout human society'. *Bulletin,* 11 October 1884, and 31 October 1885; and *Australasian,* 7 July 1882, cited in Stilz, 'Nationalism before Nationhood', 484, 487.

37 Stilz, 'Nationalism before Nationhood', 482; *Australasian,* 8 December 1883, cited in Stilz, 'Nationalism before Nationhood', p. 487. The 'factual' nature of realism was praised in Australia – as a character in J. M. Harcourt's socialist realist novel *Upsurge* declares, 'books that give information' were the only ones that were 'real' and hence worth reading. As Harcourt himself was well aware (since *Upsurge* was the first book banned by the Literary Censorship Board in 1933), its exposure of 'squalid, sordid [or] degraded' social conditions rendered it dangerous. Harcourt, *Upsurge,* p. 73.

'dirt' and 'impurity' it also undermined Australia's ability to develop, in the words of the *Australasian,* in a hygienic, 'cleanly way'.[38]

The Vizetelly affair down under

That there were tensions in Australia between British cultural dominance and Australian efforts to fashion a realist national literature – and that these revolved, moreover, around questions of racial hygiene – is evident in the response to Vizetelly's Zola translations in Australia. Thanks to the expansion of imperial communication networks, by the mid-1880s Australian booksellers such as Turner and Henderson could boast that they received 'New French novels' from Britain, including works by Émile Zola, 'by Every Mail'.[39] Among the impressive list of French novels carried by the Sydney bookseller was *Piping Hot* (a translation of *Pot Bouille*), one of the works later targeted in the Vizetelly trials. Advertised simply as 'a realistic novel' and illustrated lavishly 'with 104 engravings from designs by French artists', the novel was priced at a fairly prohibitive 7s 6d.[40] But less expensive translations of Zola's novels were also available in Australia at this time, including those by Vizetelly and Co. – translations that, as in Britain, had become a source of anxiety.[41] Copies of Vizetelly's translation of Zola's *Nana* were seized four years prior to Henry Vizetelly's 1888 trial in London in a police raid on a Sydney bookshop, although it was only after the trial that anxiety over Zola's works reached such a crescendo that his name became as 'familiarly invoked as if he were a resident of Sydney'.[42] The impact of the trial was in fact arguably greater 10,000 miles away in the Australian colonies than it had been in Britain. For not only did it serve to trigger the creation of a new biopolitical system for the regulation of the obscene

[38] *Australasian,* 8 December 1883, cited in Stilz, 'Nationalism before Nationhood', 487. 'The innovation of modern "realism" under the aegis of Émile Zola and his imitators' was thus responsible, as an observer remarked in the mid-1930s, for 'inaugurat[ing] a new reign of terror for the booksellers' by fostering a frantic campaign to keep books that were forbidden in England out of Australia. 'Book Bans from John Cleland to Mae West', n.p., n.d., clipping in Vol. 201, Mss. Z/Q991/N, ML.

[39] Advertisement in *The Publisher: Australian Literary News,* 1 October 1886, 14.

[40] *The Publisher,* 1 October 1886, 14. This edition does not seem, however, to have been a translation by Vizetelly and Co., since Vizetelly's edition, first published in 1885, contained only sixteen engravings.

[41] *The Publisher* contains advertisements for translations of a range of Zola's novels priced as little as 2s 6d.

[42] Jarvis, 'Realism', pp. 77, 82. Zola's works, and those of other French realists, were also targeted by the Victorian Customs Department (when in 1887 it made a seizure of such works), and by a growing number of libraries (through refusing to carry them). Hubber, 'Literary Pest-Germs', p. 109.

in Australia, but in constructing Britain as a source of moral and bodily contamination that Australia needed to protect itself from, such a system served ultimately to undermine, rather than enhance, the metropole's own national-imperial regulatory project.

The alarm over the trial was first raised, less than a week after Vizetelly's first conviction, by the Victorian *Daily Telegraph*.[43] Fearful of Holywell Street publishers dumping their now unsaleable Zola translations on Australian shores, the paper declared such translations to be a 'subtle and deadly infection' that was as great a danger to Australia as 'having the Pacific poisoned by the deporting of French criminals to an island 2,500 miles distant from our shores'.[44] The significance of this analogy between the body, space and contamination was not lost on the Victorian Chief Secretary and French literary connoisseur (as well as future Australian prime minister) Alfred Deakin, who immediately initiated a hunt for translations of Zola's novels in Melbourne.[45] An exhaustive police search revealed that while many were available for sale, none, in the opinion of the Chief Commissioner of Police H. M. Chomley, were 'so prurient in character as to induse [sic] the majority of justices to issue warrants for their seizure'. Chomley informed Deakin, however, that he would be willing to bring a prosecution against these works should the government so desire. With the proceedings of the London trial clearly in mind, Deakin asked Chomley to look specifically for *La Terre* and to 'purchase a copy off some bookseller who usually sells this class of works'. After several weeks of instituting a 'very careful search', however, Chomley reported that 'it cannot be found that "La Terre" is on sale anywhere in Melbourne'. Even an establishment such as that of Mrs Lacey of Fitzroy, which claimed to have all of Zola's works available for borrowing, did not have a copy of the work in question, which led the Commissioner of Police to conclude that the novel was not yet available in Australia. Chomley was therefore ordered to get 'the next worst book of Zola's works on sale'.[46]

43 The *Daily Telegraph* was, notably, both an evangelical and pro-imperial paper.

44 Coleman, *Obscenity*, p. 4.

45 'Suppressing M. Zola', *Daily Telegraph*, clipping in VPRS 3992, Unit 269, 6783, PROV. That Victoria was the first Australian colony to respond in such a manner to the trial was probably a result of several factors: that of the six Australian colonies it was the largest importer of books from Britain; that it contained the greatest number of evangelical and non-denominational churches in Australia; and that it had a Chief Secretary who, while he was an admirer of French fiction and regarded literature as a powerful educational tool, believed that the 'rudimentary' nature of culture in Australia meant that such a tool had to be tightly controlled. See La Nauze and Nurser, *Walter Murdoch and Alfred Deakin*, pp. 6–7; and Mss. 1540, NLA.

46 Memo from Chief Commissioner's Office to Under-Secretary, 8 November 1888, VPRS 3992, Unit 269, 6783, PROV. Since Deakin issued specific instructions to look

The 'next worst book of Zola's' that the police could turn up in Melbourne was a translation of *Thérèse Raquin*. In the face of ongoing criticism from the *Daily Telegraph* – which accused the Victorian government of 'an amazing and scandalous reluctance ... to suppress that plague of obscene literature which afflicts us' (one which 'resemble[s], indeed, both for offensiveness and abundance, the plague of frogs which once afflicted Egypt') and demanded 'that our law courts shall not be more lenient to "putrid" literature than are the English law courts; and [that] our public authorities shall not be less vigilant to suppress a moral plague of this kind than the English Government has been' – Deakin submitted it to the Victorian Attorney-General for his opinion on the probable success of a prosecution against it.[47] For the Attorney-General, however, the chance of success was slim, since while the novel was 'a most unwholesome and objectionable book' it did not appear to be obscene under the meaning of the 1876 Victorian Obscene Publications Act. He was also reluctant to submit the novel to trial, since 'A prosecution means a very serious affair and would require to have [sic] all the objectionable passages alleged to be obscene set out'. Deakin thus decided to take no action against *Thérèse Raquin* but requested the police to keep an eye out for translations of Zola's more reprehensible novels, particularly those 'upon which the English conviction was obtained', and asked the Victorian Customs Department to see if they could do anything to stop such works from entering the colony.[48] But while the customs agreed to stop all future importations of Zola's novels and to submit them for examination, the Minister for Customs was fearful, like the Attorney-General, that such a confiscation might be challenged in the Supreme Court and that a prosecution would not be successful.[49] Hence when a shipment of Zola's novels arrived in Melbourne early in 1889 (possibly Vizetelly's newly expurgated translations), after a careful examination the Customs Department allowed the books to land since they consisted of 'Zola's less objectionable books', and *La Terre* was not

for *La Terre* rather than for its translated title, *The Soil,* it is not entirely clear whether he was interested in finding only translations of Zola's works or their originals as well.

47 'Suppressing M. Zola'. According to the Chief Commissioner, 'Although the vendors give out that they have all Zola's works on sale, they have in fact but few, and those now left on hand are comparatively of harmless character'. Chief Commissioner to Under Secretary, 15 December 1888, VPRS 3992, Unit 269, 6783, PROV.

48 Memo, C. A. Smyth to Under-Secretary, 8 January 1889, VPRS 3992, Unit 269, 6783, PROV.

49 The Customs Department's hesitation to undertake such a confiscation, which it had the power to do under the Victorian Customs Act of 1883, reveals that this was something it rarely resorted to. Acting Secretary for Customs to Under-Secretary, 28 January 1889, VPRS 3992, Unit 269, 6783, PROV.

among them. Vizetelly's second conviction in London that May, however, set alarm bells ringing again in Victoria. A search was once again made for *La Terre*, and while the Commissioner of Police revealed that a number of booksellers had claimed to have sold the work, 'they admit they are influenced by the last prosecution of Vizetelly in England', and have vowed to stock no further copies of it.[50]

There was nothing further that the police could do to deal with the trade in Zola's works in Melbourne. However, as the Minister for Customs had already implied, there already *was* a tool in place by 1889 that would provide for the regulation of imported publications. This was the Victorian Customs Act of 1883, which gave customs the power to seize and destroy 'obscene' publications. As Brian Hubber argues, 'it only needed a more zealous [Customs] minister to put [the Act] in motion'.[51] Luckily for Deakin one came along in the form of the newly appointed 'Orangeman and apostle of Empire' James Brown Patterson, who immediately assured Deakin that 'every assistance will be rendered by this Department in putting a stop to the sale and importation of such works'.[52] He was true to his word, for within a month of his appointment he made a seizure, widely lauded in the Australian press, of a shipment of 162 French novels imported by the radical bookseller Edward Cole.[53] While for the Melbourne *Age* it was fitting that such 'filthy and revolting' works should be seized by customs and 'burned on the pyre that consumes confiscated cigars at the Customs House', the anti-establishment Sydney *Bulletin* sounded a note of caution, declaring that 'Jingo Patterson may be all right for dealing with the undervaluations of pianos and piece-goods, but in the name of commonsense, why is such a man allowed to regulate the literature of a country?'[54] The *Bulletin* was, however, alone in raising such a cry of alarm, and the press silently acquiesced when Cole and Patterson, keen to avoid facing a decidedly uncertain verdict in the courts, struck a bargain in which Cole consented to the destruction of his shipment in return for Patterson's sanction that he disclaim all responsibility for having ordered the books (thus establishing a mutually reinforcing relationship between customs and the Australian book trade that was to last for the next seventy years).

50 Memo from Chief Secretary to Chief Commissioner of Police, 14 May 1889, VPRS 3992, Unit 269, 6783, PROV.

51 Hubber, 'Literary Pest-Germs', 9.

52 Coleman, *Obscenity*, p. 3; and Memo from Acting Secretary of Customs to Under-Secretary, 14 June 1889, VPRS 3992, Unit 269, 6783, PROV.

53 Coleman, *Obscenity*, p. 3.

54 *Daily Telegraph*, 8 December 1888, VPRS 3992, Unit 269, 6783, PROV; *Age*, 17 August, 1889; and *Bulletin*, 17 July 1889, cited in Coleman, *Obscenity*, p. 6.

The Victorian Customs Department likewise met with no resistance when it stopped a consignment of translations of Vizetelly's series of French 'Boulevard Novels' in September 1889 and covertly destroyed it.[55]

Unlike in Britain, therefore, no translations of Émile Zola's works were ever actually tried in Victoria, nor – since the regulatory campaign was soon taken up in other Australian colonies – in either the other colonies or later in the Commonwealth.[56] Although the Australian colonies had their own laws for the regulation of obscenity, the conviction of Vizetelly in a British court was regarded as sufficient legal, political and social justification for the exclusion from Australia of Zola's works, or for the destruction of those discovered there. In light of the fact that most of the books and a large volume of the periodicals circulating in Australia by the late nineteenth century were, like Australia's obscenity laws, imported primarily from the imperial metropole, such a belief was not, perhaps, entirely unreasonable.[57] It was, however, a product of more than simply faith in the justice of British law. For in a year that marked both the immense promise of Australia's future, thanks to the celebrations for the centennial of its founding, as well as profound skepticism, courtesy of the land-boom crash (which was to plunge Australia into a severe economic depression in the 1890s), the Vizetelly trials hit home for the first time in Australia the biopolitical dangers to the emergent nation of a print culture that was largely imported. Such tensions were evident in a growing desire to fashion a 'pure', 'clean' and 'white Australia' – the phrase 'White Australia policy' was used in print for the first time that year – through keeping 'foreign bodies' ranging from humans (1888 also witnessed a renewed attempt to prohibit Chinese immigration) to books from infiltrating Australian borders. Following the trials, publications imported from Britain or purveyed to Australia through imperial networks thus began to be conceptualized as a 'foreign invasion', a 'moral infection' that was 'swamping' Australia and 'sapping the vitality of [its] manhood' – one which was, moreover,

55 Hubber, 'The Victorian Customs Department', 6.

56 Both South Australia and New South Wales began prohibiting the importation of Zola's works at the time of the Vizetelly trials, but the latter retained its vigilance in the matter for several decades. Such zealousness by no means, however, led to the eradication of Zola's works from Australia – the Broken Hill Mechanics Institute listed a number of Zola's novels in their 1899 catalogue, while the Mechanics Institute at Orange was offering no fewer than twenty-five of his works in 1914. *New South Wales Parliamentary Debates*, July 1889, pp. 3044, 3039; A1023, AAS; and Lyons and Taksa, *Australian Readers*, pp. 141–2.

57 Victoria was the first colony to pass an Obscene Publications Act in 1876 (which was modelled on the 1857 English Act). By 1902 all the states of the new Commonwealth possessed similar legislation, to which the federal government added in 1901 with stringent Customs and Post Office Acts.

virtually impossible to combat once it permeated Australia's borders.[58] Such an awareness led to the emergence of a new understanding of the relationship between literature – and, over the course of the next decade, language – space and hygiene, and of the cultivation of new techniques to manage such contagion.

The problem with British publications as it began to be conceptualized in the late nineteenth century was summed up succinctly several decades later by one of the individuals most responsible for consolidating the system designed to regulate them, Commonwealth Customs Minister T. W. White. For White literature shaped not only the development of the individual but the progress of nations.[59] The trouble for Australia, however, was that while it had a renowned literary heritage (which enabled it to claim 'some of the greatest names in the world's history as poets and prose writers, including the immortal Shakespeare'), a good system of public education and a broad network of lending libraries (which meant that 'access to books, the "food and medicine of the soul", is not confined to a wealthy few'), thanks to the contraction of distance between metropole and dominion wrought by 'quickened communications' it had become a 'dumping ground' for 'obscene and indecent writing' from Britain (which, he surmised, may even have been printed explicitly for export). Since 'A free sale of poisons is not permitted by chemists', for the sake of the nation – and, perhaps even more pressing, for the empire as a whole (since 'it must not be placed in jeopardy by the weak units within it') – it was thus incumbent upon Australia to make itself 'cleaner [through] their exclusion'.[60]

It was such concerns over the dangers of British publications or those purveyed through imperial networks that led, in the aftermath of Australia's constitution as a nation-state, to the construction of a system of literary regulation that would protect Australia's strength, purity and 'whiteness', and with it that of the empire. Some protests were

[58] 'Book Bans from John Cleland'; and *New South Wales Parliamentary Debates*, Assembly, 12 July 1889, p. 3044. In the decade following the Vizetelly trials the Australian colonies witnessed numerous attempts (many of which resulted in legislation) to pass laws to keep out not only imported publications – with their 'highly spiced reports of disgraceful proceedings in the old world' – but, since it was 'being flooded by importations of objectionable literature', specifically *British* publications. *New South Wales Parliamentary Debates*, Assembly, 12 July 1889 pp. 3032–3; and *Victoria Parliamentary Debates*, Assembly, 12 July 1892–3, p. 412.

[59] For Australia not only was it 'by raising reason, learning, and enlightenment to the highest level that the nation will progress intellectually', but without literature the biopolitical project of 'peopling our outback would be immeasurably increased'. 'Report of "The Star" Public Debate', 26 February 1935, Mss. 9148, NLA.

[60] 'Report of "The Star" Public Debate', and 'Migration and Secondary Industries', Mss. 9148, NLA.

undoubtedly made as to the powers, derived from Victorian customs law, to be accorded to the new Commonwealth Department of Trade and Customs to regulate imported literature. As Senator Stewart of Queensland declared, the law in relation to obscene publications in Victoria had become 'so strained ... that articles which do not properly come under that definition', including 'respectable' British publications such as *Reynolds Newspaper*, had been excluded.[61] Moreover, Stewart warned his fellow senators, were the Commonwealth to adopt such a system, it would be 'putting the cart before the horse', for instead of trying questionable publications in the courts 'any landing-waiter in the Commonwealth might find in a volume of Zola a phrase which might appear to be indecent to his prurient or too vivid imagination, and might stop the importation of that work on the ground that it was indecent or obscene'.[62] While Stewart's concerns received some support, with one senator going so far as to argue that 'I do not know that any of Zola's novels are so very bad that they must be excluded from the community', by 1901 the problem for Stewart was that *all* imported publications had become construed as threats to the Australian 'community'.[63] They therefore had to be excluded from the geo-body of the nascent nation-state through whatever means possible – most notably through the powers accorded to the new Commonwealth customs – to 'protect' Australia from literary contamination, including from its imperial metropole.

Hygiene, quarantine and White Australia

To understand the relationship between hygiene and the regulation of imported publications in Australia we need to examine how 'whiteness' had come to be conceived of by the late nineteenth century, and its role in shaping what came to be known as the 'White Australia' policy. 'Whiteness' in Australia was not, to begin with, defined solely in terms of colour – particularly from the interwar period when Aborigines began to be reclassified as 'white'; nor, in spite of the emergence of a small but powerful eugenics movement in the early twentieth century that advocated programmes such as the sterilization of the 'unfit' and the

[61] *Parliamentary Debates: Commonwealth of Australia*, 15 August 1901, p. 3767, and 28 June 1901, pp. 1793–9. See also Stewart's comments during the debate on the Post and Telegraph Bill, *Parliamentary Debates: Commonwealth of Australia*, 17 July 1901, p. 2597.

[62] *Parliamentary Debates: Commonwealth of Australia*, 15 August 1901, p. 3767.

[63] *Parliamentary Debates: Commonwealth of Australia*, Senate, 29 August 1901, p. 4259.

detention of 'mental defectives', solely in biological terms.[64] 'Whiteness' instead referred to a wide range of cultural, mental and bodily attributes that were united by a concern with purity, hygiene and cleanliness, not only of the individual, but of the social and, from the turn of the twentieth century, emergent national body. That whiteness – and the need to protect it from contamination – came to assume such prominence in Australia was a product of the intimate relationship that emerged during the course of the nineteenth century between race, space and place. The annexation of the whole (and in the settler imaginary, 'empty') continent in 1829, combined with its distance from the mother country, gave settlers a unique sense of spatial identity.[65] On the one hand, Australia's isolation 10,000 miles from Europe – what Geoffrey Blainey has memorably termed the 'tyranny of distance' – and its vast and natural borders afforded a sense of geographical protection from physical and, to a lesser extent, cultural contaminants. On the other hand, its location and its very boundedness served to heighten its sense of vulnerability to external threats, which was magnified in the late nineteenth century in the face of the collapse of distance and the growing interaction between different peoples wrought by global and imperial networks. Not only was Asia – perceived as dirty, diseased and debased – brought much closer to Australia, so too was the 'old world', which, it was believed, had grown corrupt and degenerate.[66]

Although the climate initially generated further fears, fostering a belief that British bodies were degenerating in an alien environment, by the

[64] Legislation to detain 'mental defectives' was adopted in Tasmania (1920), Victoria (1922), Queensland (1938), and New South Wales (1939), although efforts to pass legislation for the sterilization of the 'unfit' in New South Wales, Victoria and Western Australia in the 1920s and 1930s all failed. So too did eugenic efforts to enshrine a biological understanding of race in Australia, as is clear in the proposed resolution to the 'Aboriginal problem' in the interwar period. This entailed the reclassification of Aborigines as 'dark' or 'archaic' Caucasians and their elimination through absorption – a solution which offers evidence, as Patrick Wolf observes, that 'Aborigines' physical substance cannot really have been seen as deficient or the last thing white authorities would have set out to do would have been to incorporate it into the white gene pool'. Wolf, 'Land, Labour and Difference', 874. For an analysis of Australian eugenics see Garton, 'Sound Minds'.

[65] Ang, 'From White Australia', pp. 51–69.

[66] The late nineteenth century witnessed not only growing activity in Australia's Pacific 'back yard' by the French, Russians and Germans, but the spectacular rise of Japan as a global power, which served to exacerbate anxieties about British corruption and racial decline. Fears that Britain would surrender Australia to the 'Yellow Peril' had also begun to emerge in Australia as early as the 1880s, and were fuelled by the signing of several Anglo-Japanese treaties in the following decades (evidence for *Truth* 'that Britain has now entered a period of national and racial abasement'). Walker, 'Race Building', p. 35; and 'Britain Betrays Us! Australia Delivered to the "Yellow Peril"', *Truth*, 12 November 1905, n.p.

late nineteenth century a new symbiosis had emerged between race and place. Place – the sunny climate, open spaces and natural resources – had made possible, it was believed, the emergence of a new social system free from the 'cake of customs' that bound the old world such as class, aristocracy and pauperism. It had also led to the generation of a 'Coming Man', who would renew a race grown enfeebled by modern industrial civilization.[67] Epitomized by the bushman, a tough and hardy pioneer for whom egalitarianism (espoused through mateship and radical democracy) was his guiding principle, the 'Australian legend' served to hold Australia up as 'a special place where "prophecy" better than history' was the essence of its character.[68] The First World War served to enhance such a sense of prophecy by demonstrating that, rather than simply safeguarding British racial supremacy, Australia had produced a race that was better 'Physically and in mental efficiency ... than any other', including the 'race' from which it sprang.[69]

Carrying out such a legacy entailed, however, an onerous responsibility, one that necessitated 'eternal watchfulness' and 'ceaseless organisation'.[70] Central to this project was collapsing 'the boundaries that now separate one part [of Australia] from another', in the words of future Australian Prime Minister G. W. Barton – namely through federation – and erecting new, hygienic ones both within and around Australia.[71] The drive to erect such hygienic barriers emerged not only, however, in conjunction with the federation movement but was in fact part of the impetus behind it.[72] Beginning in the late nineteenth century a host

[67] Cole, '"The Crimson Thread of Kinship"', 518.

[68] Veracini, 'Historylessness', 79; and Davison, 'Sydney and the Bush'.

[69] Meudell, *Australia for the Australians*, n.p. Australians were still anxious, however, to ensure that such a race was still viewed as 'British'. Williams, *The Quarantined Culture*, p. 158.

[70] Octavius Beale, letter to Alfred Deakin, 27 September 1906, Mss. 1540/15/2678–2695, NLA. Beale was head of his self-funded New South Wales Royal Commission on Secret Drugs, Cures and Foods, which sought to determine the effects of contraceptives and abortifacients on the Australian 'race'. See Pringle, 'Octavius Beale'.

[71] G. B. Barton, 'The March of the Colored Alien: And the Future Nationality of Australia', *The Star*, 10 January 1899, n.p., clipping in C4205/1, Box 1, Vol. 4, NAS. Efforts to erect hygienic boundaries to manage the white race are evident from as early as the 1860s and 70s through the passage of Contagious Diseases Acts. While in Britain such Acts were restricted to garrison towns and were aimed at improving defence, their remit was much broader in Australia (extending, in the case of Victoria, to the entire colony) – evidence for Judith Smart that their purpose was to secure 'the fitness not only of young men but of society as a whole and, most especially, of future generations'. Furthermore, such laws not only remained on the books in Australia (again in contrast to Britain), but were supplemented through the course of the early twentieth century. Smart, 'Sex, the State', 107.

[72] Bashford, *Imperial Hygiene*, p. 120. The hygienic measure most closely bound to federation was undoubtedly the drive to create a federal quarantine system. Quarantine became,

of hygienic measures were therefore implemented that were designed to whiten out the diseased and degenerate elements within both the individual and, by extension, the national body. Until the First World War such measures focused primarily on increasing the production of 'white' bodies in order to create the 'walls of men' necessary to defend White Australia.[73] Although Australian losses in the war fuelled ongoing concerns about the birth-rate, in the interwar era concerns with quantity were matched with a growing eugenic desire to increase the quality of the white bodies thus produced.[74] Reproduction, childbirth and infant welfare thus became increasingly bureaucratized, and motherhood rationalized.[75] Even masculinity, a cornerstone of Australian identity, was transformed through such measures as the 'family wage', which was designed to fashion a 'Domestic Man' who would assume his responsibilities to the family, nation and race.[76] With their bodies both the subjects and objects of racial governance, White Australia thus rendered hygiene and citizenship synonymous.

But securing Australia as a home for the advancement of the white race required more than simply the hygienic management of that race in

significantly, the only public health power granted to the federal government in the Commonwealth constitution, which resulted in the establishment of a Federal Quarantine Service in 1909. Bashford, *Imperial Hygiene,* p. 126.

[73] C. Von Hagen, 'White Australia: The Need for Defensive Preparedness', *Daily Telegraph,* 2 June 1905, n.p., clipping in Mss. Z/Q991/N, ML. Such an impetus was driven by what Neville Hicks describes as 'a spectacular decline in the Australian birth rate' from the 1880s, when family sizes averaged six or seven children, to the 1920s, when they dropped to two or three. Concerns over the decline led to the establishment of both the Royal Commission on the Decline of the Birth-Rate in 1903 and the Royal Commission on Secret Drugs, Cures and Foods three years later, and to efforts to prevent the sale and purchase of contraceptives and abortifacients. Hicks, *'This Sin and Scandal',* p. xv; and Foster, 'Joseph Symes', 9–11, and 'The Collins Prosecution'.

[74] Of the 330,000 Australian men who served overseas in the war, 60,000 died and another 150,000 were injured – a casualty rate of two-thirds. Australians were well aware that the onus was thus on them to reproduce. As late as the 1950s one unfortunate man was forced to importune customs officials to release his shipment of condoms (which had been prohibited imports since 1904) because 'his wife was under the apprehension that condoms made in Australia were no good because they wanted to increase the population ... and consequently a certain percentage had holes in them by Government decree'. Denoon and Mein-Smith, *A History of Australia,* pp. 269, 291; and John Hall interview, Box 15, Mss. Acc 96/76, NLA.

[75] See Rodwell, 'Domestic Science'; and Reiger, *The Disenchantment of the Home.* For a cautionary note on the limitations of such reform see Allen, 'Octavius Beale Re-considered'.

[76] The concept of the 'family wage' – sufficient to support a wife and three children – was enshrined in Australian welfare policy in the 1920s. Denoon and Mein-Smith, *A History of Australia,* p. 236; and Lake, 'Frontier Feminism', p. 99.

Australia.[77] It also necessitated excluding all 'undesirable' bodies from the Commonwealth, ensuring the departure of those already there, reducing their ability to reproduce and lowering their life expectancies.[78] Although non-white bodies were the initial target of such exclusionary policies, by the eve of federation the hygiene of 'white' bodies, particularly those from Britain, had become the primary source of concern.[79] As Bashford argues, while the key purpose of the 1901 Immigration Restriction Act – the first Act passed by the new Commonwealth legislature and the cornerstone of Australian immigration policy for most of the twentieth century – was to keep out 'colored aliens', 'the real work of this medico-legal border control was undertaken on those who *were* seeking entry . . . whites'.[80] During the following decades 'undesirable' whites came to be excluded on both medical and, since moral states and

[77] In light of the fact that the 'white' race had reached the limit of its expansion, as works such as C. H. Pearson's seminal *National Life and Character* (1893) argued, Australia was in fact vital to the renewal and growth of the race – an argument that made possible the representation of the biopolitical drive to fashion a white Australia 'not as a narrow, parochial policy, but as an expansive gesture of racial solidarity'. Walker, 'Race Building', p. 40.

[78] Markus, 'Of Continuities and Discontinuities', p. 176. The measures taken to exclude unwanted bodies included the monumental Immigration Restriction Act (1901); the Pacific Island Labourers Act (1902), which authorized the deportation of Melanesian sugar workers; the repeal of a provision allowing Chinese residents to bring their wives and families to Australia (1905); the withdrawal of Commonwealth subsidies from mail lines employing 'coloured' labour (1905); the denial of pensions to all non-Europeans born outside the Commonwealth (1908); the banning of non-Europeans from sugar cultivation (1913); protections for Australian seamen against non-European labour (1913); and the imposition of restrictions on the number of Maltese and Italian immigrants allowed to land in each state (1920s). Other measures, such as the passage of laws to restrict the production and consumption of opium, were designed to encourage 'undesirable' immigrants to depart for friendlier shores. For those who could not leave, namely Aborigines, the measures employed were largely of a segregative nature (barring, by the interwar period, the removal from their families of children who were perceived to be half-caste), as well as the denial of citizenship and welfare benefits. Such policies led to the gradual 'whitening' of Australia's population between federation and the Second World War. Day, *Smugglers and Sailors*, p. 299; Willard, 'The History of the White', 7; Carney, 'The History of Australian Drug Laws'; and Markus, 'Of Continuities', pp. 176–7.

[79] As the labour paper the *Worker* emphatically declared, 'No man should be allowed to land upon Australia's shores at all be he sixty thousand times ten thousand times an Englishman or ten million times a Briton unless he can present a good moral and physical record'. Following federation British immigrants were in fact forced to do so through the implementation of a range of new restrictions such as a mandatory pre-departure medical test. *The Worker,* 19 September 1891, cited in Guyatt, 'The Publicists', p. 255.

[80] Bashford, *Imperial Hygiene,* p. 151. Although the New South Wales Immigration Restriction Act of 1898, under which paupers, the insane, felons and individuals 'suffering from a loathsome or contagious disease' were refused entry, was the first Australian Act to mark the transition from a discourse of racial difference to one that focused on the hygienic status of whites, such provisions (along with the exclusion of

tendencies were also biologized, on moral grounds as well.[81] Such measures would ensure, as the *Australian Star* maintained, that the 'healthy, clean-living race' in Australia would be protected 'from the foul stains that the age, the social conditions, and the sins of the older races have bred in the bone until it has become a hereditary curse'.[82]

That protecting Australia's purity from contamination by the bodies of unhygienic Britons was one of the chief goals of the 'White Australia' policy is clear in an examination of Australia's quarantine system as it emerged in the late nineteenth century.[83] Not only were more ships from Britain than from Asia, relative to their numbers, detained by Australian quarantine officials, but they were held for lengths of time that were often as long as double those of ships from Asia – in spite of the fact that the time–distance barrier between Britain and Australia was far in excess of the accepted incubation period of most known diseases.[84] Moreover, the period of quarantine of incoming ships was determined not by their date of arrival at port, but by the date of the last case of illness on board, which reveals that, as Krista Maglen argues, the aim of Australian quarantine practices was 'to create distance from individual cases of

'idiots' and the insane) were included in the 1901 Commonwealth Act. The confidential guidelines issued to customs officers in turn expanded such exclusionary practices to include individuals 'suffering from any serious physical incapacity, such as blindness, loss of limbs, epilepsy, phthisis, consumption, or tuberculosis in any form'. By the First World War efforts were being made to weed out such 'defectives' before they reached Australia by requiring ships' masters and medical officers, as well as medical officers at the point of departure, to certify to the health, or lack thereof, of their passengers. *Immigration Restriction Act 1901–1910: Confidential Notes for the Guidance of Officers*, A1, 1911/10657, AAC; and Bashford, *Imperial Hygiene*, p. 153.

81 Cases of barring individuals on medical grounds include that of a Glasgow manufacturer in 1905 because he was blind, and that of an unfortunate individual in 1931 described only as a 'freak' 'on the ground that loathsome or revolting types might under certain conditions be dangerous to the beholder'. The most notorious case of 'moral' exclusion was undoubtedly that of Mrs Mabel Freer, who in 1936 was denied entry into the Commonwealth for being 'a person of undesirable character' (a verdict apparently based on her adulterous shipboard affair with an Australian army officer). 'Immigration Restriction Act, Striking Case in Tasmania', *Sydney Morning Herald*, 5 May 1905, 85; A425/1 43/4388, AAC; and *Parliamentary Debates: Commonwealth of Australia*, 152, p. 1659, quoted in Martin, *Robert Menzies*, p. 255.

82 'The Restriction of Aliens', *Australian Star*, 18 November 1897, p. 3.

83 The first colonial Quarantine Act came into force in New South Wales in 1832 (in response to a cholera outbreak in Britain), but a system of mass quarantine was not introduced in Australia until 1881 following a smallpox outbreak in Sydney. Infected vessels and their cargo were fumigated and isolated, and *all* their passengers, not simply those who were diseased, were detained at geographically isolated quarantine stations. Anderson, *The Cultivation*, p. 93; and Maglen, 'A World Apart', 201.

84 Maglen, 'A World Apart', 209. Since by the late nineteenth century most ships from Britain made the voyage to Australia without stopping in Asia (or anywhere else) on the way, Britain itself was clearly the target of Australian quarantine. Maglen, 'A World Apart', 206–7.

disease' – namely the bodies of white immigrants – rather than simply from disease founts.[85] Although by the turn of the twentieth century strict maritime quarantine had come to be largely abandoned in Europe as a public health strategy, in favour of sanitary reform, with the creation of the Commonwealth in 1901 'A national maritime quarantine "line" was created, which *was* the border of the new nation' (emphasis in original).[86] Space and place thus made possible the implementation of a cordon sanitaire – which, since Australia had an 8,000 mile long natural border, made possible the control of contact with 'foreign bodies' to a degree unparalleled by other states – around the geo-body of the emergent nation-state. The two key meanings of water in this period, 'water as part of hygiene and the water of oceans, its currents, its dominance and its yielding of wealth', thus came effectively together in Australia as it set about constructing not only one of the most rigorously enforced systems of quarantine in the world, but one that was unsurpassed in scope and longevity.[87]

Australia's quarantine system employed, furthermore, one of the most unique and effective methods in the world for keeping undesirable bodies outside the geo-body of the nation-state: the dictation test. First adopted by New South Wales, South Australia and Western Australia in 1898, the dictation test, although greeted with considerable hostility upon its assumption, became the cornerstone of Australia's immigration policy in 1901.[88] While it was initially applied only to all 'coloured immigrants' by 1909 it was being applied to all 'whites' who were 'suffering from any physical incapacity', and by 1912 to those who were deemed undesirable 'for economic, political, or moral reasons'.[89] As the regulatory target shifted from non-white to white bodies, customs

[85] Maglen, 'A World Apart', 211. The unsanitary condition of Australian towns and cities relative to Britain's did, however, necessitate caution, particularly since vaccination rates in Australia were much lower than in Britain.

[86] Bashford, *Imperial Hygiene,* p. 116.

[87] Mohanram, 'White Water', para. 11; and Maglen, 'A World Apart', 197, 211.

[88] Palfreeman, 'The End of the Dictation Test'. The reason for such hostility was two-fold: because the Australian colonies were forced to adopt this particular method of exclusion, first developed in Natal, at the behest of the British government (over concerns of the effects of such a race-based policy on its wider national and imperial interests); and because, as the *Australian Star* concluded, 'if a coloured alien, speaking his own language is undesirable he does not become any the less undesirable because he may know English, German, or Italian'. 'The Restriction of Aliens', p. 3.

[89] Secretary, Department of External Affairs, to Customs Collectors, 24 June 1903, A1/15, 1903, 3997, AAS; 'Immigration Restriction Acts 1901 and 1905'; and Yarwood, 'The Dictation Test', 19. See also 'Restriction of Immigration: The Workings of the NSW Act: Immigrants Debarred from Landing', *Sydney Morning Herald,* 6 January 1899, 35; 'White Aliens', *Daily Telegraph,* 18 April 1902, 75; 'The Stelling Case', *Daily Telegraph,* 23 December 1903, 100; and A1, 191/10657, AAS.

Collectors were advised that, since it was 'not desirable that persons should be allowed to pass the test . . . before putting it to anyone the Officer should be satisfied that he will fail'. Such an outcome could be ensured either by giving a test in English that contained such tortuous terms that it would be impossible to get them all right, or by applying the test to the particular individual concerned 'in some other language of which he was ignorant'.[90] As former customs official Wal Moore contended, the test thus became 'the ultimate weapon to keep people out of Australia'.[91]

It was a weapon, moreover, that was based on, and in turn fostered, an intimate relationship between hygiene, language and the body. The existence of such a relationship was certainly clear both for the *Australasian Medical Gazette,* which in 1898 laid the blame for the declining birth-rate in New South Wales on 'indecent advertisements' and 'quack literature', which it claimed were 'eating the heart out of our young and otherwise healthy country', and for the individuals who gave evidence before the Royal Commission on the Decline of the Birth-Rate in 1904, a number of whom professed that 'indecent' publications were responsible for that decline.[92] Belief in the existence of such a relationship in fact grew as the century progressed, so that a deputation from the United Social Questions Council (which represented thirty-seven different purity organizations) could inform the Victorian Chief Secretary in 1928 that 'obscene' publications were 'doing as much harm as diseases germs' and were forcing Australia into 'committing national suicide'.[93] Moreover, as another deputation informed the Commonwealth Customs Minister in 1935, the effects of language on Australian bodies were most serious when it came to imported publications, which were 'constantly knocking at the doors of the Commonwealth for admission'. Second-hand magazines from overseas were in fact regarded as, quite literally, *physical* contaminants, as a 'source of disease and menace to health',

90 Secretary, Department of External Affairs to Customs Collectors, 24 June 1903, A1/15, 1903/3997, AAS. The notorious Mrs Freer, for example, was given a dictation test in Italian, while the Czech communist Egon Kisch was subjected to one in Scottish Gaelic (and although he also failed it, he managed, like Mrs Freer, to enter the Commonwealth by securing a High Court verdict that Scottish Gaelic was not deemed a European language for the purposes of the Act since so few people spoke it). Yarwood, 'The Dictation Test', 28.

91 Wal Moore interview, 31 March 1990, Mss. Acc 96/76, NLA. Although Moore claimed that he had never heard of anyone passing the test, there were a few isolated cases in the early years of its administration in which individuals did so, as in the 1902 case of two 'Hindoos' in Western Australia. 'A Black and White Law', *The Daily Telegraph,* 14 February 1902, 97.

92 'The Decreased Birth-Rate in New South Wales', editorial, *Australasian Medical Gazette,* 21 November 1898, 503.

93 VPRS 3992, Unit 2402, T7016, PROV.

which even the bleaching agent used in the making of paper – 'in itself a disinfectant [that] militates against disease' – was unable to combat.[94] In short, such 'degrading things . . . being dumped in Australia from foreign countries' threatened, as the Good-Literature Superintendent of the New South Wales Christian Endeavour Union Cortis H. McNeill advised Prime Minister Lyons in 1934, to 'blot our WHITE AUSTRALIA policy' (emphasis in original).[95] It was therefore up to the Customs Department to 'free Australia and give it a chance to build its national life on fit, strong, clean, and pure moral grounds'. What was needed was for the customs to enact a censorship system that functioned in the nature of a 'sanitary system' or, as another deputation member put it, as a 'quarantine to prevent plagues which would interfere with the moral health of the people from entering the Commonwealth'. Should such advice be followed, a member of the Young Nationalists advised, Australia would become a well-populated country containing a 'healthy', 'pure' and 'high-class race'.[96]

The Customs Department and the creation of a 'quarantined culture'

This anonymous cove at the Customs,
This storehouse for horrible stuff,
Is as venal, I'll bet,
As the rest of us, yet
Does he whine that his job is too tough?
No. He keeps his identity secret,
His knowledge safe under his hat;
And he lurks all alone,
Unsuspected, unknown
Such as hangmen and heroes like that.[97]

94 'Secondhand Literature', A425/122, 1939/5151, AAC. Since a 1930 inquiry into the Australian book trade revealed that the second-hand market in Australia was in part supplied through American exporters who acquired discarded books and magazines through a network of railway porters and bell hops, such matter thus contained, as Customs Minister Perkins disdainfully observed, 'egg marks and other breakfast stains'. Faced with similar concerns about the hygiene, or lack thereof, of library books, circulating libraries in Australia often employed 'sterilizing cabinets' to de-contaminate books after use. Nile, *The Making of the Australian*, p. 39; *Parliamentary Debates: Commonwealth of Australia*, 22 September 1938, p. 116; and J. Arnold, 'Choose your Author', p. 81.

95 Cortis H. McNeill to Joseph Lyons, 27 June 1934, A425/122, 1939/5151, AAC.

96 'Report of Proceedings of Deputation to the Hon. T. W. White', 10 September 1935, Mss. 9148, NLA.

97 'Den', 'The Anonymous Altruist', *The Herald*, 29 August 1935, n.p., clipping in Mss. 9148, NLA.

The Australian customs service was, undoubtedly, more than up to the task. As the Commonwealth's first Collector of Customs H. N. P. Wollaston proudly declared, '"Let the Customs do it" became the saying and a practice when any particularly disagreeable business had to be done. If the police wanted to search some suspected premises without a warrant, the Customs would be invited to make use of its powers to enable them to do so. If an officer were wanted for any special services, the Customs would be applied to'. In an unusual burst of candour for a department whose representatives were renowned for their secretiveness, Wollaston further noted that such activities gave the customs the reputation 'of being a live department', which meant that it 'would not hesitate to push the law to its utmost extent, in the public interest'.[98] What constituted 'the public interest' was for the most part determined by the department itself, although Wollaston claimed that other bureaucratic, legislative and even judicial branches of the Commonwealth were not averse to availing themselves of the extensive powers afforded to the Department of Trade and Customs – which ranged from revenue collection to protecting Australia from a multitude of external threats, including undesirable immigrants, disease, the physical contamination of impure food and the moral contamination of impure literature – should their own legal means prove insufficient for the task at hand. An examination of its powers and practices for the regulation of 'obscene' literature reveals that it was the most powerful agency for the regulation of print culture not only in the Commonwealth, but arguably in the whole empire.

Although colonial customs departments began to develop systems for the regulation of imported publications following the Vizetelly trials, it was not until after federation that regulating obscenity came to be one of the chief functions of the new Commonwealth Department of Trade and Customs thanks to the Commonwealth Customs Act. One of the first acts to be passed by the new legislature, the Act accorded the department greater powers to regulate print culture than had ever been granted to its colonial counterparts – ones that, moreover, ensured that the regulatory operations of the department would remain largely concealed not only from the public but from the rest of the government as well.[99] Central to these powers were Sections 52(c), which provided for the

[98] 'Trade and Customs: The Interesting History of a Great Department', *Life*, 15 November 1907, p. 446.

[99] South Australia became the first colony to pass legislation to prohibit the importation of 'obscene' publications or other matter in 1864 (although colonial customs departments had in fact been excluding such material since at least the 1850s), followed by Queensland in 1873, New South Wales in 1879 and Victoria in 1883. A5507, 9/2, AAC; and Day, *Smugglers and Sailors*, p. 285.

prohibition of 'Blasphemous indecent or obscene works and articles' and 52(g), a dragnet clause that provided for the prohibition of 'All goods the importation of which may be prohibited by proclamation'.[100] The latter clause, which was not to be found in any British or colonial Act, ultimately proved to be the cornerstone of the department's apparatus for the regulation of imported publications, for under it customs could issue proclamations to seize and destroy both print matter and other items such as contraceptive products that purportedly had a tendency to 'deprave and corrupt'.[101]

Such provisions made the Act a nightmare for importers, particularly since it offered neither a definition of what constituted a prohibited publication nor a mechanism for publicizing what books were actually prohibited under it.[102] It did not even provide a board or body of 'sane, sound and competent judges' to determine whether a publication should be prohibited or not, but instead, as one critic declared, gave 'every tide-waiter the duty of throwing into outer darkness any book or article which he may think is obscene, indecent, or blasphemous'.[103] Importers could challenge a seizure in court, but since the Act essentially reversed the basic tenet of British law that a person is innocent until proven guilty by placing the burden of proof that a work was not obscene upon the importer instead of the government – which as the Act's chief framer and champion, the protectionist Customs Minister Charles Kingston, admitted placed 'a Customs offence in a somewhat different position from any other offence under the criminal or quasi-criminal law' – recourse to the courts, as the framers of the Act were well aware, would be rare.[104] Such

100 Section 270, which gave the Governor-General the ability to make regulations consistent with the Act, was also used to supplement these powers.

101 The items seized under this clause were, moreover, rarely listed on the department's lists of prohibited publications.

102 Efforts to introduce amendments to require the publication of a list of prohibited publications in the *Government Gazette* failed due to fears that this would serve to increase their circulation – somewhat faulty logic in light of the fact that individual items prohibited under Section 52(g) of the Act (including 'obscene' works or other items) were listed in the *Gazette*.

103 *Parliamentary Debates: Commonwealth of Australia*, 11 July 1910, pp. 2405, 2410. While Kingston hastened to assure critics that the department would not 'be so utterly foolish that grave issues of this sort would be held to be within the duties of a minor officer', his reply was disingenuous, since the Bill gave any customs official in charge of the landing of goods the power to seize publications that he believed to be prohibited imports (although such seizures were 'subject to the supervision of his supervisor'). *Parliamentary Debates: Commonwealth of Australia*, 11 July 1910, p. 2412, and 15 August 1901, p. 3765.

104 *Parliamentary Debates: Commonwealth of Australia*, 11 July 1901, p. 3767, and 14 August 1901, p. 3678. Importers faced the loss of an entire shipment of goods should only one item within it be declared a prohibited import, as well as a fine of up to £100.

provisions made the bill, as leader of the Opposition and former New South Wales Customs Minister Reid declared, 'transcend every other Bill of the kind in the thoroughly brutal fashion in which it suppresses the individual who may happen to come in conflict with His Majesty's Customs'.[105]

Kingston did, in fact, initially attempt to use the courts to put his new powers for the regulation of imported publications into effect (doubtless because this was the quickest and easiest way to establish regulatory guidelines for the newly formed department to follow) through initiating three prosecutions in rapid succession against Melbourne booksellers, but the exposure of the department's new regulatory ideals and powers to public scrutiny rendered it subject to such ridicule that, in spite of securing convictions in all three cases, he rapidly abandoned such a course.[106] Uniformity of practice was instead cultivated through referring all questions as to what constituted an 'obscene' publication to the Comptroller General, a hierarchical system of administration which, while generating tremendous frustration among customs staff, enabled the department to institute fairly uniform standards of practice for the regulation of imported publications throughout its widely dispersed branches.[107] A problem that continued to plague the department, however, was the difficulty of coming up with guidelines as to what signified an 'obscene' or 'indecent' publication.[108] It was not until 1914, following a furore over what constituted an 'indecent' postcard, that it laid down some guidelines which, in addition to providing a definition of the

[105] *Parliamentary Debates: Commonwealth of Australia*, 10 July 1901, p. 285. While members of the nascent Commonwealth parliament were wary of the powers the bill accorded the Customs Department to regulate imported literature, and evinced 'a considerable amount of hesitation about giving these very large powers to anybody', they believed that such powers were necessary 'in the interests of decency'. *Parliamentary Debates: Commonwealth of Australia*, 11 July 1910, pp. 2440, 2442.

[106] All three prosecutions involved translations of French novels (including Zola's), but what made Kingston and his department a laughing stock was the decision to prosecute the esteemed firm of George Robertson and Co. for importing Balzac's acknowledged 'classic' *Droll Stories*, and for employing Melbourne university professor Edward Morris (who felt so 'defiled' after reading the book that he 'felt as if [he] needed a bath after it') as a prosecution witness. The police magistrate in charge of the case, while he felt obliged to convict on the grounds that the work in translation was 'indecent within the meaning of the act', nonetheless 'regretted that such a prosecution had been brought into court' and imposed a reduced fine – in the process sending Kingston a clear message that the courts did not look favourably on his new regulatory agenda. 'Impure Literature', 21 September 1901, clipping in Mss. 12720, Box 3514/3, SLV.

[107] Day, *Contraband and Controversy*, p. 7.

[108] As Wollaston put it, the problem was that 'The question of what is indecent is so largely a matter of taste that no definition can be given which is entirely satisfactory to all minds'. Wollaston, *Customs Law*, p. 35.

word 'indecent', ordained that in putting this definition into practice customs officials should not only interpret the term 'in its wider sense', but 'should be guided by their experience of what is usually considered unobjectionable in the house-hold of the ordinary self-respecting citizen'.[109] Although it is questionable how useful such a guideline was in practice, thankfully for customs officials the department banned so many publications via proclamation that such proclamations, which were issued periodically in book form as *General Orders for the Officers of the Department of Trade and Customs,* afforded more specific guidelines as to exactly what they should seize.[110]

In addition to containing proclamations pertaining to prohibited imports, the *General Orders* also included information as to how customs law should be administered. They therefore reveal both how standardized the department's procedures for regulating 'obscene' publications had become by the late 1920s and to what extent such regulation had become enshrined as part of the customary duty of customs officials. The *General Orders* for 1927, for example, informed customs officers that they were to exercise 'All possible vigilance ... to prevent the introduction into the Commonwealth of obscene or indecent books or articles', in particular photographs containing nudity (as well as all other postcards or pictures that were even 'suggestive of indecency'), literature pertaining to contraceptives (including price lists), and any children's publications that offended 'against modesty or common propriety'.[111] By the 1930s, however, new types of 'undesirable' publications had begun to flood the Commonwealth, which customs guidelines did not

109 *General Orders for Officers*, pp. 203–4. 'Indecency' was defined as: '(a) offensive to common propriety or adjudged to be subversive of morality; offending modesty or delicacy; unfit to be seen or heard; immodest; grossly obscene; (b) contrary to what is fit and proper; unbecoming'. Although the words 'obscenity' and 'indecency' were often used interchangeably, such a definition indicates that the former was conceived of as a subset of the latter.

110 Since new proclamations were issued so frequently, and customs officers were rarely supplied with more than one edition of the *General Orders* in the course of their careers, such books contained a multitude of blank pages to which new proclamations could be affixed. Of the two books of orders that I examined, one of them was issued in 1914 and contained pasted-in entries dating to the late 1920s, while the other was issued in 1927 and had been faithfully updated until 1954. While such books became chaotic and unwieldy after prolonged use, they reveal that customs employees were conscientious in keeping track of the ongoing flow of proclamations against prohibited publications. C4338/1, Box 1, AAS.

111 'The term "indecent"', customs officials were informed, 'is to be interpreted in its wider sense, and all postcards, pictures, and the like, the obvious intention of which is to cater to the immodest as well as the indecent tastes of purchasers' – or which would 'offend the average householder' – were 'to be detained'. Such matter was to be retained for a month and, if unclaimed (an action that risked a fine and possible prosecution), they were to be destroyed. *General Orders*, pp. 203–4.

provide sufficient scope to restrict. The department therefore began to enlarge once again upon its conception of 'indecent' or 'obscene' publications by issuing a proclamation in 1934 excluding 'the worst type of gangster literature', which was followed a year later by a letter to members of the Australian book trade informing them that henceforth all advertisements in imported publications that pertained to medicines for curing venereal disease, sexual impotence, 'female irregularities', abortion and alcohol or tobacco addiction were to be considered 'indecent' publications.[112] The department broadened its definition of obscenity once again in 1938 to incorporate any publication that 'unduly emphasizes matters of sex or crime' or 'is calculated to encourage depravity'.[113]

The regulatory scope of the department was extended even further in the 1930s thanks to the activities of two advisory bodies, the Book Censorship Advisory Committee (founded in 1933) and the Literature Censorship Board (which replaced the Advisory Committee in 1937), which were accorded the task of providing recommendations as to whether publications that the department considered obscene should be prohibited.[114] Although the advisory bodies did recommend the release of some of the more controversial works on the department's list of prohibited publications, and were more willing than the department to allow limited circulation to many imported works rather than prohibiting them outright, they also advocated the prohibition of many 'borderline' works, particularly classics and foreign-language publications,

[112] 425/122, 1939/5151, AAC. Realizing, perhaps, that the department was attempting to stretch the law to its extremes, instead of issuing a proclamation prohibiting such advertisements, it asked the Australian book and periodical trade to undertake a mammoth self-censoring operation to rid imported newspapers and periodicals of them. In return, the trade was permitted to continue importing publications that contained such advertisements. The most remarkable aspect of this fantastic proposal was that it actually succeeded.

[113] *Parliamentary Debates: Commonwealth of Australia*, 22 September 1938, p. 111.

[114] It was the emergence of the first concerted agitation against the censorship activities of the department that led the Lyons government to establish the three-member Book Censorship Advisory Committee (headed by Sir Robert Garran). The Customs Department was not obliged, however, to submit publications to the Committee for its opinion, nor to follow its recommendations. The failure of the Committee was signalled by the emergence of renewed agitation in the form of the Book Censorship Abolition League (formed in 1933), which the department tried to appease by abolishing the Committee and creating the Literature Censorship Board and an Appeal Censor. However, since the latter post was filled by Garran and the constitution of the Board remained virtually the same as for the Committee, the department ensured that its regulatory activities would continue undisturbed. *Parliamentary Debates: Commonwealth of Australia*, 12 December 1934, n.p., clipping in A425/127, 1943/4949, AAC.

that customs officials had previously hesitated to regulate.[115] Moreover, many of the efforts that the advisory bodies did make to liberalize customs regulation, such as expanding the Second Schedule (which was introduced in 1926 to provide access to proscribed works to individuals who would have a 'bona fide' interest in them such as doctors and scholars) and persuading customs to agree to permit booksellers to import items on this schedule provided that they only sold them to 'respectable' customers, actually had the opposite effect.[116] Booksellers, for example, became subject to increased surveillance in order to ensure that they were selling only those publications that the department explicitly permitted them to sell (and that they were selling them to the 'right' sort of people).[117] They were also increasingly co-opted by the department to become part of its regulatory system.[118] For those who failed to fulfil their obligations to the department, customs officials were empowered, as one disgruntled bookseller complained, to 'enter the bookseller's premises, search all his records, place his staff under surveillance, examine his stock and confiscate some of it' – which they often did with a large squad of officers in tow while the shop was trading.[119]

While critics of the customs' system of literary regulation feared that 'what we shall read and thereby very largely what we shall know and what we shall think . . . [is] at the mercy of customs officials' – individuals who, moreover, were 'not chosen for their positions on account of their high literary qualifications' – the department always hastened to defend both the status and educational attainments of its staff.[120] There was some justification in such a defence. Customs always sought to cultivate

[115] Coleman, *Obscenity*, p. 26; and Report, Book Censorship Advisory Committee, 28 March 1935; 8 August 1935; and 6 May 1938, A3023, Folder 1935/36, AAC. Although the department generally did submit works to the Board that appeared to have some literary merit, anything that did not continued to be dealt with by customs officials.

[116] The First Schedule consisted of publications that were completely prohibited.

[117] Report, Inspector Jamieson, Investigation Section, n.d., A425/17, 1943/5050, AAC; Letter from C. Coffey to the Collector of Customs, Melbourne, 12 September 1928, A425/17, 1943/5050, AAC; and Report, Director-General of Health, 18 October 1928, A425/17, 1943/5050, AAC.

[118] Booksellers who had proved themselves 'trustworthy' were entitled to put their books up for sale without submitting them for examination, as long as they detained 'such titles as they think might be questioned'. Page, *Australian Bookselling*, p. 125.

[119] Page, *Australian Bookselling*, pp. 125–7. A similar procedure might also be carried out at a bookseller's home.

[120] Letter from Senator Arthur Rae to Customs Minister T. W. White, 9 November 1921, A425/127, 1943/4949, AAC. For White such charges were groundless because 'the Customs officials who carry out duties in regard to the prohibitions of literature have distinct literary qualifications, and in some cases have a knowledge of three or four European languages'. Letter from White to Rae, 14 November 1921, A425/127, 1943/4949, AAC.

an image, to begin with, of being the most 'gentlemanly' of the public services. From the very formation of the colonial customs services customs officers were required, according to David Day, to be 'pillars of probity' who would help to 'foster a sense of bourgeois respectability' in colonial Australia.[121] By the mid-nineteenth century it had thus already become well established that the higher echelons of the customs services such as Landing Surveyors and Landing Waiters (who since they examined imported goods also served as literary regulators) should 'be filled by gentlemen in whom great confidence can be placed as upon the faithful discharge of their duties depend, in great measure, the accuracy and fidelity with which the public revenue is collected'.[122] With the shift from a patronage-based to a merit-based appointment system towards the end of the nineteenth century, rather than declining, such an ethos instead percolated down to the lower echelons of the customs hierarchy.[123] Thanks in part to the often phenomenally lengthy careers of customs officials, it also carried over into the new Commonwealth Department of Trade and Customs.[124] Wollaston, for example, the first Commonwealth Comptroller-General of Customs, first joined the Victorian Customs Department in 1863 at the age of seventeen. Although Nicholas Lockyer, who followed Wollaston as Comptroller General, did not enter the New South Wales Customs Department until 1896, he had in fact joined the colony's civil service (at the ripe old age of thirteen) only five years after Wollaston began his career.[125] Little wonder that, like Wollaston, he was a staunch believer in the continuance in the Commonwealth of the values of the colonial public services. These included 'remain[ing] pure', maintaining 'a splendid record of faithfulness and honesty' and 'rendering silent service to the King and to the Empire' – all of which would ensure that the Commonwealth remained

121 Day, *Contraband and Controversy*, p. 442.

122 H. R. Power, 'Historical Review of Customs Activities in Victoria', A5507, 9/2 AAC. The importance of placing gentlemen in these weighty positions is reflected in the salaries for such posts, for Landing Surveyors and the Head Landing Waiter all received the rather considerable income of £600 a year.

123 Such gentrification extended not only lower down the social scale (with the renaming of Tide Waiters, for example, who occupied a fairly lowly position in the customs hierarchy, as 'Examining Officers') but to the very outposts of the department (since even in a remote place such as Bowen, Queensland, customs officers kept out a tray for calling cards and partook of a highly formal tea ceremony upon the arrival of company. Day, *Smugglers and Sailors*, p. 404; and Day, *Contraband and Controversy*, p. 19.

124 The department's policies were thus, like much of its staff, slow to change. As Comptroller-General Kennedy (who had joined the department in 1901) noted in 1946, 'if a book was "indecent" in 1905, it should still be "indecent" in 1946'. Minute, Kennedy to Turner, 1 May 1936, A425/1, 36/2880, AAC, quoted in Day, *Contraband and Controversy*, p. 245.

125 McDonald, 'The Former Customs Clerks', 32–44.

'untarnished by evil traditions'.[126] In the case of the customs this service was to be best rendered by recruiting young men 'with fair primary educational qualifications straight from the schools'.[127] Such candidates could then be moulded into the department's own image and made part of the customs 'family'.[128]

Yet in spite of the young age at which customs officers were recruited, they were by no means ignorant. Entry to the Clerical Division of the Commonwealth Customs required a fairly impressive knowledge of English literature from 1558, a basic knowledge of mercantile law and knowledge of one out of a possible eight subject areas (which included French and German, along with modern European history, English history, constitutional law, the economic development of Australia and social science).[129] But such knowledge did not exactly prepare new recruits for the task of regulating 'obscene' publications.[130] Many a greenhorn clerk, who had envisioned a customs career as one of action and adventure 'chasing smugglers' or 'sitting back in a fast motor boat running around outside the port', instead found himself dumped in a cramped office and ordered to pour over imported publications looking for obscene words or images – which in light of the sheer volume of material to be examined made the job, according to one former clerk, 'rather boring after a time'.[131] Although such a task was technically relegated to Examining Officers many of the department's branches were so small that even statistics clerks were often obliged to assist in it.[132]

126 Lockyer, *Some Ideals*, pp. 14–15, 16.

127 Lockyer, *Some Ideals*, p. 12.

128 This sense of 'family' was fostered through the paternal figure of the Collector, who in addition to offering personal training to new recruits organized departmental picnics and other excursions. The fact that the customs was 'a traditionally Catholic-dominated section of the public service' (which may help to explain its attitude towards birth control literature and products) also served to cultivate such a sense. Day, *Contraband and Controversy*, p. 102.

129 *New South Wales Regulations*. See, for example, *Regulations under the Public Service Act*. As the Queensland *Standard* acknowledged in 1935, the officials responsible for regulating print culture in the Customs Department 'in most instances have received quite a good education in the general acceptance of that very much maligned word. They have probably taken honours in English, graduated with distinction in mathematics, and understand all the mysteries of geometry' (although this did not, it hastened to note, 'equip them to decide what adult Aussies should read'). *Standard*, 29 June 1935, n.p., clipping in Mss. Z/Q991/N, ML.

130 Training was, moreover, virtually non-existent. New recruits were simply provided with a copy of the department's *General Orders* and the *Tariff Guide* (although 'A lot of people didn't have them because they weren't available') and expected to get on with it. Dick Serle interview, 1 April 1990, Mss. Acc 96/76, NLA.

131 Dick Searle interview; and John Hall interview.

132 Dick Searle interview. Such 'casual' censors would, however, have done little more than refer 'questionable' material to a superior.

The fear that the customs system for the regulation of imported publications was conducted by entry-level clerks with insufficient qualifications was therefore somewhat justified.[133] But not only did such clerks take their responsibilities in this matter extremely seriously – ogling obscene material and handing it around surreptitiously 'was generally', as one former Examining Officer noted, 'regarded as taboo' – but the seizing officer was simply expected to take the publication, 'document it, envelope it up and give it to his senior officer'.[134] If a senior officer believed that the material in question was blatantly obscene (as in the case, for example, of postcards with nude images on them) he had the power to destroy it 'on the spot'. However, any material about which there was some doubt or that was believed to have some literary or scientific merit was forwarded to the Investigations Section in each state, which until the creation of the Book Censorship Advisory Committee was the heart of the department's regulatory apparatus. Although staffed by only third-grade clerks who were rarely university-educated, the literary knowledge and linguistic skills of such personnel were often quite impressive. Charles Brossois, for example, who worked in the New South Wales Investigations Section for three decades, recommended that *The Works of Aristotle, the Famous Philosopher,* be prohibited importation since its contents had not, in fact, been written by Aristotle (which he determined based on the author's references to Galen, who was born over four centuries after Aristotle's death) and hence its licentiousness could not be justified by its antiquity; while South Australian Investigations clerk E. R. Nain wrote reports that read more like literary reviews (in which, as in his report on Aldous Huxley's *Eyeless in Gaza,* he extolled 'the author's views on art, science, religion, ethics, Communism [and] Hitlerism').[135]

Investigations clerks examined the publications that were submitted to them and made recommendations as to their fate, but clerks were not the final arbiters. That responsibility instead rested with as many as half

[133] The department, like the rest of the Commonwealth Public Service, was divided into four divisions, with the fourth the lowest. In the case of customs the First Division consisted of the Comptroller-General, the second of Collectors, and the third and fourth made up the bulk of the department's staff.

[134] Stephen Gallagher interview, 14 November 1989, Mss. Acc 96/76, NLA. The seriousness with which such a responsibility was carried out may have been a product, in part, of the department's reward system, through which customs officers who seized prohibited goods (including print matter) were entitled to a portion of the fines paid by those convicted of importing such goods. See *Victoria Parliamentary Debates*, 13 November 1895, pp. 3152–4; 29 January 1897, pp. 5080–1; and 5 November 1895, p. 3067.

[135] Brossois, Report, 31 July 1929, A425/126, 1943/2670, AAC; Report to Collector, South Australia, 19 August 1936, A425/1, 36/11759, AAC.

a dozen individuals higher up the hierarchy in the department's regulatory system. If clerks such as Brossois and Nairn recommended that a particular publication be permitted importation then their advice was generally followed by their superiors, the various state Collectors of Customs.[136] However, if they recommended that a particular publication be deemed a prohibited import, then further advice could be sought from Collectors, the Comptroller-General, senior clerks in the Central Office's Correspondence and Records Section, external 'experts' such as the Director-General of Health (often called upon in the case of medical books), the Solicitor-General, the Attorney-General, the book censorship advisory boards (after 1933) and, ultimately, the Minister for Customs, who, if he chose to exercise it, had the final say as to a work's destiny.[137]

The Customs Minister could also, if need be, call upon other branches of the Commonwealth's apparatus for regulating 'obscene' publications, namely the Post and Telegraph Department and the various state police forces, the remit of which, in contrast to that of customs, extended to the regulation of indigenous as well as imported publications. The powers accorded to the post to regulate print culture were, like those given to the customs, considerable. The first Commonwealth Post and Telegraph Act (which, like the 1901 Customs Act, was one of the first pieces of legislation passed by the new Commonwealth parliament) gave the department the power to remove any newspaper containing indecent or obscene matter from the postal register; to refuse to deliver and to destroy any newspaper or parcel containing an indecent or obscene book, article, or picture; to refuse the delivery of postal articles to anyone suspected of being engaged in an 'obscene, indecent or immoral business'; to refuse to send or receive 'blasphemous indecent obscene offensive or scandalous' telegrams; to make anyone guilty of sending an indecent article through the post liable for a fine of up to £100 or two years in prison; and to give the Postmaster-General the power (with the consent in writing of the accused) to serve as judge and jury of those charged with offences against the Act. The Act also granted the Governor-General the power to make any regulations that were deemed necessary

[136] Collectors also revealed an often surprising amount of literary knowledge. See, for example, letter from Comptroller-General Abbott to the Literary Censorship Board, 10 March 1937, A425/127, 1943/4949, AAC.

[137] Customs Ministers such as Frank Tudor (minister in 1908–9 and 1910–13), a working-class unionist who had trained as a hatter, were often the least qualified members of the department's system of literary regulation, although some, such as T. W. White, who wrote a book on the First World War (*Guest of the Unspeakable*), were published authors.

for carrying out the Act, a clause that would later prove exceedingly useful to postal censors. Like the customs, the Post Office could thus prohibit or restrict the circulation of newspapers, books and other matter sent through the post without recourse to the courts.[138]

The department employed two main means of regulating the circulation of 'obscene' publications in Australia. The first was to prohibit the receipt of all mail by anyone suspected of using the Post Office to conduct, in the words of the 1901 Act, 'obscene, indecent or immoral business'.[139] Such a policy was in marked contrast to that of the British warrant system, through which only individual publications or postal matter *sent* by known traders in 'obscene' wares could be prohibited, and only at the behest of the Home Secretary – not, as in the Australian case, by the Postmaster-General.[140] The second means through which the department regulated the trade in 'obscene' publications was through prohibiting traders in 'obscene' wares (such as contraceptive publications or products) – information about which it obtained by employing detectives to monitor their activities – from holding private post boxes.[141] The department was also not averse to using threats to deter individuals from sending 'obscene' matter through the post.[142] Yet though the Post

138 The first annual report on the Post Office in 1912, for example, reveals that the Melbourne General Post Office (the only one to list 'obscene' postal matter separate from other prohibited items) had prohibited 121 items from being sent through the post because of their alleged obscenity. MP341/1/0, 1912/6293, Box 47, AAM.

139 For example, upon the complaint of a Sydney resident in 1903 about receiving a price list of indecent publications from Spain, the Postmaster-General immediately decreed, without further investigation, that the offending Spanish firm would henceforth be prohibited from receiving any letters from Australia. A similar fate met Durjodhan's Herbal Home of Calcutta for sending 'obscene' advertisements to the Commonwealth. Nor were Australian businesses spared such treatment. A6662, 79, AAC; and MP341/1/0, 1934/8305, Box 161, AAM.

140 The real radicalism of the Post and Telegraph Act, however, was that it offered a definition of 'indecent or obscene matter' – namely 'any drawing or picture or advertisement or any printed or written matter in the nature of an advertisement if it related to venereal or contagious diseases affecting the generative organs or functions or to nervous debility or other complaint or infirmity arising from or relating to sexual impotence or intercourse or sexual abuse or to pregnancy or to any irregularity or obstruction of the female system or to the treatment of any complaint or condition peculiar to females or may reasonably be construed as relating to any illegal medical treatment or operation' – and that moreover, such matter, as far as the Act was concerned, related entirely to the reproductive capacities of the body.

141 See, for example, MP341/1/0, Item 1905/3186, Box 155, AAM. The legal basis of the department's prohibition of contraceptive products and publications such as advertisements was, like that of the customs, unclear. Although Alfred Deakin, in his guise as Attorney-General, determined as early as 1902 that contraceptives were not indecent or obscene within the meaning of the Post and Telegraph Act (which meant that the department was therefore obliged to carry them), Deakin's verdict was not definitively adopted until 1934. MP 341/1/0, 1934/8205, Box 161, AAM.

142 Payne, 'Aspects of Commonwealth Literary Censorship', pp. 43–51.

and Telegraph Department may have had a variety of legal means at its disposal to regulate the transmission of 'obscene' postal articles, these only applied to materials in the public domain (such as advertising circulars or newspapers), not the private (such as letters and items sent in closed packets).[143] The Post Office therefore had considerably less power than the customs to regulate the trade in 'obscene' publications in Australia.[144]

The same held true for the police, which in contrast to the Customs and Postal Departments had no legal means to prohibit or otherwise restrict the sale and circulation of obscenity except through the courts.[145] In light of the undesirable publicity prosecutions garnered, the general policy of the police towards the sellers or purveyors of 'obscene' wares was to have a 'quiet word' with a publisher or bookseller regarding an undesirable work, which they generally only did upon receipt of a public complaint.[146] Upon receiving such complaints, far from employing underhand methods to 'suppress reading matter which offends their sensibilities', as Bill Hornadge claims, in contrast to the policies of both the customs and Post Office, the Australian police generally, in fact, tried to consider the motivations and expectations of both the producers and consumers of such commodities when attempting to determine their alleged obscenity.[147] When Detective

[143] The Post and Telegraph Act of 1901 prohibited the seizure of obscene postal items unless they were sent in open packets or bore obscenity on the outside, which made it impossible to put a stop to the activities of an individual such as the Melbourne chemist R. J. Pouton, who for over twenty years sent advertisements pertaining to 'irregularities of the female system' through the post in sealed envelopes. MP341/1/0, 1934/8205, Box 161, AAM.

[144] There were numerous attempts to amend the law to give postal officials the powers they believed they were lacking, but none of these came to fruition. See MP273/1, Item 1919/6439, AAM.

[145] The police did have some powers to regulate the trade in obscene publications, most of which were acquired in the two decades prior to federation. Between 1890 and 1900 Victoria alone passed four acts that gave its police the power to deal with 'obscene' matter. These included the Police Offences Act of 1890 (which provided up to two years in jail for anyone who exposed an obscene book print or picture in a public place); the Wrongs Act of 1890 (which made it an offence to publish obscene or blasphemous matter, even in reference to true incidents); the Crimes Act of 1891 (which made it an offence to affix any obscene matter to a wall, window, etc., or to print or distribute advertisements relating to sexual matters); and the Crimes Act of 1900 (which extended the law in the matter of advertisements and pictures pertaining to sexual matters). These powers were increased once again in 1907 with a new Police Offences Act that prohibited the exposure or sale of indecent postcards.

[146] The police did, however, seek increasing recourse to the courts after the successful prosecution for obscenity of J. M. Harcourt's *Upsurge* in 1933.

[147] Hornadge, *Chidley's Answer*, p. 48. Following the receipt of numerous complaints in 1938 about a photograph of a nudist wedding in the *Sun* newspaper, for example, Sergeant Third Class George H. Fleming reported that in his opinion the photograph

A. S. Burvett of the Victorian Police was assigned the task in 1911 of investigating William Chidley's *The Answer*, for example, Burvett not only warned Chidley that he did not have to sell copies of *The Answer* to him if he did not want to run the risk of prosecution, he also let the printer off with nothing more than a warning to register his press and type.[148] As in the case of both the customs and the Post Office such generosity was notably absent, however, when it came to purveyors of birth control literature or products or matter pertaining to sexual diseases.[149]

The phenomenal system of literary regulation developed by the Commonwealth customs (in conjunction with the post and police), a system designed specifically to regulate *imported* rather than indigenous publications, reveals that for the customs erecting a cordon sanitaire around Australia to keep out undesirable print matter was an essential component of the administration of the White Australia policy, and was as vital to its mission to protect Australia from contaminants – including from its imperial metropole – as was its quarantine system to keep out impure bodies. The linkages between the two were certainly clear to critics of the system, as is evident in a 1936 radio skit entitled 'Rabelais Calls on the Minister for Customs'. In the skit Rabelais drops in on the Minister for Customs to find out why his works are banned in Australia, to which the minister replies:

> We want to keep this southern air of ours pure and free from the contamination of the murky blasts of Europe, ancient or modern. Here we have a continent free

was not at all indecent, not only because it contained no 'suggestions of indelicacy and immodesty', but because 'Even the most biased person ... would ungrudgingly concede that considered purely as an item of news interest, the solemnizing of a wedding under unusual circumstances' was noteworthy, so that 'from a publisher's viewpoint, there is some justification for the publication of the picture'. George H. Fleming, report, 3 June 1938, 4/6633, B2423 (1938) to B2765 (1938), SRC.

148 Burvett's attitude was not unusual, for the files of the Victorian Chief Secretary's papers are filled with complaints about various supposed obscene publications, photographs, and other ephemera that were investigated by the Melbourne police but for which no action was taken, such as the complaint in 1903 regarding mutoscope films with titillating titles such as 'How Bridget Served the Salad Undressed' or 'A Midnight Romp', or protests in 1928 over the sale of ceramic 'novelty dogs' that were capable of mimicking the act of defecation. 3922, 1286, AAM; and 4/6634, B2805–B459, SRC.

149 Between 1890 and 1920, not only did all states pass laws to regulate the sale and circulation of such matter (which Victoria and Tasmania added to in 1935 with the passage of Police Offences (Contraceptives) Acts), but the police were extremely dogged in pursuing complaints pertaining to it (generally under pressure from religious and social purity groups). See, for example, 4/6633, B2606–B5226, SRC; and 4/6633, B2423–B2765, SRC.

and untrampled by the foetid conventions of an evil minded old world, and the Ministry of which I have the honour to be a member is determined to keep Australia white in every sense of the word.

This entails ensuring that the country's populace remains 'free, pure, and unsullied'. Rabelais then enquires what is to prevent him from staying in Australia and printing copies of his works there, to which the minister replies that the dictation test will do so, and asks him if he can speak Esperanto. Rabelais cannot and fears that he would fail the test were it to be administered in such a language, to which the minister replies: 'That's the idea ... We pick a language that we know you *will* fail in.' Rabelais thereupon decides to abandon both Australia and his literary endeavours and to head for Hollywood, which he thinks will be pleasing to the minister since celluloid 'burns much better' than paper.[150]

The goal of such a system of what we might term cultural quarantine was undoubtedly to produce what John F. Williams has termed a 'quarantined culture', which aimed to protect Australia from 'alien influences', including an imperial metropole that, critics feared, had begun to demonstrate such 'hedonism' that it generated anxieties 'about the future of the race'.[151] While such a system came to fruition, as he argues, in the 1920s, when 'the desirability of isolation and the need to protect the emerging new race from potentially corrupting encounters was fairly ingrained into a culture whose "beau ideal" had been the solitary bushman', it in fact existed from the very founding of the Commonwealth and much of the groundwork for it was laid well before.[152] Nor was such a system designed purely to protect 'high' culture, as he argues. The range of materials that customs sought to keep out of Australia reveals, instead, not only that popular culture was more at stake, but those elements of culture that undermined the self-regulatory abilities of Australian bodies. As Williams rightly notes, the ultimate aim of the system was therefore to protect Australians 'from themselves'.[153]

Obscenity and the body

Common to virtually all of the acts, prosecutions, seizures and debates on obscenity in Australia has been a focus on constituting the body,

[150] A425/1, 36/10165, AAC. It is worth noting that the Customs Minister in 1936 was actually named White, a factor that the satire was clearly playing upon.
[151] Williams, *The Quarantined Culture*, p. 7; and *Telegraph*, 29 November 1913, n.p., cited in Williams, *The Quarantined Culture*, p. 49.
[152] Williams, *The Quarantined Culture*, p. 245.
[153] Williams, *The Quarantined Culture*, p. 7.

particularly the female body, as obscene.[154] As Lynda Nead has revealed, in modern Western aesthetics the nude female body is a key marker of the border between art and obscenity. When rendered as high art the female nude serves as a metaphor for the value and significance of art since 'It symbolizes the transformation of the base matter of nature into the elevated forms of culture and spirit.'[155] In thus containing the 'marginal stuff' of the female body, the aesthetically framed female nude also works to control female sexuality – and, by extension, that of the viewers of such images.[156] Representations of the nude that sexualized the female body – that, in other words, showed 'little sense of propriety', in the words of Sergeant Third Class George Fleming of Sydney, or that revelled in 'suggestiveness' – served not only to undermine such control, but to incite the viewers of such images to 'commit acts of lewdness'.[157] But whether or not an individual would be incited to commit such acts also depended on the location or form in which such images were displayed, as well as on the nature of the viewer. As one Australian judge commented in 1930 in regard to an issue of *Art in Australia*, it was no defence to claim that the nude photographs depicted in the magazine were simply reproductions of the works of great masters, since 'it would depend on circumstances whether such reproductions of naked women were obscene or not'. While they would not be considered obscene if displayed in museums and 'looked at merely as beautiful works of art', it would be 'monstrous to say that a collection of 500 photographs of naked women in all imaginable attitudes, offered for sale as these were, and some of them actually exhibited in the window of a shop in a public thoroughfare within 100 yards of King Edward's School, where 500 boys were educated, was not obscene and indecent'.[158]

The same held true for the body itself. While in Australia, as in Britain, representations of the body were not regarded as inherently obscene, even when unclothed, where Australia differed from its metropole was in the extent to which it strove to construct the body *itself* as obscene – at least when displayed in public. William Chidley was certainly not alone in finding himself hauled before a police court in

[154] That the female body was a particular source of concern is clear in the *General Orders* for customs officers, which proscribed 'the importation of photographs of females' figures in the nude when photographed from living models' but made no reference to images of male bodies. *General Orders for Officers*, p. 204.

[155] Nead, *The Female Nude*, p. 2. It was only the face, however, that served to reflect a woman's true beauty, since it served as a window to her moral state. Grewal, *Home and Harem*, p. 31.

[156] Douglas, *Purity and Danger*, p. 121.

[157] 4/663, B2423–B2765, SRC.

[158] Coleman, *Obscenity, Blasphemy, Sedition*, p. 40.

1912 for appearing in public in nothing but a neck-to-knee bathing costume, for at the time of his conviction it was illegal to wear such a costume even on Victoria's sunny beaches after ten in the morning, and on Sundays at any time of the day or night. Australia's proscription of the display of the body almost seems to amount to torture when we consider its scorching climate and splendid beaches stretching out along an 8,000-mile coastline. Since such proscriptions began during the convict period, with the passage in New South Wales of an 1833 Act prohibiting bathing in Sydney Cove or Darling Harbour between the hours of 6 am and 8 pm, they were perhaps intended to. Although most of the prohibitions in regard to bathing were removed by the end of the First World War, and over the next two decades the beach came to replace the bush as the archetypal site of Australian culture (with the bronzed lifesaver the new national icon), prohibitions against the display of the body – particularly the female body – continued to exist.[159]

Not only was the body thus constituted as obscene in Australia, so too were its natural functions, in particular articulations or representations of, or even mere allusions to, acts such as urination, defecation or menstruation. It was a belief in the inherent obscenity of the representation of such acts that led the customs to prohibit the importation in 1929 of pottery figurines from Germany that issued pellets 'in imitation of excreta', and that spurred the Victorian Commissioner of Police to launch a prosecution in 1916 against a 'grossly offensive' postcard that depicted a man and a woman entering adjacent toilet cubicles and that carried the apparently lewd phrase 'Two minds with but a single thought'.[160] Depicting the functions of diseased bodies was deemed as dangerous as those of healthy ones if not more so. In 1924, for example, the Postmaster-General attempted to prohibit transmission through the post, on the grounds of its alleged obscenity, of a pamphlet offering a cure for kidney complaints – because, he believed, it was 'offensive to the moral sense of a large number of people'.[161] Literature pertaining to sexual diseases, impotence or the category generally defined vaguely as 'female complaints' was even more problematic. Beginning with the Victorian Crimes Act of 1891, which prohibited 'Advertisements relating to sexual diseases or intercourse', Australia passed a multitude of Acts that constituted any references to sexually diseased bodies as

[159] Denoon and Mein-Smith, *A History of Australia*, p. 433. For a fuller examination of the prohibitions against sea bathing see Dunstan, *Wowsers*, ch. 6.

[160] Memo, Ernest Hall, 30 April 1929, A51/1206, SP906/1, AAS; and Memo, Commissioner of Police to Chief Secretary, 4 October 1916, VPRS 3992, Unit 773, U10586, PROV.

[161] MP341/1/0, 1934/8205, Box 161, AAM.

obscene. Under these Acts any printed matter relating to impotence (often more delicately referred to as 'nervous debility'), to 'any complaint or infirmity arising from or relating to sexual intercourse', or references to any 'disease affecting the generative organs or functions' or to 'female irregularities' were decreed obscene.[162] Not only were representations of sexually diseased bodies both male and female thus obscene under the law, but references to even the healthy sexual functions of the female body (such as menstruation or pregnancy) were specifically constituted as obscene under such Acts, such as advertisements pertaining to female sexual hygiene (even for products such as Lysol) or to menstrual pain.[163] Any allusions to the 'normal' sexual functions of the female body were therefore constituted as abnormal and clearly dangerous.[164]

So too were efforts to restrict the 'normal' functions of the reproductive body. As Rosemary Pringle argues, in Australia 'The moral order was seen as the basis of all order, and birth control as a form of "moral pollution"'.[165] Whether literature pertaining to contraceptives and to contraceptive products themselves could be classified as obscene provoked heated debate in Australia from the 1880s onwards, although several early and prominent judgments against the censorship of either birth control literature or products did hold out the hope that such items would be allowed to be as freely circulated in Australia as they were in Britain following the failed prosecution against Charles Bradlaugh and Annie Besant in 1877 for re-publishing Henry Knowleton's 1832 tract

[162] See, for example, the Victorian Crimes Act of 1900; the Post and Telegraph Act of 1901; the Western Australian Obscene Publications Act of 1902; the New South Wales Venereal Diseases Act of 1918; the Tasmanian Obscene Publications Act of 1917; and Customs Minister Abbott's letter to the book trade in 1935 which outlined the types of advertisements to which the Customs Department objected, A425/122, 1939/5151, AAC. For an examination of some of the most noteworthy cases pertaining to the publication, dissemination or reception of printed matter relating to sexually diseased bodies, see *ex parte* Rummans, *The New South Wales Weekly Notes*, 18 July 1901, pp. 118–20; *ex parte* Hawe, *State Reports, Queensland*, pp. 21–7; and *Kiernan* v. *Lipman*, *Victorian Law Reports* (1920), pp. 81–7.

[163] It was none other than former Victorian Chief Secretary Alfred Deakin, in his guise as Commonwealth Attorney-General, who in 1902 established Commonwealth policy relating to the sexual functions of the female body with his legal advice that 'advertisements relating to the treatment of ailments peculiar to females are indecent or obscene'. Memo, Chief Inspector Harry, Postal Service, 8 October 1934, MP 341/1/0, 1934/8205, Box 161, SRC.

[164] In 1919, for example, *Damaged Goods*, a didactic film on the dangers of syphilis, was prohibited from public display in Melbourne because of a scene in which the female lead is shown 'lying on a bed preparing for accouchement' in a position which, in addition to her 'pronounced condition', made the scene both 'painful and disgusting'. 4/6633, B4493–B3002, SRC. See also *Kiernan* v. *Lipman*.

[165] Pringle, 'Octavius Beale', p. 20.

The Fruits of Philosophy.[166] The most important judgment was undoubtedly that given by New South Wales Supreme Court Justice Windeyer in the Collins case of 1888, which ironically concerned Annie Besant's updated version of *The Fruits of Philosophy* published following her trial, *The Law of Population: Its Consequences and Bearing upon Human Conduct and Morals*.[167] Windeyer granted Collins's appeal that he had not been selling an obscene publication by arguing that neither the 'suggestion that families should be limited by the prevention of conception' nor the discussion of either the sexual functions of the female body or of intercourse 'is an idea in itself obscene' (although he acknowledged that, depending on the circumstances under which language is published, they could be).[168] But while the verdict came to be seen as 'a moral triumph for freethought' in Australia, it was a triumph that was extremely short-lived.[169] Far from leading to the open dissemination of literature pertaining to birth control, as numerous critics have claimed, the judgment was generally ignored by later lawmakers, jurists and bureaucrats.[170] As a member of the Victorian Legislative Assembly declared a year following the judgment, even if a court found that a work such as *The Law of Population* was not obscene, 'That of course makes it none the less obscene'.[171] The Windeyer judgment was, in fact, disregarded no less than two years after it was made, by the Victorian Customs Act of 1890, which provided not only for the prohibition of

[166] In 1885, for example, Thomas Walker, president of the New South Wales Branch of the Australian Secular Association, was discharged on appeal by the New South Wales Supreme Court for displaying 'obscene' diagrams during a lecture on birth control. *Bremner* v. *Walker*, *New South Wales Law Reports*, VI (1885), p. 284.

[167] William Whitehouse Collins, like Walker a prominent freethinker (he edited both the Melbourne *Liberator* and the Sydney *Freethinker and New South Wales Reformer*), was convicted by a Sydney police magistrate in May 1888 for selling Bradlaugh and Besant's pamphlet. Foster, 'The Collins Prosecution', 78.

[168] Windeyer, *ex parte Collins*, p. 8. For Windeyer, since the pamphlet was published 'in the interests of truth' to provide important medical information, then it could not be 'prejudicial to general morality and decency'. The most radical aspect of Windeyer's judgment, however, was his contention – which challenged the explicitly class-based nature of obscenity regulation since *R.* v. *Hicklin* – that 'Information cannot be pure, chaste, and legal in morocco at a guinea, but impure, obscene, and indictable in a paper pamphlet at sixpence'. Windeyer, *ex parte Collins*, pp. 15, 11.

[169] Coleman, *Obscenity*, p. 71.

[170] Coleman, *Obscenity*, p. 76; and Foster, 'The Collins Prosecution', 79. This was easy to do because it diverged so significantly from the Hicklin judgment. Even the very court that had passed such a stunning judgment essentially reversed it fourteen years later (in *Potter* v. *Smith*), while courts were often forced to acquit based merely on technicalities rather than out of support for Windeyer's verdict. *The New South Wales Weekly Notes*, 19 (5 June 1902), p. 103. See also *Cuming* v. *Pinnock and Another*, *The Queensland Law Journal* 5 (1892–3), pp. 30–1; and *Porter* v. *Taylor and Another*, *The Argus Law Reports*, XII (1906), pp. 614–16.

[171] *New South Wales Parliamentary Debates*, 12 July 1889, p. 3045.

obscene publications but for the proscription of 'other blasphemous indecent or obscene articles', which gave the Victorian customs the power to prevent the importation of both literature pertaining to birth control and birth control products themselves. The Victorian customs was no more averse to using its powers to restrict access to contraceptive literature or products than was the Commonwealth Customs Department when it was given the same powers a decade later. By 1904 it had, in fact, become such common practice for the Commonwealth customs to seize contraceptive materials that when the New South Wales Royal Commission on the Decline of the Birth-Rate published its report in that year, recommending that the importation, sale and distribution of contraceptives and advertisements pertaining to them be prohibited, the customs met with no opposition when it legitimated its own policies by immediately issuing a proclamation prohibiting the importation of such 'obscene' items.

The Customs Department went to great lengths to keep contraceptives and literature pertaining to them out of Australia (in spite of the fact that the manufacture of contraceptive items such as condoms was never illegal in Australia).[172] Items that were clearly intended for contraceptive purposes, such as condoms, were automatically excluded.[173] Other products that might have contraceptive properties were subjected to intensive scrutiny, with everything from their labels to accompanying explanatory leaflets or advertisements examined for any language that could be constituted as 'obscene'. Although initial shipments of 'borderline' products were generally admitted, importers were notified that should they wish to import such products in future all offending language must be removed from their accompanying literature. Thus an importer of Dr Raspail's Female Pills of Apiol and Steel was notified in 1909 that the department objected to the leaflet that accompanied the

[172] While this discrepancy may seem bizarre, customs were able to prevent items such as condoms from entering the Commonwealth simply by declaring them 'obscene items' under the Customs Act; for the states to prohibit their manufacture or sale would have necessitated the passage (and public discussion) of legislation to that effect. In 1958 customs claimed that imported contraceptives had been prohibited to prevent the 'dire results to public health' that would ensue should 'any disease . . . be introduced with the articles if they were not manufactured and distributed under sanitary conditions', although such a health rationale was not given when contraceptives were first officially declared prohibited imports in 1904. B13/13, Box 3, AAM.

[173] Customs were by no means alone, however, in declaring contraceptive products and literature obscene. Both Western Australia and Tasmania followed suit with similar clauses in their Obscene Publications Acts in 1902 and 1917, respectively, while Victoria's Police Offences (Contraceptives) Act of 1935 prohibited the advertisement, display and unsolicited distribution of contraceptives and contraceptive literature. MP 341/1/0, 1935/8405, Box 161, AAM.

product since it referred to the pills as a 'preventive' that had a great effect in 'bringing about all that can be desired' in the case of 'female irregularities and complaints'.[174] Not only did the department tell importers which words needed to be excised, it even offered alternative re-writes, and in the case of Dr Raspail's Female Pills suggested that the words 'defective menstruation' or 'restoring the flow if due to anaemia or want of tone' might be substituted for the passages that it objected to.[175] Such re-writes were often, to say the least, highly creative, and in addition to obscuring the purpose of a product they often endowed it with an entirely different set of curative properties than the ones claimed by the manufacturers. In the case of Toyle's Pennyroyal and Steel Pills, for example, the department recommended that in the leaflets accompanying the product the words 'Eruptions', 'Depression of Spirits', 'Langour', 'Lassitude', 'Hysteria' and 'kindred complaints' be replaced with the words 'connected with the stoppage of the periods from chill or similar causes'.[176] Were importers or manufacturers unhappy with the department's linguistic choices they were free to submit their own modifications to a state Collector for his approval.[177]

But not only was matter that posed a direct threat to the reproductive capacities of (white) Australian bodies labelled as obscene; so too was matter that did so more indirectly by depicting marriage or the role and status of women in a derogatory light or by undermining their reproductive responsibilities. H. N. Wollaston, in his new guise as chief film censor, warned film importers in 1917 that he would be on the look-out for 'any scene [which treated lightly] those laws or rules which govern the relations of the sexes, in married and single life' – concerns that motivated regulatory policies ranging from efforts to pass an Obscene Evidence Publications Bill in New South Wales in 1889 to the issuing of a Customs Department General Order in 1914 that defined indecency as 'what is usually considered objectionable in the house-hold of the ordinary self-respecting citizen' and another in 1938 that sought to prohibit from entry into Australia any literature that 'unduly emphasizes

[174] Such terms generally referred to abortion.

[175] T and C 09/15568, 24 November 1909, A6280/1, Box 2, AAC.

[176] T and C 09/16201, 7 December 1909, A6280/1, Box 2, AAC.

[177] The attempt to prohibit the use of particular words in Australia was by no means restricted to contraceptive products. Words such as 'Aussie', 'Returned Sailor', and 'Repatriation' were prohibited by the government during the First World War, with the word 'Anzac' remaining prohibited over a decade later. The Australian flying ace Kingsford Smith thus had to suffer the indignity in 1932 of having his airplane impounded by the Australian Customs Service because the word 'Anzac' was painted on the fuselage. Order 93, *Commonwealth of Australia Gazette*, 28 October, 1920; SP331, Book 8, AAS; and SP906/1, Box 74, A52/7800, AAS.

matters of sex or crime' or 'that is calculated to encourage depravity'.[178] Although the latter general order, number 14(a), was issued as a means of dealing primarily with American detective fiction, under it works such as *Modern Girl Book,* which according to customs clerk T. A. Fisher gave young girls 'an altogether erroneous conception of the qualities on which mutual attraction rests' (because the theme of its stories was 'the purely physical attraction between members of the opposite sexes'), were also prohibited.[179] An example of the potential dangers of such 'erroneous conceptions' was offered by *Beckett's Budget,* with its stock in trade of salacious stories culled from court proceedings. For the *Budget,* what was newsworthy about court cases such as that concerning fifteen-year-old Ethel Jager, who in 1927 accused her family's middle-aged lodger of raping her, was not that the girl was raped, but that she dared to bring such a case to court and that she told her story, moreover, 'without any outward suspicion of embarrassment or diffidence, and showed that she was quite au fait with phrases, expressions, and terms not generally included in the accepted vocabulary of a dainty miss of 15'. Ethel Jager's knowledge, whether or not it was obtained against her will, thus reeked of a 'juvenile and adolescent immorality' that revealed 'the extent to which general unwholesomeness exists' in Australia 'hidden, as it is, by a veneer of "respectability" and hypocrisy'.[180] But while the *Budget* may have prided itself on alerting readers to the existence of such immorality, for the paper's critics, in doing so the *Budget* served to foster its spread, and thus had to be stopped by any means possible.[181]

[178] In Bertrand, *Film Censorship in Australia,* cited in Bashford, *Imperial Hygiene,* p. 148; and *General Orders*, p. 204. A later Chief Censor, Crewswell O'Reilly, was so troubled by films that depicted marriage or women's virtue in a negative light that he often re-wrote entire scenes to ensure that such matters were depicted more positively. See his response to the film *The First Born,* A425/1, 37/9526, AAC. Such concerns also drove the customs prohibition of works such as James Joyce's *Dubliners* and Basil Tozer's *The Story of a Terrible Life*. For the indefatigable Edward Brossois, the problem with the latter was its lengthy musings 'in defence of sexual gratification of unmarried females' and the conviction of its main character, a 'procuress', that girls were beginning to shy away from marriage since 'they find they can without difficulty obtain much that marriage offers, so why marry and lose their liberty and encumber themselves?' A425/127, 1943/4766, AAC. Brossois was even more condemnatory of works that dealt with miscegenation, particularly those that dared to depict liaisons between white women and non-European men. See A425/127, 1943/5104, AAC.

[179] A425/122, 1939/715, AAC. For Assistant Comptroller-General of Customs H. F. Morris, while *Modern Girl Book* 'may not be obscene or indecent' it could nonetheless 'reasonably be classified as literature calculated to encourage depravity'.

[180] 'Ethel Jager Admits Previous Immorality and Now Accuses Man of Fifty', clipping in 4/6634, B2606–B5226, SRC.

[181] The various machinations to put a stop to the *Budget* – between the New South Wales government (which passed an amendment to the state's Obscene Publications Act to prevent the paper's circulation), the police (who secured a conviction against it for

By the Second World War the obscene had come to be defined in Australia in ways that differed drastically from Britain, from which it had derived both its early censorship legislation and its aesthetic tradition. Not only was contraceptive advertising never illegal in Britain (let alone the sale of contraceptive products), but salacious journals in the vein of *Becket's Budget* had been freely circulating there since the mid-nineteenth century, with little apparent sign of turning young British women into social deviants. Although the desire to control bodies (to prevent them from committing 'immoral' or 'undesirable' acts) is at the root of all projects to regulate the obscene, Australian regulators desired not only to *inhibit* the behaviour of Australian bodies but to actually *promote* a mode of sexual behaviour that was deemed beneficial to the nation – namely to increase the birth-rate among white married couples. This meant that the body needed to be de-sexualized and reinscribed as a site, quite literally, of national production. Like the American anti-obscenity crusader Anthony Comstock, who 'understood the world fundamentally in economic terms', Australian officials defined the obscene according to their fears about the dangers of 'waste and dispersal'.[182] Explicit references to the female body, the depiction of women as social deviants and the advertising of contraceptives (and even more so the sale of contraceptives themselves) all served to discourage the specific sexual practices on which the future of Australia was seen to depend: namely the production of large numbers of racially pure, culturally homogeneous children that were, to borrow a phrase from Homi Bhabha, 'almost the same, but not quite' as those produced in Britain.[183]

Settler coloniality, literature and history

In Australia, as in Britain, the late nineteenth century thus witnessed the emergence of a new biopolitical project to protect the strength and purity of 'white' bodies from external contaminants, including obscene publications. But Australia, unlike Britain, was a white settler society whose concerns about hygiene were, as we have seen, considerably greater than those of its imperial metropole. This particular hygienic project therefore differed from the one undertaken in Britain in two key ways. The first was that, as Brian Lloyd and George Gilbert observed in the 1930s in the first sustained polemic against Australia's system for the regulation

publishing an obscene article) and the Post Office (which prohibited it from being sent through the post) – succeeded in driving it out of business. 4/6634, B2606–B5225, SRC.

182 Kendrick, *The Secret Museum*, p. 143.

183 Bhabha, 'Of Mimicry and Man', p. 153.

of print culture, 'the Australian public [was regarded as being] more susceptible to pollution than the British'.[184] Australia had a tremendous fear, they argued, of 'dirt, real or imaginary' (including, since it is 'dirt in the wrong place', of obscenity).[185] It thus had, as another observer remarked several decades later, a 'phobia about protection', and hence the 'sexual obsession in censorship' was simply 'part of a larger pattern of protectionism, in which we Australians have, since Federation, attempted to hide ourselves away in a pure, all-white paradise'.[186]

The second difference between this particular biopolitical project in Australia versus Britain was the means through which it was carried out. Unlike in Britain, where the hygienic drive to regulate the obscene first emerged through social purity and hygiene organizations, in Australia it both originated as and largely remained a state project. This is not to say that the colonial and later Commonwealth governments carried out such a project without the support of civil society – far from it. They received both support and pressure from religious groups (such as the eighty religious organizations that in 1894 sent a joint deputation to the Victorian Customs Minister to protest against the importation of penny dreadfuls),[187] medical organizations (such as the various medical associations that participated in a deputation, along with the Council of Churches and the White Cross League, to the Victorian Minister of Education in 1909 to complain that 'the Postal Department allowed itself to be used in relation to objectionable purposes'),[188] library associations (such as the Library Association of Australasia, which with the creation of the Customs Department's Second Schedule in 1926 became a virtual arm of the department's system of literary regulation),[189] women's groups (such as the National Council of Women or the Country Women's Association, which engaged in their own campaigns to 'save our people, young and old ... from this contamination' by

[184] Lloyd and Gilbert, *The Censorship*, p. 10.
[185] Lloyd and Gilbert, *The Censorship*, pp. 25–6, 40.
[186] Dutton, 'Moral Protectionism', p. 96.
[187] Coleman, *Obscenity*, p. 145. Organizations such as the Council of Churches continued such pressure after the formation of the Commonwealth. See, for example, A425/122, 1939/5151, AAC.
[188] *Parliamentary Debates: Commonwealth of Australia*, 20 October 1909, p. 4743. The 'objectionable purposes' to which they alluded were the circulation of advertisements for contraceptives through the post, which the Australian medical profession regarded as a blight not only on the 'moral tone of the community' but on the status of the profession. Editorial, 'Alleged Criminal Abortion in the Australasian Colonies', *Australian Medical Gazette*, 20 October 1898, p. 454.
[189] Librarians were given the right not only to import works on the Second Schedule but to determine who had access to them. Pollak, *Sense and Censorship*, p. 16; and Payne, 'Aspects of Commonwealth Literary Censorship', pp. 54–5.

'obscene' publications),[190] purity leagues (such as the Indecent Literature Committee, launched in Melbourne in 1912, and the Council for Civil and Moral Advance, established in Sydney after the First World War, which were concerned, respectively, with the peddling of obscene publications by Afghan hawkers and with cinema advertisements)[191] and hygiene associations (such as the Health Society and the Council of the Federation of Health, which in 1919 participated in a deputation to the New South Wales Chief Secretary's Department for the regulation of cinema advertisements).[192] But the state not only dominated the campaign to regulate obscenity in Australia – particularly of imported publications – it also managed to co-opt such groups into its regulatory project to a degree unparalleled in Britain.

The Australian book trade offers the most phenomenal example of such co-option. Australian booksellers had always, as the bookseller C. T. Clark claimed in 1899, 'had a tendency to keep the public in the straight path' (which meant that they often 'lost heavily through purchases of volumes that people should have read, but would not'), a tendency that encouraged the Customs Department in the 1920s to begin to shift some of the increasingly onerous burden for regulating imported publications to booksellers.[193] Rather than resisting such a burden, Australian booksellers assumed it with relative equanimity – even when, in 1934, the Customs Department sent a letter to all known importers of foreign magazines reminding them about the department's regulation concerning 'the importation of a certain type of cheap publications in which crime is glorified or which are derogatory to national sentiment' and warning them that 'unless action be taken ... either to discontinue the importation, within a reasonable time, of publications bearing objectionable advertisements, or to secure the exclusion from such publications of the objectionable advertisements, this Department will be compelled to take action to prohibit their importation'.[194] The response of the trade was to send a deputation to determine exactly

[190] E. A. V. Sterne, Country Women's Association of Western Australia, to Prime Minister Joseph Lyons, 1 May 1936, A425/122, 1939/5151, AAC.

[191] Coleman, *Obscenity*, pp. 158, 160.

[192] File 4/6633, B4493 (1928) to B3002 (1931), SRC.

[193] 'The Book Trade in New South Wales', *Sydney Morning Herald*, 9 February 1899, clipping in Miscellaneous Papers 1899–1934, Mss. 3315, ML. Booksellers who were deemed trustworthy were given the right to import works from the Second Schedule and to sell them to people with a '*bona-fide*' interest in them.

[194] Memorandum from Abbott to Collectors of Customs, 5 April 1935, A425/122, 1939/5151, AAC. 'Objectionable advertisements' included: 'Medicines for use in the cure of venereal disease or the alleviation of female irregularities or for influencing the course of pregnancy'; 'Medicines for the correction of sexual impotence'; 'Sex publications the importation of which, taking the advertisements as a guide to the nature of the

what advertisements the department objected to and how the trade could put a stop to them.[195]

Members of the trade were willing to comply with the department's unorthodox request in part because they feared for their livelihoods (in Australia booksellers had to pursue their business, according to Lloyd and Gilbert, with 'the trepidation of a sly-grog shop proprietor'), but this was by no means the only reason.[196] Some members supported it because they believed that crime and detective magazines did 'not make desirable reading for the citizens, particularly the younger generation, of this country', while others were so concerned about the debilitating effects of 'obscene' advertisements in foreign magazines (generally advertisements for contraceptives, abortifacients and aphrodisiacs) that they had already taken the initiative to have shipments expurgated before they were sent to Australia.[197] Though not all members of the trade held such opinions, those who did not were forced to comply with them through peer pressure. Compliance necessitated blacking out all offending advertisements from imported publications, which was not only an incredibly exhausting and time-consuming task but, since what constituted an 'objectionable' advertisement was open to doubt, a challenging one as well. Thus the bookseller A. C. Butfield, who when a new shipment of magazines arrived had to work, along with his staff, 'until as late as 3 am in order to tear out or black out advertisements such as are objected to by the department', found himself under investigation (after being informed on by his colleagues) for failing to black out all aberrant advertisements from his magazines. The problem, as the embarrassed Investigations Officer Charles Brossois discovered, was that Butfield was ignorant as to the uses of items such as 'Liquid Latex' or of 'novelties' such as 'Tillie and Ma' and 'Papa and Mama'.[198] Butfield's method of obliterating advertisements also left them partly visible, the solution to which, as proposed by New South Wales Collector G. F. A. Mitchell, was to employ a stamp with a 'rosette pattern', which he maintained not only effectively eradicated the offending advertisements but had 'a dazzling

works, would be prohibited as indecent'; 'Novelties described as risqué, pictures in intimate poses and rare photos in the nude which apparently would be prohibited as indecent, if imported'; and 'Drink and tobacco habit cures which, if imported, would be prohibited'. Acting Customs Minister Abbott to magazine importers, 22 July 1935, A425/122, 1939/5151, AAC.

195 Minutes of meeting between Sydney booksellers and the Assistant Minister of Trade and Customs, 23 June 1934, A425/122, 1939/5151, AAC.

196 Lloyd and Gilbert, *The Censorship and Public Morality*, p. 52.

197 George Batchelor Pty Ltd to Abbott, 27 July 1935; and Barwick and Minter to Abbott, 26 July 1935, A425/122, 1939/5151, AAC.

198 Brossois to Abbott, 21 November 1935, A425/122, 1939/5151, AAC.

effect on the eyes'.[199] By late 1935, all members of the trade had apparently adopted such stamps and were obliterating what Sydney bookseller Samuel Wood estimated to be half a million advertisements each month from imported magazines in an effort to defend Australia against foreign immorality.[200]

In light of such widespread support for the government's system for the regulation of print culture it should perhaps come as little surprise that it was not until 1934 that an organization, the Book Censorship Abolition League, was formed to challenge it.[201] The agenda of the League, however, was limited to the rather astounding demand – one that acknowledged the extent of Australia's cultural colonization by Britain – that the government 'admit into Australia those books on economic and political subjects which freely circulate in Britain'.[202] As its president Macmahon Ball argued at a debate on literary regulation at Melbourne Town Hall in 1935, the League did not, therefore, 'stand for the abolition of all restrictions on printed matter'. They in fact maintained that not only did 'the Government [have] the right to ban books which incite violence in Australia', but they were strongly opposed to the entry into the Commonwealth of works of an 'immoral' nature.[203]

[199] Mitchell to Abbott, n.d.; and Abbott to Butfield, 17 December 1935, A425/122, 1939/5151, AAC.

[200] Such a large number of advertisements meant that the task of obliterating them made importing magazines no longer economically viable for the trade, which, in addition to leading to the collapse of such an outlandish regulatory system, led the customs to issue a new proclamation in 1938 against the importation of any publication that was in any way 'derogatory to national sentiment'.

[201] It was the increasing proscription of so-called 'seditious' works after the First World War – through such means as government proclamations, Crimes Acts and customs regulations, all of which were designed to combat communism, anarchism, and later fascism, but by the early 1930s were being used to prohibit a wide range of material deemed injurious to the nation – that generated a growing public awareness of, and opposition to, the nature of the Commonwealth's system of literary regulation.

[202] 'Report of proceedings of deputation to the Hon. T. W. White'. While such a demand left a member of the government asking incredulously, 'But is not one of our principles the right of self-government?', Ball strove to substantiate it by arguing that 'Great Britain has a longer cultural tradition', and hence 'British statesmen have shown much more imagination and wisdom than others in dealing with political writings which may be unpalatable to the Government in power'. The League circulated a petition with this plea in 1935 and obtained half a million signatures. Such a request had widespread backing – the deputation included representatives from the Australian Natives Association, the Australian Journalists Association, the Trades Hall Council, the Young Nationalists, the Douglas Credit Movement, the Australian Tramways Union, the Rationalist Association and the Australian and Unitarian Churches. 'Book Bans from John Cleland'.

[203] Report of 'The Star' Public Debate'. See also 'Report of Proceedings of Deputation to the Hon. T.W. White'; Mss. 10061, SLV; and Holt, 'Censorship, Citizenship and Democracy'.

As the *Central Queensland Herald* insightfully observed some months following the debate, opposition to Australia's system of literary regulation was largely a failure because 'the bulk of its critics have been content to accept the necessity of the principle'.[204]

This is not to say that there was not more widescale opposition to the state project to regulate the obscene in Australia. But while opponents of the system railed against it, at least when it impinged on their own reading habits (as A. G. Stephens of *Bulletin* fame demanded to know in 1901, when a copy of Pierre Louys's *Les Aventures du Roi Pausole* was detained by customs, 'why should I, as a student of French literature, be limited in my range by any censorship whatever?'), they invariably supported it when it came to the reading habits of others, particularly those with less cultural capital – and hence presumably less ability to regulate themselves (it was thus fitting, according to Stephens, that 'cheap English translations of the grosser French authors' should not be 'exposed for public sale').[205] Even in the case of Lloyd and Gilbert, who acknowledged that Australia's system for the regulation of print culture as it had developed by 1930 was designed to control particular segments of the population, and who were opposed to the state regulation of the reading matter of children (which they felt should be left up to parents) and adolescents (since this would simply lead to greater 'auto-erotic abuse'), they not only supported the regulation of the reading matter of 'the ignorant', 'yokels', women and 'the vicious', but felt that the states should be given greater powers to control indigenous print culture in order to deal with the 'mephitic miasma' of the press coverage of divorce court cases, the 'persistent sickly eroticism of cinema films' and 'the unrestricted obscenity suggested by the ... advertisements in the press of "books of nature", contraceptive literature, and the like, these being obviously designed to allure the adolescent and the prurient'.[206] What Lloyd and Gilbert were ultimately calling for, therefore, was not the destruction of the system, but that it should incorporate governmental forms of power – of, in other words, practices of the self and of expert agencies – in order to more effectively control white Australian bodies.

What is notable about both the support for and opposition to the system for the regulation of print culture in Australia is the tremendous and unquestioned power accorded to the state. As Stephen Castles *et al.*

[204] 'Australian Culture and the Censorship', *Central Queensland Herald*, 10 October 1935, n.p., clipping in Mss. Z/Q991/N, ML.

[205] A. G. Stephens, 'The Customs and a Mangled Book', *The Register*, 12 February 1902, clipping in 4205/1, AAS.

[206] Lloyd and Gilbert, *The Censorship*, pp. 33, 52.

contend, 'Contrary to ideas of the open frontier of individualism, the state played a central role in Australian development.'[207] This is clear both in the case of literary regulation – the enumeration and management of literary crimes such as sedition was, after all, central to both the founding and construction of settler colonial society in Australia – and in the realm of public health, as 'medical and sanitary interventions enabled a new kind of governmentalization of the colonial state in which quantification, distribution and administration of an indigenous or a white "settler" population was both achievable and produced new kinds of subjects for rule'.[208] We have seen how, by the early twentieth century, the conviction had become enshrined that (white) Australians had to be governed and to govern themselves along hygienic lines in order to be accorded the rights of citizens. This does not mean, however, that a clear shift from disciplinary (such as quarantine) to governmental forms of power, or from sovereign power to self-governance, took place in Australia. Such a clear-cut shift did not take place in Britain either, since sovereign power is always, as Stephen Legg asserts, 'concerned with biopolitics'.[209] But the nature of settler coloniality meant that in Australia it remained justifiable, to an extent greater than in Britain, to limit the liberty of the individual for the sake of the health and purity of society at large.[210] Even though no less a figure than A. A. Phillips, cultural critic and coiner of the concept of 'cultural cringe' – and, less well known, a one-time member of the Literature Censorship Board – could try to

[207] Castles *et al.*, 'The Bicentenary', 58.

[208] Bashford, *Imperial Hygiene,* p. 34. Sedition was both enumerated and managed in late eighteenth- and early nineteenth-century Britain through, in part, exiling offenders to Australia (a reminder of the role that, Richard Burt argues, 'dispersal' and 'displacement' play in literary regulation) and silencing them (often literally through the use of torture devices such as the ironwood gag). Since Australia was thus a repository of what had to be excised and silenced from Britain it should come as little surprise that by the 1820s the conviction had become enshrined not only that a free press, in the words of New South Wales Chief Justice Francis Forbes, was 'not suited' to Australia (since 'the direct tendency of the press is . . . to equalize mankind; and the direct policy of our little state is only an enlarged prison discipline') but that 'wherever Englishmen went they carried as much with them "as the nature of things will bear"', and the 'nature of things' in Australia did not bear the extension of such liberties. Burt, 'Un-Censoring in Detail', p. 17; Herman, 'The Origins of a Free Press'; and Pullan, *Guilty Secrets,* p. 38.

[209] Legg, *Spaces of Colonialism,* p. 4. Sovereign power could not but be concerned with biopolitics since it evolved 'around the "terrains of existence" of biopolitics and discipline'. Legg, *Spaces of Colonialism,* p. 6.

[210] Such limitations were arguably imposed, furthermore, from an earlier age. As Grant Rodwell demonstrates in the case of preschooling, 'The notion of quarantine' – of segregating children with 'poor heredity' (as manifested in 'immoral behaviour' such as masturbation) from their peers – 'pervade[d] the early history of the Australian kindergartens'. 'Curing the Precocious Masturbator', 87.

ironically deny that Australia's system of literary regulation was not an example of that cringe (namely that it was not a sign that Australia was 'a provincial and anti-intellectual community tak[ing] refuge from frightening challenges under the umbrella of convention') but rather a product of 'an accident of cultural geography' (namely the fact that most of its publications were imported), he was unable to hide the relief he felt not in 'liberating' the system, as was his original intention, but in being able to 'draw [a] line' demarcating those books that 'could do no good and might do some harm' to Australian society.[211] Phillips thus offers evidence that in liberal systems of rule rights and freedoms are bestowed on those deemed capable of bearing them, and since Australia was a white settler society in which the hygiene of the individual equated to that of the whole it was thus necessary, as Geoffrey Dutton observed in the case of literary regulation, to protect Australians 'mostly from themselves'. All individuals, in other words, had to be assumed to be incapable of self-governance – and to believe that 'there is someone higher up or somewhere else who will decide what is best for you' – in order to ensure the protection of 'white Australia'.[212]

Denying responsibility for individual action and investing it in a source of external authority was about more, however, than a desire to protect 'whiteness'. It was also a product of the desire for historical oblivion, which as Lorenzo Veracini argues is a key trait of settler ideological formations. According to settler ideology, settler societies are places where 'history could and had to be abandoned' – the history, that is, of the 'old world', which is represented as corrupt and degenerate – in order to organize a regenerated body politic.[213] In these new Arcadias the land is envisioned as being unmarked by social relations and inhabited by a settler community disassociated from previous social determinants – as, in other words, 'a people without history in a place without history'.[214] The arrival of the settlers is thus a foundational moment that marks the end of history. But this rhetorical evocation of a lack of history coexists with a competing effort to reclaim history: a tension, Veracini argues, born of efforts both to fashion a 'society that is *other*' (and thus devoid of history) and to create '*another* society', a new Britain or Europe that is connected to the 'old' via history.[215] In Australia 'the expectation was that [it] should have a special history and that this uniqueness was that there would be little of it', but the tension between

211 Phillips, 'Confessions of an Escaped Censor', 508, 509.
212 Dutton, 'Moral Protectionism', p. 97.
213 Veracini, 'Historylessness', 271.
214 Veracini, 'Historylessness', 273.
215 Veracini, 'Historylessness', 275.

fashioning a society that is both *other* and *another* generated a situation in which history was both claimed and denied simultaneously.[216] But since history was not generated in Australia (since the construction of a regenerated body politic would produce a historyless future) it could only be claimed, according to such a narrative, if it was made somewhere else (hence the power of the ANZAC legend). Threats to Australia's historylessness by unwanted manifestations of history were correspondingly perceived to come from elsewhere, namely the 'old world', and hence had to be 'stopped on their way in – on inbound ships, international waters, [and] at the beach'.[217]

'Place' and 'race' became so central to Australian settler identity because they were perceived to be constant and unchanging – and hence were not history. Protecting the geo-body of the nation by keeping it 'white' was, in fact, viewed as a means of preserving Australia's 'classlessness' (and hence historylessness) since it would ensure that a new and inferior 'class' (in both racial and economic terms) did not come into being in Australia.[218] According to Radhika Mohanram, such a 'fantasy of whiteness, not riven by class, gender, sexual and regional dimensions' could be played out only in contexts such as Australia 'because it is only there that the white can function as universally representative'.[219] But place and race were not, as the settler imaginary implied, immutable. In the case of place, rather than being an Arcadian garden Australia was a scorched and arid land – a 'utopia emptied of otherworldliness'.[220] Race was an even more problematic construct, not only because 'whiteness' was threatened by place (by the climate, by contact with non-whites, and so on) but because the 'whiteness' of Australians was undermined by their coloniality. As Marilyn Lake argues, Australians came to place such stock in 'whiteness' – in particular their identity, in the words of the *Sydney Morning Herald,* as 'a clean white British people' – as a means of 'distinguish[ing] themselves from other (coloured) colonized peoples'.[221] White Australia was thus

216 Veracini, 'Historylessness', 277.
217 Veracini, 'Historylessness', 276.
218 The belief that the influx of 'non-white' races would produce class conflict was a staple argument in Australia against their immigration from the 1830s onwards. See Curthoys, 'Liberalism and Exclusionism'.
219 Mohanram, 'White Water', para. 23.
220 Crozier, 'Antipodean Sensibilities', 848, 849.
221 C. W., 'Australia. VII – The Australian Ideal', *Sydney Morning Herald,* 13 July 1907, clipping in Mss. Q331.6/W, ML; and Lake, 'Between Old World "Barbarism"', p. 85. Lake refers to a passage in Francis Adams's *The Melbournians,* in which the character Susie MacGhie, recently returned from London, declares: 'I don't see why Australians shouldn't be proud of being Australians, and not be ashamed of owning it, as they are

'a rejection of the possibility of history'.[222] Such a rejection, however, necessitated 'reworking the distinction between civilized and non-civilized as a distinction between the democratic New World and the non-democratic Old World'.[223] She demonstrates how Australian feminists sought to do this by defining themselves as 'free' in comparison not only to Aboriginal women (who were oppressed by 'primitive barbarism') but to British women (oppressed by 'Old World barbarism') – which as Angela Woollacott has demonstrated also enabled them to conceive of themselves as more modern than British women.[224]

We can see such a process at work in the case of the regulation of the obscene. Drawing upon Freud's concept of 'parapraxis' (more commonly known as the 'Freudian slip', which entails the substitution of a wrong name for a forgotten one), Nicole Moore observantly posits that the excising of 'certain kinds of sex and sexual meaning' from Australian society has been a means of forgetting or repressing 'certain historical experiences and knowledges', although she does not explain the rationale behind this excising drive, or exactly what these repressed experiences and knowledges were.[225] She is perhaps unable to since more than particular experiences or knowledges were at stake here: Australia's system of literary regulation was, in short, a rejection of the very *possibility* of history. The goal of the system was to prevent Australia from being contaminated by the history of the mother country – the mother that, while it had nurtured the 'race', had now become corrupt and degenerate. The 'tyranny of distance', rather than being seen as a hindrance to the development of a 'pure', 'clean' and historyless society, was therefore instead seen as a key means of achieving it. As Christina Stead and

in England. One woman asked me once if I wasn't a Kaw-lonial, just as if you'd asked if you weren't a Haw-tentot or a Esquim-maw. I said no; I was an Aw-stralian' (85). But it was not only the British who viewed Australians in such terms – so too did settlers in other colonies. As one irate member of the Commonwealth Representatives declared in 1909, Anglo-Indians regarded Australia 'as an uncultivated land peopled by semi-barbarians instead of a country in a high state of civilisation'. This fear of being mistaken for 'semi-barbarians' undoubtedly explains some of the antipathy to the working-class sex reformer William Chidley, who found himself frequently before the courts in both New South Wales and Victoria in part for dressing, as the press regarded it, 'like an Indian coolie'. *Parliamentary Debates: Commonwealth of Australia*, 6 December 1909, p. 7076; see also 'Challenged Book: Penalty Imposed', *Herald*, 1 March 1912, n.p.; and 'An Apostle of Joy', *The Bookfellow*, 15 February 1916, n.p., clippings in Mss 143/6, ML.

222 Veracini, 'Historylessness', 278.

223 Lake, 'Between Old World "Barbarism"', 85.

224 Wollacott, 'White Colonialism and Sexual Modernity'.

225 Moore, 'National Parapraxis', 302. While it 'often appears uncontrolled, arbitrary and unprincipled' Australia's system for the regulation of print culture is instead, Moore argues, 'highly calibrated'.

Nettie Palmer observed at the 1935 Congress of Writers for the Defence of Culture in Paris, the Australian government was 'taking advantage of the distance of Australia from Europe' in order to 'ban books which would keep Australia in touch with progressive English and European thought'.[226] The system was thus a 'prophylactic', in the words of the *Daily Mail,* against such forms of 'contagion', and a means, moreover, of obscuring the reality of Australia's own *historical* rather than history-less past.[227] As one irate victim of the system raged at 'this wretched colony' over the seizure of a shipment of imported magazines in 1925, Australians may have been full of 'brag and pride', but it was all a mask, he implied, for 'the arrival of the First Fleet'.[228]

[226] 'Censorship in Australia', *Courier-Mail,* 27 June 1935, clipping in Mss. Z/Q991/N, ML.
[227] *Daily Mail,* 23 January 1933, clipping in A425/1, 37/9526, AAC.
[228] SP 906/1, A51/10990, AAS. As Marilyn Lake argues, 'The imposition of "purity" could be seen as especially important in the Australian colonies, given the possibility of contamination from the convict legacy'. Lake, 'Frontier Feminism', p. 97.

5 Localizing the global in exploitation colonies: regulating the obscene in India

While by the 1880s Australian colonies may have become the largest single market for British books and periodicals, India was a close second. Thanks to initiatives such as the launch of government-sponsored English education in the 1830s and the establishment of hundreds of schools and colleges, by the mid-nineteenth century India had become a growing market that British publishers were eager to cultivate. The nature of the market in India – such as its size and linguistic diversity, the differences in the types of publications that were popular there compared with Britain, and the fact that reprints (largely pirated) of British books could be sold much more cheaply than works imported from London – meant, however, that British publishers faced much stiffer competition there than in Australia.[1] In spite of such obstacles, between 1850 and 1863 book exports from Britain to India (primarily of 'useful' books such as schoolbooks, histories and grammars) more than doubled, which meant that 'a substantial amount of what Indians read, particularly through the 1870s, arrived printed and shipped from Britain'.[2] Although the rapid expansion of the Indian publishing industry meant that book exports to India from Britain peaked in 1864 (at a total value of £313,772), the exemption of British publications from the 3 per cent 'foreign' print tax, coupled with imperial copyright laws – which operated as what L. T. Hergenhan has termed 'a kind of imperialist "protection" policy' – enabled British publishers to retain 95 per cent of the market share of book imports into India.[3]

[1] Additional problems were posed by the linguistic diversity of India and the differences in the types of publications that were popular there.

[2] Joshi, *In Another Country*, p. 39.

[3] Joshi, *In Another Country*, pp. 18, 39; and Hergenhan, 'English Publication', p. 76. Until the passage of the International Copyright Act in 1886 books published in Britain retained their copyright throughout the empire but those published in British colonies did not. However, since the law served to strangle nascent publishing industries in British colonies the British book and periodical trades were able to maintain their imperial dominance even after the passage of the Act. For debates on copyright in India see, for

That India was one of the most lucrative markets for British publishers is evident in the import figures for books and other printed matter. By 1887 half as many book packets were imported into India from Britain as were sent within India, and a reduction in parcel rates between the two in 1889 served to raise the volume of imports even higher.[4] Within less than a decade book and newspaper imports from Britain had reached such immense proportions that the Postmaster-General of India noted with some awe in his annual report for 1894–5 that 'The great bulk of the mail from the United Kingdom consists of newspapers and packets of which more than five millions are now received in the year, filling some five hundred mail bags every week'.[5] Imports doubled again within the next decade, and by 1911 India was importing over twelve million packages of books and newspapers a year from Britain, a peak that they were not to scale again for several decades.[6]

The Vizetelly affair in India

Until the 1880s the Indian government was, however, largely oblivious as to the scope of the trade in imported publications in India, since it was convinced that 'India is not a reading country'. Colonial officials therefore remained confident that 'There [were] not ten tradesmen altogether, European and Native, who import[ed] books', and of those who did they '[got] them in small quantities' from England.[7] By the end of the decade such complacency had, however, been shattered. The culprit, once again, was Vizetelly's Zola translations. Shortly before Vizetelly's first trial in July 1888, the former Viceroy Lord Northbrook informed the Secretary to the Government of India, A. P. MacDonnell, that 'I have lately received some rather painful communications from India as to the very filthy works – translations from the very worst of French novels by M. Zola – which, it is alleged, are sold along with other pernicious trash at the Railway stations in India'. Northbrook asked

example, 49/August 1877, 184–204/May 1877, and 317–28/June 1886, Judicial, A, Home Department, NAI; 27–32/February 1888, 37–9/January 1902, and 138–9/January 1903, Books and Publications, A, Home Department, NAI; 59/July 1910, Books, Deposit, Home Department, NAI; and 119/November 1913, B, Commerce and Industry, NAI.

4 207–10/February 1887, Separate Revenue (Post Office, General), A, Finance and Commerce Department, NAI.

5 81–3/January 1895, Separate Revenue (Post Office, General), A, Finance and Commerce Department, NAI.

6 6–10/October 1911, Post Office, A, Department of Commerce and Industry, NAI. See also the reports for 1925–6, 1929–30 and 1934–5.

7 317–18/June 1886, Judicial, A, Home Department, NAI.

MacDonnell to investigate the matter and, if necessary, take action under the Indian Penal Code. Northbrook's concern was not with the dangers such 'pernicious trash' posed to European readers but, since 'one of the most important matters of all is to prevent if possible such food as this being administered to young natives', to the growing numbers of English-educated Indians.[8]

Northbrook's request was by no means the first time that the attention of the Indian government had been drawn to the sale of 'obscene' books circulating in India, including the works of Zola. Government officials were in fact besieged with a host of appeals in the late 1880s from educators, newspaper editors and affronted railway passengers that the government take action against translations of French novels and other works of questionable morality circulating in India. The problem with such works, as the Rector of St Xavier's College, A. Neut, declared, was that 'Most of the modern French writers in the light literature are harmful, and tend to destroy, if not always, the moral sense, at least the not less important sense of respect of authority' (to him 'the strength of the English nation'), and in India this 'strength' was being undermined by the fact that not only were Indian schoolboys reading such texts in English, but also in vernacular translations. For Neut such 'bad reading' thus constituted 'the greatest danger for the morality of the boys'.[9]

Neut's concerns were expressed in response to a government inquiry regarding the necessity of introducing 'moral education' into Indian schools and colleges. The inquiry, spear-headed by MacDonnell, was a product of the perceived moral crisis that English education had precipitated among Indian youth. 'So far from having that refining influence on students which might have been expected', English education, MacDonnell noted with some alarm, had 'cut loose the rising generation from many of the moral and social bonds of their forefathers' and in the process 'rendered them less submissive to their teachers, less respectful to their parents, and less courteous to all persons with whom they come into contact'. While MacDonnell remained convinced that 'Western education if persevered in must in time bring with it Western principles of discipline and self-control' (since 'A moral vacuum is as impossible as a physical vacuum'), others were less sanguine.[10] For W. Lee-Warner, Esq., Secretary to the Government of Bombay,

[8] C. U. Aitchison to A. P MacDonnell, 17 July 1888, 384/July 1888, Public, Deposit, Home Department, NAI.

[9] A. Neut to A. Croft, 19 December 1887, 14–17/October 1887, Education, A, Home Department, NAI.

[10] Note by A. P. MacDonnell, 12 August 1886, 36–9/January 1888, Education, A, Home Department, NAI.

> The best efforts in the schoolroom to impress character are seriously endangered by the wreckage caused by literature, and by the supply of books which the Professor cannot control. The Indian school life based almost entirely on the day system offers, to a much less degree than the English school, resistance against external influences that surround the rising generation. If the European schoolboy can neutralise the teaching of the school-room by recourse to bad books, such as the works of Emile Zola or the naturalist school, the facilities for obtaining bad literature in India are not counteracted by numerous libraries, a well-conducted press, and a pure drama.[11]

Nor, for numerous critics, were they counteracted by a 'pure' home life, since Indian students breathed in the 'impure' atmosphere of the home 'without any antiseptics since childhood' (and continued to breathe it in even 'with the antiseptics of school and college teaching and discipline').[12] This meant that 'books that are innocuous to the comparatively pure and healthy morals of English boys may not be so to the more inflammable minds of Indian boys'.[13] Moreover, since the purportedly septic nature of Indian home life made 'the mind of Indian youth a *tabula rasa*' when it came to 'ideas of right and wrong', then in India the book was quite literally 'everything, for the master cannot supply what it fails to give'.[14]

Yet in spite of such concerns, nothing was done to tackle the problem.[15] A request from Northbrook, however, necessitated a response, so the Viceroy Lord Dufferin immediately sent a dispatch to all local

[11] W. Lee-Warner, Esq., Secretary to the Government of Bombay, to Secretary to the Government of India, Home Department, 2 October 1888, 36–9/January 1888, Education, A, Home Department, NAI.

[12] H. B. Grigg, Director of Public Instruction, Madras, to Chief Secretary to the Government of Madras, 6 April, 1889; and A. Monro, Inspector of Schools, Fifth Division, to Director of Public Instruction, Madras, n.d., 17–72/September 1889, Education, B, Home Department, NAI. Such impurity was allegedly wrought both by the ignorance of Indian mothers and wives (which made obtaining 'a high standard of moral and cultivated feeling' impossible) and by the fact that 'with existing social arrangements a pure minded boy or girl of 13, in the European acceptation of the term, can hardly by any possibility exist'. Grigg to Chief Secretary to the Government of Madras, 6 April 1889; and Opinion of T. B. Kirkham, Esq., Educational Inspector, Central Division, 20 June 1888, 17–72/September 1889, Education, B, Home Department, NAI.

[13] L. Garthwaite, Esq., Inspector of Schools, Sixth Division, to Director of Public Instruction, Madras, n.d., 17–72/September 1889, Education, B, Home Department, NAI.

[14] Grigg to Chief Secretary to the Government of Madras, 6 April 1889; and Dr J. Murdoch, Secretary of the Madras Branch of the Christian Vernacular Education Society to the Director of Public Instruction, Madras, n.d., 17–72/September 1889, Education, B, Home Department, NAI.

[15] While one colonial official noted that 'I have seen many complaints in the papers about these filthy books', he had clearly felt no impetus to do anything about them. The Police Commissioner in Calcutta had likewise ignored requests to take any action against

governments asking them to conduct a search for Zola's novels and other 'indecent and immoral' literature.[16] Once the search was underway, such literature began turning up everywhere. Reports started pouring in that translations of Zola's novels were being sold in the cantonment in Poona, that European booksellers such as Vest and Co. and Higginbotham and Co. and Indian booksellers such as V. Kalayana Rama Iyer were selling them in Madras, Thacker, Spink and Co. in Calcutta, and A. H. Wheeler and Co. all over the place.[17] Wheeler's was in fact selling no fewer than twenty-two of Zola's novels at its railway bookstalls, including two of those later convicted in the Vizetelly trial (*Nana* and *Piping Hot*), along with translations of other French novels by authors such as Gustave Flaubert and Alphonse Daudet. Then books of an even more dubious character began to turn up. Bengal, for example, sent along a catalogue of popular sexology books from the Calcutta Phrenological Institute's Book Depot with titles such as *Amativeness – Or the Evils and Remedies of Excessive and Perverted Sexuality* and *Home Treatment for Sexual Abuses*. And with none of the above books priced above one and a half rupees, they were widely accessible to both European and Indian pockets.[18]

But in spite of Northbrook's prodding to take action against such works under the obscene publications provisions of the Indian Penal Code, neither the provincial nor Indian governments were particularly inclined to do anything about them, even after the first Vizetelly trial heightened awareness in India about the 'dangers' of such works.[19]

popular sexology books, while Conway Gordon, Director-General of Railways, noted that he had received a deputation in 1887 complaining about the literature sold at bookstalls on the North-Western Railway, but that since in its contract with bookstall proprietors A. H. Wheeler and Co. the railway had reserved for itself no authority over the works sold at railway bookstalls he did nothing about it. Such action was in any case inadvisable, Gordon suggested, since 'it is impossible to keep people pure & moral by act of Parliament'. Aitchison to Sir Charles Elliott, n.d., Benjamin Aitken to J. P. Hewett, 22 November 1888, and Gordon to Charles Smith, 19 July 1888, 384/July 1888, Public, Deposit, Home Department, NAI.

16 Dispatch from Governor-General to Chief Secretaries to the Governments of Madras, Bombay, Bengal, the North-Western Provinces and the Secretary to the Governor of the Punjab, 4 July 1888, 384/July 1888, Public, Deposit, Home Department, NAI.

17 The Bombay Commissioner of Police turned up copies of almost all of the French novels that Wheeler's had for sale, along with a host of 'similar publications' at the city's main bookshops. Commissioner of Police to W. Lee-Warner, Esq., Chief Secretary to the Government of Bombay, 30 January 1889, Vol. 163, J.D. 371/1889, Publications, Judicial Department, MSA.

18 J. Murdoch to C. U. Aitchison, 2 October 1888, 384/July 1888, Public, Deposit, Home Department, NAI.

19 Perhaps anticipating that the Indian government would be less than enthusiastic in carrying out his request, Northbrook also wrote a letter to John Murdoch, head of the Christian Vernacular Education Society in Madras, asking that he also investigate the matter. Murdoch complied by reprinting a catalogue of A. H. Wheeler and Co. and

As one government official laconically remarked at the start of the investigation, while some of Zola's novels were 'very objectionable', they were nonetheless 'not Hollywell [sic] literature, & not worse than several English works I have seen'.[20] The Special Commissioner of Police, Madras, felt that although some questionable literature might be available in Madras, 'There is no such sale of indecent or immoral publications in this town as would amount to a public scandal' – which meant, as far as he was concerned, that no action need therefore be taken.[21] The Chief Secretary of the Central Provinces, Sir John Edgar, felt that the only action the Indian government need take was to tell Wheeler's to stop selling the novels for which Vizetelly had been prosecuted in London, since the effects of such literature were, as far as he could see, not worth worrying about. As far as the native population was concerned, Edgar was convinced that 'Nothing from Europe can harm [them] when they have ready access to [such literature] in their own tongue', while 'The Eurasian hobble-de-hoy' would do little more than simply 'gloat over it'.[22] Neither Edgar nor any other government official regarded such works as a danger to the European population in India.

Thus despite the fact that the disciplinary power of the colonial bureaucracy was launched to survey and document the sale of 'obscene' publications throughout British India, such responses ensured that very little was actually done about them. Wheeler's was asked to desist from selling Zola's more notorious works, the major Indian booksellers were issued warnings by their local police against selling obscene publications, and that, as far as the Indian government and most of the provincial governments were concerned, was the end of the matter.[23] Officials actually revealed themselves to be more concerned about the consequences of taking action against Zola's works than about not doing so, for a crusade launched against translations of French novels could quickly outstrip the government's ability to control it; the impetus to regulate the obscene could easily spread to the vernaculars, and if that

sending it to the Indian government, along with a request that the government put a stop to the sale of such publications. Murdoch to C. U. Aitchison, 2 October 1888.

20 Charles Smith to C. U. Aitchison, n.d., 384/July 1888, Public, Deposit, Home Department, NAI.

21 Special Commissioner of Police, Madras, to Chief Secretary to the Government of Madras, 10 August 1888, 384/July 1888, Public, Deposit, Home Department, NAI.

22 Sir John Edgar to Macdonald, 6 February 1889, 353–68/June 1889, Public, Deposit, Home Department, NAI.

23 '"The Soil", "Nana", and "Piping Hot", by Zola, published in English by Henry Vizetelly', were, however, listed as prohibited imports under the Sea Customs Act, although they remained the only 'obscene' works ever specifically listed as prohibited imports in colonial India. *The Preventive Service Manual*, n.p.

happened, as one worried administrator put it, 'We should have our hands full'.[24] Even when copies turned up of the translations for which Vizetelly had been prosecuted in London, local governments simply decided to let the matter drop.[25] Unlike in Britain and Australia, in India the Vizetelly affair did not, therefore, lead to the generation of a new biopolitical project to regulate the obscene. The Indian government, in fact, actively resisted undertaking such a project. To understand the reason for this we need to examine the relationship between aesthetics and governmentality in India, or rather the state's failure to establish such a relationship through the technology of 'aesthetic imperialism'. For by the 1880s this particular technology of colonial governmentality had revealed itself to be not only a failure, but a threat to the very moral framework upon which the project of colonial governmentality depended.

Aesthetic imperialism

One of the central technologies of government in colonial India, aesthetic imperialism, was a means of fashioning 'a brand-new population that would conform to the liberal philosophies fashionable in Europe'.[26] Since in India it was impossible for the British to educate Indians as they did their own working classes (thanks to both their policy of religious neutrality and the existence of a well-entrenched learned class), English literature, which had not yet emerged as a discipline in England, was called upon to instruct Indians in the regulation of individual conduct and to generate a confluence of interests between rulers and ruled – to, in the words of the *Oriental Herald*, 'insensibly wean their affections from the Persian muse, teach them to despise the barbarous splendour of their ancient princes, and totally supplanting the tastes which flourished under the Mogul reign, make them look to this country with veneration'.[27] What made literature purportedly capable of carrying out such an ambitious task was its relationship to beauty. In the *Third Critique*, Kant describes beauty as 'the result of an internal struggle between reason and morality for adequate comprehension of an object that

[24] Anonymous note, 30 May 1889, 353–68/June 1889, Public, Deposit, Home Department, NAI.

[25] *Piping Hot*, for example, was discovered for sale in Calcutta, but although the Commissioner of Police was convinced that the book 'abounds in vicious suggestions' and was 'published for the sole purpose of ministering to the depraved taste of casual readers' the Bengal government decided to take no action. Lambert to Chief Secretary, 14 February 1889, 353–68/June 1889, Public, Deposit, Home Department, NAI.

[26] Schwarz, 'Aesthetic Imperialism', 574.

[27] 'On the Inefficacy of the Means Now in Use for the Propagation of Christianity in India', *Oriental Herald* (1825), cited in Viswanathan, *Masks of Conquest*, p. 6.

defies description in the strict terms of either, as in fact the subject's appreciation of its own cognitive power in competing against itself for this comprehension'.[28] Literature served to make this cognitive mechanism for realizing a non-cognitive truth sensible by giving it material form. What a literary education therefore offered was training in aesthetic sensitivity which, in light of the Kantian belief in the universality of subjective experience, was a deeply socializing practice.[29] Furthermore, 'since the aesthetic condition per se was one of self-correction and approximation to an ideal realizable finally in its individual performance', the systematization of such an aesthetic experience taught individuals how to discipline themselves.[30]

India was regarded as being a suitable place for such an experiment in light of the fact that, as the *Calcutta Review* opined, 'the East has been the land, where the excellent practice of inculcating truth through the pleasing guide of fiction first took its rise ... [and] the Hindu mind, while it is exceedingly attached to metaphysical and abstract truth, is yet at the same time passionately fond of fictitious narratives'.[31] There were, moreover, some important potential benefits to be derived from the development of a literary curriculum in India. The first was that, since British rule in India was autocratic and hence violated liberal principles of government, literature would enable the government to become, if only to a limited extent, representative through fostering the generation of an Indian civil society in which the products of Indian presses – imbued, of course, with the appropriate aesthetic principles – would function as the voice of the people (the registration of Indian publications, instituted in 1867, would, in turn, enable the documentation of such a voice).[32] Secondly, educating Indians through English literature would serve, as Gauri Viswanathan has so memorably phrased it, as a 'mask of conquest' that defined 'the Englishman's true essence ... by the thought he produced' rather than by his behaviour and actions.[33] It would therefore operate to camouflage the economic exploitation, systemic violence and oppression of the colonizers.[34]

[28] Schwarz, 'Aesthetic Imperialism', 570.
[29] Aesthetic judgments, for Kant, were both 'at once subjective and universal'. Eagleton, *The Ideology of the Aesthetic*, p. 93.
[30] Schwarz, 'Aesthetic Imperialism', 571.
[31] *Calcutta Review* (1850), cited in Schwarz, 'Aesthetic Imperialism', 580.
[32] Schwarz, 'Aesthetic Imperialism', 574. The reports produced on Indian publications thus served, as Uma Kalpagam asserts, 'as an illustration of liberalism in practice'. Kalpagam, 'Colonial Governmentality and the Public Sphere', 45.
[33] Viswanathan, *Masks of Conquest*, p. 6.
[34] As Terry Eagleton observes, while culture 'sketches the ghostly outline of a non-dominative social order' (since the cultural domain is one of non-coercive consensus)

It was English literary fiction that was to be accorded the primary task of cultivating the aesthetic development of young Indian minds.[35] A work such as *Robinson Crusoe*, for officials such as Thomas Macaulay, was 'worth all the grammars of rhetoric and logic in the world', since it not only taught rhetoric, grammar and logic by example rather than by rule (as well, of course, as the rudiments of British character, and the 'correct' relationship between ruler and ruled), but it did so in an exciting form that encouraged the internalization of such knowledge.[36] Such a 'soft route' to regulation thus served to '[dispose] its reader toward a correct, controlled discipline of rules that seemed voluntary even though it was elaborately learned'.[37] Furthermore, since English literature was perceived to cultivate an appreciation of the beautiful – for, in the words of one missionary journal, its 'qualities of loveliness and purity ... [and] high thought and feeling' made it seem 'rather the production of angels than men' – it could equip Indians both mentally and morally to receive the 'truth' while bypassing their resistance to proselytization.[38]

It was not until 1835, when the East India Company first officially devoted itself to the teaching of English to its Indian subjects – since the 'Orientalist' model of education, which entailed the teaching of Indian languages and literatures, had according to James Mill failed 'to make a favourable impression ... upon the minds of the natives' – that a highly literary curriculum was developed in India.[39] But by the 1850s English education had produced little in the way of either Anglicization or conversion, which led to the development of a new approach to inculcating the virtues of English literature in Indian hearts and minds. This entailed combining the aesthetic values of English literature with indigenous forms of thought and sentiment through translating English

'it does so by mystifying and legitimating actual dominative social relations'. Eagleton, *The Ideology of the Aesthetic*, p. 97.

35 Indian literature was regarded as being completely unsuitable for such a task, since not only did it employ allegory to accord sanctity to Indian social customs that, for British critics, were immoral (which meant that it 'contained neither the moral nor mental cultivation essential for good government'), but Indians read it not as intellectual production but as divine authority (which meant that it entailed the exercise of blind faith rather than reason). Tharu and Lalita, 'Empire, Nation', p. 209.

36 Schwarz, 'Aesthetic Imperialism', 568.

37 Schwarz, 'Aesthetic Imperialism', 569

38 Schwarz, 'Aesthetic Imperialism', 572. While the East India Company maintained an official policy of religious non-interference, in reality it ran what Schwarz refers to as a '"crypto-confessional state" saturated by evangelical patronage'. Clergymen who visited government schools were often astonished at the students' knowledge of Christianity. Schwarz, 'Aesthetic Imperialism', 573; and Viswanathan, *Masks of Conquest*, p. 88.

39 Viswanathan, *Masks of Conquest*, p. 39.

literary texts into the vernaculars (which were perceived to lack a comparable literary tradition to India's classical languages and hence the same degree of falsehood, ignorance and error). By the 1860s, thanks to both changes in government education policy (namely the shift from subsidizing English to vernacular education) and the aid of organizations such as the Vernacular Literature Society (VLS), or Bangla Anubadok Samiti (Bengali Translators' Society), there were signs that such a project had, at last, begun to succeed.[40] Not only had Indian readers taken avidly to didactic fiction, especially 'classical' English works such as *Rasselas* and *The Pilgrim's Progress* (in both English and translations), but Indian writers had begun to adopt the novelistic form to produce reams of novels in suitably purified vernaculars that addressed problems of social and religious reform.[41]

The problem for advocates of the governmental technology of aesthetic imperialism, however, was that such productions were unable to compete either with popular English fiction of the likes of G. W. M. Reynolds, by far the most popular English-language author in India, or with the productions of what had grown to be a vast Indian publishing industry.[42] Although Europeans knew little about it – since 'A person may be twenty years in Calcutta', according to the Irish missionary (and head of the VLS) James Long, 'and scarce know that any Bengali books are printed by Bengalis themselves' – Long estimated in 1855 that two million books had been published in Bengali alone in the past decade, an output that made Calcutta a rival to London as a centre of literary production.[43] While the bulk of this trade consisted of educational works

40 Oddie, *Missionaries*, p. 82. The Indian government was so convinced as to the importance of translations for Indians' moral and intellectual development that it regarded the introduction of copyright law, which would prevent 'free translations', as being 'detrimental to the progress of the country'. 184–204/May 1877, Judicial, A, Home Department, NAI; and Appendix I, 119 ser 1/November 1913, Commerce and Industry, B, NAI. See also 37–39/January 1902, Books and Publications, A, Home Department, NAI.

41 Such works were widely translated in India because for the Indian reader they offered 'a view to improving himself in relation to the knowledge of the culture of his masters'. Balagopal Varma, 'Some Thoughts on English Fiction and the Reading Public', cited in Joshi, *In Another Country*, p. 73.

42 As Priya Joshi has revealed, while institutions such as the Calcutta Public Library may have tried to cultivate a taste for 'graver reading' among their Indian patrons by removing the works of Reynolds and other authors from their shelves, the ensuing spectacular decline in Indian subscribers forced them to abandon such an agenda. Joshi, *In Another Country*, pp. 57–8.

43 *Returns Relating to Publications in the Bengali Language, 1857*, cited in Ghosh, 'Cheap Books', 178; Roy, 'Disciplining the Printed Text', p. 33; and Schwarz, 'Aesthetic Imperialism', 563. Long made the first effort to catalogue Bengali publications in 1852 in *Granthavali, An Alphabetical List of Works Published in Bengali*, which

(such as the bestseller *Shishubodh*, which contained mythological tales and *sloka*s and was written almost entirely in verse), religious texts (such as missionary tracts and Puranic literature), and almanacs and popular medical texts, by the mid-1870s fiction, drama and farces (many of which were translated from English) – which schoolboys and college students particularly relished – had begun to gain in popularity over older literary forms.[44]

Along with a flourishing book trade, a vibrant newspaper industry had also arisen throughout India by the second half of the nineteenth century.[45] As a Home Department dispatch observed somewhat nervously in 1890, the Indian press had expanded rapidly in the past decade, for while 'Ten years ago it numbered about 180 journals all told ... it now numbers about 450, besides 100 Periodicals', which together had a circulation of 250,000 copies.[46] By 1905 there were 1,359 newspapers and journals circulating in India, for Home Department member H. H. Risley an overwhelming 'mass of heterogeneous material ... the mere bulk of which, to say nothing of its chaotic character, renders it unmanageable'.[47] While the circulation figures of most Indian newspapers were fairly small, such figures said little about the actual dissemination of a publication, for 'These newspapers are widely circulated from hand to hand; they are read aloud to listeners; [and] the statements made in them are repeated by readers or listeners to others'.[48] They were therefore readily accessible to both reading and listening audiences.

contained a list of 1,084 titles. Roy notes that in the second half of the nineteenth century the publishing industry 'was perhaps the largest indigenous enterprise in Calcutta'. Even as late as 1911 the publishing industry in Calcutta dwarfed that of industries such as jute, employing almost six times as many employees. Roy, 'Disciplining the Printed Text', pp. 33, 30.

44 Ghosh, 'Cheap Books', 179, 181; and Roy 'Disciplining the Printed Text', p. 47. Such translations were so common that they often far outstripped the publication of original works of fiction in Indian languages. In 1893, for example, of the thirty-two works of fiction published in Gujarati in the Bombay Presidency, no fewer than twenty-two of them were translations of English works. Although such translations were often of works by popular British authors such as Mary Elizabeth Braddon and Maria Edgeworth, many of them were of much more ephemeral authors such as Dick Donovan, Glydnen Hall, Alfred Colbeck and Robert H. Sherard. Vol. 28 Comp. 1003/1894, Judicial Department, MSA.

45 The two did not expand at the same rate, however, and the growth of both varied greatly from province to province. See Roy, 'Disciplining the Printed Text', pp. 30–1; Boyce, *British Policy*, p. 48; and Vol. 8 Comp. 1003/1894, Judicial Department, MSA.

46 319–323/1890, Public, Home Department, NAI.

47 Barrier, *Banned*, p. 9; and 178–80/July 1907, Political, A, Home Department, NAI.

48 Dispatch, C. U. Aitchison, G. Chesney, and J. Westland, 6 November 1888, 319–23/ January 1890, Public, Home Department, NAI; see also 153/January 1909, Political, B, Home Department, NAI. By the mid-1880s over 20 million newspapers were being sent through the Indian post, over 30 million by 1900, and by 1909 the figure had topped a

Literacy was in fact a highly variable phenomenon in India in the late nineteenth century. Although the Indian census of 1881 recorded literacy rates of only 6.6 per cent among Indian men and a mere 0.3 per cent among Indian women, such figures do not fully account for the large swathe of Indians with rudimentary reading skills.[49] In Bengal, for example, a wide network of Bengali and Persian schools had existed since the seventeenth century and catered not only to the higher caste and service populations but, through elementary vernacular schools, or *pathshalas*, and Vaishnava *tols* (centres for higher learning), to lower-caste groups, considerable numbers of whom attended to attain sufficient literacy (in Bengali and often Persian) in order to serve as clerks, letter-writers and accountants in zamindari, government and commercial establishments.[50] The numbers of such 'functionally literate' groups had expanded considerably by the mid-nineteenth century thanks to new educational opportunities and cheap print technology.[51] But what made print accessible to illiterate, listening audiences, was the fact that much of the new print culture preserved the formats, genres and uses of oral traditions such as speech and song (not to mention the printed image).[52] As a Bengali newspaper noted in 1873, 'There is not a peddling shopkeeper who does not spend the hours between his midday meal and his resumption of business in the afternoon in reading something or other, and very few even among the unlettered peasantry are willing to forgo the pleasure of hearing popular books read to them by some fortunate neighbour who understands better than they the mystic symbols of the alphabet.'[53]

Although male literacy undoubtedly exceeded that of female, such 'pleasures' were by no means restricted only to men, nor only to elite women. In addition to the growing numbers of higher-caste girls being educated in the zenana, by the 1850s it was not uncommon for lower-caste girls (even the children of prostitutes) to be sent to school, like their

phenomenal 50 million. See Indian Posts and Telegraphs Department, *Annual Report*, 1886–7, 1899–1900 and 1908–9.

49 Joshi, *In Another Country*, p. 42. Literacy rates were, moreover, highly variable – the literacy rate in Calcutta according to the 1876 census, for example, was 60 per cent, with Hindu men making up the bulk of the literate. Literacy in both the vernaculars and English increased over the following decades (with 3.4 per cent of the population literate in English by 1921) thanks to the tremendous growth in English secondary schools and colleges. Banerjee, *The Parlour*, p. 122; and Chatterjee, 'The Disciplines', pp. 9–10.

50 Ghosh, *Power in Print*, pp. 31, 33.

51 Ghosh, *Power in Print*, p. 108.

52 Ghosh, *Power in Print*, p. 153.

53 Banerjee, *The Parlour*, p. 139. One report from the early nineteenth century estimated that every copy of a newspaper had on average ten hearers. Ghosh, *Power in Print*, p. 166.

brothers, until they had acquired functional literacy.[54] High female literacy also existed among particular segments of the population, such as Vaishnavas.[55] Those who lacked such basic reading skills were read to; in wealthier households often by a raconteur hired for the purpose.[56] Growing numbers of women therefore had access, like men, to Indian print culture.

That 'cheap literature and [a] vernacular press' had come to 'surround the rising generation' was bad news for the advocates of aesthetic imperialism.[57] Not only was it impossible to even attempt to cultivate the aesthetic sensibilities of the bulk of the population that was avidly imbibing the products of Indian presses (since 'for every 12 boys under instruction 88 are growing up without schools'), but even among the 12 per cent of the population that colonial education could reach 'the best efforts made in the schoolroom to impress character' were being 'seriously endangered by the wreckage caused by . . . the supply of books which the Professor cannot control'.[58] But there were growing signs, by as early as the 1850s, that such 'wreckage' was being effected not only by 'bad books', but by aesthetic imperialism itself. For rather than being unsuccessful, this particular governmental technology was in fact '*too* successful, for in combating learning and culture [it] inevitably signified the transmission of ideas of moral autonomy, self-sufficiency and unencumbered will' (emphasis in original).[59] Rather than generating a confluence of interests between rulers and ruled, aesthetic imperialism instead served to do the opposite.[60] While in England the aim of teaching 'improving' literature was to foster the leadership qualities deemed necessary in a governing elite, the goal in India was instead to produce 'a class of interpreters between us and the millions whom we govern'.[61]

54 Ghosh, *Power in Print*, p. 157.
55 Ghosh, *Power in Print*, p. 176.
56 Joshi, *In Another Country*, p. 42.
57 W. Lee-Warner, Esq., Secretary to the Government of Bombay to Secretary to the Government of India, Home Department, 2 October 1888.
58 C. Browning, Esq., Inspector-General of Education, Central Provinces, to Secretary to the Chief Commissioner, Central Provinces, n.d.; and W. Lee-Warner, Esq., Secretary to the Government of Bombay to Secretary to the Government of India, Home Department, 2 October 1888. In light of the lively market in 'scrap' paper, there were also questions as to whether much of the 'useful' literature advocated for Indian readers, and provided by organizations such as the VLS, was ever read at all.
59 Viswanathan, *Masks of Conquest*, p. 143.
60 It was, not surprisingly, the novel that emerged as one of the chief forums for anti-colonial and nationalist critiques. Joshi, *In Another Country*, p. xvii.
61 T. B. Macaulay, Minute on Indian Education, 2 February 1835, in Sharp, *Selections from Educational Records*, p. 116. Although a growing awareness of the potential dangers of aesthetic imperialism led Governor-General Lord Hardinge to pass a resolution in 1844 according preference for appointment to public office to Indians who had pursued a

Such a discrepancy between content and intent meant that instead of entering a realm of aesthetic universality whose object was rational, enlightened progress, the Indian subject thus produced was imitative, superficial, and intellectually shallow (the 'babu' of British – and much Indian – scorn). The product of a clash between aesthetics and ideology, of the Arnoldian literary curriculum versus the logic of colonial governmentality, such a subject could, moreover,

> become hyperrational, divorced from either English or Indian loyalties, suspicious of religion and prone to self-doubt. It experienced the skepticism of the divided subject unrepresentable to itself: aesthetic irony could just as easily be turned toward politics or society. Its language was unsteady, and it had periods of self-consciousness.[62]

For Indian writers such a situation necessitated creating a subjective voice that could balance the inner realm of Indian experience with the encroaching realm of colonial modernity, a struggle that for individuals such as Krupabai Satthianadan proved impossible in the face of a cultural dislocation so profound that she was wracked by a self-division bordering on madness.[63] While her heroine Saguna proudly imbibes English literary works such as Spenser's *Faerie Queen* such reading, 'rather than socializing her into the hierarchies of a colonial landscape as the Macauldian model for English education would have it . . . render[ed] her ill equipped to deal with the world she inhabit[ed]'.[64]

The response of the government to such a problem was to switch from a humanistic to a practical model of education.[65] Such a shift in policy

course of study in English literature, the difficulty was that not only were there not enough posts available, but the highest position that Indians could aspire to (at least until the reform of the Indian Civil Service that began in the second half of the nineteenth century) was that of copying clerk, which required little more than a rudimentary knowledge of English.

62 Schwarz, 'Aesthetic Imperialism', 578.

63 Lokugé, 'Introduction', p. 8. Satthianadhan, whose parents were Brahmin converts to Christianity, is generally credited with being the first English novelist in India. She wrote two novels, *Saguna* (published in the *Madras Christian College Magazine*, 1887–8) and *Kamala* (again published in the *Madras Christian College Magazine*, 1892–3), and a number of stories.

64 Joshi, *In Another Country*, p. 180.

65 Instead of moral and intellectual elevation, the goal of education became that of 'confirm[ing] individuals into the social class to which they were born', and to initiate social change by the cultivation of differentiation instituted through laws, institutions and government. But by the early 1880s higher education had in fact ceased to become the primary educational objective of government. While two new universities were founded (in Lahore in 1882 and Allahabad in 1887), in the last two decades of the century the government established only one new college (compared to the establishment by Indians of a total of seventy-six aided and private colleges), and only 134 English secondary schools (compared to the Indian establishment of

came too late, however, not only to address the crisis in subjectivity unleashed by English education, or the thwarted expectations that it raised, but to hide the moral crisis at the heart of aesthetic imperialism. For while the goal of colonial educators was to effect the inculcation of a Christian morality in Indian hearts and minds, they were at the same time forced to disavow such a project, for domination, as Homi Bhabha argues, 'is achieved through a process of disavowal that denies the difference of colonialist power'.[66] What had to be disavowed in the case of aesthetic imperialism was the conflict in truth claims that it generated. While the culturally unambiguous text voices its truth claims by displacing others, the culturally ambiguous text instead relies on the progress of history, which in demonstrating the relative applicability of one idea over another serves to establish its validity. In India the English literary text was caught, however, between these two poles – between 'process and state, observation and assertion, [and] identity and difference' – and was therefore characterized by ambivalence, since while colonial educators were forced to treat it as culturally ambiguous (in order to disavow their goal of inculcating Christian morality, or for missionaries the more explicit goal of conversion), they at the same time actively resisted such an approach. For Viswanathan the tension wrought by this process of disavowal was so profound that it 'threatened to destroy the whole edifice of British control from within'.[67] But such a process also undermined British control from without, for this disavowal of Christian moral 'truths' served, in turn, to *relativize morality*: to deny, in other words, the very universality of moral truth that aesthetic imperialism had endeavoured to inculcate. In thus renouncing their culture as the embodiment of moral truth, the British thus laid themselves open to charges of immorality, or even of threatening the sanctity of a superior Indian morality.

That such critiques would eventually emerge was inevitable in light of the fact that the technology of aesthetic imperialism – a technology that demonstrates that colonies were not only sites where governmentality was dislocated, but where new techniques were invented (and later transported back 'home') – ultimately undermined the larger project of colonial governmentality that it aimed to advance.[68] As Adam Smith argued in the *Theory of Moral Sentiments* (1759), a key text in the Indian curriculum, literature encouraged a process of self-evaluation and

830 aided and private). Viswanathan, *Masks of Conquest*, p. 146; and Chatterjee, 'The Disciplines', p. 9.

66 Bhabha, 'Signs Taken for Wonders', cited in Viswanathan, *Masks of Conquest*, p. 96.

67 Viswanathan, *Masks of Conquest*, pp. 97–8.

68 Schwarz, 'Aesthetic Imperialism', 574.

self-enlightenment.[69] Indians were regarded as being inherently capable of undergoing such a process, since they had 'great natural sagacity, quickness and apprehension, sound intellect, sound reasoning and eloquence of expression'. What prevented them from doing so, however, was the despotic nature of their systems of government, which destroyed 'every principle intended by nature to promote the improvement of man'.[70] Such dormant principles could be rejuvenated through a historical approach to the reading of English literature, which in addition to rousing Indians to an awareness of the flaws in their own society would lead to a realization of the benefits of society in the West. Historical training thus 'reconstitut[ed] the object of instruction as the restoration of the Indian to his original state of goodness' by taking him '*back* to a true self'.[71] Such an educational approach necessitated finding a way of fashioning such subjects without undermining British rule – a task that, ultimately, proved impossible. By the second half of the nineteenth century it had become apparent that English education had indeed made Indians capable of governing the self, but that in the process it had destroyed not only, as MacDonnell had been well aware, their reverence for their own culture and religion but much of the culture itself – and, since the British had 'implant[ed] no other [culture] of a holier and purer kind', they were thus preventing Indians from being able to do so.[72]

Although such concerns were not explicitly voiced in the debates over Zola's works in India, they were in the case of later British requests for the Indian government to undertake the regulation of the obscene, particularly in regard to the Obscene Publications Agreement and Treaty. While 'a good many rankly obscene books and pictures' were imported into India, as the Director of the Criminal Intelligence Department (CID), C. R. Cleveland, declared in 1912, the Indian government, like its Australian counterpart, was opposed to adhering to both accords – although for considerably different reasons.[73] The problem was not only

69 In Viswanathan, *Masks of Conquest*, p. 128.

70 'Facts Illustrative of the Character and Condition of the People of India', *Oriental Herald* (October 1828), cited in Viswanathan, *Masks of Conquest*, pp. 129, 130.

71 Viswanathan, *Masks of Conquest*, p. 132.

72 John Murdoch, Education in India: Letter to His Excellency the Most Honourable Marquis of Ripon, Viceroy and Governor-General of India, cited in Viswanathan, *Masks of Conquest*, p. 134.

73 C. R. Cleveland to Home Department, 1 December 1912, 193–204/April 1913, Judicial, A, Home Department, NAI. While the Indian government eventually adhered to both accords, after considerable pressure, because it was 'unwilling to appear not to be in sympathy with an object which is in itself excellent', it did little to implement them. See note by H. Wheeler, Home Department, 24 July 1913, 246–7/ August 1913, Judicial, A, Home Department, NAI; and C. R. Cleveland, circular to

that regulating the obscene was 'work of doubtful effectiveness and character' (which made Cleveland loath to 'undertake anything in the nature of a regular bureau of obscenity') but that India was a *victim* of, rather than participant in, the international trade in 'obscene' publications.[74] For while India was riddled with the 'obscene' effluvium of Britain, its empire, and – through its communications networks – the world, such traffic flowed only in one direction.[75] Although for some such a one-way flow was attributable to the fact that Indian 'obscene' publications were 'from their lack of allusiveness and artistic merit unlikely to appeal to the taste of Western nations', a concern more widely articulated when it came to the crime of obscenity – and one that ultimately made the efforts of the British to regulate the obscene in India a virtual impossibility – was that 'India was more sinned against than sinning'.[76] As the debates on the Obscene Publications Treaty make clear – debates that significantly occurred in the new 'Indianized' legislatures made possible by the Government of India Act – by the 1920s such a belief ultimately made it possible for Indians to initiate their own biopolitical project to regulate the obscene: a project that, as in Australia, necessitated defending India from being 'polluted' by its imperial metropole.

Obscenity and the failure of colonial aesthetics

This does not mean that the colonial state completely abstained from efforts to regulate the obscene in India. The first obscenity statute in the empire was in fact passed in India in 1856 (a year before the passage of such an Act in Britain), and not only did the state undertake numerous prosecutions for obscenity, but from the mid-nineteenth century segments of civil society in India ranging from missionaries to Indian reform organizations to, by the early twentieth century, nationalists and social hygiene groups, waged ongoing battles both to pressure the government to regulate the obscene and to spur Indian society to self-regulation.[77]

Local Governments, 28 March 1914, 388–93/April 1914, Judicial, A, Home Department, NAI.

74 C. R. Cleveland to Home Department, 5 July 1912, 193–204/April 1913, Judicial, A, Home Department, NAI.

75 See 332/33, Judicial, Home Department, NAI.

76 S. P. O'Donnell, Esq., Secretary to the Government, United Provinces, Judicial (Criminal) Department, 24 April 1912, to Mr Crook, Home Department, 193–204/ April 1913, Judicial, A, Home Department, NAI; and *Extract from Council of State Debates*, 11 March 1924, 570/1923, Judicial, Home Department, NAI.

77 Rather than regulating the obscene through Police Acts, as was the case in Britain, a special act to 'prevent the public sale or exposure of obscene books and pictures' was deemed necessary in India since rather than having a 'limited sale' and being 'conducted

Aesthetic imperialism, or by the late nineteenth century the broader project of colonial governmentality of which it had served as a technology, necessitated that the state offer at least a token response to such pressure. But unlike in Britain or Australia, in India state efforts to regulate the obscene never coalesced into a biopolitical project, since the contradictions in the moral framework of British rule as revealed by aesthetic imperialism made that an impossibility. The Vizetelly affair, rather than serving as the trigger for such a project, instead became a byword for an opportunity lost. It was not unusual, for example, to find the Anglo-Indian press judging an anti-Catholic tirade in the *Indian Watchman* in 1892 by its similarity to the works of 'Zola and the pornographic school', to find references in 1907 to certain 'obscene' articles in the Arya Samaj journal *Musafir* as attributable to the fondness among Parsis for 'certain sorts of French novels, which can be easily obtained in India', or even to find a government official over three decades after the affair justify his refusal to concede to a bishop's request to put a stop to the sale of literature of dubious morality in cantonments by reference to the Vizetelly affair.[78]

It was initially pressure by the ubiquitous James Long that first spurred the government to do something to regulate the obscene at a time, significantly, when faith in aesthetic imperialism had not yet been entirely lost. The English language may not have proved to be the appropriate means through which to cultivate Indian moral and intellectual development, but there was still hope that it was possible to achieve such an outcome through the vernaculars. Although both the East India

secretly', as was purportedly the case in Britain, in Calcutta 'The sales [of such matter] were extremely common; indecent books were thrust into the hands of passengers in all the principal streets and thoroughfares of this city'. They were, moreover, extremely inexpensive. Contrary to British law the Act also 'provid[ed] against the importation of obscene books and prints'. While 'obscene' images were undoubtedly a source of concern (since 'pictures spoke an universal language'), the chief target was clearly English-language matter, since 'the number in this country that was able to read and understand English, was very far from being few'. *Proceedings of the Legislative Council of India*, 14 July 1855, Vol. I, pp. 528–35.

78 *Bombay Gazette*, 5 May 1892, Vol. 185 Comp. 885/1892, Prosecutions, Judicial Department, MSA; 20/January 1907, Public, Deposit, Home Department, NAI; and Note signed simply 'M', 20 June 1923, 355 no. 1–2/1923, Judicial, B, Home Department, NAI. One reason the Vizetelly affair may have continued to resonate in India was Zola's popularity there – as the Lahore Assistant Inspector-General, Railway Police, claimed in 1889, 'The works of Emile Zola had a very large sale, and his works perhaps were the best investment Wheeler and Co. had compared with that of any other author'. Booksellers such as Thacker, Spink and Co. were still advertising their sale of such works into the mid-1890s. Mr Christie to C. L. Lopper, 18 March 1889, 353–68/June 1889, Public, Deposit, Home Department, NAI; and *The Englishman*, 1 May 1894, n.p.

Company and wider missionary opinion were opposed to reintroducing legislation, discarded in 1835, to regulate print culture in India, Long's revelations both of the scale of vernacular publishing in Bengal and of the popularity of 'Battala' publications (produced in the region of Calcutta that, for British critics, was the equivalent of London's Holywell Street) generated sufficient concerns to enable the passage of the Obscene Publications Act.[79] But although several individuals were prosecuted, in spite of continued laments that 'the vernacular, which we take so much pains in utilizing as an organ of education in the masses, [has] ... become a vehicle of immorality', the provisions of the Act remained virtually a dead letter even after it was absorbed into the Indian Penal Code in 1861.[80]

Beginning in the 1870s there was, however, a revival of interest in these provisions, although the pressure to implement them came not, this time, from the British public in India, but from the Indian. Although Indian reformers had long been vociferous in their critiques of the purported obscenity of vernacular print cultures, what eventually drove the government to act was a petition submitted by the Municipal Committee of Ulwar, which protested that the sale of obscene publications in Rajputana was preventing the spread of female education ('on account of the fear entertained by all respectable men', in the words of Political Agent C. T. Cadell, 'of the morals of their wives and daughters being corrupted by bad books falling into their hands, should they be able to read them').[81] Reluctant to appear to condone such 'corruption', the Indian government requested the provincial governments in the North-Western Provinces and Punjab (in 1871 the latter had rejected a plea from the Punjab Reform Association to take action against 'obscene' publications) to initiate

[79] James Long, 'Returns Relating to Publications in the Bengali Language in 1857', *Selections from the Records*, p. xxv. Although Charles Metcalfe had famously 'liberated' the Indian press in 1835, within a decade a system of press surveillance began to emerge that, by the 1870s, had been adopted by all the provincial governments (not to mention the launching of various press patronage schemes to influence the 'tone' of the Indian press). Books became subject to surveillance from 1867 with the passage of the Press and Registration of Books Act. Boyce, *British Policy*, p. 42; and Barrier, *Banned*, pp. 52–5, 71.

[80] Reports on Native Presses in the NWP for 1862, 1863, 1864 and 1865, *Selections from the Records of the Government of India, 1849–1937*, V/23/121, Part 44, Article 1 (IOL), cited in Gupta, *Sexuality, Obscenity, Community*, p. 50.

[81] Cadell, to Colonel J. C. Brooke, Governor-General's Agent, Rajpootana, 39–42/April 1873, Judicial, B, Judicial Department, WBSA; and *The Friend of India*, 11 September 1873. When it came to such publications, for Cadell it was, furthermore, 'impossible to prevent their dissemination throughout Native States as long as they are printed by thousands in British territory'. Complaints about the dangers of female reading became increasingly common from the 1860s. See Ghosh, 'Cheap Books', 191.

prosecutions against the perpetrators of the trade. The Bengal government, long inured to such pleas, soon followed suit.[82]

The success of such efforts emboldened the state to undertake a spate of prosecutions for obscenity in the 1880s and 1890s.[83] But it was, vitally, *the opinion of Indians*, rather than that of the British public in India or even in many cases of the colonial government, that led to the initiation of such prosecutions.[84] While Partha Chatterjee argues that for the colonial state only the opinion of the British public 'counted as public opinion', and that, furthermore, 'the question of the appropriate relationship between government and the public came to be defined primarily around the freedoms of the British Indian press', the case of 'obscene' publications proves otherwise.[85] The Indian and provincial governments in fact turned down repeated requests from members of the British public in India to initiate prosecutions for obscenity. The Bombay government, for example, rejected a request from the Bombay Catholic Union in 1892 to initiate a prosecution against the editor of the *Indian Watchman* for publishing an 'obscene' anti-Catholic tirade on the grounds that while 'the sale of obscene literature for the purpose of demoralizing the purchasees or those who may obtain possession of the books is an offence of so abominable a kind that the Govt [sic] ought certainly to suppress the offence by prosecuting the offenders on every proper occasion', the government was not the only possible prosecutor, and hence 'it would ... be wise of Govt [sic] to leave the duty of prosecution to the other party to the controversy'.[86] The Indian government displayed even less sympathy in 1903 towards the outraged request of one Colonel Perry that it take action against the *Pioneer* for distributing 'obscene' advertisements. As far as the government was concerned, 'only the strongest of cases would justify the Government of India

[82] 39–42/April 1873, Judicial, B, Judicial Department, WBSA; and 'The Society for the Suppression', 179–204.

[83] The most important of these are all Bombay cases. See *Queen-Empress* v. *Indarman*, *Indian Law Reports*, 3 Bombay (1881), p. 837; *Queen-Empress* v. *Framji D. Taraporewalla*, Criminal Appeal 219 (1891), in Ratanlal, *Unreported Criminal Cases*, pp. 620–2; and *Queen-Empress* v. *Parashram Yeshvant*, *Indian Law Reports*, 20 Bombay (1895), p. 193.

[84] As Tanika Sarkar argues, when it came to socio-moral reform in India, 'colonial initiative ... [was] generally a belated and forced surrender to Indian reformist pressure'. Sarkar, *Hindu Wife*, p. 196. The colonial state was besieged with requests, particularly from the 1880s onwards (with the formation of organizations such as the National Social Conference), to regulate not only the 'obscene' but 'immoral' behaviour ranging from *nautch* performances to Holi celebrations, not to mention issues such as the age of consent.

[85] Chatterjee, *The Nation*, p. 22.

[86] H. Birdwood, n.d., Vol. 185 Comp. 885/1892, Prosecutions, Judicial Department, MSA.

in moving', and since Colonel Perry did not contact the editor of the *Pioneer* in a 'courteous and temperate' manner to ask him to cease distributing such advertisements, but instead wrote 'under the impulse of extreme indignation and an avowed desire for personal violence', then he was 'not entitled to approach the Government of India in the character of a member of the public who, having exhausted the means of private remonstrance, is compelled to have recourse to public authority'.[87] As another exasperated colonial official noted in regard to a similar case in the late 1890s, 'these people' – namely members of the British public – 'ought to understand that it is not the business of the Government to descend into the arena in such matters'.[88]

Indian public opinion, on the other hand, was in fact so important to the colonial state that it generally refused to take action to regulate 'obscene' publications unless convinced that such opinion would sanction it, for as an official in Punjab noted in 1890, such efforts 'can only be usefully or successfully applied where public opinion is on the whole in sympathy with the repressive measure'.[89] The efforts of the Association for Moral and Social Hygiene in the 1920s and 30s to combat 'obscene' advertisements in the Indian press were thus met with the galling response from the Indian government that it would be more supportive of such efforts if 'Associations representative of Indian opinion' had initiated them. In the absence of such 'representative' opinion the Association was advised to 'agitate the question in the Press and see what views are expressed on it; in this way would public opinion be formed'.[90] The support of the Indian public (or rather one of the many 'varieties of public', in this case the reading public, that were regarded as holders of authoritative opinion in colonial India) was so necessary to the colonial state's efforts to regulate the obscene because, in contrast to either Britain or Australia, the sovereignty of the state was not supported by the popular will.[91] Colonial governmentality in India was therefore

87 Notes by R. Greeven, J.M. Macpherson and T. Raleigh, 9 April 1903, 292–3/April 1903, Public, A, Home Department, NAI.

88 Vol. 11 Comp. 1512/1897, Judicial Department, MSA. Indian governments were, however, appreciative of the generally enthusiastic assistance rendered to them by British booksellers in India to regulate the obscene. See, for example, note by J.H. DuBoulay, Secretary to the Government of India, Home Department, 10 April 1917, 134/May 1917, Judicial, A, Home Department, NAI.

89 J.R. Drummond, Esq. to Commissioner and Superintendent, Delhi Division, n.d., 457–83/October 1890, Public, A, Home Department, NAI.

90 M.G. Hallett to Meliscent Shephard, Association for Moral and Social Hygiene, 16 November 1935, 115/35, Political, Home, NAI.

91 Kalpagam, 'Colonial Governmentality and the Public Sphere', 35.

forced to function in the absence of a social contract between the state and its subjects. As Uma Kalpagam argues:

> The institutionalization of the public use of reason through a liberal political sphere by the colonial state sought to achieve the dual goals of both improving the moral conduct of the people as well as have an effect on the government of the state and in the process tried to reconcile the requirements of general interests with the requirements of political legitimacy.[92]

The Indian public thus produced, however, was caught in a dialectic of acceptance of colonial governmentality (in order to improve its techniques) and a rejection of it (in particular of its rationality).[93] Such instability meant that it was vital for the state to ensure that it did not further undermine the Indian public sphere through technologies of rule to which it was firmly opposed. This did not mean, however, that the state responded to *all* pressure from the Indian public to regulate the obscene, since this would entail more labour than was in fact necessary to ensure the governance of colonial conduct. As the Bombay government noted in regard to a plague of such requests from the Bombay-based Students' Social Purity League in the 1890s, 'The question [was] perhaps a little awkward', since while it was willing to initiate a prosecution if a case 'seemed to urgently require [it]', it was also fearful of being 'flooded with all the doubtful literature published in Bombay in order that one or two publishers who may have gone too far may be prosecuted'.[94]

One way out of such a bind, and by far the most common method adopted, was to endeavour to influence colonial conduct more informally, through issuing 'warnings by the police under executive instructions that the relevant sections under the Penal Code may be invoked if the moral tone of the paper or advertisement [or book] is not improved'.[95] Such an approach was often taken, for example, in the case of the Arya Samaj, which had a penchant for publishing lubricious anti-Puranic and

92 Kalpagam, 'Colonial Governmentality and the Public Sphere', 37–8.

93 Kalpagam, 'Colonial Governmentality and the Public Sphere', 41. For Kalpagam it is in the public discourses of social reform that this dialectic of acceptance and rejection is most evident.

94 Note by H. Birdwood, 10 June 1893, Vol. 48 Comp 865/1893, Judicial Department, MSA. Indian governments faced the same dilemma when Indian authors or publishers submitted book manuscripts to them to enquire whether they were suitable for sale. See, for example, 212B/1938, Political, Executive Br., Home Department, NAI.

95 Such intervention often did the trick, since it was 'often the fear of such action' that kept offending items (including those that 'may after all stand the test of obscenity in a court of law') 'away from the public gaze'. Note by D. L. Das, 22 July 1940, 136/40, Judicial, Home Department, NAI. See also 353–68/June 1889, Public, Deposit, Home Department, NAI; 174–6/June 1911, Political, B, Home Department, NAI; and Vol. 173 Comp 1757/1910, Judicial Department, MSA.

anti-Islamic tracts that endangered not only the morals but the peace of the Indian public.[96] Other approaches included asking publishers to 'surrender' 'obscene' texts in order to evade prosecution, or on occasion to issue expurgated editions of their works.[97] Known dealers in 'obscene' wares might also find their imports kept under surveillance by the Sea Customs Department, or their correspondence subjected to the 'particular attention' of the Post Office.[98]

Such procedures were applied selectively by the colonial state, across both time and place, since in contrast to Britain or Australia (in particular the latter) it did not develop a coherent system for the regulation of 'obscene' publications – as acknowledged by the government itself, its system was instead an 'abstract entity'.[99] It was, to begin with, split between the Indian and provincial governments.[100] The Indian government operated largely as what Gerald Barrier refers to as a 'nerve center' in overseeing the regulatory mechanisms of the provinces, reserving to itself only the power to prohibit the importation of publications under the Sea Customs Act, and to decide how publications seized by the Post Office or customs were disposed of.[101] It was the provincial governments that assumed primary responsibility for regulating the obscene through such means as the Post Office (by issuing orders for the interception of 'obscene' works or for the de-registration of newspapers to prevent their transmission through the post), the Sea Customs Department (through adjudicating customs decisions relating to 'obscene' items), and the courts (through initiating prosecutions). To determine what to regulate, the provincial governments relied on networks of advisors ranging from Oriental Translators to Inspectors-General of Police to district magistrates (who oversaw the registration of literature and printing presses in the *mofussil*), although the nature of such networks varied from province to province.[102] The police assisted such activities by checking on the

[96] See, for example, note by Denizel Ibbetson, 8 February 1905, 23–4/May 1904, Public, A, Home Department, NAI; and King, 'Images of Virtue and Vice'.

[97] See 1398/1922, Judicial, B, Home Department, NAI; and 101/June 1912, Police, B, Home Department, NAI.

[98] See 326–27/November 1902, Public, A, Home Department, NAI; and 241–2/1911, Public, B, Home Department, NAI.

[99] 233/38, Political, Home Department, NAI.

[100] The system of literary regulation in Britain and Australia was also, of course, divided between the central and local governments in the former and the Commonwealth and state governments in the latter, but in both cases – particularly in the Australian – the central government retained more control over it than was the case in India.

[101] See note by H. A. Stuart, 9 March, 1907, 210–11/September 1907, Public, A, Home Department, NAI.

[102] Thus in Bombay and the Central Provinces the Oriental Translator held the main responsibility for bringing 'obscene' publications to the attention of the police, while in

registration of printing presses, monitoring the activities of known purveyors of 'obscene' wares, searching for such publications (on the order of a magistrate) and serving in an 'advisory' capacity at Indian post offices.[103]

The need to ensure (Indian) public support for the regulation of the obscene and the heterogeneity of the state's regulatory mechanisms – not to mention the reluctance of colonial officials to put those mechanisms into operation – offers evidence as to why the colonial state was unable to transform efforts to regulate the obscene into a viable project of colonial governmentality. There were, however, two additional, and arguably more significant, reasons. The first was the fact that, as in Australia, officials, magistrates and judges drew on the precedents set by English common law for the regulation of the obscene, which meant that the Hicklin test became, once again, the standard common law definition of obscenity in yet another completely different context from the one in which it had originated. As the birth control campaigner R. D. Karve wearily observed, in India the Hicklin judgment became 'a mantra which every judge refers to ... whatever the decision he has to give'.[104] In theory the Hicklin test actually worked *better* when applied to a colonial context such as India than it did in Australia (or, for that matter, in Britain), since by acknowledging that 'Matter which might deprave the minds of one class of youth might be common subject of conversation of youths of another class or race' it essentially made allowance for the possibility that the British and Indians might have divergent notions as to what constituted obscenity.[105] As Home Department member Mr Hobhouse noted in 1876 in a debate on the Dramatic Performances Bill,

Madras this job went to a Deputy Inspector-General for Criminal Investigation (who worked with four translators and their establishments). A similar system prevailed in the United Provinces. Bengal divided the job between an Oriental Translator (who handled literature) and the head of the Special Branch of the Bengal Police (who handled the press), while Punjab relegated the job solely to a Deputy Inspector-General of its Special Branch, and Burma to a Deputy Inspector-General of Police for Railways and Criminal Investigation. The registration of Indian publications was likewise conducted by a motley assortment of officials in the various provinces, ranging from a Registrar of Books in Madras to the Director of Public Instruction in East Bengal and Assam. Note by H. C. Woodman, 26 April 1910, and by A. L., 13 May 1910; and 41–9/January 1912, Political, B, Home Department, NAI.

103 See Secret Letter D-363, 12 June 1923, 67/39, Political, Home Department, NAI. A special branch of the police, the Criminal Intelligence Bureau, also dealt with 'obscene' publications.

104 *Reason* (June and July 1940), n.p., clipping in 211 p.t. II/1938, Political, Examination Br., Home Department, NAI.

105 Note by H. A. Stuart, 11 October, 1906, 17/January 1907, Public, Deposit, Home Department, NAI. The two most important cases that enshrined the Hicklin judgment in Indian common law were *Queen-Empress* v. *Indarman* in 1881 and *Queen-Empress* v. *Parashram Yeshvant* in 1895.

since the British in India were 'foreigners, accustomed to a different standard [of obscenity]' from Indians, however much the government 'might try to judge people by their own standard, they were likely to err'. The benefit of the Hicklin judgment was therefore that it 'did not set up any absolute or ideal standard of decency or purity'.[106]

Yet this was also the key problem with the Hicklin test when put into effect in India, since it led to the development of a dual conception of obscenity, namely subject matter that might be deemed offensive to Indians and material that Europeans might find offensive. Reconciling the two posed almost insurmountable problems, since the difficulty lay in determining whether to take action against something that might 'deprave and corrupt' Indians but not Europeans, or vice versa. As one colonial official judiciously noted in 1890, while the government should not 'tolerate everything that native opinion does not condemn', it would nonetheless be 'most ineffectual and unwise to attempt to raise the native standard by punishing offences against our own'.[107] In practice this meant that the aesthetic or moral concerns of the rulers generally gave way to the literal or perceived anxieties of the ruled; for the Rangoon Collector of Customs 'obscene' thus meant 'obscene relative to the average inhabitant of the Indian port in question'.[108]

But such a policy also put British officials in the awkward position of trying to protect such 'average inhabitants' from being 'corrupted' by matter that would 'ordinarily not be regarded as obscene in Europe' but that they were supposedly disgusted by.[109] In doing so they ran foul, not surprisingly, of Western-educated elites, who, while they embraced the technique of aesthetic imperialism, rejected its rationality. British officials therefore often found themselves having to defend certain aspects of Indian culture against the charges of Western-educated elites that they were obscene. Religious images, which had been exempt from prosecution for obscenity since 1856, were a particularly sensitive issue.[110] After assuring his listeners that 'there are few people in the

[106] *Abstract of the Proceedings of the Council of the Governor-General of India*, p. 341.

[107] D. Ibbetson to S. S. Thorburn, 21 February 1890, 547–83/October 1890, Public, A, Home Department, NAI.

[108] A. E. Boyd to Secretary, Central Board of Revenue, 28 October 1927, R. Dis. 1271/Cust 27, Customs Duties, Central Board of Revenue, NAI.

[109] Note by P. C. Bamford, Director of Criminal Intelligence, n.d., 597/27, Judicial, Home Department, NAI. See also D. Dis. 1040/Cust 25, Customs Duties, Central Board of Revenue, NAI.

[110] The 1856 Act to Prevent the Sale or Exposure of Obscene Books and Pictures included an exception that 'Nothing contained in this Act shall apply to any representation sculptured, engraved, or painted, on or in any temple, or on any car used for the conveyance of idols', which was in turn incorporated into the Indian Penal Code

country who have more to do with obscene literature than I have', the Director-General of Posts and Telegraphs, Sir Geoffrey Clarke, declared in 1925 that:

> in the history not only of Hindu religion but of all religions, phallic emblems and things of that sort were designed for a particular purpose and have behind them really no intention and no idea of obscenity. These emblems did not convey any ideas of that kind at all to the people who originally designed them and it is only modern civilization, if I may call it that . . . that has placed a wrong interpretation on these things.[111]

Such a statement was a critique, on the one hand, of colonial modernity, in particular the technology of aesthetic imperialism. But on the other it targeted Western-educated elites who, since they viewed erotic religious images as obscene, revealed that they had not yet learned to cultivate aesthetic disinterest.

Yet in spite of the institutionalization of the Hicklin judgment in India, for the British there were 'limits of decency which must not be transgressed'.[112] These fell into three broad categories: realistic depictions of sexuality; sexual representations that undermined Indian patriarchies; and delineations of the sexual mechanics of the body in a non-scientific manner. In the case of the first limit, the concern for British officials was not, to begin with, realistic works of an erotic nature in English, which were regarded as being little more than mildly titillating for Indian readers. The manner in which Indians read English realistic novels may explain the reason for such a belief, since as the critic Ram Chandra Bose confessed, when reading such literature he

> hurried over graphic descriptions of scenes which to me are outlandish; inventories of articles of furniture which it will never fall to my lot even to dream of buying; vivid pictures of costumes which I scarcely expect to see; and portraitures equally realistic of drawing-rooms in which I should probably feel myself and be felt to be a fish out of water.[113]

English reality (or, we may assume in the case of Zola's works, French reality rendered into English) was simply too alien and alienating to appear either real or meaningful to Indian readers.[114] In the case of such

(although after the word 'idols' the much broader and more contentious phrase 'or kept or used for any religious purpose' was added).

111 *Legislative Assembly, Debates*, V, 20 (20 February 1925), n.p., clipping in 570/23, Judicial, Home Department, NAI.

112 *Indian Law Reports*, 3 Allahabad p. 840.

113 *Madras Christian College Magazine* (1889–90), cited in Joshi, *In Another Country*, p. 129.

114 Joshi, *In Another Country*, p. 129. See also Mukherji, *Realism and Reality*.

realistic works, Indian readers were therefore ironically able to distance themselves, if not quite cultivate aesthetic disinterest, to a degree that Europeans were not. Realistic works in the vernaculars were, however, another matter. In 1924, for example, the Bombay Commissioner of Police initiated a prosecution against the *Sahel Sapata* for publishing a story about a man who seduces women in a house that is thoroughly 'Indian' on the inside (it is filled, we are informed, with 'Swadeshi furniture'), but that contains a bathroom with a swimming-pool-sized bathtub surrounded by pictures of 'European ladies in a naked condition' and of 'attractive scenes depicting modern ideas about the sports of sexual love' that he had ordered from Germany.[115] It was not the reference to depictions of naked European women that led to concerns with a story like this (since, as we shall see, such images circulated fairly freely in colonial India), but rather its endless iteration of erotic details, which served to make the scenes it depicted real for Indian readers. Thus while the intent of a work such as *Manavi Prapanch*, prosecuted by the Bombay government in 1913, may have been 'to depict a realistic picture of Hindu society', for District Magistrate L. J. Mountford the 'nauseous detail' in which it described 'How temples are used for immoral purposes, how widows resort to abortion to hide their shame, [and] how blackguard sadhus lure women into their meshes and corrupt their morals' rendered it capable of 'depraving and corrupting' Indian readers.[116]

In the case of the second limit, which entailed the upholding of indigenous patriarchies (regarded as necessary, as numerous scholars have demonstrated, for the maintenance of colonial rule), almost any depictions of sexuality that threatened to subvert them – even if they contained 'no grossly indecent details' or 'obscene language' – were regarded by British officials as obscene.[117] Matter that portrayed rampant female sexuality or that inverted sexual hierarchies was subject to particular attention, as in the case of a story in an 1893 issue of the *Jam-e Jamshed* about a prostitute who had such a 'relish of prostitution' that to her 'one man or four men is just the same'; while the *Hindu Punch* was prosecuted in 1890 for publishing a story about an old Hindu priest who, 'with a view to give her opportunities of misbehaving herself', often

[115] 'Lalkaka's New Wife', *Sahel Sapata* (20 August 1924), 65-II/24, Political, Executive Br., Home Department, MSA. While the Commissioner of Police attempted to proceed against the publisher of the paper, Nathalal Kalyanji Mehta, he was living in the princely state of Baroda. Since publishing an obscene publication was not an extraditable offence under the Indian Penal Code, the Bombay government ended up abandoning the prosecution.

[116] 24 pt. III/1913, Books and Publications, Judicial Department, MSA.

[117] *Kailaschandra Acharjya* v. *King-Emperor*, *Indian Law Reports*, 60 Calcutta, pts. I–XII (1933), pp. 208–9.

left his wife at home for long periods of time and affixed a sign over the door reading 'Ramchee pooja' (which while translated as 'the worship of Rama', if read backwards and separated into different syllables, according to the Bombay Reporter on the Native Press, read 'go and have sexual connection').[118] Stories about rape were also often deemed obscene, particularly when carried out by family members, and virtually anything that referred to sodomy even if, as in the case of the *Rameshdâr Atmakathâ*, it contained 'pious remarks ... as to the ruinous effects of such a vice'.[119] Such a work posed the threat, it was feared, that 'immature readers would ... be tempted on reading the book to seek such experiences'.[120]

At stake in the third and final limit that for British officials should not be transgressed, the delineation (in non-scientific language) of the sexual functions of the body, were considerably different concerns, namely the confrontation between British and Indian ideas about the body, how to regulate it, and the acceptable parameters of public discourse about it. Works on 'sexual science', generally written in Sanskrit and based on religious texts (*kamashastras*), had circulated freely in India throughout the period of colonial rule. But while prior to 1900 such works, according to the Director of the Linguistic Survey of India, George Grierson, were 'impossible to get except through secret channels', in the late nineteenth century 'imitations or translations' had begun to appear, and by the 1920s were being 'openly advertised and published' and were, moreover, obtainable almost everywhere.[121] So too were advertisements for such works, often more explicit than the texts themselves, as well as for aphrodisiacs and virility enhancers. The problem for the British was not only that even educated Indians were 'very fine in their open allusions to matters and subjects to which it is considered amongst Europeans indelicate or even improper to refer to', but that most Indians regarded such texts or advertisements not as 'stimulat[ing] immorality

[118] 'A handsome prostitute who smoked opium', *Jam-e Jamshed* (22 December 1893), n.p., clipping in Vol. 177 Comp. 644/1893, Judicial Department, MSA; and G. M. Saithe, Esq., Reporter on the Native Press, to J. Monteath, Esq., Acting Secretary to the Government, Political Department, 20 February 1890, Vol. 163A J.D. 1101/1890, Prosecutions, Judicial Department, MSA. Upon the advice of the Public Prosecutor that the article in the *Jam-e Jamshed* would not obtain a conviction, the Bombay government decided to refrain from prosecution.

[119] For example, the editor of the Bombay magazine *Theatre*, Ratilat Sukhal, was convicted in February 1934 of publishing a series of stories featuring rapes, which were carried out primarily by family members or individuals close to the family. 49/1934, Political, Executive Br., Home Department, MSA.

[120] *Kailaschandra Acharjya* v. *King-Emperor*.

[121] George Grierson to Sir Arthur Hirtzel, 27 August 1925, 669/25, Home Department, NAI.

but rather act[ing] as a warning against its probable results'.[122] The enshrinement of the Hicklin test in India, however, meant that 'allowance must be made for local sentiment', and when local sentiment regarded 'seminal fluid ... [as] the very essence of the human body', then little could be done to regulate advertisements that offered treatments to restore virility that has been destroyed by 'masturbation, [and] excessive sexual enjoyment' or to cure 'flaccidity and crookedness of man's private parts'.[123]

In the 1890s and early 1900s some efforts were, however, made to prosecute *kamashastra* literature and advertisements for using 'unscientific' (and hence obscene) language, but since it proved 'impossible to lay down any general rule' as to what constituted an 'obscene' versus a 'scientific' advertisement or text, the verdict was generally that they were not obscene.[124] By the First World War, such works therefore circulated

[122] E. Ferrers Nicholson, Esq., Bombay Public Prosecutor, to Commissioner of Police, 19 December 1902, Vol. 164 Comp. 391/1903, Judicial Department, MSA; and F. G. Hartness Anderson, District Magistrate, Surat, to Secretary to Government, Judicial Department, 29 June 1910, Vol. 173 Comp. 1757/1910, Judicial Department, MSA. While British officials may therefore have found *kamashastra* works such as *Fareb-un-Nisa Yaani Aurton Ke Makr* (*The Deceits of Women*) too obscene to even translate, they were forced to concede that since 'to the Hindu, procreation is a religious necessity', then 'the offer of some medical aid to the childless and impotent could hardly be called "obscene"' (nor, for that matter, could items that 'profess[ed] to increase the pleasure of sexual intercourse'). 88/1934, Political, Executive, A, Home Department, MSA.

[123] Legal opinion by G. H. B. Kendrick, Advocate-General, 29 April 1911; *Rangpur Darpan*, 15 August 1910, 174–76/June 1911, Political, B, Home Department, NAI; and advertisements from the *Akhbar-i-Soudagar* (27 July 1910), p. 3, and *Rajasthan* (23 July 1910), p. 5, Vol. 173 Comp. 1757/1910, Judicial Department, MSA. As one official noted in regard to such advertisements in 1906, 'because [they] would not be allowed in England, it would not necessarily follow that the managers of newspapers who insert them in India should be prosecuted'. Note by J. P. Hewett, 1 December 1906, 17/1907, Public, Deposit, Home Department, NAI.

[124] Vol. 173 Comp. 1757/1910, Judicial Department, MSA. Moreover, since as the District Magistrate of Surat observed in 1910, 'The terms used [in such advertisements] are ordinarily Sanscrit [sic] derivatives and the language probably such as only the more or less educated could understand', an individual such as Thakkar Datt, proprietor of the *Desh Upkarak*, was able to escape conviction for publishing 'obscene' advertisements based on the 'technical and recondite terms' that were employed in them. Hartness Anderson to Government, 29 June 1910; and *King-Emperor* v. *Thakkar Datt*, *The Criminal Law Journal of India*, 17 (1917), p. 129. Although Indian governments did occasionally secure convictions for the publication of such matter (see, for example, 239/1929, Political, Home Department, MSA, and *Sarat Chandra Ghose* v. *King-Emperor*, *The Indian Law Reports*, 32 Calcutta (1904), pp. 247–8), fear of failing to do so meant that they generally declined to prosecute (see Vol. 107 A/1890, Judicial Department, MSA; Vol. 198 Comp. 1037/1895, Judicial Department, MSA; Vol. 11 Comp. 1512/1897, Judicial Department, MSA; Vol. 171/1902, Judicial Department, MSA; 150/1936, Political, Executive Br., Home Department, MSA; 163/1936, Political, Executive Br., Home Department, MSA; and 211 pt. II/1938, Political, Executive Br., Home Department, MSA).

with relative impunity in India. So too did English-language sexology literature, including works such as H. C. Fischer and Dr. E. X. Dubois's *Sexual Life During the World War* ('a daring revelation of the varied kinds of sexual vices that were in practice during the days of the Great War'), Joseph Fishman's *Sex in Prison*, A. Hesnard's *Strange Lust: Psychology of Homo Sexuality*, and eugenics works such as Walter Gallichan's *Sterilization of the Unfit*.[125] After the Bombay High Court's decree in 1892 that 'there is nothing obscene ... in advocating checks to conception' (an opinion substantiated by reference to the New South Wales verdict of Justice Windeyer), contraceptive literature and advertisements were also allowed to circulate freely, including works on 'coital technique' when presented in the guise of birth control information (even if they were 'exotically illustrated').[126] So too, after another Bombay court ruling three years later that nudity was not, in itself, obscene, were images of the nude white female body.[127]

The problem of the female nude reveals that regardless of the 'intellectual rapacity' with which colonial states attempted to produce knowledges about the people over whom they ruled, such knowledges were not only reconstructed and reassessed through being experienced and enacted, they often coexisted with 'a kind of despair' on the part of the colonizers in the face of the reality of the colonial situation.[128] As the Lieutenant-Governor of Bengal, Sir Richard Temple, declared in 1876, all 'Publications which are designed to bring contempt upon us nationally, must ... tend to bring our sovereignty into some disrepute also'.[129] But since the core of British claims to a higher morality was the 'purity' of their women, publications that cast their morals in a derogatory light struck, as another critic observed, 'at the very roots of our social and moral fabric'.[130] Such concerns meant that colonial officials often agonized over whether to regulate a wide assortment of publications that threatened to undermine such a fabric, ranging from popular fiction such as the works of the often-targeted G. W. M. Reynolds (the 'grossly

125 Advertisements for books in the *New Book Digest*, July 1938 and October–November 1938, 212B/1938, Political, Executive Br., Home Department, MSA.

126 Ratanlal, *Unreported Criminal Cases*, p. 620; and advertisement in *New Book Digest*, October–November, 1937, 212B/1938, Political, Executive Br. Home Department, MSA. Where the law drew the line, however, was in relation to literature or advertisements relating to abortion (since under the Indian Penal Code abortion was a criminal offence).

127 *Queen-Empress* v. *Parashram Yeshvant*.

128 Thomas, *Colonialism's Culture*, pp. 15–16.

129 Minute, 13 June 1876, 214–31/September 1876, P.V. Vol. 232, Judicial Department, NAI.

130 M. A. Rowson, 'Demoralising Effects of Indecent Films', *Eastern Times*, 19 June 1935, 2/1/34, Political, Home Department, NAI.

false view of English morals and character' in which purportedly gave Indian students a poor view of European women), religious tracts (that in evoking a 'similarity between the Hindu and Romish systems of consecrating women to the service of religion' threatened to make Christianity 'a scandal among the heathens'), and cinema posters (renowned for their images of 'scantily clad women').[131] They even considered regulating the behaviour of European women themselves, whether in their dress (which if not sufficiently modest did 'untold harm' to British prestige), their employment (in the case of European prostitutes or even barmaids, who 'cannot but bring us into contempt in the eyes of the natives of this country'), or in their sexual activities (as in the case of masturbatory aids such as 'finger ticklers', or as the Indian government termed them 'rubber appliances for the sexual abuse of women').[132] Colonial officials were generally forced to concede, however, that their desire to regulate such behaviour or matter was born of the fact that 'our self-esteem is wounded by the grossly incorrect view they give of English morals'.[133] Since to give in to such wounding would have served to undermine the very moral logic of colonialism then matter that could be 'published with impunity in England' had to be allowed to circulate freely in India – including images of the female nude.[134]

While some colonial officials sought to throw aesthetics and the Hicklin test to the wind and proscribe if not the circulation, at the very

131 H. Parsons, Secretary of the Calcutta Missionary Conference, to Sir John Woodburn, Lieutenant-Governor of Bengal, n.d., 24–33/1902, Municipalities, A, Home Department, NAI; Rev. W. E. S. Holland, Warden, Oxford and Cambridge Hostel, Allahabad, to H. W. Orange, Esq., Director-General of Education, 27 June 1907, 13/August 1907, Public, Deposit, Home Department, NAI; 'A Shameful Calumny', Letter to the Editor from 'A Catholic Layman', *Bombay Gazette*, 5 May 1892, Vol. 185 Comp. 885/1892, Prosecutions, Judicial Department, MSA; and 2/1/34, Political, Home Department, NAI. Cinema posters tended to evoke greater concern than the films themselves, thanks in part to the activities of the provincial film censor boards and the efforts of the British Board of Film Censors to establish guidelines for filmmakers regarding subject matter that could undermine British prestige. See Chowdhry, *Colonial India*, p. 54.

132 Meliscent Shephard to F. A. R. Sempkins, Esq., Secretary to the National Vigilance Association, 7 August 1933, GB/106/4NVA/S.88/2, Box 107, WL; Petition, Calcutta Missionary Conference, n.d., 24–33/1902, Municipalities, A, Home Department, NAI; and 198–200/March 1906, Judicial, A, Home Department, NAI. As 'Appliances for the cure of Chlorosis, or Green-Sickness', which 'European girls suffer[ed] at the time of their puberty in the hot climate of India', the purpose of 'finger ticklers', according to their importer Fothergill and Co., was 'to help girls to preserve their chastity in private, without their having recourse to commit adultery, or to have immoral intercourse'. 'The Bengal government, however, unconvinced as to their medicinal purpose, declared 'finger ticklers' and all other 'objectionable rubber items' (including 'imitations of the male and female sexual organs') prohibited imports.

133 Note by H. A. Stuart, n.d., 13/August 1907, Public, Deposit, Home Department, NAI.

134 Note by H. A. Stuart, n.d., 13/August 1907.

least the importation of nude images of European women (on the grounds that 'the internal traffic' in such images 'is carried on by making reproductions of pictures previously imported'), the general policy was to endeavour to regulate only those images that would be deemed obscene in Britain, namely those which, thanks to their exposure of pubic hair or their depiction of a 'crude' pose or 'vulgarity of expression', might 'suggest lewd thoughts in the minds of persons looking at them'.[135] Prosecutions for such matter were, occasionally, successful. This was not the case, however, with images that had a pretension to either art or science. Magazines that purportedly aimed to '[help] photographers in taking photos of the nude female figure' or 'to prove the case for the nudist cult' were therefore – regardless of the 'particular kind of shop' in which they were sold or the 'particular class of public' to which they were sold – permitted free circulation in India.[136] Thus while in a colony such as Basutoland the discovery that 'brass finger rings containing photographs of nude white women' were being sold to the local inhabitants led to the passage in 1912 of an Obscene Publications Proclamation which made the selling of such items a crime punishable by not only a fine of up to £250 and two years hard labour, but the administration of twenty-four lashes (which should preferably be administered, according to the Right Honourable Viscount Gladstone, High Commissioner for South Africa, by the 'cat', by far 'the best instrument' for such a task since 'Its severity can be easily adjusted & ... it can be used according to the physique of the offender'), in India the dictates of colonial governmentality and the enshrinement of the Hicklin test

[135] Note by P. C. Bamford, Deputy Director of Criminal Intelligence, 6 July 1927, 597/27, Judicial, Home Department, NAI; and *King-Emperor* v. *Krishnaji Anand Joshi and Prushotm Sadashiv Joshi*, Esplanade Police Court, Bombay, 2 February 1926, R. Dis. 319/Cust 26, Customs Duties, Central Board of Revenue, NAI. The Commissioners of Police in both Bombay and Calcutta made efforts in the 1920s to deal with the circulation of such images by ensuring their prohibition at the docks, but the Sea Customs Department proved less than cooperative. See, for example, R. Dis. 1271/Cust 27, Customs Duties, Central Board of Revenue, NAI; and D. Dis. 1040/ Cust 25, Customs Duties, Central Board of Revenue, NAI.

[136] J. M. Sladen, Secretary to the Government of Bombay, Home Department, to Secretary to the Government of India, Home Department, 23 June 1939, 131/39, Judicial, Home Department, NAI. When in 1937 the Madras government pressured the Indian government to prohibit the importation of the English nudist journal *Health and Efficiency* on the grounds that it would 'give a wrong idea of western civilisation', the latter responded that not only was the magazine not obscene, but that it could not be prohibited 'merely on the ground that its purpose is likely to be misunderstood in India'. C. F. Brackenbury, Esq., Chief Secretary to the Government of Madras, to Secretary to the Government of India, Home Department, 3 December 1937; and Government of India to Government of Madras, 4 January 1938, 372/37 Judicial, Home Department, NAI.

rendered the regulation of such works, let alone the punishment of those who circulated them, a virtual impossibility.[137]

With the law having deemed that religious imagery and contraceptive literature were not obscene, and that most material pertaining to sexuality and the body did not merit legal intervention, the net effect of the institutionalization of the Hicklin judgment in India was to give it, by the 1890s, what was undoubtedly the most liberal obscenity law in the empire. This is not to say that the state made no efforts to regulate the obscene after the 1890s – indeed, prosecutions for obscenity actually peaked in the following decade in the face of the emergence of new forms of 'obscenity'. But since in obscenity trials the colonial courtroom became what Robert Darnton terms a 'hermeneutic battlefield' where each side attempted to obtain 'symbolic dominance through textual exegesis', the failure rate of such prosecutions was high.[138] Moreover, the sheer size of the task by the early twentieth century made even contemplating regulating the obscene a virtual impossibility, since the state was no more able to check the use of 'obscene' language during festivals such as Holi than it was to sort through all of the post received by the Sea Post Office (up to 2,000 mail bags a day by 1909).[139] The chaos of the state's systems to regulate the 'obscene' generated further checks, as did the virtual autonomy of these systems.[140] The reach of

137 Acting Resident Commissioner of Maseru to Gladstone, 15 July 1911; note by Gladstone, 14 January 1912, DO 119/865, NAUK.

138 Darnton, 'Un-British Activities', 87. Translation issues played a large role in these textual battles, since as the pleader and president of the Simla Municipal Committee E. S. Cullin noted in 1890 in the case of Urdu, 'The term employed in vernacular editions of the Indian Penal Code to express the term *obscene* is *fahish* or *fahsh*, which does not, I believe, connote the Urdu equivalents for the word "indecent", which . . . are "*be-adab, beemtiyáz, násháista, nahamwár, namuláim, besobh*"'. The Police Act used yet another word, *behayái*, a linguistic complexity that Cullin claimed would ensure that 'many an indecent ad or writing would escape punishment'. Memo, E. S. Cullin, 19 February 1890, 457–83/October 1890, Public, A, Home Department, NAI.

139 As the City Magistrate of Nasik asserted in 1888 in response to a complaint about the ineffectiveness of the police in checking the use of 'obscene' language during the Holi festival, it was 'impossible for a handful of Police . . . to watch the action of every person among the twenty-two thousand residents of Nasik, at a time when the minds of the people are excited and bent upon carrying out the customs of the festival, the object of which has a tendency to obscenity'. Mr Richardson, City Magistrate of Nasik, to Magistrate First Class, Nasik, 21 June 1888, Vol. 117, J. D. 974/1888, Judicial Department, MSA; and 14–18/October 1909, Political, A, Home Department, NAI.

140 The efforts of the Indian government in 1890 to do something about 'obscene' advertisements, for example, while welcomed by some provincial governments, were greeted with considerable reluctance by others (particularly Bengal), which forced the Home Department to limply concede that it should not 'go further than we have done to press Bengal or other Governments to greater activity' in the matter. Provincial governments wishing to put a stop to the infiltration of 'obscene' matter from other provinces faced similar difficulties. 457–83/October 1890, Public, A, Home

these systems extended, furthermore, only throughout British India, which meant that the state was as helpless to put a stop to the activities of individuals such as Major Fallon, author of *The Escapades of Erotic Edna* and safely ensconced in the princely state of Hyderabad, as it was to stop *The Romance of Lust* from being sent from the French territory of Chandernagore through the Indian post.[141] Such vulnerability reveals that British efforts to regulate the obscene were always made, as Tapti Roy argues, 'from a position of externality'.[142]

The colonial state did not, however, operate entirely from a position of externality. Indeed, the second major reason that the state was unable to transform its efforts to regulate the obscene into a coherent project of colonial governmentality – and an additional and generally overlooked cause as to why governmentality was inevitably dislocated (and hence reinvented) in a colonial context such as India – was that, thanks to the progressive Indianization of the state from the 1880s Indian officials ranging from magistrates and judges at the higher end of the state apparatus to the thousands of postal, customs and police officials at the lower end came to play an ever-increasing role in these systems. While such transformations gradually *lessened* the externality of such regulatory systems, they nonetheless threatened to undermine the fragile rationale of such systems. The state therefore responded to this process by endeavouring to prevent Indians from playing key roles in such regulatory systems and even, in the case of the Post Office and Sea Customs Department, by excluding them from employment in the branches of these departments directly responsible for regulating the obscene.

Department, NAI; Note by H. Stokes, 1 January 1911, 174–6/June 1911, Political, B, Home Department, NAI; and Vol. 15 Comp. 945/1893, Judicial Department, MSA.

141 247/43, Public, Home Department, NAI; and 5/March 1911, Political, Deposit, Home Department, NAI. The Dewan of Nawanagar, for example, was less than sympathetic to the efforts of the Bombay government to put a stop to the dissemination of a publication printed in Nawanagar entitled *Important Disclosures*, not only because its author had 'thousands & thousands of such pamphlets printed in Calcutta and Bombay' and distributed them throughout India, but because 'if the long arm of the British Government [was] unable to reach him' it was 'too much ... to expect more from this state'. Dewan of Nawanagar to Agent to the Government of Bombay, Katiawar, 25 January 1906, Vol. 202/1906, Judicial Department, MSA.

142 Roy, 'Disciplining the Printed Text', p. 53. Such prosecutions were by no means a complete loss for the colonial state, since they provided valuable lessons about how to more effectively apply the law to deal with 'seditious' publications – which, first criminalized in the 1870s (although the first conviction against them was not secured until 1898), had by the end of the nineteenth century become perceived as a greater threat to colonial rule. See A. C. Trevor, 30 July 1898, 329–44/May 1898, Judicial, A, Home Department, NAI. See also 131–3, Judicial, A, Home Department, NAI; 161–9/October 1878, Judicial, B, Home Department, NAI; and 290–334/October 1881, Judicial, A, Home Department, NAI; 345–76/May 1899, Public, Home Department, NAI; and 260–286/October 1891, Public, Home Department, NAI.

A brief look at the size and nature of the Post and Telegraph Department offers some insights into why British officials were wary of according powers to regulate the obscene to Indian officials. By the 1880s there were 9,763 post offices in India, a figure which had almost doubled by 1906 to 16,775 and by 1935 had risen to 23,629 – two-thirds of which, moreover, were staffed by what were referred to as 'non-departmental agents' (such as school teachers and shopkeepers).[143] Indian employees, unsurprisingly, made up the bulk of this vast department. Thanks to the department's notoriously unremunerative pay scale, such employees were, moreover – at least according to British critics – 'from a different and in some sense inferior class of men to that from which other Departments draw their employees'.[144] Such a lament was chanted repeatedly by senior postal officials, who jockeyed endlessly for higher rates of pay in order to attract more qualified candidates, particularly in the *mofussil*.[145] As Justice Sir Cecil Walsh observed with some distaste in 1930:

> The ordinary up-country post-office, or district sub-post-office ... is not a pleasant place either to look upon, or to work in. It is generally dark & airless, & seems to be permeated with *khaki*-coloured paper, dust, & a general air of untidiness ... A heavy cloud of physical and mental nostalgia hangs over the place, and the lassitude which appears to affect the staff is to be found, only too often, in the supervision, whose lack of grip leads inevitably to a looseness of discipline.

The hazards of the job may have contributed to the poor quality of job applicants, for postal employees, particularly those in rural areas, were subjected to an amazing variety of dangers in the course of their employment: in 1906 alone five postal officials were murdered, the department was the victim of twenty-three highway robberies, one postal employee was eaten by a tiger and another by a crocodile, and numerous others succumbed to fires, avalanches and a cyclone.[146]

The vast numbers of Indian postal officials, not to mention the low esteem in which they were held, led the Indian government in 1909 to withhold authority to detain or open 'obscene' postal matter from all but

[143] 71–3/February 1892, Post Office, A, Finance and Commerce Department, NAI; 1–5/December 1906, Post Office, A, Commerce and Industry Department, NAI; and Indian Posts and Telegraphs Department *Annual Report* (1934–35). The department already contained over 40,000 employees by the 1880s.

[144] *Proceedings of the Sub-Committee, Public Service Commission*, p. 9. Such a complaint was also frequently made about the police. See Verma, 'Consolidation of the Raj', 109.

[145] See 1–3/September 1907, Post Office, A, Department of Commerce and Industry, NAI; and 25–7/February 1908, Post Office, A, Department of Commerce and Industry, NAI.

[146] 1–5/December 1906, Post Office, A, Department of Commerce and Industry, NAI.

'post offices where European or Eurasian postmasters are ordinarily employed', since as far as the government was concerned 'To extend this authorization to all postmasters would ... be impossible and quite useless'.[147] The powers of search and seizure were, however, also accorded to senior officers in the Sea Post Office and the Railway Mail Services – the arms of the department that, despite Indian protests, the government managed to maintain as European preserves until virtually the end of colonial rule.[148] The Preventing and Appraising branches of the Sea Customs Department, whose responsibilities included the seizure of 'obscene' publications, were likewise safeguarded as 'a close preserve for Europeans and Anglo-Indians'.[149] When in the 1920s the department was forced, under Indian pressure, to hire more Indians as Preventive and Appraising staff, it responded by relaxing the maximum age of recruitment for such appointments (by raising it to twenty-five) and seeking out Indian officers from disbanded regiments to hire – provided, however, that they were unmarried, debt-free, and could speak and write English fluently.[150] They also had to accept a low rate of pay, factors which effectively ensured that the number of 'acceptable' applicants for such posts remained low.[151]

Yet in spite of the government's insistence that Indians had to be excluded from such posts since 'the qualifications for these appointments

[147] C. J. Stevenson-Moore, 19 January 1909, 14–18/October 1909, Political, A, Home Department, NAI. Although postal officials were accorded the power to detain publications that were banned under the Sea Customs Act in 1882, it was not until 1898 that they were able to detain postal articles that were believed to contain 'obscene' materials, and not until 1912 that such power was extended to articles that bore obscenity on their covers. Granting even such limited powers of search and seizure provoked considerable controversy (as did according such powers to the police). See Post Office (Amendment) Act, 1912; Note by C. Kerisi, 15 November 1922, 1398B/1922, Judicial, Home Department, NAI; and 520–610/1898, Separate Revenue, A, Finance and Commerce Department, NAI. See also 270/September 1907, Post Office, A, Commerce and Industry Department, NAI.

[148] *Proceedings of the Sub-Committee*, p. 9.

[149] 'Report of the Proceedings of the Standing Finance Committee', May and June 1921, 2/March 1922, Customs Establishments, Department of Commerce, NAI.

[150] 'Report of the Proceedings of the Standing Finance Committee'.

[151] By 1925 75 per cent of the department's Preventive Officers and 39 per cent of its Appraisers were European, and by 1929 Europeans and Anglo-Indians together still made up 67 per cent of the Sea Custom's Department's entire staff. D. A. Diss 123/29, Customs Establishment, Central Board of Revenue, NAI. See also 2621–4/December 1894, Statistics and Commerce, Customs, B, Finance and Commerce Department, MSA; 44–57/January 1904, Statistics and Commerce, A, Finance and Commerce Department, NAI; 1–8/February 1905, Customs, A, Department of Commerce and Industry, NAI; and 'Comparative statement showing the number of Europeans, Anglo-Indians, Hindus, Mahommedans, etc. employed in the various subordinate customs services at all the Custom Houses', 7/January 1913, Customs, Department of Commerce and Industry, NAI.

are such as no examination of the ordinary kind will test' – qualifications that, moreover, Indians were perceived to lack – in contrast to Australia the qualifications for such posts were minimal.[152] Since Preventive staff were primarily responsible for guarding vessels, thwarting the illicit landing of cargo, and searching ships, such posts were generally filled by former soldiers and police officers, who were not renowned for their educational abilities. Although such posts were not normally filled through examination, on the rare cases that they were (when a suitable candidate could not be found), the test was so simple that anyone with an elementary-level education should have been able to pass. Appraisers – who were accorded the chief responsibility for determining whether a publication should be deemed obscene and who had the power to confiscate and destroy such works – had better clerical skills, but unlike Australian Preventive staff they seem to have had less than promising literary backgrounds.[153] The same held true for most of the other European officials responsible for regulating the obscene in colonial India. District magistrates were often regarded as a particularly 'ignorant lot'. As a member of the Legislative Assembly pronounced in 1925, the average district magistrate would gladly proscribe the works of Tolstoy, Goethe, and even the Canticles of Solomon 'because he knows no better' – and he knew even less, of course, about Indian literature.[154]

If the colonial state's system to regulate the obscene was to have any possibility of success it therefore needed to rely more on polyglot officials such as G. N. Sathe, the Registrar of Native Publications for the Bombay

[152] K. G. Gupta, Secretary to the Board of Revenue, Lower Provinces, to Secretary to the Government of Bengal, Financial Department, 5 August 1890, 55–7/April 1889, Salaries, Establishment, A, Finance and Commerce Department, NAI. As one disparaging official remarked in 1889, Indians' 'physical (and moral) defects' meant that not 'one out of fifty could ride eight miles in the hour along the high road; and not one out of a hundred would have the pluck to lead a party of his own men to arrest a gang of smugglers who shewed [sic] the least signs of resistance'. That such beliefs continued to persist may explain why as late as 1910 the department found it necessary to warn its officers that 'Striking a Native' could lead to dismissal. W. S. Meyer, Esq., Secretary to the Commissioner of Salt, Abkari and Separate Revenue, Madras, to Secretary to the Government of Madras, Revenue Department, n.d., 55–7/April 1889, Salaries, Establishment, A, Finance and Commerce Department, NAI; and *The Preventive Service Manual*, p. 5.

[153] Packages were first inspected by Examiners. Appraisers were assisted in determining the given obscenity of a particular work by the list maintained by the Sea Customs Department of literature that had been previously examined but that it did not regard as obscene. If still in doubt they could consult the Special Branch of their local police force or the Central Board of Revenue. *Appraiser's Manual of Standing Orders at Calcutta Custom House*, Vol. II., n.d., D. Dis. 751-Cust I/38, Customs Duties, Central Board of Revenue, NAI; and *Madras Customs Standing Orders*.

[154] *Legislative Assembly, Debates*, V, 20. Fortunately for readers of Tolstoy and Goethe, the verdicts of district magistrates could be appealed to a higher court.

Presidency, rather than on Europeans such as the Bombay Director of Public Instruction, E. Giles. While Sathe's reports on Indian publications may have critiqued colonial rule for the neglect of vernacular literature and for forcing it 'to depend on third and fourth-rate' authors, those of Giles, as the *Indian Spectator* charged, demonstrated that he was 'Neither by temper, training nor association ... fitted for the work of appraising the merits of vernacular literature', since he lacked the 'culture and scholarship such as could appreciate the delicacies of foreign thought and diction, and sympathize with the feelings and sentiments, the hopes and aspirations of an alien people'.[155] But the difficulty, once again, was how to 'maintain a reasonable standard of "decency" when a European and a Native Magistrate' – or, for that matter, European and Indian officials – 'would have totally different ideas on the subject'.[156]

There was one way out of such a bind. It was first raised in 1874 by John Robinson, the Bengali Translator to the Government, at the very nascence of the state's efforts to regulate the obscene. It would be far wiser, Robinson advised, for the state to abstain completely from such a project and hand the task of regulation over to newly emergent Indian organizations such as the Society for the Suppression of Obscenity, which had been founded the previous year.[157] Containing an impressive array of Hindus, Christians, Brahmos and Muslims who were, in the words of Keshub Chunder Sen, 'all united in this great work by a common morality', the explicit aim of the Society was to enforce the law against 'obscene' publications and to improve it if necessary.[158] The larger goal, however, was to further 'the progress of the country' through the 'promotion of pure, and the suppression of undoubtedly vicious, literature'.[159] The problem to date, as Syed Ameer Ali lamented at the Society's launch, was that 'There is a certain *vis inertia* among our people

155 Vol. 17 Comp. 700/1893, General Department, MSA; and 'The Director of Public Instruction, Bombay, and the Author of *Sansarika'*, *Indian Spectator*, 16 September 1900, p. 731, clipping in Vol. 13 Comp. 700/1900, General Department, MSA. Giles took over writing the Reports on Publications Registered for the Bombay Presidency from Sathe in 1899, but following the mêlée that greeted the publication of the article in the *Spectator* the task was handed over to the Oriental Translator.

156 Note by P. P. H., 11 October 1890, 457–83/October 1890, Public, A, Home Department, NAI. Indian magistrates, to the frustration of British officials, often failed to convict in what were for them clear-cut cases of obscenity. See, for example, 212B/1938, Political, Executive Br., Home Department, NAI.

157 John Robinson to Secretary to the Government of Bengal, 7 March 1874, 463–4/ March 1874, Judicial, B, Judicial Department, WBSA.

158 'The Society for the Suppression', 192. Sen, who was also on the Executive Committee of the British, Continental and General Federation for the Abolition of Government Regulation of Prostitution, was a great advocate of such organizations. Levine, *Prostitution, Race*, p. 104.

159 'The Society for the Suppression', 179.

which makes them feel the strongest disinclination to give themselves any extra trouble in order to promote public welfare or bring an offender to justice'. The Society aimed to 'supply this want of public spirit on the part of our fellow-countrymen' through 'act[ing] as a silent yet active police on the conduct of those wretches who pander to the morbid tastes of a certain class of the Indian community'. The colonial government had supplied both the legal tools and the education to provide the framework for India's uplift; now it was up to Indians, Ali made clear, to implement those tools and to complete the 'unfinished character' of that education by shaping its moral component.[160]

If, as Gyan Prakash argues, the first vivisection performed by an Indian in 1836 represents the beginning of the emergence of biopower in India, of the subjection of Indians to a new form of surveillance and control and, with it, the birth of their constitution as modern subjects, then Robinson's proposal represents its triumph, or rather the possibility that for the British the project of colonial governmentality *had in fact succeeded* in colonial India.[161] Such a statement goes against the grain of our understanding of the nature of colonial governmentality in India, namely that, as Prakash argues, 'the state considered the colonized to be incapable of self-governance'.[162] The 1870s, after all, witnessed the first all-India census and with it the emergence of what Nicholas Dirks has termed 'the ethnographic state', which governed through the construction of difference between the bodies of the colonizers and those of the colonized.[163] But it could be argued that the maintenance of colonial rule necessitated the multiplication of difference between rulers and ruled *precisely because* in the eyes of the British such difference had in fact ceased to exist – at least as far as a segment of the colonized population was concerned, namely those educated under the aegis of aesthetic imperialism. For as Susan Bayly contends, the decade after the introduction of the census witnessed a marked reversal of the longstanding belief in Indian degeneracy, at least for many British ethnologists, who maintained that 'degeneracy was being reversed' in India thanks to Indian revival and reform movements, which meant that 'Asia's Aryans

[160] 'The Society for the Suppression', 183.
[161] Prakash, 'Body Politic', pp. 189–90.
[162] Prakash, 'Body Politic', p. 215.
[163] Dirks, 'The Ethnographic State', pp. 43–60. While Dirks, Arjun Appadurai, Bernard Cohn and others have regarded the census as being symptomatic and productive of both the emergence of biopolitics in India and the governmentalization of the state, Sarah Hodges contends that the term 'population' is consonant with terms such as 'rainfall' or 'cultivation' and hence does not function 'as a key node for understanding or governing'. Hodges, 'Governmentality', 1158. See also Appadurai, 'Number in the Colonial Imagination'; and Cohn, 'The Census'.

were dangerously ready to recover the vigor and competitive greatness that [were] implanted in their racial heritage'.[164] As exemplified by the introduction of local self-government by the Ripon administration in the early 1880s, such educated elites had in fact *proved* that they were capable of governing the self – for the British aesthetic imperialism had, after all, failed because it had succeeded too well.[165] As the *Calcutta Review* pontificated in 1873, it was

> a pleasure to see a healthy tone of morals, fast winning its way into Bengali fiction. Time was when the *Vidyasundara* or *Jivantara* or some other equally indecent tale in verse would have been thought good reading by many grown up natives ... In these happily-stern days, everything savouring of indecency or childishness, anything that does not either afford innocent amusement or add a little to our stock of knowledge, is sure to be put down with a high hand, consigned by the unanimous verdict of critics to the dead store of the pastry cook or the boxmaker; while works of real merit, like the *Durgeshanandini* [a historical novel by Bankim Chandra Chattopadhyay] ... are read and re-read until there are others to supply their place.[166]

Since, as Robinson averred, the 'respectable native gentlemen' who made up the Society for the Suppression of Obscenity were 'far better acquainted with the meaning of the vulgar phrases used in the books' and would be better able to 'detect their tendency' than he could, and since they were moreover willing to unite to 'save India from the curse of public obscenity, indecency, and impurity' (the Society had, in fact, already sent five books to Robinson for inspection), then it appeared to him 'that the end may be secured without taking up the attention of any of the Public Officers of the Government, except those connected with the Police'.[167]

But in acknowledging that aesthetic imperialism had produced Indians who were capable of governing the self, the British were also

164 Bayly, 'Race in Britain and India', pp. 81, 82. The theory of Aryan kinship as developed in India by officials such as W. W. Hunter in his *Annals of Rural Bengal* (1868) demonstrates that the British, as Bayly argues, 'did not invariably insist on hard and fast separations between white and nonwhite peoples, or between rulers and the colonized' (although the belief in an Aryan 'revival' did begin to wane by the 1920s). Bayly, 'Race in Britain and India', p. 78.

165 Such failure was clear, for example, in the case of education, since while on the one hand the colonial state was happy to let Indians take the initiative in developing institutions to discipline young Indian bodies, by the turn of the twentieth century 'educational institutions, especially in Bengal, had ... largely passed into a disciplinary domain where the discursive forms of a specifically nationalist modernity were already in command'. Chatterjee, 'The Disciplines', p. 11.

166 *Calcutta Review* (1873), cited in Banerjee, *The Parlour*, p. 173.

167 John Robinson to Secretary to the Government of Bengal, 7 March 1874, 463–4/ March 1874, Judicial, B, Judicial Department, WBSA; and 'The Society for the Suppression', 195.

forced to expose the moral contradictions in this particular technology of colonial governmentality – and, in turn, British justifications for colonial rule. For since obscenity is not inherent in a text or object but is dependent on the responses of the viewing subject, if Indians did not see anything indecent about a text or object that a British observer might regard as blatantly obscene then clearly it was the British observer who was rendering it thus. There were still, to be sure, British critics who regarded Indian culture as distasteful, immoral and a hindrance to Indian 'progress'.[168] But by the early twentieth century it was not uncommon for individuals such as Colonel Sir Henry Stanyon to proclaim that 'There is no country perhaps which has a stronger objection to anything like a public display of indecency and obscenity than India'.[169] Such a sentiment was in part a product of a new celebration of the 'primitive', which as Marianna Torgovnick has revealed was 'an attempt to imagine the primitive as a source of empowerment – as a locus for making things anew, to preserve what is worth preserving and change what deserves to be changed'.[170] It was yet another means, in short, of producing difference, but in contrast to the agenda of the ethnographic state the primitive had become essential to the very construction of modernity, to 'making modernity reconcilable with itself', by incorporating what modernity was perceived to lack.[171] Instead of denigrating Indian popular culture (namely what was 'uncorrupted' by Western influences), many British officials had thus come to see such culture as 'natural' and 'inherently pure' – as one district magistrate enthused, 'A naked Bhil man is an Apolloe [sic] like joy to behold'.[172]

[168] By the early nineteenth century the view of Indian art, for example, as being a sign of the lack of progress and amorality of Indian civilization had come to replace earlier perceptions of its monstrosity. Mitter, *Much Maligned Monsters*, pp. 211, 215; and Gupta, '"Dirty" Hindi Literature', 94.

[169] *Legislative Assembly, Debates*, IV, 26 (8 March 1924). As Philippa Levine observes, colonized peoples were often regarded, on the one hand, as being defined by sexuality, while on the other as being prudish, which for her 'suggests a complex of anxieties among the rulers about how best to justify and to maintain British rule'. Levine, *Prostitution, Race*, p. 181.

[170] Torgovnick, *Gone Primitive*, p. 45.

[171] Gelder and Jacobs, *Uncanny Australia*, p. 1. For the British it was also possible to celebrate the primitive both because modern power was engaged in the task of eliminating it and because it served as a means of undermining (and dealing with the humiliations wrought upon them by) Indian nationalism. Collingham, *Imperial Bodies*, p. 187.

[172] W. C. Tudor-Owen, Esq., District Magistrate, Panch Mahals, 10 June 1924, 5823/1924–6, D Branch, Home Department, NAI. It had also become common for British critics to celebrate Indian art not only as 'a lofty and adequate expression of the religious emotion of the people' but as 'a possession of priceless value' that 'ought to be regard[ed] with the utmost reverence and love'. Letter to *The Times*, 28 February 1910, cited in Mitter, *Much Maligned Monsters*, p. 270.

But in thus discarding colonial aesthetics by blaming the 'prurient false modesty' that they had introduced for corrupting such joy, the British also laid themselves open to charges that it was *British culture*, not Indian, that was inherently debased and obscene.[173]

Ashlil, aesthetics and Indian elites

Although British officials may have begun to believe by the late nineteenth century that the project of colonial governmentality had rendered Western-educated elites capable of governing the self, the irony is that it had the opposite effect on the Indians thus educated. As the *Bharat Samskarak* enthusiastically declared in 1876 in response to the passage of one of the few colonial legislative enactments for the regulation of the obscene, the Dramatic Performances Act, 'If we cannot discipline ourselves, we can get others to do it for us'.[174] The belief of such elites in their inability to govern the self can be traced back to the late eighteenth century, well before the development of aesthetic imperialism as a governmental technology, to British-initiated efforts to transform Indian vernaculars into what Bernard Cohn has termed 'languages of command' – for use, in other words, as technologies of rule.[175] Since a language reflects 'a social group's self-understandings of its beliefs, values, and identities', as Anindita Ghosh argues, it thus 'offers valuable definitions of itself and its "others"'.[176] Such projects of linguistic reform, in seeking not only to 'rationalize' a language such as Bengali (since according to the grammarian N. B. Halhead it was full of 'Persian, Arabic and Hindostanic terms, promiscuously thrown together without order and meaning') but to purge it of its 'vulgarity', thus generated tremendous self-doubt about indigenous culture, values, virtues and morals, particularly since support from pundits, munshis and the literati was vital to carrying them out.[177]

With Sanskrit recognized by Orientalist scholars as the 'classical' language from which most of India's vernaculars derived, Brahmin pundits, with their knowledge of India's 'authentic' past, came to play a particularly important role in shaping 'the new codes of acceptability'

173 W. C. Tudor-Owen, 10 June 1924.
174 3 March 1876, cited in Ghosh, *Power in Print*, p. 93.
175 Cohn, *Colonialism and its Forms*, pp. 16–56.
176 Ghosh, *Power in Print*, p. 2.
177 *A Grammar of the Bengali Language*, cited in Gosh, *Power in Print*, p. 69. In contrast to the chaste *sadhu* style of Bengali (that contained *tatsama*, or Sanskrit loan words), which was used largely by pundits and the courtly literati and was restricted primarily to poetry, the *chalet* style was used mostly by the common people and was employed largely in business and administration.

in India's vernacular languages through a process of Sanskritization and 'purification'.[178] Such a reformist project was in turn taken up, from the early nineteenth century, by the urban intelligentsia, first the nouveau riche aristocracy (which included high-caste merchants, bankers, banians and landowners) and, from the 1860s, by the emergent middle class (which consisted of small merchants, professionals and landholders) who had been schooled in colonial aesthetics. Such respectable people, or *bhadralok* as they were known in Bengal, founded clubs, societies and literary journals to establish literary standards, purge the vernaculars of Persian, Arabic, and colloquial elements and 'purify' them of obscenity. Such a 'sanitizing drive' grew from mid-century.[179] While for the Bengali *madhyabitta sreni*, or middle classes, the novels, dramas and poetry of Battala were particularly subject to such sanitizing, as were folk traditions such as *jatras, panchalis* and *kobi* contests (since, as the renowned author Bankim Chandra Chattopadhyay opined, these offered clear evidence that 'obscenity is the national vice of the Bengalis'), their counterparts elsewhere had other targets.[180] In the United Provinces, for example, the Hindi literary form of Braj Bhasha, once celebrated for its erotic poetic tradition on the life and loves of Krishna, was discarded in favour of Khari Boli, which lacked such a dubious past.[181]

Since Indian elites were placed in a two-fold position of subordination and domination – a position that is crucial, as Partha Chatterjee contends, for understanding the hegemonic aspirations of bourgeois nationalism – such a project was vital, firstly, for negotiating their subordination to colonial power by ensuring that their languages and literatures could 'stand the test of scrutiny by outsiders'. But it was also critical for establishing their dominance, through constructing new linguistic hierarchies (and with it new hierarchies of religion, gender and caste), over what in Bengal were known as the *chhotolok* or *itarjan* (namely, those who lacked status and civility), and in particular over those new lower-middle-class groups who thanks to the spread of vernacular education had become competitors with such elites for scarce jobs. The 'purification' of Indian vernaculars was thus a means for Indian elites to shore up their fragile status in a rapidly changing colonial world.[182] It was also critical, however, for overcoming their perceived

[178] Ghosh, *Power in Print*, p. 47.
[179] Ghosh, *Power in Print*, p. 79.
[180] *Bangadarshan* (Pausch 1280 [1873]), cited in Banerjee, *The Parlour*, p. 184. See also Banerjee, 'Bogey of the Bawdy'.
[181] Gupta, *Sexuality, Obscenity*, pp. 209–10.
[182] For an overview of the factors that served to undermine such elites see Sarkar, *Hindu Wife*, pp. 8–18.

racial degeneracy, a belief in which had been engendered by colonial ideology and made manifest by colonial conquest and the degradation of colonial rule.[183] Since the blame for 'sapping the vigor of the race' was laid by the British at the feet of Indian men (who were accused of being so lacking in self-control that they engaged in sexual intercourse with child brides and as a result produced weak and sickly offspring), such accusations also engendered a crisis in Indian masculinity.[184] This was in turn furthered by aesthetic imperialism. Influenced by the construction of middle-class domesticity in England, in which women were upheld as forces of domestic stability and familial love, the British regarded English literature, in particular the literary romance, as being able to 'create romantic bonds of attraction in the colonial relationship and, in doing so, to propagate a kind of colonial domesticity of middle-class love in India' – but between English and Indian *men* rather than between men and women.[185] As Schwarz argues, 'the colonial subject interpellated by the affectionate discourse of English literature in the imperial romance' was thus 'directed to occupy conflicting positions: both English *and* Indian, resembling but not being, masculine *and* feminine, symbolically split along the age-old axis of the body and the mind'.[186] Such interpellation, in thus feminizing Indian men in the public sphere, in turn transformed their behaviour in the private sphere, fostering an agenda that Pradip Kumar Bose regards as 'a change from the government *of families* to government *through the family*' (emphasis in original).[187]

For such elites the current era was therefore envisioned as one of decline, debasement and bodily decay, concerns that in the late nineteenth century were further magnified for the Hindu upper castes (and taken as a sign that the age of *kaliyug* had indeed arrived) by the enumerative technologies of colonial governmentality, which revealed that Muslims and the lower castes were reproducing at a faster rate than they were.[188] But since race in India was largely conceptualized, as Indira Chowdhury-Sengupta contends, in cultural and linguistic terms (as yet another supporter of the Dramatic Performances Bill, the Honorable Raja Narendra Krishna, affirmed, 'No members of a nation that aspired to be reckoned as a civilized race should indulge in ... obscene exhibitions'), Indian elites were convinced that 'only the adoption of [the] English language and manners could regenerate them' – or, we

183 Chatterjee, *The Nation*, p. 36; and Ghosh, *Power in Print*, p. 51.
184 Sinha, 'Gender and Imperialism', p. 226.
185 Schwarz, 'Sexing the Pundits', p. 236.
186 Schwarz, 'Sexing the Pundits', p. 238.
187 Bose, 'Sons of the Nation', p. 125.
188 See Appadurai, 'Number in the Colonial Imagination'; and Datta, 'Dying Hindus'.

might add, aesthetic norms – and save them from racial degeneracy.[189] It was thus Indian elites, not the British, who transformed the regulation of the obscene into a biopolitical project in order, in the words of the Students' Social Purity League, to 'Promote the cause of Personal and Social Purity' and 'cultivate . . . habits of [a] pure, holy and healthy life'.[190]

There were two main targets of this particular project. The first, a means of restoring Indian masculinity (and, in line with British concerns, of maintaining indigenous patriarchies), was depictions of women as sexual beings. While orthodox Hindus such as Sanatan Dharmists regarded women as the bearers of Hinduism (since they were believed to be ruled by scripture and thus uncorrupted by Western education or the depredations suffered by Hindu men in the colonial public sphere), and Hindu reformers such as Arya Samajists viewed them as the repositories of a new, reformed Hinduism (from which practices such as child marriage and enforced widowhood would be abolished), both deemed women, like their Muslim counterparts, as the embodiment of virtues such as chastity, purity and self-sacrifice.[191] By the early twentieth century Indian women were increasingly held up, furthermore, as the antithesis of Western women, who were viewed as idle, useless and of loose morals.[192] For Indian critics the display of white female bodies in 'respectable' journals was 'not very pleasing . . . and some times [sic] shocking', as were the 'nakedly obscene' scenes in European films and cinema posters (since 'In India . . . even women of evil fame will not consent to display their bodies in this shameless manner').[193] Such concerns necessitated regulating not only contemporary works such as the play *Kamala* (based on Marie Corelli's novel *Thelma*), in which a female character declares she has 'grown emaciated by pining away for union' with a man, but 'classical' works of literature such as the Telugu

[189] Chowdhury-Sengupta, 'The Effeminate and the Masculine', pp. 289–91; *Abstract of the Proceedings of the Council of the Governor-General of India*, Vol. XV, 14 March 1876; and Banerjee, *The Parlour*, p. 72.

[190] Students' Social Purity League, 'Pure Thoughts, Pure Words, and Pure Deeds' (n.d.), Vol. 44 Comp. 1259, 1892, Judicial Department, MSA.

[191] Sarkar, 'Orthodoxy, Cultural Nationalism', p. 172; and Katrak, 'Indian Nationalism', pp. 395–406. See also Sinha, 'Gender in the Critiques of Colonialism'.

[192] Grewal, *Home and Harem*, p. 25. In a discourse that completely reversed the British division between 'home' and 'harem', the Indian woman became viewed as the embodiment of the spiritual world, in contrast to her English counterpart, who symbolized the material. Grewal, *Home and Harem*, p. 54.

[193] *Legislative Assembly, Debates*, IV, 26 (8 March 1924), and Arjun Das, 'Display of Obscene Posters', letter, *Tribune*, 17 May 1935, 570/1923, Judicial, Home Department, NAI. European women were also credited with having a penchant for obscenity. Gupta, *Sexuality, Obscenity*, p. 45.

courtesan and poet Muddupalani's *Radhika Santwanam* (*Appeasing Radhika*), which for the novelist and social reformer Kandukuri Veerashalingam was 'shamelessly fill[ed] ... with crude depictions of sex'.[194] In order to avoid portraying Indian women in such sexual terms, Gandhi advised Indian writers to 'think of women as your own mother', which he averred would ensure that 'the chastest literature will flow from your pens'.[195]

The second target of this project was to regulate matter that divorced sexuality from the reproductive imperative. Not only had the project of colonial governmentality shifted 'The potential subjectivity of Indian subjects ... into the cultural logic of reproduction', but for the British there was an intimate connection between courage, strength and virility, and since virility implied not only 'one's ability to spend semen' but also 'one's ability to control the conditions under which it was spent', then the failure to exert self-control implied both physical and moral weaknesses, the consequences of which affected both the individual and the race.[196] For Indian men such concerns grew in the early twentieth century with the emergence of eugenics in India, which as Sarah Hodges reveals 'was taken up with remarkable vigour'.[197] Eroticism, in thus undermining self-control, therefore became conceptualized for the Indian middle classes as the hallmark of 'a decadent, feminine and uncivilised culture', and literature that celebrated it, such as *shringar ras* poetry (which celebrated the love of Radha and Krishna), *ashlil* (obscene).[198]

194 Vol. 184 Comp. 1318/1911, Judicial Department, MSA; and Kandukuri Veerashalingam, *Andhra Kauvla Charitramu*, cited in Tharu and Lalita, 'Introduction', p. 3. It also necessitated purifying 'female speech', or *meyeli bhasha* as it was known in Bengal. Ghosh, *Power in Print*, p. 64.

195 Gandhi, *To the Women*, cited in Kakar, *Intimate Relations*, p. 127.

196 Dirks, 'Castes of Mind', 76; and Alter, 'Celibacy, Sexuality', 56. It was not only Indian men who had to be taught 'lessons of self-restraint' in order to avoid 'the disastrous consequences of indiscriminate propagation', but India's 'potential *sickly* and *diseased* mothers' (emphasis in original). 'The Bombay Baby and Health Week IV', *Jam-e-Jamshed*, 26 March 1928, clipping in 58/1928, Political, Home Department, NAI. See also Bose, 'Sons of the Nation'; Sen, 'Motherhood and Mothercraft'; Manna, 'Approach towards Birth Control'; Guha, "The Unwanted Pregnancy'; Anandhi, 'Reproductive Bodies'; and Ramusack, 'Embattled Advocates'.

197 Hodges, 'Indian Eugenics', p. 118. Although the first pseudo-eugenic organization, the Hindu Malthusian League, was founded in Madras in 1882, it was not until the interwar period that the eugenics movement in India gained serious currency with the formation of organizations such as the Sholapur Eugenics Education Society in 1927 and Dr A. P. Pillay's Society for the Study and Promotion of Family Hygiene in 1935 (which published the internationally renowned journal *Marriage Hygiene*). While clearly influenced by the eugenics movement in the West, Indian eugenicists claimed that the caste-based marriage practices of Hindus revealed that eugenics was, in fact, inherently Indian. Hodges, 'Indian Eugenics', p. 136.

198 Gupta, '"Dirty" Hindi Literature', 98.

For Bankim Chandra Chattopadhyay, Bengali literature was so imbued with such a sensibility that it was completely devoid of 'manly feeling'; a sign, for him, of 'an effeminate and sensual race'.[199] In the face of such beliefs, the Telugu Translator to the Madras Government found himself 'blush[ing] to admit' that Telugu poets had no 'hesitation in freely indulging in depraving and lascivious descriptions of the details of sexual intercourse'.[200]

Anything that undermined the procreative imperative therefore had to be regulated, such as Pandey Bechan Sharma 'Ugra's' best-selling 1927 short story collection *Chaklet* (*Chocolate*), which like *Ramesdhar Atmakatha* contained vivid portrayals of sexual acts between males. The primary concern, however, was *kamashastra* literature, British complacency about how it reflected Indian sensibilities notwithstanding.[201] For critics such as Banarsidas Chaturvedi, editor of *Vishal Bharat* and leader of the anti-obscenity Ghasleti Andolan movement in the United Provinces, *kamashastra* works in fact demonstrated India's cultural and moral inferiority to the British.[202] The journal *Madhuri* went so far in 1925 as to blame *kamashastra* literature for India's conquest and colonization, declaring that the 'kamshastra [sic] was composed at a time when there was an excessively luxurious orientation in India, and in the end this only resulted in our enslavement'.[203] Failing to regulate such matter would, moreover, make overcoming such enslavement impossible. For Deputy Commissioner Rao Bahadur R. S. Thakur, not only had 'the modern tendency of freer expression of thought in unrestrained language ... resulted in the throwing off of the many helpful restraints which preserved the cleanliness and dignity of social intercourse', but through such matter 'the virus will spread with uncontrollable rapidity and [will]

199 Bankim Chandra Chattopadhyay, *Bankim Rachanabali*, cited in Schwarz, 'Sexing the Pundits', 235.

200 M. R. Ry. G. Kanakaraju Garu, 'Minute of Dissent to the Report of the Registrar of Books and the Chairman of the Telugu Board of Studies', n.d., 101/1912, Police, B, Home Department, NAI.

201 Such works therefore generally met with convictions at the hands of Indian judges. See *Kailaschandra Acharjya* v. *King-Emperor*.

202 Gupta, '"Dirty" Hindi Literature', p. 115. This helps explain why Indian critics of such matter drew upon all the stock phrases of Victorian moralism in critiquing it. Inveighing against advertisements in 'the gutter press', the editor of a Gujarati paper, for example, declared in 1901 that 'nothing can be more shocking than the foul words and expressions used in describing the nature and symptoms of [sexual] diseases' in such advertisements, and requested that something be done to stop this 'nefarious traffic' in order to purify the press and make it safe for 'the respectable classes of the reading public'. K. N. Kabraji, 8 September 1901 to C. H. Hill, Esq., Vol. 171/1902, Judicial Department, MSA.

203 Gupta, *Sexuality, Obscenity*, p. 157.

demoralize with a thoroughness appalling in its extent and impossible to eradicate'.[204] As another former colonial official declared in the case of *kamashastra* works and advertisements, 'the state of Indian society needs much moral elevation before undertaking Swaraj [self-rule]', since obtaining 'Swaraj with such [a] degenerate high class society' would entail the 'death & annihilation of millions of dumb voiceless Indians'.[205]

While Indian languages were considerably altered by the endeavours of reformist elites, their efforts to regulate the obscene were less successful. The problem, to begin with, was their deployment of colonial aesthetics – which, as the British were well aware, were far from universal. Although the concept of *aslilatva* (obscenity) existed in Sanskrit poetry, for example, the presence of 'obscene' images in a poem was regarded not as a moral wrong but as a literary fault. Such wrongs were not, moreover, universally condemned; as the eleventh-century literary critic Abhinavagupta claimed, they could serve an important purpose – what determined whether they should be considered obscene or not was whether the author's intention was to sexually excite his or her readers (although since in Hinduism *kama* (the satisfaction of desire) was perceived to be one of the 'four aims of man', the representation of sexuality itself was not taboo).[206] While religious texts such as the puranas prohibited obscenity, words that could be interpreted as obscene through induction (*taksana*) but were not obscene in their primary meaning were not regarded as obscene.[207] Thus in Indian aesthetics 'the "problem" of obscenity was an intellectual one, not a practical one', since 'Literary critics argued, but did not presume to prescribe'.[208] It was therefore possible for even respectable presses like the Abhyudaya Press or the Chand Press to publish *kamashastra* works, and for the authors of these works, such as Pandit Krishnakant Malaviya (nephew of Madan Mohan Malaviya) or Manishankar Govindji Shastri, to declare their texts aesthetically sound treatises on matters such as how to obtain sexual fulfilment in marriage or the means of overcoming the problem

204 Opinion of Rao Bahadur R. S. Thakur, Deputy Commissioner, Hoshangabad, 570/1923, Judicial, Home Department, NAI.

205 Khan Bahadur Jacob B. Israel, retired Deputy Collector, Bombay, to Secretary to the Government, Home Department, 18 April 1928, 113/1928, Political, Home Department, MSA.

206 Masson-Moussaieff, 'Obscenity in Sanskrit Literature'. The other aims are *dharma* (performance of religious duty), *artha* (worldly pursuits) and *moksha* (the seeking of salvation).

207 Dwivedi, 'Concept of Obscenity', 72.

208 Masson-Moussaieff, 'Obscenity in Sanskrit Literature', 202.

of 'self-abuse'.[209] That for Indians there was 'no one simple derivative framework of European aesthetics that could be accepted ... with any unanimity' is clear even in the case of government officials, who to the chagrin of their British counterparts often trumpeted such beliefs.[210] As Rao Bahadur M. Rangachariyar, Registrar of Books for the Madras Presidency, and M. R. Ry. G. Venkataranga Rao, Chairman of the Telugu Board of Studies contended, there were 'forms of literature in which even [obscene] descriptions may appropriately find a place'.[211]

It was also impossible for this project to succeed because it was largely undertaken by the upper middle classes, not the lower – the latter were instead avidly consuming the *kamashastra* literature, Battala productions and other matter that their social betters sought to regulate. For not only did older oral-performative traditions, spoken languages, scribal cultures and literary genres such as *qissas* and *kahanis* adapt themselves to the new commercial print forms (due in large measure to the sizeable body of printer–publishers of relatively plebeian origin who had emerged thanks to the spread of basic literacy), but Indian readers engaged in 'a thousand diverse patterns of consumption ... that flouted disciplinary devices'.[212] Such new consumption patterns were driven largely by what Ghosh, following Sumit Sarkar, terms 'lesser bhadralok' or 'petty bhadralok', who were primarily a service population living on the margins of the elites.[213] While Viswanathan notes that 'English literature marked the boundaries between classes', in reality it marked the lines of division *within* the middle class; the upper echelons of the middle class may have scorned the lower for their ignorance of English (as well as, of course, of colonial aesthetics), but those thus scorned in turn mocked the linguistic pretensions of the 'babus' in such formats as farces, which were hugely popular in the last quarter of the nineteenth century.[214] Such farces not only reversed the moral hierarchy of the reformist project (by accusing the elites of declining standards of morality), but they did so in a racy and abusive

[209] Petition by Manishankar Govindji Shastri to the Governor of Bombay Presidency, 29 January 1906, Vol. 202/1906, Judicial Department, MSA; and Gupta, *Sexuality, Obscenity*, p. 160.

[210] Ghosh, *Power in Print*, p. 100.

[211] Report by Rao Bahadur M. Rangachariyar, Registrar of Books and M. R. Ry. G. Venkataranga Rao, Chairman of the Telugu Board of Studies, 4 December 1911, 101/1912, Police, B, Home Department, NAI.

[212] Ghosh, *Power in Print*, p. 18.

[213] Ghosh, *Power in Print*, p. 21.

[214] Viswanathan, *Masks of Conquest*, p. 152.

language that strove to reclaim respectability for the literatures and cultures of the lower orders.[215]

The lower middle classes were not the only threat to this particular biopolitical project. An additional problem for reformist elites was that, as Himani Bannerji argues in the case of Bengal, 'the moral utterances and social projects of the ... middle-class intelligentsia did not form a monolithic whole, but rather consisted of ideological-discursive strands which converged, competed with and contradicted each other'.[216] Whereas some members of the upper-middle-class elite may have condemned Battala literature or *shringar ras* poetry in public while secretly consuming it in private, others were entirely opposed to efforts to regulate the obscene for fear that they would undermine Indian culture.[217] Indeed, from the 1870s a section of the Indian intelligentsia began to embrace what they regarded as the 'pure', 'earthy' or 'authentic' colloquial traditions of Indian culture, and like their lower-middle-class critics, farces – often in a risqué language – were a key medium through which they did so.[218] In contrast to the farces of the lower-middle classes, however, those produced by playwrights such as Amritlal Basu or Girish Ghose ridiculed both the colonial state and their own affectations.[219] With former 'notions of the "polite" and "vulgar" ... beginning to lose currency' by the early twentieth century, even advertisements for aphrodisiacs – which, significantly, offered compensation for a masculinity that had been perceived to be lost – were being printed in huge numbers in 'respectable' newspapers.[220]

But as is clear in the 1912 appeal trial of Kherode Chandra Roy Chowdhury, previously convicted for obscenity for publishing *Natu Chori* (*The Theft of Tops*), an Oriya poem on the lives of Radha and Krishna, defining the obscene was still open to considerable negotiation. For the Calcutta High Court Justice N. R. Chatterjea, *Natu Chori* could not be regarded as obscene because the term *rati* as used in the poem was not meant to be interpreted as 'carnal intercourse', but rather as 'spiritual union', since the poem 'was not a description of Radha and Krishna as human beings and [hence] must have a spiritual meaning'. Moreover, since to Hindus Radha and Krishna were gods, 'those who believe in

215 Ghosh, 'Valorising the "Vulgar"', 161. Women likewise flouted disciplinary conventions in their reading tastes, especially in their consumption of romance novels – tastes which were shared not only by elite women such as those who belonged to the Tagore household, but those lower down the social scale. Ghosh, *Power in Print*, p. 162.

216 Bannerji, 'Attired in Virtue', p. 69.

217 Ghosh, *Power in Print*, pp. 26, 104.

218 Ghosh, 'Valorising the "Vulgar"', 151.

219 Ghosh, *Power in Print*, p. 193.

220 Ghosh, 'Valorising the "Vulgar"', 155; and Gupta, *Sexuality, Obscenity*, p. 73.

their divinity would not take immoral ideas from a story such as is described in the book'.[221] The numerous witnesses called during the course of the trial, however, revealed far less certainty in their interpretation of the work. Girish Chandra Bhattacharjee, Head Clerk of the Registration Office, claimed that while he would not refuse to register the book on the grounds of obscenity he nonetheless found it too obscene to read before his mother and other elders. Another witness, a retired Inspector of Schools, declared that he did not regard the book as obscene but considered 'his own idea of purity [as] different from that of ordinary Hindus'. A third witness regarded the work as obscene but felt that other similar works were not obscene if they were 'looked at from the spiritual point of view'.[222] The bewildering array of opinions witnesses offered reveals that negotiating the boundaries between 'pure' and 'obscene', 'polite' and 'vulgar', 'authentic' and 'corrupt' remained a highly fraught process.

By the 1920s, however, older colloquial and literary traditions came increasingly to the fore as the intelligentsia strove to celebrate – and in the process to fashion – India's 'national' culture.[223] The Indian government's introduction of a new Obscene Publications Bill in 1924, its reluctant concession to signing the Obscene Publications Treaty, was therefore not heralded, by either Indian members of the newly expanded legislatures or the Indian public, with quite the same breathless enthusiasm with which they had greeted the Dramatic Performances Act over four decades previously. The most contentious issue, once again, was over the Exception to the Indian Penal Code that exempted religious images from prosecution. Some critics, such as Pandit Shamlal Nehru, clearly still clung to the dictates of colonial aesthetics. Nehru argued that the Exception should be dropped from the Indian Penal Code because rather than protecting Hinduism, it had the effect of vilifying it, since 'No religion teaches us to exhibit obscene engravings or pictures' such as those found on some Indian temples (which should, furthermore, be 'screened off from the public gaze').[224] But far more common in the debates on the bill was the view expressed by C. Duraiswami Aiyangar, who protested that Hindu religious images had a 'a sublime and esoteric significance' that made it impossible to view them as obscene. For Aiyangar, India had in fact never produced such a thing as an 'obscene'

221 *Kherode Chandra Roy Chowdhury* v. *King-Emperor, Indian Law Reports*, 39 Calcutta (1912), 384–5, 386.
222 *Kherode Chandra Roy Chowdhury* v. *King-Emperor*, 387.
223 Ghosh, *Power in Print*, p. 106.
224 *Legislative Assembly, Debates*, V, 20 (20 February 1925) and IV, 52 (15 September 1924), n.p., clippings in 570/1923, Judicial, Home Department, NAI.

publication; hence it was impossible to find an 'Indian obscene picture or publication ... either in India or outside it'.[225]

Such views were in large measure a product of the tremendous changes that had transformed Indian nationalism from a primarily elite affair to a mass movement – one that reached out to peasants, tribals, women, and, through Gandhi's Non-Cooperation and Khilafat campaigns, to Muslims. It was during this period, furthermore, that the modern state – based on the democratic ideals of universal adult suffrage and social justice – came to be seen as 'the single, determinate, demographically enumerable form of the nation'.[226] But the participation of such diverse groups unleashed myriad new social and political demands, as well as ideas about the form that such a state should take, all of which challenged the existing social order. By the 1920s public discourse was also 'rife with references to race, eugenics and a type of international Darwinism which saw relentless competition between communities, nations or races', which generated new bodily anxieties.[227] In light of the growing nationalist awareness that a large and healthy population was a national resource, fears of physical deterioration became imbued with a nationalist significance, and the body itself was increasingly politicized. For Hindus the apparent ongoing decline in their numbers vis-à-vis those of Muslims (thanks both to their lower reproductive rates and low-caste conversions) fostered the emergence of a 'new organistic perspective of Hindu society which viewed the strength of the organic whole as inseparable from the well-being and fitness of its different but mutually-dependent constituent parts'.[228] Efforts to construct this whole ranged from *shuddi* (purification or 'conversion') and *sangathan* ('consolidation') campaigns to bodily reform. While the lower castes undertook new projects of bodily reform in an effort to acquire higher caste status, Charu Gupta argues that 'a moral panic of sorts gripped a section of the ... Hindu middle-class, creating anxieties regarding questions of sexuality' – and with it the drive to 'cleanse literature of all of its perceived obscenities' – as a means of fashioning a modern collective Hindu identity.[229] In the process the Indian biopolitical project to regulate the obscene developed a new impetus.

[225] *Legislative Assembly, Debates*, IV, 26 (8 March 1924).
[226] Chatterjee, *The Nation*, p. 238.
[227] Watt, 'Education for National Efficiency', 340.
[228] Watt, 'Education for National Efficiency', 340.
[229] Gupta, *Sexuality, Obscenity*, p. 30. Such anxieties were driven in part by changing women's roles generated by the spread of education among women, their participation in new public activities (such as the Non-Cooperation and Khilafat movements) and new ideals of companionate and monogamous marriage. Gupta, *Sexuality, Obscenity*, p. 24.

Obscenity, hygiene and colonial governmentality

It was at this point, therefore, that the concerns of upper-caste Hindus began to diverge from those of the nationalist elite. For the latter sought not only to celebrate the colloquial and 'authentic' in Indian culture, but to reject colonial aesthetics in their entirety for making them *see* Indian culture as obscene in the first place. As Bipin Chandra Pal asserted in 1924 in the case of religious images, 'no one in India has ever looked upon these ... in the sense in which erotic literature is looked upon by Europeans'.[230] Colonial aesthetics, rather than purifying Indian culture, was thus responsible for corrupting it by *producing*, or marking out, obscenity where it had previously not existed. Thus as Gandhi declared in 1927 (in a scornful review of Catherine Mayo's *Mother India*), he had been unaware that the 'Shivalingam [an idol that is generally regarded as a phallic symbol of the god Shiva] ... had any obscene significance at all' until he encountered a missionary book, which revealed 'the obscenity of many practices which we have hitherto innocently indulged in'. He refused, however, to concede to colonial aesthetics, contending that 'even now when I see a Shivalingam neither the shape nor the association in which I see it suggests any obscenity'.[231]

But where the concerns of the nationalist elite did merge with those of the Hindu upper caste was in their belief in the corrupting influence that obscenity had on Indian bodies – although for them such influences did not emanate from Indian print culture, but rather from the barrage of 'obscenities' flooding into India through Britain's imperial networks.[232] As Dr Sir Deva Prasad Sarvadhikary observed in the Council of State, 'circulars of [a] flaring type disgracing Charing Cross shop windows' were pouring into India, and since Indians were 'apt pupils' – and since, moreover, 'whatever is in print is gospel truth, and particularly if it happens to be in English, the language of the rulers, it is doubly gospel' – they 'think it is a right thing to take the cue where the teachers left

230 *Legislative Assembly, Debates*, IV, 26 (8 March 1924). Pal had not managed, however, to reject colonial aesthetics in its entirety, since, as he confessed in his memoirs, he had a penchant for 'rather prurient publications' in his youth. Bipin Chandra Pal, *Memoirs of My Life and Times, 1857–1884*, cited in Gupta, *Sexuality, Obscenity*, p. 163.

231 'Drain Inspector's Report', in *Collected Works of Mahatma Gandhi*, cited in Viswanathan, *Masks of Conquest*, p. 126. It was because foreigners had 'no idea of sublimity and no idea of religious eroticism', for another critic, that they regarded such matter as obscene. *Legislative Assembly, Debates*, IV, 26 (8 March 1924).

232 India, as even members of the government were forced to admit, was being swamped with 'productions which are of [such] a filth and even bestiality' that they posed a 'demoralising' danger even graver than 'the traffic in pernicious drugs, [or] even that in women and children'. *Legislative Assembly, Debates*, IV, 26 (8 March 1924), and *Extract from Council of State Debates* 4, 19 (11 March 1924).

off'.[233] The unfortunate irony for the British was that since in India linguistic and social stratification had served to preserve a pure, unadulterated form of English (Indians were in fact often credited by the British with speaking a 'purer English than we speak ourselves'), then Indians had come to judge the British by the standards that aesthetic imperialism had set for them – and as in Australia, modern British print culture was found to be not only severely wanting, but a danger to the strength and purity of Indian bodies.[234] For Pal it was vital, therefore, that India accede to the Obscene Publications Treaty, since India needed to 'protect [its] own innocence against the invasion of these kinds of lit and cards and paintings that may be imported into India from Europe', or, as another critic remarked, to prevent matter from overseas from 'corrupt[ing] the morals of the people of this country'.[235]

For the British, as John Kelly argues, what 'was necessary to define the colonial vision of virtue and civilization was the image of a cultural gap between the rulers and ruled, a gap in social achievement, [or in] social-evolutionary time' – a gap that aesthetic imperialism had, moreover, sought to foster.[236] It had, for a time, succeeded in doing so. But by the 1920s an ascendant and increasingly race-conscious Indian nationalist elite was eager to expose the flaws in the moral logic of colonial aesthetics, even more so after 1929 when *swaraj*, envisioned in Gandhian terms as both moral improvement and political emancipation, became the explicit goal of the Indian National Congress. Obscenity, like the English woman, thus became a symbol of the depraved state of Western culture. Rather than the British 'bringing about in [India] a less barbarous and more civilized state [of] morality', as they had envisioned, by the 1930s even 'the lower classes' had come to have a 'very poor idea of the morals of the white races'.[237] In the face of such morality, as one critic opined, 'How can we expect our children to grow up Brahmcharis [sic]?'[238]

When it came to obscenity, the mistake for the British had been to rely on governmental power to effect its regulation rather than, as in Australia, on sovereign power, particularly when it came to dealing with imported publications. Unlike the Australian government, its Indian

233 *Extract from Council of State Debates*, 4, 19 (11 March 1924).
234 *Parliamentary Papers, 1852–53*, Evidence of Charles Trevelyan, cited in Viswanathan, *Masks of Conquest*, p. 116.
235 *Legislative Assembly, Debates*, IV, 26 (8 March 1924); and Letter from G. A. Khan, Esq., Officiating Commissioner, Chhattisgarh Division, to Secretary to the Government CP, Legal Department, 28 June 1924, 570/1923, Judicial, Home Department, NAI.
236 Kelly, *A Politics of Virtue*, p. 12.
237 Fraser, 29 June 1907, 178–80, Political, A, Home Department, NAI; and the Hon. Khan Bahadur Dr Sir Nasarvangi Choksy, *Council of State, Debates*, 11 February 1935.
238 Arjun Das, 'Display of Obscene Posters'.

counterpart made little effort to erect a cordon sanitaire to keep 'obscene' imported matter from infecting Indian bodies. The state was not averse to implementing such cordons when the health and purity of white bodies was at stake, through such means as building civil lines and barracks away from polluting 'black towns' (and even, in the case of New Delhi, building an entirely new city alongside the old), or ensuring that the bodies of those Indians with whom the British came into the closest contact (such as servants, soldiers and plantation workers) were vaccinated.[239] But, particularly after the 1870s, it rarely resorted, on the grounds of public order concerns, cost, and the detrimental impact on trade, to erecting such cordons to protect Indian bodies, even in the case of a catastrophic disease such as cholera.[240] While by the 1860s the linkage between cholera and pilgrimage had become apparent and India had long been recognized as a source of global cholera epidemics, the Indian government actively resisted the efforts of the 1866 Constantinople Sanitary Conference to introduce quarantine for pilgrims to prevent the spread of the disease by arguing in favour of the outmoded 'miasmic', or atmospheric theory of cholera causation as opposed to the widely accepted waterborne theory.[241] Although the Indian government was forced to introduce quarantine to deal with the outbreak of plague in 1896, it did so primarily to protect Indian trade, and since 'most IMS officers were unfamiliar with, or displayed little enthusiasm for, these new "technologies" of prevention' and since quarantine had, moreover, met with widescale resistance, it was abandoned.[242] With the Indian state thus torn by 'the conflicting rationalities of the biopolitical and economic spheres', a disease that was recognized by 1884 as being widely preventable was by 1900 killing almost half a million Indians per year.[243]

Yet not only, as one sanitary officer enthused in 1894, would 'the achievement of true hygiene' in India bring the '"Golden Age" sung of by poets and dreamt of by ... dreamers through countless years', but

[239] Legg, *Spaces of Colonialism*; and Arnold, *Colonizing the Body*, p. 135.
[240] Harrison, *Public Health*, p. 79.
[241] Harrison, *Public Health*, p. 106. Sheldon Watts contends that such resistance stemmed from the desire of Britain to protect its shipping from interference by foreign governments. Watts, 'From Rapid Change to Stasis'.
[242] Harrison, *Public Health*, p. 145.
[243] Legg, *Spaces of Colonialism*, p. 209; and Watts, 'From Rapid Change', 324. As Vijay Prashad argues, for the colonial state hygienic measures had to be 'essentially based on the idea of their being *profitable* in a pecuniary point of view', a belief that helps explain the Indian government's paltry expenditure on public health (a mere £0.0025 per person between 1888 and 1894). Prashad, 'The Technology of Sanitation', 116; and Watts, 'From Rapid Change', 339.

it was a moral obligation on the part of the British to make India hygienic.[244] But as is clear in the case of obscenity, regarded by both the British and Indians alike as a hygienic threat, fulfilling such an obligation required the generation of a confluence of interests between rulers and ruled, which 'in a colonial situation in which notions of racial superiority, and cultural distance' predominated was virtually impossible, particularly in light of the fact that 'government priorities would always favour the former'.[245] Moreover, British perceptions of Indian bodies, in the words of one medical officer, as 'walking disseminators of the most repulsive forms of filth' actually increased in the late nineteenth century with the rise of bacteriological theories of disease causation, and hence by the turn of the century most British officials had become convinced 'that there was little prospect of Indians being educated out of their "filthy habits"'.[246] They did not give up entirely, however, on promoting Indian hygiene through education; by 1914 hygiene was in fact being taught in all government schools.[247] But by the First World War the state may have become more sanguine about taking a less active role in Indian hygiene since nationalists had begun to display a more active interest in it, although for decidedly different reasons, and with markedly different goals.[248] In spite of such difficulties, the irony is that in India – a colony with an autocratic state that, furthermore, lacked hegemony – imperial hygiene was implemented primarily through governmental means.

But that the British did not make greater efforts to make India hygienic, whether through governmental, sovereign or disciplinary power, was arguably because they actually *needed* it to remain unhygienic in order to ensure both their own bodily and moral superiority.[249] For the spatial distance they sought to maintain between British and Indian bodies

244 Grant, *The Indian Manual of Hygiene*, cited in Harrison, *Public Health*, p. 139.

245 Harrison, *Public Health*, p. 234. For the British the link between obscenity and hygiene in India was clear in places such as Puri, which they regarded as epitomizing all that was 'obscene, degrading, and epidemiologically dangerous about Hindu India'. Arnold, *Colonizing the Body*, p. 187.

246 Robert Caldwell, *Military Hygiene*, cited in Harrison, *Public Health*, p. 70.

247 Harrison, *Public Health*, p. 88. There were, however, concerns about some of the hygienic texts being taught, such as Babu Jadunath Mookerjea's *Saral Sarir Palan*, or 'Easy Treatise on the Preservation of Health', which according to one critic threatened to 'corrupt the minds of children' through its 'undisguised and quite unnecessary references to the lowest functions of the animal body'. P. Wagstaff, Esq., Secretary to the Agent and Superintendent, East Indian Railway Aided Schools, to the Inspector of European Schools, Bengal, 3 May 1887, 14–17/October 1887, Education, A, Home Department, NAI.

248 The first all-India Sanitary Conference was held in Bombay in 1911.

249 Chandavarkar, 'Plague, Panic', p. 211.

(through such means as surrounding bungalows with large compounds or placing servants' quarters at a respectable distance from European living spaces) also served to signify the hierarchical relationship between such bodies. So did the hygienic management of the European household. As Collingham notes, 'household manuals of advice for the woman newly arrived in the tropics argued that it was imperative not only for the health but also for the *prestige* of the entire community that European principles of sanitation should be applied within the household'.[250] That it was in fact impossible to close off British bodies from contamination by Indian ones or to maintain the home as a preserve of European hygiene provoked ever greater efforts to try, which meant that hygienic discourse was able to pervade the private sphere in British-Indian homes to a far greater degree than in Britain.[251] Moreover, the 'tendency to treat the individual body as a barometer of social morality meant that the neglect of any of those practices which distinguished the colonizer from the colonized was virtually taboo'.[252] Thus while Indian boarding schools, as Satadru Sen demonstrates, may have sought to employ physical training as a means of enhancing the self-governing abilities of Indian schoolboys, the problem was that the bodies thus educated threatened to undermine the bodily distinction of the British.[253] Ensuring the distinction of British bodies, and with it the maintenance of imperial rule, thus necessitated preventing Indian bodies from adopting the very qualities that set those bodies apart. As was the case with so many aspects of Indian culture ranging from *sati* to child marriage, obscenity therefore provided necessary 'evidence' of the immorality of Indian culture.[254] Failing to sufficiently regulate the obscene was thus a means, in short, of maintaining the moral and bodily distinction of British rule.

For the British, their inability to transform the regulation of the obscene into a project of imperial hygiene resulted in the very outcome that colonial officials were so anxious to prevent, namely that 'the

[250] Collingham, *Imperial Bodies*, pp. 166–7.

[251] Collingham, *Imperial Bodies*, p. 167. A sign that such discourse succeeded, according to Sanitary Commissioner J. T. W. Leslie, was clear in the dramatic decline (of 62 per cent) of death rates for European soldiers in India between 1904 and 1913. Guha, 'Nutrition, Sanitation, Hygiene', 397.

[252] Collingham, *Imperial Bodies*, p. 179.

[253] Sen, 'Schools, Athletes and Confrontation', pp. 60, 58.

[254] In the case of the debates on obscenity between Indians and the colonial administration in Fiji, John Kelly argues that the British 'enjoyed provoking the Indians to live up to their image of them as ... immoral, and perhaps even needed ... [such] debates as continuing evidence of the Indians' alleged degradation of character'. Kelly, *A Politics of Virtue*, p. 225. See also Heath, 'Sanitizing Modernity'.

governing race [was] being discredited'.[255] The trouble was that aesthetic imperialism had produced what Gyan Prakash refers to as an 'embattled zone of governance', and since for Indian nationalists the problem with colonial institutions of power was that they 'were not modern enough', in doing nothing either to protect Indian moral and hence bodily integrity through regulating the Indian obscene, or to prevent the 'dumping of pornography' in India, Indians were able to usurp the project of colonial modernity and – in contrast to Australia, which sought to deny history – to *reclaim* history for themselves.[256] For Indian nationalists history became such an empowering discourse, as Sudipta Kaviraj argues, because 'it could produce a giant anachronism in popular consciousness, making all periods in a nation's history appear a preparation for what [they were] carrying out at the present time'.[257] But preparing for the present necessitated resurrecting a past in which disciplines of self-subjection were perceived to have trained Indian bodies in the service of the nation, a process of resurrection through which the 'golden age' of Hinduism became projected as an ancient and clearly *Indian* version of the modern West.[258] Such a vision, while permitting 'the assimilation of archaic Hindu disciplines of self-subjection into the logic of modern governmentality', generated an ongoing struggle to 'restore' the Indian body to its original pristine condition and protect it from matter that threatened to corrupt it – including 'obscene' publications.[259] Rather than being a historical vanguard, the British, in not only failing to modernize India along hygienic lines but in polluting it with their own degeneracies, could thus be reconceived, as in Australia, as backward and degenerate, and as a threat to the fashioning of a pure, clean and hygienic Indian modernity.

[255] Note by J. H. F., n.d., 193–204/April 1913, Judicial, A, Home Department, NAI. The state's concerns with the governing race being discredited because of its lack of effort to either improve or protect Indian morality played a significant role, however, in spurring it to regulate 'sedition', since the first two sedition trials in India (of the *Bangabasi* in 1891 and Tilak's *Kesari* in 1898) involved articles that denigrated British morality. See 260–86/October 1891, Public, A, Home Department, NAI; and 345–76/May 1899, Public, A, Home Department, NAI.

[256] Prakash, 'Body Politic', p. 204; Chatterjee, *The Nation*, p. 15; and 'A Reader', letter to the editor, *Gem*, 30 July 1938, 1-I/1938, Political, Home Department, NAI.

[257] Kaviraj, 'On the Construction', p. 47. The idea that India's history was marked by a decline into degeneracy that only the British could save it from was one of the most powerful legacies of colonial rule, since while Indian historians rejected the narrative of European reason they embraced the objectifying procedures of knowledge propagated by colonial modernity. See Chatterjee, *Nationalist Thought*.

[258] Prakash, 'The Body Politic', p. 211; and Nandy, *The Intimate Enemy*, p. 26.

[259] Prakash, 'The Body Politic', p. 211.

Conclusion: Retangling empire, nation, colony and globe

Several years prior to the first Vizetelly trial, the impoverished autodidact and future sex-reform campaigner William James Chidley (1860?–1916) read a translation of Zola's *Nana*.[1] Although *Nana* was by no means the first French novel that Chidley had read, nor even the first work by Zola (he had recently read *L'Assommoir*), it had a tremendous impact on him. As he records in his 'Confessions', a remarkable account of nineteenth-century sexuality:

> *Nana* disturbed my diseased nerves, and showed me how much I had injured myself, what a strong hold lust had on me. I tried to become abstemious, and spoke to Ada [his common-law wife], asking her to help me, telling her I think or dream nothing but lust. She agreed willingly, for she was easily led, and I ceased to go in quite so heavily – for a time. But lust is a demon that can play a waiting game.[2]

While the impetus behind the various attempts to regulate English translations of Zola's works in England, Australia and India was the belief that they undermined the self-governing abilities of their readers, for Chidley *Nana* in fact served to convince him that he needed to cultivate self-control in order to ensure his bodily strength and purity.

Chidley's path to attaining self-control was, however, long, torturous and intimately bound with reading. As an adolescent he became, he believed, 'nervous and ill' as a result of reading works such as Reynolds's *Mysteries of Paris*, Smollett's *Roderick Random*, and Shakespeare's works as masturbatory aids.[3] What 'saved' him from decline and degeneracy was, he was convinced, his constant 'hunt for a new light', which in spurring him to plough through a phenomenal range of metaphysical, phrenological, philosophical, poetical and critical reading matter led him to Walt Whitman.[4] It was Whitman's *Leaves of Grass* (1855) – to which,

[1] McInerney, *The Confessions*, p. 125.
[2] McInerney, *The Confessions*, p. 125.
[3] McInerney, *The Confessions*, p. 40.
[4] McInerney, *The Confessions*, p. 125.

he confessed, he 'clung ... as I did to any book that seemed to lift me from the deterioration that still followed me' – particularly his poem on the coming man, 'The Answerer', that first gave Chidley an inkling of the means to ensure not only his own self-governance but that of others (through 'preach[ing] a doctrine of Love against lust').[5] But it was ultimately Émile Zola who revealed to Chidley what he regarded as the secret to the governance of the self, for it was upon reading Zola's *Hélène, A Love Episode* that Chidley realized that '*I had the clue – the secret to all in Zola – and in life*' (emphasis in original).[6] Zola's novel convinced Chidley both of the degenerative effects of 'unnatural' intercourse and of his mission, through his 1911 sexological treatise and public proselytization, to teach others how to govern the self – a mission of no less significance, he believed, than to save the human race from decline and degeneracy.

Chidley's mission was somewhat broader than that of his famous and slightly younger contemporary Mohandas Karamchand Gandhi, whose struggles to control the self are so well known. 'Man is man', as Gandhi argued in his treatise on his experiments in self-governance (*The Story of My Experiments With the Truth*), 'because he is capable of, and only in so far as he exercises self-restraint'.[7] Gandhi, like Chidley, berated himself for what he saw as the sexual excesses of his youth, which he believed threatened to make him 'prey to disease and premature death', or to '[sink] into a burdensome existence'.[8] Whereas Chidley's path to controlling the self entailed altering the way in which he – and mankind – had sex, Gandhi pursued the path of *brahmacharya*.[9] For Gandhi *brahmacharya* necessitated not only 'bodily restraint' through celibacy but, since the senses were '[s]o overpowering ... that they can be kept under control only when they are completely hedged in on all sides, from above and beneath', it also required 'control of the senses in thought, word and deed'.[10] Although Swami Vivekananda had first called upon *brahmacharya* as a means of building a nation of heroes, Gandhi transformed it

[5] McInerney, *The Confessions*, pp. 143, 151.
[6] *Hélène, a Love Episode*, was a translation of Zola's *Une Page d'Amour*. McInerney, *The Confessions*, p. 208.
[7] Gandhi, *An Autobiography*, p. 317.
[8] Gandhi, *An Autobiography*, p. 13.
[9] Erections, for Chidley, were the chief problem with the way that mankind had sex. For him 'natural' sex occurred only when the male partner had a soft – and hence controlled – rather than an erect penis (which would only be possible, he argued, if the male felt purely love rather than lust towards his partner). Sex was also to take place only for procreative purposes. A version of this article was published in the *British Medical Journal* in 1915. 'Erection', Box 6, Mss 143/6, ML. See also Darby, 'William Acton's Antipodean Disciples'.
[10] Gandhi, *An Autobiography*, p. 210.

into a discourse on national integrity, since for him 'the nation required an end of wasteful expenditure of time and energy', including sexual expenditure.[11] Morality was therefore for him a problem in which truth and biology were mutually imbricated, since while *satyagraha* ('truth-force') was vital to freeing India from colonial rule, it could not be achieved without *brahmacharya.*

But while Chidley demonstrates that the political rationality of governmental power was well developed in Australia – regardless of whether the Australian state thought otherwise – whether Gandhi's concerns represent the triumph of governmental power in India is far less clear. Gandhi was undoubtedly 'a translated man', since he not only imbibed much of his philosophy from the West but engaged with Indian philosophy through the medium of translation.[12] When he called for celibacy as a means of generating moral power in the pursuit of *swaraj* his logic therefore owed as much to European thinking as it did to South Asian discourses on aesthetically generated energy (*tapas*).[13] It is also true that, by the turn of the twentieth century, *brahmacharya*, like aspects of sexuality in the West, had become medicalized and was often discussed 'in moral and ethical terms that highlight[ed] the importance of "self-control" and "self-knowledge"'.[14] Yet not only was Gandhi deeply hostile to Western medicine, but the discourse and practice of *brahmacharya* that he drew upon to develop his own project of self-governance emerged, as Alter argues, 'from a history quite different from that which has produced medicomoral discourses on masturbation, fornication, sodomy, adultery and so forth'.[15] While in the West, Joseph Alter contends, the subject of sexuality is the self – and hence 'the problematic nature of sexuality refers directly to the health of the individual and his or her self-conception as an autonomous, free agent' – in Hindu society (from which the concept of *brahmacharya* emerged) 'the individual is not primary or indivisible, but is, rather the contingent, constituent product of more primary "dividual" elements and processes'.[16] This means that, regardless of its obsession with self-control, *brahmacharya* is 'not a problem of "self-knowledge" in the purely intersubjective sense of which Foucault clearly writes', but is instead 'a knowledge of the transcendental Self, which is only partially realized in any particular

[11] Gupta, *Sexuality, Obscenity*, p. 68. As he argued in 1920, 'it is our duty for the present moment to suspend bringing forth heirs into slavery'. Alter, *Gandhi's Body*, pp. 11, 209–10.
[12] Alter, *Gandhi's Body*, p. x.
[13] Kelly, *A Politics*, pp. 18–19.
[14] Alter, 'Seminal Truth', 275.
[15] Alter, 'Seminal Truth', 276.
[16] Alter, 'Seminal Truth', 277.

individual'.[17] It aims to regulate life, furthermore, on a psychosomatic level rather than on the psychic level of emotion or on the intersubjective level of action; morality for the *brahmachari* is thus associated with a regime of health that is delineated more in biological than ideological terms.[18] While for both Chidley and Gandhi the discourse of sexuality and health was therefore conceived of in terms of embodied truth, they sought to attain such truth through, on the one hand, 'a hermeneutics of truth about the body', and, on the other, through 'an embodiment of truth in somatic terms'.[19]

In order to understand the principal elements of the male *brahmachari*, it is necessary, according to Alter, to begin with semen rather than with the self. As Wendy Doniger argues, in Hinduism semen is considered a product of life-blood; hence to retain semen is 'to preserve one's very life, to *save* one's life – literally, as one would save money'.[20] To retain semen is more than to preserve one's life, however, for the unspent semen travels upwards to the head and provides the *brahmachari* with, according to Gandhi, 'wonderful potency'.[21] In the Kundalini Yoga tradition the yogi, by drawing his semen to his third eye, converts it into soma, and in so doing ensures his immortality.[22] But since even for the ordinary man 'the phallus that draws up its seed is symbolic of the perfect man' – and since it takes, moreover, one month to make the amount of semen spent in just one ejaculation – for the *brahmachari* the effect of the loss of any semen threatens biomoral degeneration, or as Doniger terms it 'a kind of death'.[23] For the *brahmachari* the control of desire (*kama daman*) is therefore a means of controlling semen (*virya nirodh*) rather than being an end in itself.[24] It is not, moreover, based on moral grounds, since virtue for the *brahmachari* is not a product of what he does but of what happens to his body as a result of his retention of semen. *Brahmacharya* does not, therefore, entail a management of sexuality through the disciplinary techniques of failure and confession, with failure being met by punishment. Semen loss is instead greeted simply with regret – which could explain why Gandhi, Alter suggests, was able to speak so frankly about his battles to control the self.[25] It is clear,

17 Alter, 'Seminal Truth', 277.
18 Alter, 'Seminal Truth', 276.
19 Alter, 'Seminal Truth', 277.
20 Doniger O'Flaherty, *Women, Androgynes*, p. 45.
21 Gandhi, *An Autobiography*, p. 317.
22 Doniger O'Flaherty, *Women, Androgynes*, p. 45.
23 Doniger O' Flaherty, *Women, Androgynes*, pp. 44, 35; and Alter, 'Seminal Truth', 283.
24 Alter, 'Seminal Truth', 282.
25 Alter, 'Seminal Truth', 288.

therefore, that 'brahmacharya and semen loss are not simply culturally conditioned expressions of some hidden anxiety about the self'.[26]

Whether or not the same can be said of all or even some of the Indian efforts to regulate the obscene remains unclear, but my purpose in concluding with a micro-analysis of the relationship between semen and the governance of the self in India and Australia is to posit that this may, indeed, have been the case. For while ample work has demonstrated the nature of colonial governmentality in India, much remains to be done to determine exactly what its impact was on Indian minds and bodies. Considerable attention has been paid, for example, to colonial constructions of caste, particularly as embodied in the census, but whether or not Indians actually internalized such constructions (through, as Nicholas Dirks and others have claimed, a process of self-objectification), or whether they simply manipulated such constructions to their own advantage, is far from clear.[27] The problem is that Foucault's insights into the micropolitics of power and knowledge reveal the way that bodies are worked upon by configurations of power, but they do little to illumine how people both respond to and deconstruct such configurations – of the role of the body, in other words, in serving as a site where agency and power must take account of each other – nor of the myriad forms such configurations can take.[28] Such an oversight, while problematic in any context, is particularly troublesome in a context such as India in which different practices of bodily regulation continued to coexist. What such coexistence meant, however, was that in India colonial governmentality was forced to negotiate with indigenous knowledges about the body (what Alter terms a 'complex referentiality of somaticity'), which made the body a site for an alternative history of the nation.[29] In Australia, on the other hand, it was, perhaps, colonial governmentality's refusal to negotiate with indigenous knowledges that fostered an obsessive

[26] Alter, 'Seminal Truth', 286. According to Hindu ideas of sexuality it is thus the lack of boundedness of the *male* body in which danger lies rather than, as in Western sexual traditions, that of the female body. In Hinduism the flow of fluids from women's bodies is literally life-giving, particularly in the case of milk. Female chastity is thus conceptualized in very different terms from in Western sexual traditions, since a woman acquires virtue 'not by performing asceticism (for then she would be denied access to her supplementary source in the male), but by remaining "chaste" in the socially sanctioned way: by letting milk flow'. Doniger O'Flaherty, *Women, Androgynes*, p. 58.

[27] See Dirks, 'The Ethnographic State', and Cohn, 'The Census'. See also Bandyopadhyay, 'Popular Religion and Social Mobility'; and Constable, 'Early Dalit Literature and Culture'.

[28] Alter, *Gandhi's Body*, p. xvii.

[29] Alter, *Gandhi's Body*, p. xviii.

hermeneutics of truth about the body – and which, in turn, closed off such possibilities.[30]

Uncovering such histories necessitates, as this book has aimed to demonstrate, 'render[ing] permeable and then creatively trespass[ing] across rather rigidly external boundaries' – to undertake, in other words, 'A new departure towards comparative and connective histories'.[31] Comparing Australia and India may seem, at first glance, an unwieldy construction, but I chose India because it is my primary area of expertise, and Australia because the archives led me there (due principally to the importance of Australia as Britain's chief literary market).[32] Australian archives yielded, furthermore, a particularly rich collection of customs materials relating to the regulation of obscenity. While the same did not hold true for Indian archives, such documentary discrepancies serve as a useful reminder that archives are cultural artefacts.[33] Although scholars of empire have long been aware that 'We cannot just *do* colonial history based on our given sources', for the comparative colonial historian considering how archives are constituted and what is excluded

[30] As Chidley's sad story illustrates, the Australian state was so fearful of the effects of his proselytization that he was prosecuted at least thirty times in Sydney alone (not to mention numerous prosecutions in Melbourne), and when this failed to silence him he was twice incarcerated in a mental institution – and on one occasion he tried to put an end to his tortured battles to control the self by attempting to take his own life. See George Black, New South Wales Chief Secretary, letter, *Mirror*, 3 May 1916, and *Truth*, January 1914, clippings in Mss. 143/6, ML. As Drs Chisholm Ross and Chill argued at one of Chidley's insanity hearings, his penchant for lecturing '"young and presumably innocent persons" about his "sexual obsessions"' made him 'a menace to certain sections of the public' and a person 'not fit to be at large'. Edwards and Hall, 'The Case of William Chidley', 137.

[31] Bose, 'Post-Colonial Histories', 146.

[32] India and Ireland would also prove a fruitful comparison in light, firstly, of the complex history of literary regulation in the latter. By the nineteenth century this involved two distinct forms of regulation, one 'private Catholic' (dominated by the pulpit and the confessional) and the other 'more secular ... and more public' (dominated by Protestant organizations such as the National Vigilance Association, which was at one stage of its existence presided over by the vice-regents of Ireland, the Earl and Countess of Aberdeen). Such a comparison would also prove fruitful, secondly, because of the historical linkages between the two (which a growing body of scholarship has begun to document). Mullin, *James Joyce*, 20.

[33] Archives in both Australia and India, however, yielded little in the way of samples of the 'obscene' matter subject to regulation, which in part explains the unfortunate lack of images in this book (although additional problems were posed by misfortunes in shipping and microfilming, since a large assortment of my photocopies of Australian archival material, including visual images, disappeared in the post, and a file containing a valuable collection of visual material disappeared into the bowels of the copying department in one Indian archive, never to reappear). Materials of course do exist, as Charu Gupta has demonstrated in the case of *kamashastra* advertisements, but since my primary interest was in the regulation of 'obscene' material rather than in the material itself I did not pursue such avenues of research. See Gupta, *Sexuality, Obscenity*.

from them – to question why, for example, in India Vizetelly's Zola translations represented what Annabel Patterson refers to as one of 'those famous puzzling cases of *noncensorship*' (emphasis in original) – is particularly pressing.[34]

But since empires were inherently transnational phenomena, it is equally pressing to uncover the myriad connections between metropoles and their colonies, especially the ways in which empire and nation served to constitute each other.[35] In the case of Britain such mutual imbrications have, however, received relatively little scholarly attention, even from scholars of the 'new imperial history', who, in spite of discarding the idea of nation and empire as separate spheres, continue to regard Britain largely as a 'fixed referent, the a priori body upon which empire is inscribed' – a sign, for Antoinette Burton, of historians' fear of 'countenanc[ing] the notion that the nation is not only *not* antecedent to empire, but that as both a symbolic and a material site the nation ... has no originary moment' – and that it is, furthermore, 'precarious, unmoored, and, in the end, finally unrealizable'.[36]

The response of this book to such challenges has been to explore empire as a set of changing and contested relations, as 'a spatialized terrain of power' (one that was, moreover, precariously shifting and vulnerable), rather than viewing metropole and colonies as discrete domains, as well as not only to untangle 'empire, nation ... colony, and globe' but to *retangle* them in productive ways in order to generate new understandings about the nature of colonial power and how it operated in markedly different contexts.[37] For not only does the concept of *colonialism* still '[need] much more specification – contextual and historical – than is conventionally given', but we need to move beyond the postcolonial blender (in which Foucault, Fanon and Lacan are mixed together and then poured onto any colonial context, subject population, or time period) to reorient our conceptual apparatus in a way 'that allows theory to grow out of the different phases of colonial rule' – in, however, multiple contexts – rather than vice versa.[38] The glaring postcolonial legacies not only of colonial boundary-marking but of the moral frameworks through which such boundaries were

[34] Patterson, *Censorship and Interpretation*, p. 17.

[35] Levine, *Prostitution, Race*, p. 17. We should perhaps be as wary, however, of the term 'transnationalism' as of the term 'nation' – as Grewal and Kaplan warn. The term has become so ubiquitous – they identify no fewer than five different uses of it – 'that much of its political valence seems to have been excavated'. 'Global Identities', 664.

[36] Burton, 'Introduction', pp. 5, 7.

[37] Burton, 'Introduction', p. 5.

[38] Bose, 'Post-Colonial Histories', 136; and Thomas, *Colonialism's Culture*, p. ix.

constructed make such a task imperative. For not only is the postcolony, as Achille Mbembe argues, 'a particularly revealing, and rather dramatic, stage on which are played out the wider problems of subjection and its corollary, discipline', but it is, perhaps, in the 'intimate tyranny [that] links the rulers with the ruled' that such legacies are most apparent.[39]

[39] Mbembe, *On the Postcolony*, pp. 103, 128.

Bibliography

GOVERNMENT ARCHIVAL RECORDS

AUSTRALIA

Australian Archives, Canberra

A1 Departments of External Affairs, Home and Territories, Home Affairs and the Interior: Correspondence Files, Annual Single Number Series, 1890–1969

A2 Prime Minister's Office: Correspondence Files, Annual Single Number Series, 1895–1926

A51 Book of Notes and Precedents: Papua, 1905–1924

A425 Department of Trade and Customs, Central Office: Correspondence Files, 1905–

A432 Attorney-General's Department, Central Office: Correspondence Files, 1901–

A981 Department of External Affairs, Central Office: Correspondence Files, 1821–1970

A3023 Book Censorship Board and Literature Censorship Board: Correspondence Files, 1933–1957

A5507 Department of Trade and Customs, Central Office: Historical Collection of Customs Material, 1828–1960

A6280 Department of Trade and Customs, Central Office: Confidential Instructions, 1908–1958

A6662 Governor-General: Miscellaneous Correspondence, 1887–1912

Australian Archives, Melbourne

B13 Collector of Customs, Melbourne: General and Classified Correspondence, 1898–

MP273/1 Postmaster-General's Department, Central Administration: General Correspondence Files, 1901–1939

MP341/1 Department of Posts and Telegraphs: General Correspondence 'G' Files

Australian Archives, Sydney

A1023 Collector of Customs, Sydney: Outward Telegram Books, 1897–1908

C4205 Collector of Customs, Sydney: Albums of Newspaper Cuttings, 1895–1915

C4338	Department of Trade and Customs: Wharf Handbooks
SP331	Collector of Customs, Sydney: Correspondence Files
SP906/1	Collector of Customs, Sydney: General Correspondence 'A' Series

Public Record Office, Victoria

3992	Inward Registered Correspondence III

Sydney Records Centre, State Records New South Wales

4/6633	Chief Secretary's Papers
4/6634	Chief Secretary's Papers

INDIA

Maharashtra State Archives, Mumbai

Proceedings and Files of the Government of Maharashtra, including the Judicial, Political, Police, Customs, Education, General, and Home Departments, 1888–1923

Files of the Home Department, Political, Executive Branch, 1923–1938

Files of the Finance and Commerce Department, Statistics and Commerce Branch, 1894

National Archives of India, Delhi

Files of the Central Board of Revenue, Customs Duties, 1925–1938

Files of the Finance and Commerce Department (later Commerce and Industry, then Commerce), including Customs Establishment, Post Office, Salaries, Separate Revenue and Statistics and Commerce, 1886–1939

Proceedings and Files of the Government of India, Home Department, including the Books and Publications, D, Education, Judicial, Municipalities, Police, Political, Public and War Branches, 1866–1943

West Bengal State Archives, Kolkata

Files of the General Department, 1864

Proceedings and Files of the Government of West Bengal, Judicial Dept., 1873–1923

UNITED KINGDOM

Public Record Office, Kew

CO 323	Colonies, General: Original Correspondence, 1689–1952
CUST 46	Board of Customs: Registered Papers, 1671–1966
CUST 49	Customs and Excise: Registered Papers, 1902–1993
DO 35	Dominions Office and Commonwealth Relations Office: Original Correspondence, 1915–1971
DO 119	High Commissioner for South Africa, and High Commissioner for Basutoland, the Bechuanaland Protectorate and Swaziland, and UK High Commissioner for the Union of South Africa: Correspondence, 1843–1965

FO 83	Foreign and Commonwealth Office and Predecessors: Political and Other Departments: General Correspondence before 1906, Great Britain and General, 1745–1975
FO 371	Foreign Office: Political Departments: General Correspondence 1906–1966
HO 45	Home Office: Registered Papers, 1839–1979
HO 144	Home Office: Registered Papers, Supplementary, 1868–1959
HO 155	Home Office: Statistics Entry Books, 1855–1921
MEPO 2	Metropolitan Police: Office of the Commissioner: Correspondence and Papers, 1817–1994
MEPO 3	Metropolitan Police: Office of the Commissioner: Correspondence and Papers, Special Series, 1830–1974

PRIVATE AND INSTITUTIONAL PAPERS

A. G. Stephens Papers, 4837/12, ML
Alfred Deakin Papers, Mss. 1540, NLA
Book Censorship Abolition League, Correspondence, Mss. 10061, SLV
Bush Book Club of New South Wales, Records 1909–59, Mss. 428 1/3, ML
C. T. Clark Papers, Mss. 3315, ML
Detective Inspector J. M. Christie, scrapbook, Mss. 12720, SLV
National Vigilance Association Papers, Mss. 4/NVA, WL
Newspaper Clippings, Mss. Z/Q991/N, ML
Records of the Australian Customs Service, Mss. Acc 96/76, NLA
T. W. White Papers, Mss. 9148, NLA
William Chidley Papers, Mss. 143/6, ML

OFFICIAL PUBLICATIONS

AUSTRALIA

Beale, O., *Royal Commission into Secret Drugs, Cures, and Foods* (Melbourne: Government Printer, 1908).
Coghlan, T., *Customs Statistics, 1883* (Sydney: Government Printer, 1884).
The New South Wales Statistical Register, 1893 (Sydney: Government Printer, 1894).
Childbirth in New South Wales (Sydney: Government Printer, 1901).
The Decline of the Birth Rate in New South Wales (Sydney: Government Printer, 1903).
Annual Statement of the Trade of the Commonwealth of Australia with the United Kingdom, British Possessions, and Foreign Countries for the Year 1904 and of the Customs and Excise Revenue (Sydney: John Sands, 1904).
Commonwealth of Australia Gazette (28 October 1920).
Department of the Parliamentary Library, *1901: Socio-Economic Profile of Australia*, Research Note 23 (2000–01).
General Orders for Officers of the Department of Trade and Customs (Melbourne: H. J. Green, 1927).
New South Wales, Parliament, *Parliamentary Debates* (12 July 1889).

New South Wales, Supreme Court, *New South Wales Law Reports*, 6 (1885).
New South Wales Regulations Made by the Public Service Board Under the Public Service Act 1902 (Sydney: William Applegate Gullick, 1907).
The New South Wales Weekly Notes, 18 July 1901 and 5 June 1902.
Parliamentary Debates: Senate and House of Representatives, Commonwealth of Australia (1901–1939).
Regulations Under the Public Service Act of 1895 (New South Wales: Government Printer, 1898).
Royal Commission on the Decline of the Birth-Rate and on the Mortality of Infants in New South Wales, Vol. II: *Minutes, Evidence, Exhibits, Index* (Sydney: William Applegate Gullick, Government Printer, 1904).
State Reports, Queensland: Decisions of the Supreme Court of Queensland (1907).
Victoria, Parliament, *Parliamentary Debates, Legislative Council and Legislative Assembly* (1891–1900; 1906; 1935).

INDIA

Abstract of the Proceedings of the Council of the Governor-General of India, 15 (14 March 1876).
Appraiser's Manual of Standing Orders at Calcutta Custom House, Vol. II, n.d.
The Bengal Police Manual, Vol. I (Calcutta: Bengal Secretariat Book Depot, 1911).
The Burma Sea Customs Manual Containing Notifications, Rules, and Orders Applicable to Burma, 5th edn (Rangoon: Office of the Superintendent, Government Printing, 1911).
Council of State, *Debates, Official Report* (1924).
Gordon, A. D., *Investigating Officers' Manual: Bengal Police* (Calcutta: Bengal Government Press, 1925).
Index to Police Regulations Bengal 1927, Vol. III (Calcutta: Bengal Secretariat Book Depot, 1928).
Indian Cinematograph (Rangachariar) Committee, 1927–28, Vol. II: *Evidence* (Calcutta: Central Publication Branch, 1928).
Indian Posts and Telegraphs Department, *Annual Report* (1886–7, 1894–5, 1899–1900, 1908–9, 1910–11, 1925–6, 1929–30 and 1934–5).
Legislative Assembly, *Debates, Official Report* (8 March 1924, 15 September 1924 and 20 February 1925).
Madras Customs Standing Orders for Appraisers (Madras: Superintendent, Government Press, 1909).
The Preventive Service Manual (Calcutta: Bengal Secretariat Press, 1910).
Proceedings of the Legislative Council of India, Vol. I, 20 May 1854–22 December 1855 (Calcutta: F. Carbery, Military Orphan Press).
Proceedings of the Sub-Committee, Public Service Commission, Relating to the Customs Department: Bengal, Bombay, Madras (Calcutta: Superintendent of Government Printing, India, 1887).
Proceedings of the Sub-Committee, Public Service Commission, Relating to the Postal Department (Bombay: Printed at the Government Central Press, 1887).
Selections from the Records of the Bengal Government, Vol. XXXII (Calcutta: General Printing Department, 1859).

UNITED KINGDOM

Great Britain, Parliament, *Hansard's Parliamentary Debates*, 3rd series (1857, 1887–8).
The Law Reports, Queen's Bench Division (1868).
Report from the Joint Select Committee on Lotteries and Indecent Advertisements (1908).

MAGAZINES, JOURNALS AND NEWSPAPERS (SPORADIC ISSUES CONSULTED)

Age (Melbourne, 1889)
The Argus Law Reports (1906)
Australasian Medical Gazette (Sydney, 1882–1907)
Australian Star (Sydney, 1897–9)
The Bulletin (Sydney, 1888–1904)
The Bystander (London, 1908)
The Colonial Bookseller, Newsletter and Stationer (London, 1908)
The Criminal Law Journal of India, 17 (1917)
Daily Telegraph (Sydney, 1899–1903, 1938)
The Englishman (Calcutta, 1894)
Fortnightly Review (London, 1885)
The Friend of India (Serampore, 1873)
The Herald (Melbourne, 1899–1905)
The Home (Sydney, 1928)
Indian Law Reports, Allahabad Series (1881, 1906)
Indian Law Reports, Bombay Series (1895)
Indian Law Reports, Calcutta Series (1904, 1912, 1933)
Intercolonial Medical Journal of Australasia (Melbourne, 1904)
Life: A Record for Busy Folk (Melbourne, 1907)
The New South Wales Weekly Notes (1901, 1902)
Pall Mall Gazette (London, 1887–9)
The Publisher: Australian Literary News (Sydney, 1886–9)
The Queensland Law Journal (1892–3)
Saunders, Otley and Co's Oriental Budget (London, 1859–61)
The Sun (Sydney, 1948)
The Sydney Morning Herald (Sydney, 1899–1930)
Truth (Sydney, 1905)
The Victorian Law Reports (1920)
Vigilance Record (London, 1888–9)

THESES AND UNPUBLISHED PAPERS

Bhattacharya, T., 'Print Culture in 19th-Century Bengal', unpublished PhD thesis, University of London (2000).
Colligan, C., 'Obscenity and Empire: England's Obscene Print Culture in the Nineteenth Century', unpublished PhD thesis, Queens University, Ontario (2002).

Cummins, A., 'The Transmission of Émile Zola in English Literary Culture, 1877–1895', unpublished PhD thesis, Oxford University (2007).
Hyslop, A., 'Arresting Race Deterioration: The Case of Child Welfare Reform in Victoria 1900–1914', unpublished paper, AHA Conference, Melbourne (1984).
Jarvis, D., 'Realism and Australian Critical Thought 1880–1900', unpublished PhD thesis, University of New South Wales (1982).
Johanson, G., 'A Study of Colonial Editions in Australia 1843–1942', unpublished PhD thesis, Monash University (1995).
Payne, S., 'Aspects of Commonwealth Literary Censorship in Australia 1919–1941', unpublished MA thesis, Australian National University (1980).
Wee, A., 'Trials and *Eros*: The British Home Office v. Indecent Publications 1857–1932', unpublished PhD thesis, University of Minnesota (2003).
Wyndham, D., 'Striving for National Fitness: Eugenics in Australia 1910s to 1930s', unpublished PhD thesis, University of Sydney (1996).

BOOKS AND ARTICLES

Allen, J., 'Octavius Beale Re-considered: Infanticide, Baby-farming and Abortion in NSW 1880–1939', in Sydney Labour History Group, *What Rough Beast?: The State and Social Order in Australian History* (Sydney: George Allen and Unwin, 1982), pp. 111–29.
Alomes, S., 'Australian Nationalism in the Eras of Imperialism and "Internationalism"', *Australian Journal of Politics and History*, 34, 3 (1988), 320–32.
Alter, J., 'Celibacy, Sexuality, and the Transformation of Gender into Nationalism in North India', *Journal of Asian Studies*, 53, 1 (1994), 45–66.
'Seminal Truth: A Modern Science of Male Celibacy in North India', *Medical Anthropology Quarterly*, 11, 3 (1997), 275–98.
Gandhi's Body: Sex, Diet, and the Politics of Nationalism (Philadelphia: University of Pennsylvania Press, 2001).
Altick, R., *The English Common Reader* (Chicago: University of Chicago Press, 1957).
Anandhi, S., 'Reproductive Bodies and Regulated Sexuality: Birth Control Debates in Early 20th Century Tamilnadu', in J. Nair and M. E. John (eds.), *A Question of Silence: The Sexual Economics of Modern India* (London: Zed Books, 2000), pp. 139–66.
Anderson, B., *Imagined Communities: Reflections on the Origin and Spread of Nationalism* (London: Verso, 1991).
'Long-Distance Nationalism', in *The Spectre of Comparisons: Nationalism, Southeast Asia, and the World* (London: Verso, 1998), pp. 58–74.
Anderson, W., *The Cultivation of Whiteness: Science, Health and Racial Destiny in Australia* (New York: Basic Books, 2003).
Ang, I., 'From White Australia to Fortress Australia: The Anxious Nation in the New Century', in L. Jayasuriya, D. Walker and J. Gothard (eds.), *Legacies of White Australia: Race, Culture and Nation*, (Crawley, WA: University of Western Australia Press, 2003), pp. 51–69.

Appadurai, A., 'Number in the Colonial Imagination', in *Modernity at Large: Cultural Dimensions of Globalization* (Minneapolis: University of Minnesota Press, 1996), pp. 114–38.

Arnold, D., 'Touching the Body: Perspectives on the Indian Plague', in R. Guha and G. C. Spivak (eds.), *Selected Subaltern Studies* (Oxford: Oxford University Press, 1988), pp. 391–426.

Colonizing the Body: State Medicine and Epidemic Disease in Nineteenth-Century India (New Delhi: Oxford University Press, 1993).

Arnold, J., ' "Choose your Author as You Would Choose a Friend": Circulating Libraries in Melbourne, 1930–1960', *La Trobe Library Journal*, 10, 40 (1987), 77–96.

Ashcroft, B., G. Griffiths and H. Tiffin, *The Empire Writes Back: Theory and Practice in Post-Colonial Literatures* (London: Routledge, 1989).

Ballantyne, T. and A. Burton, 'Introduction: Bodies, Empires, and World Histories', in T. Ballantyne and A. Burton (eds.), *Bodies in Contact: Rethinking Colonial Encounters in World History* (Durham, NC: Duke University Press, 2005), pp. 1–15.

'Postscript: Bodies, Genders, Empires: Reimagining World Histories', in T. Ballantyne and A. Burton (eds.), *Bodies in Contact: Rethinking Colonial Encounters in World History* (Durham, NC: Duke University Press, 2005), pp. 405–23.

Ballhatchet, K., *Race, Sex and Class under the Raj: Imperial Attitudes and Policies and their Critics, 1793–1905* (London: Weidenfeld and Nicolson, 1980).

Bandyopadhyay, S., 'Popular Religion and Social Mobility in Colonial Bengal: The Matua Sect and the Namasudras', in R. K. Ray (ed.), *Mind, Body and Society: Life and Mentality in Colonial Bengal* (Calcutta: Oxford University Press, 1995), pp. 152–92.

Banerjee, S., 'Bogey of the Bawdy: Changing Concept of "Obscenity" in 19th Century Bengali Culture', *Economic and Political Weekly*, 22, 29 (1987), 1197–206.

The Parlour and the Streets: Elite and Popular Culture in Nineteenth Century Calcutta (Calcutta: Seagull, 1989).

Bannerji, H., 'Attired in Virtue: The Discourse on Shame (lajja) and Clothing of the Bhadramahila in Colonial Bengal', in B. Ray (ed.), *From the Seams of History: Essays on Indian Women* (New Delhi: Oxford University Press, 1997), pp. 67–106.

Barnes, J., *Free Trade in Books: A Study of the London Book Trade Since 1800* (London: Clarendon Press, 1964).

Barrier, G., *Banned, Controversial Literature and Political Control in British India 1907–1947* (Columbia: University of Missouri Press, 1974).

Bashford, A., *Imperial Hygiene: A Critical History of Colonialism, Nationalism and Public Health* (London: Palgrave Macmillan, 2004).

Bashford, A. and C. Hooker, 'Introduction: Contagion, Modernity and Posmodernity', in A. Bashford and C. Hooker (eds.), *Contagion: Historical and Cultural Studies* (London: Routledge, 2001), pp. 1–12.

Bataille, G., 'Sexual Plethora and Death', in *Eroticism* (San Francisco: City Lights Books, 1986).

Baucom, I., *Out of Place: Englishness, Empire and the Locations of Identity* (Princeton, NJ: Princeton University Press, 1999).
Bayly, S., 'Race in Britain and India', in P. van der Veer and H. Lehmann (eds.), *Nation and Religion: Perspectives on Europe and Asia* (Princeton, NJ: Princeton University Press, 1999), pp. 71–95.
Beisel, N., 'Morals Versus Art: Censorship, the Politics of Interpretation, and the Victorian Nude', *American Sociological Review*, 58 (1993), 145–62.
Benton, L., *Law and Colonial Cultures: Legal Regimes in World History, 1400–1900* (Cambridge: Cambridge University Press, 2002).
Beverley, B., 'The Taste of India', *Australian Cultural History*, 9 (1990), 36–48.
Bhabha, H., 'Difference, Discrimination, and the Discourse of Colonialism', in F. Barker, P. Hulme, M. Iversen and D. Loxley (eds.), *Literature, Politics and Theory: Papers from the Essex Conference 1976–1984* (London: Methuen, 1986), pp. 148–72.
The Location of Culture (London: Routledge, 1994).
'Of Mimicry and Man: The Ambivalence of Colonial Discourse', in F. Cooper and A. L. Stoler (eds.), *Tensions of Empire: Colonial Cultures in a Bourgeois World* (Berkeley: University of California Press, 1997), pp. 152–60.
Blainey, G., *The Tyranny of Distance: How Distance Shaped Australia's History* (Melbourne: Sun Books, 1966).
Bland, L., *Banishing the Beast: Sexuality and the Early Feminists* (New York: Free Press, 1995).
Bose, P. K., 'Sons of the Nation: Child Rearing in the New Family', in P. Chatterjee (ed.), *Texts of Power: Emerging Disciplines in Colonial Bengal* (Minneapolis: University of Minnesota Press, 1995), pp. 118–44.
Bose, S., 'Post-Colonial Histories of South Asia: Some Reflections', *Journal of Contemporary History*, 38, 1 (2003), 133–46.
Bourdieu, P., *Distinction: A Social Critique of the Judgment of Taste*, trans. Richard Nice (London: Routledge and Kegan Paul, 1984).
'Censorship and the Imposition of Form', in J. B. Thompson (ed.), *Language and Symbolic Power*, trans. G. Raymond and M. Adamson (Cambridge, MA: Harvard University Press, 1991), pp. 137–59.
Boyce, M. T., *British Policy and the Evolution of the Vernacular Press in India, 1835–1878* (Delhi: Chanakya Publications, 1988).
Bristow, E., *Vice and Vigilance: Purity Movements in Britain Since 1700* (Dublin: Gill and Macmillan Ltd, 1977).
Broken Hill Mechanics Institute, *Catalogue of the Lending Library and Rules and Library By-Laws* (Broken Hill: Harman and Jacka, Printers, 1899).
Brown, M., ' "That Heavy Machine": Reprising the Colonial Apparatus in 21st Century Social Control', *Social Justice*, 32, 1 (2005), 41–52.
Budd, M. A., *The Sculpture Machine: Physical Culture and Body Politics in the Age of Empire* (Houndmills, Basingstoke: Macmillan, 1997).
Buell, L., 'Postcolonial Anxiety in Classic U.S. Literature', in A. Singh and P. Schmidt (eds.), *Postcolonial Theory and the United States: Race, Ethnicity, and Literature* (Jackson, MS: University Press of Mississippi, 2000), pp. 196–219.
Burt, R., 'Un-Censoring in Detail: The Fetish of Censorship in the Early Modern Past and the Postmodern Present', in R. Post (ed.), *Censorship*

and Silencing: Practices of Cultural Regulation (Los Angeles: Getty Research Institute for the History of Art and the Humanities, 1998), pp. 17–41.

Burton, A., 'The White Women's Burden: British Feminists and "the Indian Woman", 1865–1915', in N. Chaudhuri and M. Strobel (eds.), *Western Women and Imperialism: Complicity and Resistance* (Bloomington: Indiana University Press, 1992), pp. 137–57.

'Introduction: On the Inadequacy and the Indispensability of the Nation', in A. Burton (ed.), *After the Imperial Turn: Thinking with and through the Nation* (Durham, NC: Duke University Press, 2003), pp. 1–23.

Butler, J., 'Ruled Out: Vocabularies of the Censor', in R. Post (ed.), *Censorship and Silencing: Practices of Cultural Regulation* (Los Angeles: Getty Research Institute for the History of Art and the Humanities, 1998), pp. 247–59.

Bynum, W. F., 'Policing Hearts of Darkness: Aspects of the International Sanitary Conferences', *History of Philosophy and Life Sciences*, 15 (1993), 421–34.

Carney, T., 'The History of Australian Drug Laws: Commercialism to Confusion?', *Monash University Law Review*, 7 (1981), 165–204.

Castles, S., B. Cope, M. Kalantzis and M. Morrissey, 'The Bicentenary and the Failure of Australian Nationalism', *Race and Class*, 29, 3 (1988), 53–68.

Chandavarkar, R., 'Plague, Panic and Epidemic Politics in India, 1896–1914', in T. Ranger and P. Slack (eds.), *Epidemics and Ideas. Essays on the Historical Perception of Pestilence* (Cambridge: Cambridge University Press, 1992).

Chatterjee, P., *Nationalist Thought and the Colonial World* (Minneapolis: University of Minnesota Press, 1993).

The Nation and its Fragments: Colonial and Postcolonial Histories (New Delhi: Oxford University Press, 1994).

'The Disciplines in Colonial Bengal', in P. Chatterjee (ed.), *Texts of Power: Emerging Disciplines in Colonial Bengal* (Minneapolis: University of Minnesota Press, 1995), pp. 1–29.

Chaudhary, Z., 'Phantasmagoric Aesthetics: Colonial Violence and the Management of Perception', *Cultural Critique*, 59 (2005), pp. 63–119.

Chowdhry, P., *Colonial India and the Making of Empire Cinema: Image, Ideology and Identity* (Manchester: Manchester University Press, 2000).

Chowdhury-Sengupta, I., 'The Effeminate and the Masculine: Nationalism and the Concept of Race in Colonial Bengal', in P. Robb (ed.), *The Concept of Race in South Asia* (New Delhi: Oxford University Press, 1995), pp. 282–303.

Cohn, B., 'The Census, Social Structure and Objectification', in *An Anthropologist Among the Historians and Other Essays* (New Delhi: Oxford University Press, 1990), pp. 224–54.

Colonialism and its Forms of Knowledge: The British in India (Princeton, NJ: Princeton University Press, 1996).

Cole, D., ' "The Crimson Thread of Kinship": Ethnic Ideas in Australia, 1870–1914', *Historical Studies*, 14, 56 (1971), 511–25.

'The Problem of "Nationalism" and "Imperialism" in British Settlement Colonies', *Journal of British Studies*, 10, 2 (1971), 160–82.

Cole, J., 'Colonialism and Censorship', in R. D. Long (ed.), *The Man on the Spot: Essays on British Empire History* (Westport, CT: Greenwood Press, 1995), pp. 45–62.

Coleman, P., *Obscenity, Blasphemy, Sedition: Censorship in Australia* (Brisbane: Jacaranda Press, 1963).
Colley, L., *Britons: Forging the Nation, 1707–1837* (New Haven, CT: Yale University Press, 1992).
Colligan, C., *The Traffic in Obscenity from Byron to Beardsley: Sexuality and Exoticism in Nineteenth-Century Print Culture* (Houndmills, Basingstoke: Palgrave Macmillan, 2006).
Collingham, E. M., *Imperial Bodies: The Physical Experience of the Raj, c. 1800–1947* (Cambridge: Polity Press, 2001).
Conrad, P., 'The Englishness of English Literature', *Daedalus*, 112, 1 (1993), 157–74.
Constable, P., 'Early Dalit Literature and Culture in Late Nineteenth- and Early Twentieth-Century Western India', *Modern Asian Studies*, 31, 2 (May 1997), 317–38.
Cooper, F. and A. L. Stoler, 'Between Metropole and Colony: Rethinking a Research Agenda', in F. Cooper and A. L. Stoler (eds.), *Tensions of Empire: Colonial Cultures in a Bourgeois World* (Berkeley: University of California Press, 1997), pp. 1–56.
Coote, W. A., *A Romance of Philanthropy: Being a Record of Some of the Principle Incidents Connected with the Exceptionally Successful Thirty Years' Work of the National Vigilance Association* (London: National Vigilance Association, 1916).
Crozier, M., 'Antipodean Sensibilities', *The South Atlantic Quarterly*, 98, 4 (1999), 839–59.
Curthoys, A., 'Feminism, Citizenship and National Identity', *Feminist Review*, 44 (1993), 19–38.
'Identity Crisis: Colonialism, Nation, and Gender in Australian History', *Gender and History*, 5, 2 (1993), 165–73.
'Liberalism and Exclusionism: A Prehistory of the White Australia Policy', in L. Jayasuriya, D. Walker and J. Gothard (eds.), *Legacies of White Australia: Race, Culture and Nation*, (Crawley, WA: University of Western Australia Press, 2003), pp. 8–32.
Darby, R., 'William Acton's Antipodean Disciples: A Colonial Perspective on His Theories of Male Sexual (Dys)function', *Journal of the History of Sexuality*, 13, 2 (2004), 157–82.
Darnton, R., *The Forbidden Best-Sellers of Pre-Revolutionary France* (New York: Norton, 1995).
'Un-British Activities', *New York Review of Books*, 12 April 2001, 84–88.
Das, V., 'Gender Studies, Cross-Cultural Comparison and the Organization of Knowledge', *Berkshire Review*, 21 (1986), 58–79.
Datta, P., 'Dying Hindus: Production of Hindu Communal Common Sense in Early Twentieth Century Bengal', *Economic and Political Weekly*, 28, 5 (1993), 1305–19.
Davin, A., 'Imperialism and Motherhood', in F. Cooper and A. L. Stoler (eds.), *Tensions of Empire: Colonial Cultures in a Bourgeois World* (Berkeley: University of California Press, 1997), pp. 87–151.
Davison, G., 'Sydney and the Bush: An Urban Context for the Australian Legend', *Historical Studies*, 18, 71 (1978), 191–209.

Day, D., *Smugglers and Sailors* (Canberra: Australian Government Publishing Service, 1992).

Contraband and Controversy: The Customs History of Australia from 1901 (Canberra: Australian Government Publishing Service, 1996).

De Grazia, E., *Girls Lean Back Everywhere: The Law of Obscenity and the Assault on Genius* (London: Constable, 1992).

Dean, M., '"A Social Structure of Many Souls": Moral Regulation, Government, and Self-Formation', *Canadian Journal of Sociology*, 19, 2 (1994), 145–68.

Governmentality: Power and Rule in Modern Society (London: Sage, 1999).

Decker, C. R., 'Zola's Literary Reputation in England', *PMLA*, 49, 4 (1934), 1150–7.

DeJean, J., *The Reinvention of Obscenity: Sex, Lies, and Tabloids in Early Modern France* (Chicago: University of Chicago Press, 2002).

Denoon, D. and P. Mein-Smith, with M. Wyndham, *A History of Australia, New Zealand and the Pacific* (Malden, MA: Blackwell, 2000).

Dirks, N., 'Castes of Mind', *Representations*, 37 (1992), 56–78.

'From Little Kingdom to Landlord: Colonial Discourse and Colonial Rule', in N. Dirks (ed.), *Colonialism and Culture* (Ann Arbor: University of Michigan Press, 1992), pp. 175–208.

'The Ethnographic State', in *Castes of Mind: Colonialism and the Making of Modern India* (Princeton, NJ: Princeton University Press, 2001), pp. 43–60.

Doniger O'Flaherty, W., *Women, Androgynes, and Other Mythical Beasts* (Chicago: University of Chicago Press, 1980).

Douglas, M., *Purity and Danger: An Analysis of the Concepts of Pollution and Taboo* (London: Routledge, 1991, 1966).

Dowling, L., *The Vulgarization of Art: The Victorians and Aesthetic Democracy* (Charlottesville: University Press of Virginia, 1996).

Dube, S., *Untouchable Pasts: Religion, Identity and Power Among a Central Indian Community 1780–1950* (Albany, NY: State University of New York Press, 1998).

Dunstan, K., *Wowsers: Being an Account of the Prudery Exhibited by Certain Outstanding Men and Woman in such Matters as Drinking, Smoking, Prostitution, Censorship and Gambling* (Sydney: Angus and Robertson, 1974, 1968).

Durkheim, E., *Moral Education: A Study in the Theory and Application of the Sociology of Education*, ed. E. K. Wilson, trans. E. K. Wilson and H. Schnurer (New York: Free Press; London: Collier Macmillan, 1973).

Dutton, G., 'Moral Protectionism', in G. Dutton and M. Harris (eds.), *Australia's Censorship Crisis* (Melbourne: Sun Books, 1970).

Dwivedi, R. C., 'Concept of Obscenity (*Aslilata*) in Sanskrit Poetics', *Annals of the Bhandarkar Oriental Research Institute*, 62, 1–4 (1981), 67–76.

Eagleton, T., *The Ideology of the Aesthetic* (Oxford: Blackwell, 1990).

Edwards, G. A. and W. Hall, 'The Case of William Chidley: A Study in Psychiatry, Morality and Lunacy Law', *Australian and New Zealand Journal of Psychiatry*, 14 (1980), 133–9.

Edwards, P., 'On Home Ground: Settling Land and Domesticating Difference in the "Non-Settler" Colonies of Burma and Cambodia', *Journal of Colonialism and Colonial History*, 4, 3 (Winter 2003).

Elias, N., *The Civilizing Process*, Vol. II: *State Formation and Civilization*, trans. E. Jephcott (Oxford: Blackwell, 1982).

Forth, C. E., 'Moral Contagion and the Will: The Crisis of Masculinity in *fin-de-siècle* France', in A. Bashford and C. Hooker (eds.), *Contagion: Historical and Cultural Studies* (London: Routledge, 2001), pp. 61–73.

Foster, F., 'Joseph Symes, H. K. Rusden and the Knowleton Pamphlet', *Atheist Journal*, 8 (1980), 9–11.

'The Collins Prosecution, the Windeyer Judgment and Publications on Birth Control', *Australia 1888 Bulletin*, 10 (1982).

Foucault, M., 'Technologies of the Self', in Luther H. Martin *et al.* (eds.), *Technologies of the Self: A Seminar with Michel Foucault* (Amherst: University of Massachusetts Press, 1988), pp. 16–49.

The History of Sexuality, Vol. I: *An Introduction*, trans. Robert Hurley (New York: Vintage Books, 1990).

'Governmentality', in G. Burchell, C. Gordon and P. Miller (eds.), *The Foucault Effect: Studies in Governmentality: With Two Lectures by and an Interview with Michel Foucault* (Chicago: University of Chicago Press, 1991), pp. 87–104.

Franklin, M., *My Brilliant Career* (North Ryde, NSW: Angus and Robertson, 1990, 1901).

Frierson, W. C., 'The English Controversy over Realism in Fiction 1885–1895', *PMLA*, 43, 2 (1928), 533–50.

Fuchs, S., *Against Essentialism: A Theory of Culture and Society* (Cambridge, MA: Harvard University Press, 2001).

Galanter, M., *Law and Society in Modern India* (New Delhi: Oxford University Press, 1993).

Gamer, M., 'Genres for the Prosecution: Pornography and the Gothic', *PMLA*, 114 (1999), 1043–54.

Gandhi, M. K., *An Autobiography: The Story of My Experiments with the Truth*, trans. Mahadev Desai (Boston: Beacon Press, 1957).

Garton, S., 'Sound Minds and Healthy Bodies: Re-Considering Eugenics in Australia, 1914–1940', *Australian Historical Studies*, 26, 103 (1994), 163–81.

Gelder, K. and J. Jacobs, *Uncanny Australia: Sacredness and Identity in a Postcolonial Nation* (Carlton South, Victoria: Melbourne University Press, 1998).

Ghosh, A., 'Cheap Books, "Bad" Books: Contesting Print-Cultures in Colonial Bengal', *South Asia Research*, 18, 2 (1998), 173–94.

'Valorising the "Vulgar": Nationalist Appropriations of Colloquial Bengali Traditions, c. 1870–1905', *Indian Economic and Social History Review*, 37, 2 (2000), 151–83.

Power in Print: Popular Publishing and the Politics of Language and Culture in a Colonial Society (New Delhi: Oxford University Press, 2006).

Gikandi, S., *Maps of Englishness: Writing Identity in the Culture of Colonialism* (New York: Columbia University Press, 1996).

Gilman, S. L., 'Sexology, Psychoanalysis, and Degeneration: From a Theory of Race to a Race to Theory', in J. E. Chamberlain and S. Gilman (eds.), *Degeneration: The Dark Side of Progress* (New York: Columbia University Press, 1985), pp. 72–96.

Gilmore, L., 'Obscenity, Modernity, Identity: Legalizing *The Well of Loneliness* and *Nightwood*', *Journal of the History of Sexuality*, 4, 4 (1994), 603–24.
Gilroy, P., 'Cultural Studies and Ethnic Absolutism', in L. Grossberg, C. Nelson and P. Treichler (eds.), *Cultural Studies* (London: Routledge, 1991), pp. 188–99.
Grewal, I., *Home and Harem: Nation, Gender, Empire, and the Cultures of Travel* (Durham, NC: Duke University Press, 1996).
Grewal, I. and C. Kaplan, 'Global Identities: Theorizing Transnational Studies of Sexuality', *GLQ: A Journal of Lesbian and Gay Studies*, 7, 4 (2001), 663–79.
Guha, S., 'Nutrition, Sanitation, Hygiene, and the Likelihood of Death: The British Army in India, c. 1870–1920', *Population Studies*, 47 (1993), 385–401.
Guha, S., 'The Unwanted Pregnancy in Colonial Bengal', *Indian Economic and Social History Review*, 33, 4 (1996), 403–36.
Gunn, J., *We of the Never Never* (Hawthorne, Victoria: Hutchinson Australia Pty Ltd, 1987, 1908).
Gupta, C., '"Dirty" Hindi Literature: Contests About Obscenity in Late Colonial North India', *South Asia Research*, 20, 2 (2000), 89–118.
Sexuality, Obscenity, Community: Women, Muslims, and the Hindu Public in Colonial India (Delhi: Permanent Black, 2001).
Guyatt, B. J., 'The Publicists – The Labour Press 1880 to 1915', in D. J. Murphy, R. B. Joyce and Colin A. Hughes (eds.), *Prelude to Power: The Rise of the Labour Party in Queensland 1885–1915* (Milton, Queensland: Jacaranda Press, 1970), pp. 246–61.
Hall, C., '"From Greenland's Icy Mountains ... to Afric's Golden Sand": Ethnicity, Race and Nation in Mid-Nineteenth-Century England', *Gender and History*, 5, 2 (1993), 212–30.
Civilising Subjects: Metropole and Colony in the English Imagination 1830–1867 (Chicago: University of Chicago Press, 2002).
Hancock, W. K., *Australia* (London: Ernest Benn, 1930).
Harcourt, J. M., *Upsurge: A Novel* (University of Western Australia Press, 1986, [1934]).
Hardt, M. and A. Negri, *Empire* (Cambridge, MA: Harvard University Press, 2000).
Harris, J., *Private Lives, Public Spirit: A Social History of Britain 1870–1914* (Oxford: Oxford University Press, 1993).
Harrison, B., 'State Intervention and Moral Reform in Nineteenth-Century England', in P. Hollis (ed.), *Pressure from Without in Early Victorian England* (London: Edward Arnold, 1974), pp. 289–319.
Harrison, M., 'Quarantine, Pilgrimage, and Colonial Trade: India 1866–1900', *Indian Economic and Social History Review*, 29 (1992), 117–44.
Public Health in British India: Anglo-Indian Preventive Medicine 1859–1914 (Cambridge: Cambridge University Press, 1994).
Climates and Constitutions: Health, Race, Environment and British Imperialism in India, 1600–1850 (New York: Oxford University Press, 2000).
Heath, D., 'Communalism, Globalization and Governmentality: Some Reflections on South Asia', *Comparative Studies of South Asia, Africa and the Middle East*, 29, 3 (2009), 573–81.

'Sanitizing Modernity: Imperial Hygiene, Obscenity, and Moral Regulation in Colonial India', in S. Dube (ed.), *Enchantments of Modernity: Empire, Nation, Globalization* (New York: Routledge, 2009), pp. 113–29.

Hergenhan, L. T., 'English Publication of Australian Novels in the Nineteenth Century: The Case of *His Natural Life*', in L. Cantrell (ed.), *Bards, Bohemians, and Bookmen: Essays in Australian Literature* (St Lucia, Qld: University of Queensland Press, 1976), pp. 56–71.

Herman, J., 'The Origins of a Free Press', *Australian Press Council News*, 15, 1 (2003). Available from: www.presscouncil.org.au/pcsite/apcnews/feb03/jim.html.

Hicks, N., *'This Sin and Scandal': Australia's Population Debate 1891–1911* (Canberra: Australian National University Press, 1978).

Hodges, S., 'Governmentality, Population and Reproductive Family in Modern India', *Economic and Political Weekly*, 39, 11 (2004), 1157–63.

'Indian Eugenics in an Age of Reform', in S. Hodges (ed.), *Reproductive Health in India: History, Politics, Controversies* (Delhi: Orient Longman, 2006), pp. 115–38.

Holden, P., *Modern Subjects/Colonial Texts: Hugh Clifford and the Discipline of English Literature in the Straits Settlements and Malaya 1895–1907* (Greensboro, NC: ELT Press, 2000).

Holt, P., 'Censorship, Citizenship and Democracy: The Regulation of Literature, c. 1930–1960'. Available from: www.abc.net.au/ola/citizen/stories/trans/program9.htm.

Hornadge, B., *Chidley's Answer to the Sex Problem* (Dubb, NSW: Review Publications, 1983).

Howell, P., 'Race, Space and the Regulation of Prostitution in Colonial Hong Kong', *Urban History*, 31, 2 (2004), 229–48.

Hubber, B., ' "Literary Pest-Germs": A Study of Censorship in Colonial Australia', in W. B. Rayward (ed.), *Australian Library History in Context* (Sydney: School of Librarianship, University of New South Wales, 1988).

'The Victorian Customs Department and Respectable Limits of Taste: Émile Zola and Colonial Censorship', *Explorations: A Bulletin Devoted to the Study of Franco-Australian Links*, 9 (1990), 3–16.

Hudson, W. J. and M. P. Sharp, *Australian Independence: Colony to Reluctant Kingdom* (Melbourne: Melbourne University Press, 1988).

Hunt, A., *Governing Morals: A Social History of Moral Regulation* (Cambridge: Cambridge University Press, 1999).

Hunt, L., *The Invention of Pornography: Obscenity and the Origins of Modernity* (New York: Zone Books, 1993).

Hunter, I., D. Saunders and D. Williamson, *On Pornography: Literature, Sexuality and Obscenity Law* (New York: St Martin's Press, 1993).

Hyam, R., *Empire and Sexuality: The British Experience* (Manchester: Manchester University Press, 1990).

Innis, H., *Empire and Communications* (Oxford: Oxford University Press, 1950).

Ittmann, K., 'Demography as Policy Science in the British Empire, 1918–1969', *Journal of Policy History* 15, 4 (2003), 417–48.

Johanson, G., ' "Cultural Cringe" or Colonial Fringe?', *Melbourne Historical Journal*, 17 (1985), 78–85.

Jones, G. S., *Outcast London: A Study in the Relationship Between Classes in Victorian Society* (Oxford: Clarendon Press, 1971).

Joshi, P., *In Another Country: Colonialism, Culture, and the English Novel in India* (New York: Columbia University Press, 2002).

Joyce, P., 'The People's English: Language and Class in England, c. 1840–1920', in P. Burke and R. Porter (eds.), *Language, Self and Society: A Social History of Language* (Cambridge: Polity, 1991), pp. 159–90.

Kakar, S., *Intimate Relations: Exploring Indian Sexuality* (Chicago: University of Chicago Press, 1990).

Kalpagam, U., 'Colonial Governmentality and the "Economy"', *Economy and Society* 29, 3 (2000), 418–38.

'The Colonial State and Statistical Knowledge', *History of the Human Sciences*, 13, 2 (2000), 37–55.

'Colonial Governmentality and the Public Sphere in India', *Journal of Historical Sociology*, 15, 1 (2002), 35–58.

Katrak, K. H., 'Indian Nationalism, Gandhian "Satyagraha", and Representations of Female Sexuality', in A. Parker (ed.), *Nationalisms and Sexualities* (New York: Routledge, 1992), pp. 395–406.

Kaul, C., *Reporting the Raj: The British Press and India, c. 1880–1922* (Manchester: Manchester University Press, 2003).

Kaviraj, S., 'On the Construction of Colonial Power: Structure, Discourse, Hegemony', in D. Engels and S. Marks (eds.), *Contesting Colonial Hegemony: State and Society in Africa and India* (London: British Academic Press, 1994), pp. 19–54.

Kelly, J., *A Politics of Virtue: Hinduism, Sexuality and Countercolonial Discourse in Fiji* (Chicago: University of Chicago Press, 1991).

Kendrick, W., *The Secret Museum: Pornography in Modern Culture* (New York: Viking, 1987).

Kennedy, D., *The Highly Civilized Man: Richard Burton and the Victorian World* (Cambridge, MA: Harvard University Press, 2005).

King, C. R., 'Images of Virtue and Vice: The Hindi-Urdu Controversy in Two Nineteenth-century Hindi Plays', in K. W. Jones (ed.), *Religious Controversy in British India: Dialogues in South Asian Languages*, SUNY Series in Religious Studies (Albany: State University of New York Press, 1992), pp. 123–48.

Kingston, B., 'The Taste of India', in *Australian Perceptions of Asia*, ed. L. Jayasuriya, D. Walker and J. Gothard, special issue of *Australian Cultural History*, 9 (1990), pp. 36–81.

Kirsop, W., 'The Four Phases of Australian Book-Trade History', in *Books for Colonial Readers – The Nineteenth Century Australian Experience* (Melbourne: Bibliographical Society of Australia and New Zealand, in association with the Centre for Bibliographical and Textual Studies, Monash University, 1995).

Kwan, E., 'Making "Good Australians"', *Journal of Australian Studies*, 29 (1991), 38–49.

La Nauze, J. A. and E. Nurser (eds.), *Walter Murdoch and Alfred Deakin on Books and Men: Letters and Comments 1900–1918* (Melbourne: Melbourne University Press, 1974).

Lake, M., 'Colonised and Colonising: The White Australian Feminist Subject', *Women's History Review*, 2, 3 (1993), 377–86.

'Between Old World "Barbarism" and Stone Age "Primitivism": The Double Difference of the White Australian Feminist', in N. Grieve and A. Burns (eds.), *Australian Women: Contemporary Feminist Thought* (Melbourne: Oxford University Press, 1994), pp. 80–91.

'Frontier Feminism and the Marauding White Man: Australia, 1890s to 1940s', in R. Roach Pierson and N. Chaudhuri (eds.), *Nation, Empire, Colony: Historicizing Gender and Race* (Bloomington: Indiana University Press, 1998), pp. 94–105.

Legg, S., *Spaces of Colonialism: Delhi's Urban Governmentalities* (Oxford: Blackwell, 2007).

Lester, A., *Imperial Networks: Creating Identities in Nineteenth-Century South Africa and Britain* (London: Routledge, 2001).

Levine, P., 'Rereading the 1890s: Venereal Disease as "Constitutional Crisis" in Britain and British India', *Journal of Asian Studies*, 55, 3 (1996), 585–612.

'Public Health, Venereal Disease and Colonial Medicine in the Later Nineteenth Century', in R. Davidson and L. Hall (eds.), *Sex, Sin and Suffering: Venereal Disease and European Society Since 1870* (London: Routledge, 2001), pp. 160–72.

'The White Slave Trade and the British Empire', *Criminal Justice History*, 17, 10 (2002), 133–46.

Prostitution, Race and Politics: Policing Venereal Disease in the British Empire (New York: Routledge, 2003).

Livingston, K. T., *The Wired Nation Continent: The Communication Revolution and Federating Australia* (Melbourne: Oxford University Press, 1996).

Lloyd, B. and G. Gilbert, *The Censorship and Public Morality: An Australian Conspectus* (Sydney: Angus and Robertson, 1930).

Lockyer, N., *Some Ideals of Public Service: Paper Read before the Commonwealth Central Staffs Public Service Association, Melbourne, 14th June, 1909* (Melbourne: Thos. Urquhart, 1909).

Lokugé, C. (ed.), 'Introduction', in K. Satthianadhan, *Saguna: The First Autobiographical Novel in English by an Indian Woman* (New Delhi: Oxford University Press, 1998).

Loomba, A., S. Kaul, M. Bunzl, A. Burton and J. Esty, 'Beyond What? An Introduction', in A. Loomba *et al.* (eds.), *Postcolonial Studies and Beyond* (Durham, NC: Duke University Press, 2005), pp. 1–38.

Lyons, M., 'Introduction', in M. Lyons and J. Arnold (eds.), *The History of the Book in Australia, 1891–1945: Towards a National Culture in a Colonized Market, 1890–1945* (St Lucia, Qld: University of Queensland Press, 2001), pp. xiii–xix.

Lyons, M. and L. Taksa, *Australian Readers Remember: An Oral History of Reading, 1890– 1930* (Melbourne: Oxford University Press, 1992).

Macaulay, T. B., *Macaulay, Prose and Poetry*, selected by G. M. Young (Cambridge, MA: Harvard University Press, 1957).

The Miscellaneous Writings and Speeches of Lord Macaulay, Vol. IV (Whitefish, MT: Kessinger Publishers, 2004).

McCalman, I., *Radical Underworld: Prophets, Revolutionaries, and Pornographers in London, 1795–1840* (Cambridge: Cambridge University Press, 1988).

McClintock, A., 'Family Feuds: Gender, Nationalism and the Family', *Feminist Review*, 44 (1993), 61–80.

Imperial Leather: Race, Gender and Sexuality in the Colonial Contest (Routledge: New York, 1995).

McDonald, D. I., 'The Former Customs Clerks: Wollaston and Lockyer', *Canberra Historical Journal* 20 (1987), 32.

McInerney, S. M. (ed.), *The Confessions of William James Chidley* (St Lucia, Qld: University of Queensland Press, 1977).

Mackenzie, J., *Propaganda and Empire: The Manipulation of British Public Opinion 1880–1960* (Manchester: Manchester University Press, 1984).

Maglen, K., 'A World Apart: Geography, Australian Quarantine, and the Mother Country', *Journal of the History of Medicine and Allied Sciences*, 60, 2 (2005), 196–217.

Manchester, C., 'Lord Campbell's Act: England's First Obscenity Statute', *Journal of Legal History*, 9, 2 (1988), 223–41.

'A History of the Crime of Obscene Libel', *Journal of Legal History*, 12, 1 (1991), 36–57.

Manderson, L., 'Colonial Desires: Sexuality, Race, and Gender in British Malaya', *Journal of the History of Sexuality*, 7, 3 (1997), 372–88.

Mani, L., 'The Debate on *Sati* in Colonial India', in K. Sangari and S. Vaid (eds.), *Recasting Women: Essays in Colonial History* (New Delhi: Kali for Women, 1989), pp. 88–126.

Manna, M., 'Approach towards Birth Control: Indian Women in the Early Twentieth Century', *Indian Economic and Social History Review*, 35, 1 (1998), 35–51.

Marcus, S., *The Other Victorians: A Study of Sexuality and Pornography in Mid-Nineteenth-Century England* (London: Corgi Books, 1966).

Markus, A., 'Of Continuities and Discontinuities: Reflections on a Century of Australian Immigration Control', in L. Jayasuriya, D. Walker and J. Gothard (eds.), *Legacies of White Australia: Race, Culture and Nation*, (Crawley, WA: University of Western Australia Press, 2003), pp. 175–98.

Marsh, J., *Word Crimes: Blasphemy, Culture, and Literature in Nineteenth-Century England* (Chicago: The University of Chicago Press, 1998).

Martin, A. W., *Robert Menzies: A Life*, Vol. I: *1894–1943* (Melbourne: Melbourne University Press, 1993).

Martin, E., 'Toward an Anthropology of Immunology: The Body as Nation State', *Medical Anthropology Quarterly*, 4, 4 (1990), 410–26.

Masson-Moussaieff, J., 'Obscenity in Sanskrit Literature', *Mahfil*, 7, 3–4 (1971), 197–207.

Mbembe, A., *On the Postcolony* (Berkeley: University of California Press, 2001).

Meudell, G. D., *Australia for the Australians: And Not for Immigrants* (Melbourne: Mission Print, 1925).

Michelson, P., *Speaking the Unspeakable: A Poetics of Obscenity* (Albany: State University of New York Press, 1993).

Mills, J. H. and S. Sen, 'Introduction', in J. H. Mills and S. Sen (eds.), *Confronting the Body: The Politics of Physicality in Colonial and Post-Colonial India* (London: Anthem Press, 2002).
Mitter, P., *Much Maligned Monsters: A History of European Reactions to Indian Art* (Chicago: The University of Chicago Press, 1977, 1992).
Mohanram, R., 'White Water: Race and Oceans Down Under', *Journal of Colonialism and Colonial History*, 4, 3 (2003).
Moore, N., 'National Parapraxis: Sex and Forgetting in Australian Censorship History', *Australian Historical Studies*, 36, 126 (2005), 296–314.
Moretti, F., *Atlas of the European Novel 1800–1900* (New York: Verso, 1998).
Morgan, P., 'Realism and Documentary: Lowering One's Sights', in L. Hergenhan (ed.), *The Penguin New Literary History of Australia* (Ringwood, Vic.: Penguin, 1988), pp. 238–52.
Mort, F., 'Purity, Feminism and the State: Sexuality and Moral Politics 1880–1914', in M. Langan and B. Schwartz (eds.), *Crises in the British State, 1880–1930* (London: Hutchinson, 1985), pp. 209–25.
Dangerous Sexualities: Medico-Moral Politics in England Since 1830, 2nd edn (London: Routledge, 2000).
Mosse, G., *Nationalism and Sexuality: Middle-Class Morality and Sexual Norms in Modern Europe* (Madison, WI: University of Wisconsin Press, 1985).
Mudge, B., *The Whore's Story: Women, Pornography, and the British Novel, 1684–1830* (Oxford: Oxford University Press, 2000).
Mukherji, M., *Realism and Reality: The Novel and Society in India* (Delhi: Oxford University Press, 1985).
Mullin, K., *James Joyce, Sexuality and Social Purity* (Cambridge: Cambridge University Press, 2003).
Nadel, G., *Australia's Colonial Culture* (Melbourne: F. W. Cheshire, 1957).
Nandy, A., *The Intimate Enemy: Loss and Recovery of Self under Colonialism* (New Delhi: Oxford University Press, 1988).
National Vigilance Association, *Work Accomplished* (London: National Vigilance Association, 1906).
Nead, L., *The Female Nude: Art, Obscenity and Sexuality* (London: Routledge, 1992).
Victorian Babylon: People, Streets and Images in Nineteenth-Century London (New Haven, CT: Yale University Press, 2000).
Nesbit, B., 'Literary Nationalism and the 1890s', *Australian Literary Studies*, 5, 1 (1971), 3–17.
Nile, R., *The Making of the Australian Literary Imagination* (St Lucia, Qld: University of Queensland Press, 2002).
Nowell-Smith, S., *International Copyright Law and the Publisher in the Reign of Queen Victoria* (Oxford: Clarendon Press, 1968).
Oddie, G. A., *Missionaries, Rebellion and Proto-Nationalism: James Long of Bengal, 1814–87* (Richmond, Surrey: Curzon Press, 1999).
Ogborn, M., 'Law and Discipline in 19th Century State Formation: The Contagious Diseases Acts of 1864, 1866 and 1869', *Journal of Historical Sociology*, 6 (1993), 25–57.
'Historical Geographies of Globalisation, 1500–1800', in B. Graham and C. Nash (eds.), *Modern Historical Geographies* (London: Prentice Hall, 1999), pp. 43–69.

Osterhammel, J., *Colonialism: A Theoretical Overview*, trans. Shelly L. Frisch (Princeton, NJ: Markus Wiener Publishers, 1997).

Page, R., *Australian Bookselling* (Melbourne: Hill of Content, 1970).

Palfreeman, A. C., 'The End of the Dictation Test', *Australian Quarterly*, 28, 1 (1958), 43–50.

Pannikar, K. N., 'Indigenous Medicine and Cultural Hegemony: A Study of the Revitalization Movement in Keralam', *Studies in History*, 8 (1992), 283–308.

Patterson, A., *Censorship and Interpretation: The Conditions of Writing and Reading in Early Modern England* (Madison: University of Wisconsin Press, 1984).

Pease, A., *Modernism, Mass Culture, and the Aesthetics of Obscenity* (Cambridge: Cambridge University Press, 2000).

Pederson, S., 'National Bodies, Unspeakable Acts: The Sexual Politics of Colonial Policy-Making', *Journal of Modern History*, 63 (1991), 647–80.

Pelling, M., 'The Meaning of Contagion: Reproduction, Medicine and Metaphor', in A. Bashford and C. Hooker (eds.), *Contagion: Historical and Cultural Studies* (London: Routledge, 2001), pp. 15–38.

Pels, P., 'The Anthropology of Colonialism: Culture, History, and the Emergence of Western Governmentality', *Annual Review of Anthropology*, 26 (1997), 163–83.

Pennycock, A., *English and the Discourses of Colonialism* (London: Routledge, 1998).

Pernicious Literature, Debate in the House of Commons, Trial and Conviction for the Sale of Zola's Novels, with Opinions of the Press (London: National Vigilance Association, 1889).

Petrow, S., *Policing Morals, The Metropolitan Police and the Home Office 1870–1914* (Oxford: Clarendon Press, 1994).

Phillips, A. A., 'Confessions of an Escaped Censor', *Meanjin*, 28, 4 (1969).

Phillips, J., 'Copyright in Obscene Works: Some British and American Examples', *Anglo-American Law Review*, 6 (1977).

Phillips, R., 'Imperialism and the Regulation of Sexuality: Colonial Legislation on Contagious Diseases and Ages of Consent', *Journal of Historical Geography*, 28, 3 (2002), 339–62.

Sex, Politics and Empire: A Postcolonial Geography (Manchester: Manchester University Press, 2006).

Pollak, M., *Sense and Censorship: Commentaries on Censorship Violence in Australia* (Balgowlah, NSW: Reed Books Pty Ltd, 1990).

Porter, R. and L. Hall, *The Facts of Life: The Creation of Sexual Knowledge in Britain, 1650–1950* (New Haven, CT: Yale University Press, 1995).

Prakash, G., *Another Reason: Science and the Imagination of Modern India* (Princeton, NJ: Princeton University Press, 1999).

'Body Politic in Colonial India', in T. Mitchell (ed.), *Questions of Modernity* (Minneapolis: University of Minnesota Press, 2000), pp. 189–222.

Prashad, V., 'The Technology of Sanitation in Colonial Delhi', *Modern Asian Studies*, 35, 1 (2001), 113–55.

Pringle, R., 'Octavius Beale and the Ideology of the Birth-Rate. The Royal Commissions of 1904 and 1905', *Refractory Girl*, 3 (1973), 19–27.

Pullan, R., *Guilty Secrets: Free Speech in Australia* (North Ryde: Methuen Australia, 1984).

Ramusack, B., 'Embattled Advocates: The Debate over Birth Control in India, 1920–40', *Journal of Women's History*, 1, 2 (1989), 173–97.

Ratanlal, R., *Unreported Criminal Cases of the High Court of Bombay 1862–1898* (Bombay: Bombay Law Reporter Office, 1901).

Reiger, K., *The Disenchantment of the Home: Modernizing the Australian Family 1880–1940* (Melbourne: Oxford University Press, 1985).

Roberts, M. J. D., 'Morals, Art and the Law: The Passing of the Obscene Publications Act, 1857', *Victorian Studies*, 28, 4 (1985), 609–29.

'Blasphemy, Obscenity and the Courts: Contours of Tolerance in Nineteenth-Century England', in P. Hyland and N. Sammells (eds.), *Writing and Censorship in Britain* (London: Routledge, 1992), pp. 141–53.

Rodwell, G., 'Curing the Precocious Masturbator: Eugenics and Australian Early Childhood Education', *Journal of Australian Studies*, 11, 59 (1998), 82–92.

'Domestic Science, Race Motherhood and Eugenics in Australian State Schools, 1900–1960', *History of Education Review* 29, 2 (2000), 67–83.

Rosecrance, R., 'The Radical Culture of Australia', in L. Hartz (ed.), *The Founding of New Societies: Studies in the History of the United States, Latin America, South Africa, Canada, and Australia* (San Diego, CA: Harcourt Brace Jovanovich, 1964), pp. 275–318.

Rosselli, J., 'The Self-Image of Effeteness: Physical Education and Nationalism in Nineteenth-Century Bengal', *Past and Present*, 86 (1980), 137–41.

Roy, T., 'Disciplining the Printed Text: Colonial and Nationalist Surveillance of Bengali Literature', in P. Chatterjee (ed.), *Texts of Power: Emerging Disciplines in Colonial Bengal* (Minneapolis: University of Minnesota Press, 1995), pp. 63–92.

Ruonavaara, H., 'Moral Regulation: A Reformulation', *Sociological Theory* 15, 3 (1997), 277–93.

Said, E., *Culture and Imperialism* (New York: Vintage Books, 1993).

St John-Stevas, N., *Obscenity and the Law* (London: Secker and Warburg, 1956).

Samuel, R., 'The Discovery of Puritanism, 1820–1914: A Preliminary Sketch', in J. Garnett and C. Matthews (eds.), *Revival and Religion Since 1700: Essays for John Walsh* (London: Hambledon Press, 1993), pp. 201–47.

Sarch, A., 'Those Dirty Ads! Birth Control Advertising in the 1920s and 1930s', *Critical Studies in Mass Communication*, 14 (1987), 31–48.

Sarkar, T., 'Orthodoxy, Cultural Nationalism, and Hindutva Violence: An Overview of the Gender Ideology of the Hindu Right', in R. Roach Pierson and N. Chaudhuri (eds.) *Nation, Empire, Colony: Historicizing Gender and Race* (Bloomington: Indiana University Press, 1998), pp. 166–81.

Hindu Wife, Hindu Nation: Community, Religion, and Cultural Nationalism (Bloomington: Indiana University Press, 2001).

Saunders, D., 'Copyright, Obscenity and Literary History', *English Literary History*, 57, 2 (1990), 431–44.

'Victorian Obscenity Law: Negative Censorship or Positive Administration?' in P. Hyland and N. Sammells (eds.), *Writing and Censorship in Britain* (London: Routledge, 1992), pp. 154–70.

Schauer, F., 'The Ontology of Censorship', in R. Post (ed.), *Censorship and Silencing: Practices of Cultural Regulation* (Los Angeles: Getty Research Institute for the History of Art and the Humanities, 1998), pp. 147–68.

Schwarz, H., 'Sexing the Pundits: Gender, Romance, and Realism in the Cultural Politics of Colonial Bengal', in Henry Schwarz and Richard Dienst (eds.), *Reading the Shape of the World: Toward an International Cultural Studies* (Boulder, CO: Westview Press, 1996), pp. 224–58.

'Aesthetic Imperialism: Literature and the Conquest of India', *Modern Language Quarterly*, 61, 4 (2000), 563–86.

Scott, D., 'Colonial Governmentality', *Social Text*, 43 (1995), 191–220.

Scott, J. C., *Seeing Like a State: How Certain Schemes to Improve the Human Condition Have Failed* (New Haven, CT: Yale University Press, 1998).

Seal, A., *The Emergence of Indian Nationalism: Competition and Collaboration in the Later Nineteenth Century* (Cambridge: Cambridge University Press, 1968).

Sen, S., 'Schools, Athletes and Confrontation: The Student Body in Colonial India', in J. H. Mills and S. Sen (eds.), *Confronting the Body: The Politics of Physicality in Colonial and Post-Colonial India* (London: Anthem, 2004), pp. 58–79.

Sen, S., 'Motherhood and Mothercraft: Gender and Nationalism in Bengal', *Gender and History*, 5, 2 (1993), 231–43.

Sharp, H. (ed.), *Selections from Educational Records*, Part I: *1781–1839*, 2nd edn (Delhi: National Archives of India, 1965).

Sharpe, J., 'The Civilizing Mission Disfigured', in *Allegories of Empire: The Figure of Woman in the Colonial Text* (Minneapolis: University of Minnesota Press, 1993), pp. 57–82.

Siebert, F. S., *Freedom of the Press in England, 1476–1776* (Urbana: University of Illinois Press, 1965).

Sigel, L. Z., 'Filth in the Wrong People's Hands: Postcards and the Expansion of Pornography in Britain and the Atlantic World, 1880–1914', *Journal of Social History*, 33, 4 (2000), 859–85.

Governing Pleasures: Pornography and Social Change in England, 1815–1914 (New Brunswick, NJ: Rutgers University Press, 2002).

Sinha, M., 'Gender and Imperialism: Colonial Policy and the Ideology of Moral Imperialism in Late Nineteenth-Century Bengal', in M. S. Kimmel (ed.), *Changing Men: New Directions in Research on Men and Masculinity* (Newbury Park, CA: Sage, 1987), pp. 217–31.

'Gender in the Critiques of Colonialism and Nationalism: Locating the "Indian Woman" ', in A.-L. Shapiro (ed.), *Feminists Revision History* (New Brunswick, NJ: Rutgers University Press, 1994), pp. 246–75.

Colonial Masculinity: The 'Manly' Englishman and the 'Effeminate' Bengali in the Late Nineteenth Century (Manchester: Manchester University Press, 1995).

Slemon, S., 'Unsettling the Empire: Resistance Theory for the Second World', *World Literature Written in English*, 30, 2 (1990), pp. 30–41.

Smart, J., 'Sex, the State and the "Scarlet Scourge": Gender, Citizenship and Venereal Diseases Regulation in Australia during the Great War', *Women's History Review*, 7, 1 (1998), 5–35.

'The Society for the Suppression of Public Obscenity in India', *Counterpoint*, 2 (1978), 179–204.

Stasiulis, D. and N. Yuval-Davis, 'Introduction: Beyond Dichotomies – Gender, Race, Ethnicity and Class in Settler Societies', in D. Stasiulis and N. Yuval-Davis (eds.), *Unsettling Settler Societies: Articulations of Gender, Race, Ethnicity and Class* (Thousands Oaks, CA: Sage, 1995), pp. 1–38.

Stewart, K., 'Journalism and the World of the Writer: The Production of Australian Literature, 1855–1915', in L. Hergenhan (ed.), *The Penguin New Literary History of Australia* (Ringwood, Vic.: Penguin Books, 1988), pp. 174–93.

Stilz, G., 'Nationalism before Nationhood: Overseas Horizons in Debates of the 1880s', *Australian Literary Studies*, 14, 4 (1990), 476–88.

Stoler, A. L., *Race and the Education of Desire: Foucault's History of Sexuality and the Colonial Order of Things* (Durham, NC: Duke University Press, 1995).

'Tense and Tender Ties: The Politics of Comparison in American History and (Post)Colonial Studies', *Journal of American History*, 88, 3 (2001), 829–65.

Sutherland, J., *Offensive Literature: Decensorship in Britain, 1960–1982* (London: Junction Books, 1982).

Tadros, V., 'Between Governance and Discipline: The Law and Michel Foucault', *Oxford Journal of Legal Studies*, 18, 1 (1988), 75–103.

Tambe, A., 'Colluding Patriarchies: The Colonial Reform of Sexual Relations in India', *Feminist Studies*, 26, 3 (2000), 587–600.

Tharu, S. and K. Lalita, 'Empire, Nation and the Literary Text', in T. Niranha, P. Sudhir and Vivek Dhareshwar (eds.), *Interrogating Modernity: Culture and Colonialism in India* (Calcutta: Seagull, 1993), pp. 199–219.

Thomas, D., *The Victorian Underworld* (New York: New York University Press, 1998).

Thomas, N., *Colonialism's Culture: Anthropology, Travel and Government* (Cambridge: Polity Press, 1994).

Torgovnick, M., *Gone Primitive: Savage Intellects, Modern Lives* (Chicago: University of Chicago Press, 1990).

Trainor, L., 'British Publishers and Cultural Imperialism: History and Ethnography in Australia, 1870–1930', *Bibliographical Society of Australia and New Zealand Bulletin*, 20, 2 (1996), 99–106.

Travis, A., *Bound and Gagged: A Secret History of Obscenity in Britain* (London: Profile Books, 2000).

Travis, D., *A Long Time Burning: The History of Literary Censorship in Britain* (London: Routledge and Kegan Paul, 1969).

Tribe, D. H., *Questions of Censorship* (London: Allen and Unwin, 1973).

Tuck, M., 'Venereal Disease, Sexuality and Society in Uganda', in R. Davidson and L. A. Hall (eds.), *Sex, Sin and Suffering: Venereal Disease and European Society Since 1870* (New York: Routledge, 2001), pp. 191–204.

Uberoi, P., *Social Reform, Sexuality and the State* (New Delhi: Sage Publications, 1998).

Valverde, M., 'Moral Capital', *Canadian Journal of Law and Society*, 9, 1 (1994), 213–32.

Van der Veer, P., *Imperial Encounters: Religion and Modernity in India and Britain* (Princeton, NJ: Princeton University Press, 2001).

Van Heyningen, E., 'The Social Evil in the Cape Colony, 1868–1902: Prostitution and the Contagious Diseases Acts', *Journal of Southern African Studies*, 10 (1984), 170–97.

Veracini, L., 'Historylessness: Australia as a Settler Colonial Collective', *Postcolonial Studies*, 10, 3 (2007), 271–85.
Verma, A., 'Consolidation of the Raj: Notes from a Police Station in British India, 1865–1928', *Criminal Justice History*, 17 (2002), 109–32.
Vincent, D., *The Culture of Secrecy: Britain, 1832–1998* (Oxford: Oxford University Press, 1998).
Viswanathan, G., *Masks of Conquest: Literary Study and British Rule in India* (New York: Columbia University Press, 1989).
Vizetelly, E., *Émile Zola: Novelist and Reformer: An Account of his Life and Work* (London: John Lane, 1904).
Walker, D., 'Race Building and the Disciplining of White Australia', in L. Jayasuriya, D. Walker and J. Gothard (eds.), *Legacies of White Australia: Race, Culture and Nation* (Crawley, WA: University of Western Australia Press, 2003), pp. 33–50.
Watt, C., 'Education for National Efficiency: Constructive Nationalism in North India, 1909–1916', *Modern Asian Studies* 31, 2 (1997), 339–74.
Watts, S., 'From Rapid Change to Stasis: Official Responses to Cholera in British-Ruled India and Egypt: 1870 to c. 1921', *Journal of World History*, 12, 2 (2001), 321–74.
Weeks, J., *Sex Politics and Society: The Regulation of Sexuality Since 1800* (London and New York: Longman, 1981).
White, R., *Inventing Australia: Images and Identity 1688–1980* (Sydney: George Allen and Unwin, 1981).
Willard, M., 'The History of the White Australia Policy', *Royal Australian Historical Society Journal and Proceedings*, 8 (1922), 1–32.
Williams, J. F., *The Quarantined Culture: Australian Reactions to Modernism 1913–1939* (Cambridge: Cambridge University Press, 1995).
Windeyer, W. C., *Ex Parte Collins: A Judgment* (Sydney: W. M. Maclardy, 1889).
Wolf, P., 'Land, Labour and Difference: Elementary Structures of Race', *American Historical Review*, 106, 3 (2001): 866–905.
Wollacott, A., 'White Colonialism and Sexual Modernity: Australian Women in the Early Twentieth Century Metropolis', in Antoinette Burton (ed.), *Gender, Sexuality and Colonial Modernities* (London: Routledge, 1999), pp. 49–63.
Wollaston, H. N. P., *Customs Law and Regulations: With Notes and References* (Sydney: William Brooks, 1904).
Yarwood, A. T., 'The Dictation Test – Historical Survey', *Australian Quarterly*, 30, 2 (1958), 19–29.
Zola, E., *Piping Hot! A Realistic Novel* (London: Vizetelly and Co., 1885).
The Soil. A Realistic Novel (London: Vizetelly and Co., 1888).

Index